On Board the USS *Boise*
in World War II

On Board the USS *Boise* in World War II

The Battles and Secret Missions of Light Cruiser CL-47

Ian S. Bertram

McFarland & Company, Inc., Publishers
Jefferson, North Carolina

The views expressed in the book are those of the author and do not necessarily reflect the official policy or position of the United States Air Force Academy, the Air Force, the Department of Defense, or the U.S. Government.

Maps were created by Jesica Hanline Breece and derived from *Boise* War Diaries available in the National Archives and official U.S. Navy and Army World War II reports.

ISBN (print) 978-1-4766-9807-6
ISBN (ebook) 978-1-4766-5821-6

LIBRARY OF CONGRESS CATALOGING DATA ARE AVAILABLE

Library of Congress Control Number 2025028928

© 2025 Ian S. Bertram. All rights reserved

No part of this book may be reproduced or transmitted in any form or by any means, electronic or mechanical, including photocopying or recording, or by any information storage and retrieval system, without permission in writing from the publisher.

Front cover image: USS *Boise* (CL-47) off San Pedro, California, 14 September 1945, Catalog #: 19-N-89079 (National Archives); based on a design by Jesica Hanline Breece.

Printed in the United States of America

McFarland & Company, Inc., Publishers
Box 611, Jefferson, North Carolina 28640
www.mcfarlandpub.com

For those that fought for liberty.

Acknowledgments

A work of this magnitude and complexity is impossible for a person to do alone. I am indebted to the time and efforts of numerous people I wish to thank. You all did so much to make this book a reality, and please know any mistakes are mine.

First, I must thank Mark and Cande Fitch for sharing DB's story, log, and papers. This book would not exist without your help. Dr. Michael Neiberg and Dr. John Grenier, thank you for getting a young cadet interested in history, and then helping me learn the business of being a historian. Rex Saukonen and Mark Chiofolo, thank you for listening to my research stories and reading my drafts.

Thank you to Mike Piano, Brian Morris, Julian Oliver, and Dr. Charles Steel for ensuring this pilot did not screw up the Navy stuff. I hope I captured the honor of sailors past and present. Several agencies and people helped me piece together the *Boise* story including Mr. Mischa Brady at the Idaho Military History Museum, the National Archives, MacArthur Memorial, National Museum of the American Sailor, United States Air Force Academy Library Special Collections, the National World War II Museum, National Naval Aviation Museum, and the Naval History and Heritage Command.

Several families shared the stories and papers of their loved ones aboard the *Boise*. Thank you, Rex Moneymaker, Theresa D'Angelo Bradford, and Roger Tripp, for your contributions and support. I am indebted to the members of the Second World War Research Group for reviews and advice, particularly Dr. Jadwiga Biskupska and Richard Frank. Thank you to my editor Aysha Rehm and graphic designer Jesica Hanline Breece for making this project look good. Thank you to Elizabeth Foxwell and the outstanding team at McFarland for giving a new historian a chance.

Finally, my family has my eternal gratitude. Dad, you stoked my fire of curiosity, and Mom, you have given me a lifetime of encouragement. Thank you to my boys for putting up with the trips and the long nights of writing. I could not have done this without your love and support. Most of all, thank you to Bonnie for following me around the world to battlefields and archives, reading my drafts, and always standing with me when I doubted myself. None of this was possible without you.

Table of Contents

Acknowledgments — vi
Preface — 1
Prologue — 3

1. A Ship and a Man — 5
2. Stopgap: Java Sea — 16
3. Recovery and Diversion: India and the Pacific — 29
4. Hell at Night: Guadalcanal — 48

Interlude: Home—Philadelphia — 71

5. Covering Fire: Sicily and Italy — 83
6. The March Up: New Guinea — 107
7. Ship of the Line: Leyte Gulf — 128
8. Liberation: Luzon, Philippines — 150
9. The Long Way Home: Borneo and Operation Magic Carpet — 176

Epilogue — 188
Chapter Notes — 199
Bibliography — 221
Index — 225

Preface

I was introduced to the USS *Boise* and the memory of Donald "DB" Fitch through my wife, DB's granddaughter. I heard stories of DB's exploits from my father-in-law at family gatherings. Later, visiting my local legion post in my hometown of Ashby, Minnesota, my wife discovered that my legion was named after another *Boise* crewmember who died during the war. In 2016, my father-in-law told me that DB had left a diary—or a log, as he called it—from his time aboard the *Boise* that encompassed the entire war, along with boxes of letters, reunion papers, and correspondence. Some had been donated to the Idaho Military History Museum, but much of it, including the log, was still with the family. He asked if I would like to read through it. As a historian I was intrigued and started reading.

A year later I was visiting my alma mater, the United States Air Force Academy, and asked a mentor what I might do to ensure DB's story, and by extension *Boise*'s, could be available for future scholars. He looked at me blandly and said, "You're a historian, write a book." And thus this project was born.

Fitch's wartime diary is the backbone of this book and the framework from which everything else hangs, but it is only one input. DB's papers and stories flesh out the dates, locations, and notes he left. The book also relies heavily on *Boise*'s daily War Diaries, which are preserved in the National Archives, and the detailed reports from various battles and engagements. It uses the official U.S. Army and Navy histories from the conflict to provide context. A variety of additional primary sources were also used, including notes from various World War II commands, Japanese wartime records, and personal diaries and reflections from admirals to common sailors. Finally, a myriad of written and audio interviews with *Boise* veterans were invaluable to describing shipboard life and what it was like to survive World War II.

This book could not have been written without the countless World War II documents digitized by the National Archives, particularly the War Diaries and Deck Logs of the *Boise* and other ships. It also draws from the records of the MacArthur Memorial, National World War II Museum, National Naval Aviation Museum, and Idaho Military History Museum (which holds the only publicly available remaining artifacts from the ship).

Many of the sources were drawn from Donald Fitch's papers. His role as the chair of several *Boise* reunions left him with a plethora of letters, postcards, newspaper clippings, and recollections from his crewmates. Many included only the stories themselves with no record of where they came from. In several instances this book quotes from crewmembers who provided Fitch their thoughts but did not sign the documents. This made specific attribution impossible. I am also indebted to Mark Fitch for the dozens

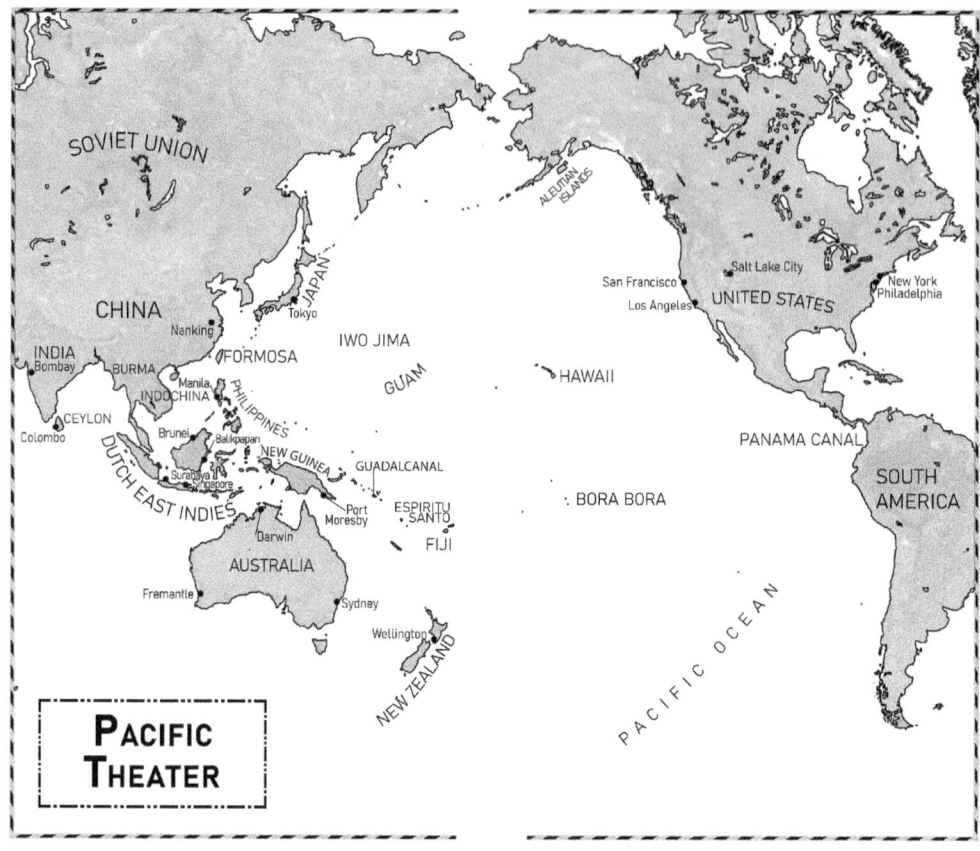

Boise **sailed much of the Pacific and Indian oceans during the war and fought in key battles off Guadalcanal, across New Guinea, and in the Philippines.**

of hours I spent with him talking about his father, the reunions he assisted his father in planning, and the stories that are the lifeblood of a sailor's life.

I had the chance to visit the locations of several *Boise* battles. There is no substitute for walking the areas around Gela, Lingayen Beach, or Corregidor when it comes to understanding the terrain and, in the case of this book, being able to contemplate what it was like for naval gunfire to rain down on a soldier's position.

DB wrote several times "Still Here" to reflect the monotony of shipboard life. But his phrase also reflects the story of the *Boise*. Despite every hardship, the ship and the men persisted. Even when the enemy gave them their worst, they remained.

Finally, this book uses place names as they were known during the war, with modern references provided in some cases. Ship designations are included only when they help differentiate vessels with the same name or add to the narrative. This work also quotes the authentic words of the men who fought the war, even when they used outdated and racist terms that were then and are now inappropriate, but it is essential for the reader to understand the raw emotions and hatred that only warfare can breed.

Prologue

The ship plowed through inky black waters, trying to hide from the waning moon that highlighted their every movement. The overly bright night sky could not penetrate the black water, and the ship desperately sought to blend into the nothingness of the sea. They were being chased; the crew felt the pursuit in their bones. Like a deer fleeing a forest fire, the ship was flying from an opposing onslaught, one that was mercilessly sinking ships, destroying aircraft, and killing men.

Somewhere off their port bow was the island of Mindanao in the southern Philippines. To the starboard side was open ocean. Behind them by a day was Manila Bay. Above them was the threat of enemy airplanes, although significantly less at night. Below lurked the threat of enemy submarines and, perhaps worse, the ocean itself. Any could kill the ship in a heartbeat.

The crew manned their battle stations. It was their first time at General Quarters during wartime. The ship's captain had little information, and the crew knew even less.

On the ship it was December 8, 1941. In America it was still December 7, and most citizens on the mainland learned they were at war by lunchtime. Japanese planes had struck Pearl Harbor, the main base of the U.S. Pacific Fleet. Fear, despair, and sometimes panic grew in the hearts of every American as they listened to their radios, heard of the devastating destruction and loss of life, and felt rage at being attacked without cause.

Pearl Harbor was not the only target of the Japanese blitz. Planes of the Imperial Japanese Army and Navy followed dawn across the globe and struck U.S. and Allied targets in Wake Island, Guam, the Philippines, and elsewhere.[1] They hoped to hit America and its Allies hard and fast to remove them from the war quickly while also ensuring access to natural resources that the Japanese home islands lacked such as iron, rubber, and, most importantly, oil. Europe was already embroiled in war, and few of the Allied powers had military resources with which they could respond. If America could be hurt badly enough in the opening phase of the war, Japanese leaders hoped President Roosevelt would negotiate a favorable peace treaty.[2] They wanted to control the Pacific, and the attacks of December 1941 were a brilliant opening move.

The men knew little or none of that. They knew they had left Manila Bay just before the first Japanese bombs fell in the area. By a stroke of luck or the vagaries of military planning, their ship had escaped the deadly fate of so many others. They now lived in uncertainty. They were ordered to fall back to a rendezvous point in the Dutch East Indies where surviving Allied ships could regroup and plan a counterattack.[3]

The ship was the USS *Boise*, a light cruiser designed to support larger surface ships but large enough and with plenty of firepower to act independently if needed. Their skipper was Captain S.B. Robinson, a veteran sailor who was operating with as much uncertainty as his crew. At the helm of this 10,000-ton warship was Donald Bird Fitch, a wiry young man from Salt Lake City. Known as "DB" or "Duck Butt" to his friends, the man must have felt fear and purpose as he steered the vessel on its course. He probably did not realize it at the time, but his position would give him a front-row seat to some of the U.S. Navy's greatest triumphs and tragedies and the terrible price exacted by each.

For now, he carried out his captain's orders by sailing into the dawn. Few words passed through the pilothouse save for small corrections from the navigator and occasional watch reports from the ship's various compartments. At this moment, DB's shipmates relied on his ability to keep them safe. They would rely on him, and each other, repeatedly in the coming months. Their very survival now relied on the engines running, the guns firing quickly and accurately, the radar and watchmen spotting the enemy before they could fire, and the damage control parties to fight fires and keep the sea out. If they could accomplish these actions and thousands of others, while underway and under fire, and with more than a little bit of luck, there was a chance they could survive this war.

And along the way, the *Boise* and DB just might make history.

1

A Ship and a Man

The USS *Boise* was a picturesque fighting ship. It had a graceful, sleek hull with twin masts towering above the superstructure and dual smokestacks in the center. Designated as light cruiser CL-47, it looked like it was built to leap through the waves, head held high, looking for a fight. Veterans of the *Boise* remembered their ship proudly as "the light-heavyweight of the Fleet ... she was big enough to pack a murderous wallop, yet fast enough to flash through and around the enemy, her graceful lines made her a ship of deadly beauty."[1]

Boise was the sixth of nine *Brooklyn*-class cruisers to roll out from America's shipyards, commissioned before the start of World War II. Its sister ships would play prominently in the coming conflict. They would serve in every theater, dealing out punishment to all Axis nations. They would also pay for their role in the war with bent steel, fire, and the blood of their men.

The *Brooklyn*-class light cruisers were the result of international shipbuilding treaties in the 1920s and '30s. The major naval powers of the world wished to avoid an arms race that could spark a Second World War. Countries around the world were worried about who was building what types of ships, how many, and whether their own fleets and interests were at risk. In 1922, a conference in Washington, D.C., led to agreements on the construction of aircraft carriers and battleships.[2] The London Naval Conference of 1930 updated the previous treaty and addressed concerns over smaller vessels. The resulting treaty focused heavily on the requirements for cruisers and destroyers.

Cruisers were smaller ships used for a variety of roles including screening for larger warships, convoy escort, economic raiding, and fighting similarly sized enemy ships. The U.S. was particularly worried about the capability of Japanese cruisers outfitted with 8-inch guns, and was desperate to limit their production.[3] The treaty ultimately dictated a ratio of 10/10/7 in total ship tonnage between the United States, Great Britain, and Japan, respectively, an increase in the number of allowable ships for Japan.[4] The U.S. was allotted 180,000 tons to build heavy cruisers with guns larger than 6.1 inches, and 143,500 tons for light cruisers carrying 6-inch guns or smaller.[5] These light cruisers became *Brooklyn*-class ships.

Boise's keel was laid on April 12, 1935, at the Newport News Shipbuilding and Drydock Company in Newport News, Virginia. It was named after the capital city of Idaho, and on December 3, 1936, Alice Salone Clark, the daughter of Idaho's governor, was on hand to christen the ship with a bottle of water from the Snake River. Miss Clark smashed the bottle across the bow of the thirty-seven-million-dollar warship as it launched for the first time.[6]

The new warship bristled with firepower. From bow to stern, it packed more firepower than a U.S. Army artillery battalion. The forward half of the ship had three turrets with three 6-inch guns each. The center Number 2 Turret stood taller than Turrets 1 and 3. Three long barrels extended over Turret 1 when the guns were trained forward, aesthetically but not functionally protecting each other like the interlocking shields of a Greek phalanx. Aft were two more turrets, with Turret 4 stacked above number 5 closest to the stern. Each turret was unique, custom-built for the *Boise*, and slightly different from the turrets of its sister ships. The turrets were recorded as assembly numbers 126–130 in the Bureau of Ordnance's "Gun Mount and Turret Catalogue."[7] This meant if any turrets were damaged, there were none available for speedy repair. Each was as unique as the ship itself, with its own details, quirks, and "gremlins" that required the crew to master and develop a sense of ownership over their specific equipment.

The Mk-16 6-inch guns were a new addition to the fleet. They were designed for rapid-fire and used a new "semifixed" type of ammunition. The new "super heavy" armor-piercing (AP) ammunition, weighing 130 pounds each, had nearly twice the penetrating power of previous rounds. This allowed the guns to produce a murderous volume of fire: Up to ten rounds per gun every minute. This meant a full broadside from the *Boise* could send 150 shells at a target every minute. During testing on other *Brooklyn*-class ships, the *Savannah*'s captain recorded their target was "simply smothered." The *Honolulu*'s skipper wrote that his ship's gunnery "looked almost like a stream of bullets playing on the targets, which were almost continuously obscured and drenched by water."[8] The guns could hit targets nearly fifteen miles away when fully elevated, although effectiveness and accuracy decreased with range.[9]

Between the fore and aft turrets were eight 5-inch guns, four on each side of the

USS *Boise* (CL-47) during sea trials, 1938 (National Archives: 19-N-19153).

ship's central structures, to defend against enemy aircraft. These could also be used against close-in targets, for firing star shells at night, and for keeping submarines submerged. Eight .50 caliber machine guns were also mounted amidships for last-ditch protection against aircraft and to defend the ship in port against small boats.[10]

To find the enemy and aim all that firepower, *Boise* used everything from men with binoculars to the most modern sensors and even aircraft. The *Boise* had the "SC" search radar aboard and would receive the newest generation "SG" radar early in the war. The SG was more accurate than previous generations and could sweep the seas for surface ships up to 15.7 miles away. The system was highly capable, but also highly classified, which meant few leaders knew its true capability. *Boise*'s masts also carried fire control radars to aim the guns. A Mk-3 Fire Control Radar (FCR) directed the 6-inch guns, and a separate Mk-35 FCR controlled the 5-inch guns.[11] These systems were a considerable improvement from manually aimed firepower.

At the stern, *Boise* had two gunpowder-powered aircraft catapults to launch scout planes.[12] The planes were stored below the deck in a hangar, raised to the main deck by an elevator, and lifted into position via a crane at the stern of the ship. The crane was also used for recovering the planes after they accomplished water landings. In 1940, *Boise* carried three SON-1 seaplanes, a slight variation of the SOC-3 Seagull that was common on U.S. battleships and cruisers.[13] The SON/SOC was a single-engine, open-cockpit, fabric-winged biplane first delivered to the Navy in 1935. It carried the pilot and a radioman who also operated a .30 caliber machine gun in the rear. SOCs could fly up to 157 mph and, if flown judiciously, stay aloft for ten hours. They could be equipped with floats for water landings, a critical component since cruisers lacked flight decks.[14] They were extremely slow compared to contemporary fighter aircraft, but they were stout, lightweight, and could spend a long time airborne searching for targets and radioing back gunnery effects to their host ship.

Boise certainly packed a punch, but it had to be able to take punishment as well or was no good to the fleet. Protection from enemy fire came mostly from speed and armor. Unfortunately, to get one a ship typically had to trade the other. Since the *Brooklyn*-class design board wanted ships that were fast enough to keep up with the fleet yet were still limited in total weight thanks to the London Treaty, that meant the ships could not become armored behemoths. The best solution was to protect key sections of the ship to ensure it could take a hit and keep fighting or retreat and survive to fight another day. The General Board decided the armor scheme would be similar to that of the *New Orleans* (CA-32), and it would protect vital components against 6-inch-gunfire at a 90° target angle from 10,000 yards. The ship had belts of armor protecting vital areas. The belt was 5 inches thick around the machinery sections and 2 inches protected the magazines housing the ammunition for each gun. The magazines were further protected by 6 inches of armor wrapping the barbette of each turret. A barbette was essentially an armored tube that protected each turret's critical functions, from the magazine below decks all the way up to the elevators that lifted the shells to the gun. The deck was covered with 2 inches of armor, and the gunhouses themselves had 6.5 inches on the face, 3 inches on the roof, 1.5 inches on the sides, and 1.25 inches on the rear.[15] All told, the ship was supposed to be armored against the same 6-inch projectiles it fired, hopefully making for an even match in a firefight.

Despite the armor, some officials questioned if *Brooklyn*-class cruisers were tough enough to survive modern war. Many thought that "too much structural integrity had been sacrificed to save treaty-mandated weight." Their concerns were made manifest after a 1939 storm in San Pedro where the *Savannah* was docked. The ship ran over its own anchor chain, which "sliced through her bow, causing such severe damage that she had to be dry-docked." Rear Admiral Husband E. Kimmel, the commander of the Battle Force cruisers, noted after the anchor chain incident that if a mild storm could cause significant damage while the ship was in port, there was no way it could hold a position in the battle line during combat.[16]

The *Boise*'s four massive turbine engines could crank out 100,000 shaft horsepower that spun the four propellers. It carried enough fuel to cruise 10,000 miles at 15 knots. Two 1,000-kilowatt diesel generators provided backup electricity to the ship. Officially the ship could reach a speed of 32.5 knots with all eight boilers pushed to their max, and even hit 33.7 knots during speed trials.[17] The crew joked they could squeeze a few extra knots "when the galley ranges were lighted off."[18] The ship likely did well in rough weather as well. Reports from *Savannah* during a storm with 65–70 knot "winds abeam," or directly hitting the side of the ship, noted that the vessel could still sail at 20 knots and "the ship rode easily and was dry on deck. The battery could have been worked easily."[19]

The sailors' existence consisted of the 608 feet and 4 inches of main deck, with several levels below and a limited number above. Descending from the main deck, a sailor would be on the second deck full of living spaces, offices, and the hangar at the rear. Further below on the third deck was more living space, various mechanical workshops, and dedicated space for the ship's contingent of Marines. Continuing down, a man would find himself on the first platform with machinery spaces, the boiler rooms, and berthing for some of the unluckier crewmembers. Finally, the lowest true deck of the ship known as the second platform was various stores and weapons magazines. Even further below was the hold filled with spaces for fuel oil, diesel fuel, and fresh water. Below it all was the inner bottom with space for additional stores.[20]

The main deck hosted the main batteries and most of the secondary batteries. It also included the galleys, bakery, and butcher shop. Forwardmost were the captain's cabin and special spaces to host admirals or other VIPs. Above the main deck were two structures fore and aft of the funnels. Climbing up from the captain's spaces would reach radio central and all ship communications. Above that was the bridge with the pilot house and chartroom, and still further up was the fire control room with the best enclosed views from the ship. The secondary fire control for the aft turrets was located aft of the funnels. Above both structures were the masts adorned with lights, radars, antennae, pendants, and flags.[21]

Decks were partitioned with fireproof bulkheads and hatches that could be sealed watertight. Behind the aft secondary fire control was the derrick for lifting supplies, parts, and launching boats. Below the main deck was everything needed for the ship and nearly 900 men to function, including a small sick bay and somehow space for men to sleep, eat, and store their limited belongings. Life rafts were mounted wherever they were easily available, including on the sides of each gunhouse.[22] Space was always at a premium for a fighting ship built to spend significant time away from port.

A ship is nothing without the men who run it. *Boise*'s official complement was 52 officers and 816 enlisted men. It would go to war with sailors doing a myriad of jobs including machinists, clerks, gunners, mechanics, pilots, and pharmacists. There was also a complement of Marines onboard to help secure and defend the ship.[23] For the ship to sail, for it to fight, for it to survive, every one of those men needed to know his duty and be able to do it under the absolute worst of circumstances. Their individual abilities, prior achievements, and training would only get them so far. To come home alive meant they had to work together and trust each other.

To bond as a crew and learn their roles and their ship, the initial complement of men sailed the ship on a shakedown cruise to Cape Town, South Africa, and Monrovia, Liberia, in August 1938 under the steady hand of Captain B.V. McCandlish, a Naval Academy graduate who won a Navy Cross during World War I.[24] The ship, and the crew, successfully completed their sea trials by January 1939, so they sailed west to join the Pacific Fleet and undertook duties between the West Coast and Hawaii. *Boise* was assigned to Cruiser Division 9, part of the Pacific Fleet's Battle Force.[25] In August 1940, Captain McCandlish passed command to Captain Stephan B. Robinson.[26] From July to November 1940, *Boise* was honored to serve as the flagship for Commander Cruisers Battle Force's Admiral Kimmel—the same admiral who doubted the strength of the *Boise*. Kimmel would gain notoriety and infamy a year later as the Commander in Chief of the Pacific Fleet when Pearl Harbor was attacked. He was subsequently fired from the position for multiple reasons that culminated in "the absence of preparedness on December 7th." *Boise* later hosted the Secretary of the Navy Frank Knox in June of 1941 while he observed Fleet maneuvers. Knox was the one responsible for firing Kimmel later that year.[27]

Boise was in Pearl Harbor in April 1941 when a young sailor from Utah stepped aboard.

Donald Bird Fitch was a man born to hustle and make ends meet, traits he probably inherited from his father. Donald was born in Summit, Utah, on March 15, 1923, to Claude Waters Fitch and Rebecca Ann Bird. Claude was an entrepreneur seemingly willing and able to make a buck regardless of an activity's legality. Originally from San Diego, by his early adult life he was a carpenter building houses in Utah. This honest work resulted in some notable architecture, as one of his constructions is registered to the National Register of Historic Places as a prime example of contemporary housing.[28] He married Rebecca Ann Bird of Salt Lake City in 1912 in Kamas, Utah. Three years later their first son, Harold, was born. The family bounced around southern Utah for the next few years, adding William Joseph in 1918 and daughter Alice Maxine a year later.[29]

By 1923 the family had landed in Delta, Utah, for Donald's arrival. Claude was the owner of the local Amoco gas station, where he sold fuel and heating oil to the surrounding farms and Civilian Conservation Corps camp. He may have also run a side business dodging prohibition law with a distillery under the local theater stage. Apparently, the smell of popcorn cooking helped hide the smell of moonshine. It is unknown how much Donald knew of the family side business, but his father's willingness to subvert the law was a spirit Donald would exhibit later on in the Navy. Rebecca spent years running a boarding house that helped the family maintain finances in between Claude's schemes. Family members remember her as a saint for putting up with Claude.[30]

Donald's early days in the hardscrabble town of Delta taught him to hunt, fish, and live in the area's wilderness. Nature became an escape for him, a place to think and heal. He would later return to his beloved Utah countryside when the war would allow, one of the few escapes from the demons that war saddles men with.[31]

By the mid–1930s the Fitch family left Delta for the city. The end of prohibition may have been an impetus for the move. Claude quickly established himself as the owner of a small-engine repair shop. Donald adapted to city life, finding ways to get a leg up on the Great Depression. Through his teenage years he attended school by day and was an underage bartender by night. His part-time job brought home a big paycheck, but inattention from lack of sleep and his troublesome attitude in class resulted in him being kicked out of multiple high schools around the city.[32]

City living added a wicked prankster skillset to his repertoire. Donald delighted in a dangerous prank of the time where local kids would slather the city trolley tracks with oil or grease. The kids would then hide in nearby bushes and eagerly await a passing trolley. When a streetcar hit the slick portions of the track, often on a hill, it would slide loose from the track as the driver scrambled to regain control of the freewheeling behemoth. Trolley operators hated when someone "greased the rails," as the cars could damage the electrical cables that powered them, creating a serious danger of electrocution to anyone in the vicinity.[33]

By late 1940, the world was sliding into chaos faster than a greased trolley. Nazi Germany followed its 1939 conquest of Poland by invading Denmark, Norway, the Low Countries, and eventually France. Great Britain pulled off their miraculous evacuation of its army from Dunkirk, and then fought off swarms of Nazi planes in the Battle of Britain.[34]

In Asia, Japan continued fighting a bitter war to conquer China. The war was characterized by the outstanding Japanese martial ability and their brutality towards opposing militaries and civilians alike. War is always full of sorrow to those caught in its grasp, but events like the orgy of violence Japanese troops unleased on the defenders and citizens of Nanking in 1937 set a high bar for inhumanity.[35]

Early 1940 saw the Chinese launch their first major counteroffensive of the war, but their forces were firmly defeated. The fighting was reaching a stalemate, and Japan was losing credibility on the international stage. Worse, they lacked secure access to the natural resources needed to continue their expansionist plans. Many Japanese leaders feared intervention by the United States or other Western nations.[36] The United States was still neutral, but President Roosevelt and others were trying to prepare the nation for war.[37]

Against this backdrop, Donald Fitch sought a change from his Utah upbringing. At age seventeen he left behind trolley pranks and bartending alike to join the Navy.[38] He did not leave specific reasons for joining the military when his nation was not yet at war, but the fact that his shenanigans had thoroughly upset his teachers, the law, and his parents probably played into it. He also did not leave an explanation of why he joined the Navy when his years of hunting in the Wasatch Mountains would have made him a natural soldier, but he would hardly have been the first young man to be struck with a wanderlust that the Navy appealed to. What he did leave was a journal, or log, of his activities during World War II. Upon his death, this simple log passed to his surviving family members. He left behind a unique perspective on some of World War II's most important battles.

Donald's military life, and the log, began on January 14, 1941. He raised his right hand at the Navy Recruiter's office in Salt Lake City and was sworn in as a Seaman Recruit making $21 a month, which was likely a steep cut from his bartending gig.[39] The next day he was on a train for San Diego and basic training, or boot camp.

The San Diego Navy Training Center opened in 1923 and focused on teaching raw sailors "core values of honor, courage, and commitment, along with the basic skills of seamanship in a team environment."[40] Each day of boot camp was packed with new experiences for the young men. Haircuts, uniform issue, customs and courtesies, marching, immunizations, and plenty of physical training. As they advanced, they began to learn the practical parts of being a sailor, including taking small boats into the harbor and practicing line handling, rope tying, and standing watch.[41]

Fitch did not record any of his thoughts on boot camp, but a man going through similar recruit training for officers in Illinois did a year earlier. The sailor left a plethora of experiences in a series of letters to his family that would have been familiar to any sailor who entered service in the months before the United States entered World War II. Gilbert Hotchkiss described a typical day early in training as:

> 5:30—everyone up—6:30—everyone dressed—barracks clean—6:45 breakfast—8:00 to 11:15 drill and classes—11:45 noon mess—1:00 to 4:00—drill & classes—4:00 to 5:30—recreation—5:45—supper—recreation till 9:30 when everyone's in bed. The recreation periods are for recreation if you have clothes washed, rolled, everything clean, etc.[42]

Hotchkiss also references the military's age-old communication system for its youngest members, the "rumor mill," which thrives in situations where men are not given enough information, so they repeat whatever they hear, and oftentimes embellish or invent information. In this case, he complains that the enlistment period will supposedly change to only four years, and that "it will be as hard to get in [the Navy] as it was before last fall [1939]." He does admit, though, that "this is only one of hundreds of rumors, and tall stories that circulate around here. You can't believe much of anything heard anywhere."[43] Also known as "scuttlebutt," rumors and stories abounded *Boise* throughout the war. Sometimes the rumors filled the void when nothing official was passed down, other times sharing them was just a way to fill time. Regardless, rumors oftentimes make up the lore that veterans remember, even if the facts may not have always remained 100 percent correct.

Donald finished boot camp in early March and returned to Utah for a few days leave. Newly minted military members are usually proud to show off their uniform. Family members also usually note a change in their service member, especially in their discipline and how they carry themselves. One can imagine these scenes between Donald and his parents while they spent time together, hopefully burying the hatchet on some of his past transgressions.[44]

He returned to San Diego on March 16 after spending his eighteenth birthday on the train. He boarded the USS *Wharton* just four days later. The *Wharton* was a twenty-year-old cargo-passenger liner that was sold to the Navy and converted into a troopship. It was on its maiden voyage making the triangular run between San Diego, San Francisco, and Pearl Harbor. Fitch was also on his maiden voyage, as this was the first time he truly put to sea.[45]

On April 5, *Wharton* pulled into Pearl Harbor. Donald noted with a bit of mid-American wonder: "Never dreamed there could be so many ships." The next day, the ship and the man were joined for the first time. Fitch reported aboard the *Boise*.[46]

Sometime shortly after arriving on the *Boise*, Donald was granted a possibly ignominious moniker that would follow him through his time aboard the ship and through the end of his days. Donald B. Fitch's nom de guerre was "Duck Butt" or just "DB," a play on his initials D.B. and his middle name Bird. Perhaps it was not the most flattering of nicknames, but it was unique, and a name that DB carried with all the pride of a pilot's call sign.

Pictures from early in the war show DB as a relaxed, swaggering young sailor. His enlistment paperwork noted he was 5 feet 11 inches tall; weighed 146 pounds; and had blue eyes, light brown hair, and a ruddy complexion.⁴⁷ He was rail thin, with a long face and friendly eyes. He seemed to prefer to wear his Dixie Cup hat pushed back to reveal a shock of dark hair, at least when there were no officers within sight. Photographs taken in early 1942 in India showed a wry, almost mischievous grin, as if he was wondering what was going on behind the scenes or perhaps how he could turn the situation to his advantage. The happy face would soon face the challenges and horrors of his generation,

Donald "DB" Fitch (Fitch Family Private Collection).

and only time would tell how war would affect the young man and his brothers aboard the *Boise*.

Years later when his family asked DB what he did during the war, he would faithfully respond that he was a USO dancer. The witty response was his way of downplaying his part on the ship and in the broader war.[48] Jokes aside, DB was trained and served as a quartermaster, or QM, one of the Navy's oldest ratings.

Not be confused with an army's quartermaster who is responsible for the supply system, the naval quartermaster's claim to fame is ship-driver. But they also assisted in multiple critical roles on the bridge. The quartermaster rating badge is rightfully a helm, or the iconic sailing ship steering wheel with eight handles extending beyond the ring.

The Navy issued guidance to its men conducting job interviews for new recruits in late 1943. They described the duties of the quartermaster as:

> Stands deck and bridge watches. Supervises enlisted personnel on the Deck in navigation (uses navigation instruments, interprets weather messages, reads charts and Pilots, determines ship's position, uses tide and current tables, applies correction to charts from "Notice to Mariners"). Must be qualified steersman. Takes bearing and soundings, plots courses, keeps deck log. Must know signaling, including whistle, bell and light signals. (On small ship, may perform all the duties of signalman.) Responsible for honors and ceremonies.[49]

Recruits should have a high school diploma with a strong math ability, 20/20 uncorrected vision, be personable, and have a good memory. DB fit most of those, minus the completion of high school. Men would be trained to use all the tools needed to steer and navigate a ship, as well as send and interpret signals with other vessels. These included "chart, sextant, navigator's rangefinder, magnetic compass, Pilots (Navigation Publications), course protractor, dividers, hand lead, sounding machine, fathometer, chronometer, gyro compass, pelorus, stadimeter, barometer, anemometer, azimuth, thermometer, blinker tube, semaphore flags, searchlight."[50] Many found the most rewarding task to be steering the ship, an experience a modern quartermaster described as a "level of freedom not really known by most people."[51]

By 1943 new recruits were given sixteen weeks to learn everything required on that long list of tasks and equipment. Judging by DB's log, he was not provided the luxury of a formal training course beyond boot camp. Instead, he learned the tools of the trade under the watchful eye of petty officers on the bridge of the *Boise*.[52]

DB and the rest of the crew spent the next five months training and conducting maneuvers around the Hawaiian Islands. He noted with delight operating around Molokai and Lani, small islands containing bombing ranges and known for little more than being home to the islands' leper colony.[53] Molokai would also be considered a few months later by President Roosevelt to be the perfect place to intern Hawaii's Japanese population in the wake of the Pearl Harbor attack, although the plan was never adopted.[54]

The men perfected operating as a crew. They took to calling the ship "Old Feeder" as both a slight against the chow and term of endearment. Most men claimed the ship's food was horrible, but it kept them going through thick and thin.[55]

While the *Boise's* crew trained, the worldwide conflagration raged. Winter and spring of 1941 saw fighting across North Africa between General Erwin Rommel's Desert Corps and the British Army. In April, a combined force of Italian, German, and Bulgarian forces invaded the Balkans. Summer was even worse, as Hitler violated his non-aggression pact with Stalin and sent his armies pouring across the western border of the Soviet Union on June 22. Japan held internal debates on whether to attack Siberia, but instead opted to push south and began occupying French Indochina in an opening move towards their "Greater East Asia Co-Prosperity Sphere."[56] The United States remained officially neutral, for the time being.

After their training period in Hawaii, *Boise* returned to the mainland. They arrived in Long Beach on September 19. For fourteen glorious days, the men did what sailors loved most: they partied. DB noted "liberty every night till six the next morning." Many of the men almost certainly drank away their pay while chasing the local Los Angeles women. DB noted that his friend Glennon ran afoul of the Shore Patrol on the last day of the month, having taken his partying to a level unacceptable even for sailors.[57] S2C William B. Glennon from Salt Lake City was charged with "(1) Disorder; (2) Breaking arrest; (3) Resisting arrest; (4) Assaulting superior officer, member of SP." He was court-martialed and later transferred from the ship to a naval prison.[58]

By October 3, *Boise* was back at sea bound for Pearl Harbor. They spent a month in and around the Hawaiian Islands.[59] Meanwhile, tensions between the United States and Japan increased. At levels much higher than DB or even Captain Robinson, the two countries were drawing ever closer to war. On November 18, the Japanese ambassador to the United States informed Secretary of State Cordell Hull "about the 'very pressing' situation in Japan and the urgent need to 'to arrest a further deterioration in the relations between the two countries.'"[60]

That same day, with the dogs of war snarling at America's door, *Boise* set sail on an operational mission to escort a five-ship troop convoy to Manila in the Philippines. At 0615 on the 23rd, DB marked an important rite for a sailor as he crossed the International Date Line for the first time. More notable for the men, on November 29 they spotted Japanese warships. Alarms sounded and the crew rushed to battle stations. The war did not start there on the open waters of the Pacific, though, and neither ship fired as they slid from each other's sights. Rumors spread a few days later that they had inadvertently sighted the Japanese fleet bound for the Pearl Harbor attack. Although the rumor persisted even after the war, the timing and known routes for the *Boise* and Admiral Yamamoto's fleet make this extremely unlikely.[61] Two days later they passed Guam, the American territory that would soon be in Japanese hands.[62]

The convoy arrived safely in Manila on December 5, 1941. Some of the crew was granted a short liberty. One sailor simply described with a wry smile and a chuckle that the stop in the city was "lively."[63] DB was able to leave the ship on the 6th to experience his own version of liveliness. According to a menu and business card he saved, he and his friend Harry had lunch at the "Plaza" which boasted first and foremost that it was air-conditioned. They spent the afternoon sightseeing, taking in the famous Walled City or "Intramuros" which held the local YMCA, and he described Manila as "much bigger than I expected."[64] That evening they visited the "Whoopee Cabaret" a few blocks from the port, which prided itself as "The Biggest Little Cabaret in the Orient." The bar's tagline was one that would appeal to many young Americans:

> Where Drinks are good
> Ladies aplenty—charming & entertaining
> Atmosphere—cheerful & homely
> Top-flight floor-show every Saturday[65]

Whatever antics the sailors and their friends found themselves in that night, one hopes they enjoyed themselves. There was no way they could have known that in just a matter of hours their world would change. These young men and millions of other Americans would be called upon to uphold solemn oaths that could, and in many cases would cost blood, flesh, tears, and lives. America was about to be plunged into World War II.

2

Stopgap

Java Sea

News of war between the United States and Japan flooded the airwaves early in the morning of December 8. *Boise* had departed Manila the previous morning and was now following the Navy's plan for war with Japan initially conceived shortly after World War I. The ship was ordered to abandon their previous orders and instead rally with the fighting strength of the Asiatic Fleet. DB wrote the night of December 8/9 that they "changed course and ran through half the Jap fleet in the [Summara] Straits" with the crew at General Quarters the whole time. They could not know that the plan was already crumbling.[1]

In 1921, the U.S. military developed plans to defend the Philippines in the event of war with Japan. America enjoyed extremely close ties to the Philippines, and the U.S. knew that it would be up to a combined force of American and Filipino troops to defend the islands. The plan was for a combined army to hold off any enemy as long as possible, and then retire to the Bataan Peninsula and hold out for reinforcements. This strategically important piece of land, along with the island fortress on Corregidor, also controlled access to Manila Bay, one of the best harbors in the region.[2]

While the Army fought for Philippine soil, the U.S. Navy would temporarily withdraw its key forces. The Pacific Fleet would muster in Hawaii to await a climactic battle with its Japanese counterparts. Meanwhile, the bulk of the Asiatic Fleet's offensive power would pull back to the Indian Ocean, leaving submarines and small craft to defend Manila Bay. When the time was right, the Asiatic Fleet's cruisers and destroyers could return to the Philippines at the head of a relief force for those holding out in the Bataan jungle.[3]

The Great Depression and other world events found the Asiatic Fleet woefully lacking in resources by 1941. When the Japanese military spread its tentacles across the world that December, there were few U.S. forces west of Hawaii to oppose them. The Asiatic Fleet counted only one heavy cruiser, its flagship the USS *Houston* (CA-30), in Philippine waters along with four scattered destroyers. Further southeast near Borneo was the light cruiser *Marblehead* (CL-12) and nine more destroyers. About two dozen submarines in varying states of readiness and repair, along with a smattering of minesweepers, tenders, gunboats, and other small craft rounded out the Asiatic Fleet roster. And, thanks to the recent convoy escort duty, the *Boise* was on loan from the Pacific Fleet.[4]

Had the military staffs in the Pacific, and more pointedly the Philippines, held to the 20-year-old plan, the majority of those forces should have hightailed towards India. But in the summer of 1941, General Douglas A. MacArthur led an effort to rethink the Philippine strategy.

MacArthur was one of the U.S. Army's best-known generals. He was the son of a Lieutenant General who won the Medal of Honor during the Civil War, fought in the Philippines, and served for over a year as the Governor of the Philippines. The father cast a long shadow over the son. Douglas graduated at the top of his West Point class, served in the Philippines, and fought first as the Chief of Staff of the 42nd Rainbow Division in World War I. Later, after becoming the Army's youngest brigadier general, he earned multiple U.S. and French medals for combat bravery. He served as a regimental and later a division commander. But through this all, he was never awarded the Medal of Honor. After the war, he was the Superintendent of his beloved West Point. He served again in the Philippines and finally as the Chief of Staff of the Army, when he accompanied his troops sent to evict the "Bonus Army" of veterans demanding payments from the Capitol during the Depression. After holding the highest job in the U.S. Army, he accepted a dual role as an American general and Field Marshal of the Philippines tasked with developing their military. He was in this position when the war started.[5]

MacArthur was also exceedingly vainglorious. One historian aptly described him as "desperate for glory."[6] Another wrote he "was a man of astonishing pomposity, megalomania, and egocentrism," but also "elicited an almost hypnotic sense of awe" in those around him.[7] Few would deny his martial ability, his intellect, or his bravery. But he was a hard man to work for who tended to surround himself with "yes-men" and was prone to long soliloquies that demonstrated his intellect.

Prior to the Japanese invasion, he persuaded the brass in Washington that with proper support from the U.S. Army Air Force the Philippines could not only withstand any attack, but act as a base from which to control the region and roll back enemy advances. By October, he had convinced his leadership in Washington that with quick reinforcements this plan was possible, and even morally necessary due to the protective relationship between the American and Filipino people. Secretary of the Navy Knox declared in October that forces could be ready to support the plan with only three months of preparation.[8]

The problem was no one told the Navy about the new strategy, and thus they could not properly prepare to support it. When Admiral Thomas C. Hart, the Commander of the Asiatic Fleet, learned of the plan he wholeheartedly concurred with its premise. In October, he went so far as to order the Asiatic Fleet to remain in Manila Harbor at the outbreak of any conflict. He surmised that with Army ground forces keeping enemy troops out of the area, and the Air Force sweeping the skies of enemy planes, his ships could await the proper time to break out and defeat the Imperial Japanese Navy (IJN). Hart was so optimistic that he put on hold any future planning that involved the Asiatic Fleet withdrawing from the Philippines until he received final instructions from the Department of the Navy in Washington.[9]

Ultimately, Hart did not hear from Washington until November 20 and those instructions had him return to the original plan of withdrawing from the Philippines. He quickly started moving combat assets away from Manila Bay, but due to the lack of planning many support vessels would still be sitting at the docks when the Japanese attacked. He also ordered the withdrawal of naval assets and Marines from China.[10] Those Marines and the riverine gunboats would aid in the upcoming defense of the Philippines, but by early December 1941, MacArthur and his boys were trusting in the Army Air Force, their Filipino allies, and their own combat capabilities. Naval support would clearly be limited.

The Japanese attacks pushed the Allies back on their heels across the Pacific and Asia. Not only did they hit Pearl Harbor on that infamous Sunday morning, they also landed troops almost simultaneously in Hong Kong, the Malay Peninsula, and Guam while conducting aerial attacks on the Philippines and Wake Island. No Allied planners thought the Japanese capable of anything that large or coordinated, and the results were devastating.[11]

Admiral Hart received word about the Pearl Harbor attack around 0300 in Manila and penned a dispatch to the Asiatic Fleet. By 0400 when he arrived at his office, the message was pushed out: "JAPAN STARTED HOSTILITIES. GOVERN YOURSELVES ACCORDINGLY."[12]

There is significant variation in how *Boise* crewmembers recalled learning they were at war. Seaman Roy Campbell recalled he was on liberty when the war started. "We were in a bar when it started, and the MPs come in, and told us we were at a state of war with Japan and to report back to our parent commands."[13] Frederick Klemm, an engine room fireman, recalled he was still in his bunk at 0800 with the ship at anchor when someone he assumed was drunk called on the PA system that "the United States is now at a state of war with Japan! Strip Ship!"[14] Joseph Fenton said they had departed Manila around midnight and were at Cebu when the war started.[15] Garnett Moneymaker wrote in his diary that they left Manila on the 6th, and that at 0615 on the 8th he had just finished convincing a friend they were not at war with Japan when they heard the war announcement on the intercom. He added, "We were not expecting such a tasty appetizer for breakfast."[16] The assistant navigator, Ensign James Starnes, was probably most qualified to comment years later, and he also recalled they were nearby Cebu.[17]

Boise would have received Admiral Hart's message quickly. Anxiety in many men skyrocketed knowing they were at war. Some had family living nearby Pearl Harbor, and information on their well-being was almost impossible to come by. Instead, the rumor mill fueled speculation and worry.

Thankfully, there was plenty of work to keep the crew busy because *Boise* needed to be "stripped" for war. Everything flammable went over the side including wooden furniture, framed pictures, drapes, rugs, cushions, and cans of polish. The white teakwood that covered the steel decks was pulled up without ceremony. Paint cans were passed around and the ship changed from white to gray in a matter of hours. They welded shut the portholes to reduce the ship's light signature and improve the watertightness of the hull. Even the "nice officer's boats" were abandoned.[18]

With much of the Pacific Fleet sitting at the bottom of Pearl Harbor and the atrophied and disorganized state of the Asiatic Fleet, MacArthur's plan for the opening of hostilities was not feasible. The Navy required time to regroup and rebuild, so the war in the Philippines would be fought initially with little support from the seafaring branch beyond gunboats and submarines. Instead of fighting from Manila Bay, *Boise* was southbound. On the 10th they rendezvoused with the *Houston* and several destroyers, along with a small convoy that included a seaplane tender and a pair of oilers. Hart had ordered this group, known as the Striking Force (TF-5) under Rear Admiral William Glassford, to Balikpapan. DB noted they were "taking them to safer waters."[19] Balikpapan was a port on Borneo, an island that is divided between present day Indonesia, Malaysia, and Brunei but in 1941 was a colony of the Netherlands.

The trip was notably slow, as the fleet did not reach Balikpapan until the 13th.[20] They likely took a circuitous route to avoid Japanese detection and tracking, and oilers were not the fastest ships of the war. They dodged at least one submarine contact, but a destroyer chased it off with depth charges. Destroyers, sometimes referred to derisively as "tin cans" or just "cans," used sonar to fix the bearing, distance, and depth of a submarine and then rushed to that location to deploy a pattern of the barrel-shaped weapons, each packed with 200–300 pounds of explosives set to detonate at preset depths. The operation was a cat-and-mouse game. Early in the war destroyers could not track submarines underneath them, so during the destroyer's last 590-foot sprint to the target wily submarine captains had a few precious moments to take extreme evasive actions. Still, the shock waves and noise from a depth charge attack could damage a submarine without a direct hit and attack the crew's morale. Best of all, it rendered the submarine impotent to attack while it evaded.[21] There is no record of a submarine being sunk that day, but there is also no record of torpedoes fired at *Boise*'s flock.

The crew was thrilled to arrive at Balikpapan because it gave them a chance to replenish their stores. Someone procured water buffaloes for the galley. Multiple sailors recalled this was their first fresh meat in weeks. The men's collective spirit sunk when the meat was not up to American standards. One man remarked that it "stinks to high heaven." Another noted that the meat was better suited for the soles of their shoes![22]

Another notable moment in DB's seafaring career took place on the 13th. The small fleet crossed the equator at 0045, an important event in the life of any sailor.[23] Normally "crossing the line" is met with a ceremony and significant fanfare aboard any ship as the newest sailors, known as "Pollywogs," are initiated into the mysteries of the deep and became "Shellbacks." The tradition goes back long before World War II, and the rite of passage is meant to induct the Pollywogs into the "Solemn Mysteries of the Ancient Order of the Deep" presided over by King Neptune. To gain Neptune's acceptance, the Pollywogs are put through a series of "harrowing and often embarrassing tasks, gags, obstacles, physical hardships, and generally good-humored mischief" hosted by the senior sailors.[24] Upon completion, Shellbacks are typically gifted a certificate full of naval lore, myths, and salty language to commemorate the experience. DB's names him as a "Trusted Shellback" who crossed the equator at 118°55'30" E and is adorned with bare-breasted mermaids flanking King Neptune.[25]

The tradition is so powerful that even President Franklin D. Roosevelt, an experienced sailor himself, was called to plead his case to King Neptune's court when he crossed the line aboard the heavy cruiser USS *Indianapolis* in 1936 while en route to South America. The ship's scrapbook from the journey is replete with pictures of Pollywogs going through various trials, being locked in stocks, and the skipper Captain Henry Hewitt passing the command to King Neptune. The Roman god was a sailor in a robe with a flowing white beard, a crown possibly made from tinfoil, and salad plates covering his nipples.[26] Sadly, with the ongoing threat of Japanese submarines that night, the crew forwent any ceremony but did note in DB's official "Enlisted Man's Jacket" that "regular initiation not performed."[27] Hopefully Neptune understood the circumstances and still granted his blessing to DB and the other young sailors.

The official War History for the *Boise* downplays the tension of the remaining weeks of 1941, stating: "BOISE was employed with units of Task Force 5 in convoying and protecting important Allied shipping which was clearing the Philippines. These operations took her at various times to Balik Papan [sic], Makassar, Soerabaya [sic], and Darwin, Australia."[28] DB added a little more color to the events. He noted on their initial arrival in Balikpapan that they took on fuel and there were only "a few white people[,] mostly natives. Speak native tongue." A few days later in Makassar, also in the Dutch East Indies, he called it "the most peaceful place I've even seen. The people waved at us from the beach and the kids came out in their canoes and dove for money." He and some other sailors got to spend Christmas Eve ashore in Surabaya on the island of Java, and the ship spent New Year's Eve off the coast of Bali while escorting another convoy.[29] Despite the mild colonial racism common at the time, DB was experiencing a whole new world with the wide-eyed wonder of a small-town American. What the official history and DB do not note is the tension and fear that must have existed and the general war situation during those days.

The overall war in the Pacific trended poorly for the Allies that December. Japanese forces from Indochina quickly occupied Thailand, and started a relentless march down the Malay Peninsula towards the British stronghold of Singapore. The British had a small naval task force in the region, but it lacked naval air cover. The Japanese found them on the 10th when British land-based fighters were unavailable. At 1100 a string of nearly one-hundred Japanese high-altitude bombers and torpedo-bombers attacked. They struck relentlessly at the battleship HMS *Prince of Wales* and the battle cruiser HMS *Repulse*, sinking both by early afternoon. This was a heavy physical and moral blow to the Allies. Singapore was now at significant risk of being cut off from outside support, and the enemy was approaching the gates.[30]

The attack highlighted the importance of controlling the skies for any navy. As the preeminent historian Samuel Morison noted, "our battleships sunk at Pearl Harbor had been 'sitting ducks,' but no free-moving battleship had yet been sunk by air power. The stock of the battle-wagon went down...."[31] Surface ships of all sizes now had serious reason to fear enemy aircraft, no matter how much maneuvering they could accomplish or lead they could throw back against those planes.

On the 22nd, the Japanese began their invasion of Luzon in the Philippines at Lingayen Gulf north of Manila. By the 27th, MacArthur declared the capital city an "open city" that the Allies would not contend in hopes of saving it. At the same time, he ordered the retreat of all remaining forces to the Bataan Peninsula.[32] With the Philippines essentially in the hands of the Japanese Empire, they eyed the rich resources of the Dutch East Indies.

In the same timeframe, the U.S. Navy promoted Admiral Ernest King to the Commander in Chief United States Fleet on December 20. He was realistic in his first statement a few days later when he declared, "The way to victory is long. The going will be hard. We will do the best we can with what we've got." In the Pacific, Admiral Chester Nimitz was promoted to the Commander in Chief Pacific Fleet after the prior leadership was fired in the wake of Pearl Harbor. King directed Nimitz to hold a line across the South Pacific from Samoa, to Fiji, to Brisbane "at all costs."[33] This was the only way to ensure continued support to Australia, New Zealand, and, if possible, the Allies still fighting in the Philippines and Dutch East Indies. If those first countries could be held, an eventual counteroffensive against Japan might eventually be possible. Everyone called on the limited power of the remaining Asiatic Fleet to support all these goals.

To further complicate matters, in January the Asiatic Fleet was officially rolled into a joint command between several nations. The new command was called ABDA after the four participating nations, America, Britain, Dutch East Indies (Netherlands), and Australia. The top commander was British General Archibald P. Wavell, and Admiral Hart soon arrived via submarine from Manila to lead the naval component, named perhaps too cleverly "ABDAFLOAT."[34] ABDA was a political nightmare, as each nation had different priorities for the limited resources. Australia was desperate to keep the Japanese out of striking distance from their north coast. The Dutch wanted to reinforce and maintain their territory, especially since their homeland was occupied by the Nazis. The British felt their national honor rested on maintaining their control of Singapore, the "Gibraltar of the East." America wanted to secure bases in Australia for eventual counterattacks. ABDA had to balance these tasks with an aged fleet that contained no aircraft carriers and no surface ships larger than a heavy cruiser.[35] *Boise* constituted a significant portion of the fleet's firepower. Admiral Hart proved unequal to the task of managing the concerns of all these nations, and before long passed naval command to the Dutch Admiral Conrad Helfrich, while Admiral Glassford became the top American commander.[36]

ABDA needed to draw a line that they thought they could defend with their limited capability. Their plan by early January 1942 was to maintain the safe harbors for support in Australia, while reinforcing the islands of Java and Sumatra with all available land forces to counter the Japanese. They were also trying to keep convoy lanes open from the Indian Ocean to Singapore so the British could reinforce the garrison.[37] To accomplish this, they hoped to keep the Japanese from breaking into the Java Sea, a task that was bound to be difficult due to ABDA's serious deficit in airpower.

The men were busy during this time as the ship moved between various ports in support of convoys between Australia, Java, and other islands in the area. They kept constant vigil for Japanese aircraft and submarines. DB recorded stops in Darwin on the 6th, Surabaya on the 11th, where they took Admiral Glassford aboard, and Saleh Bay in Sumbawa on the 13th for refueling, and finally on to Timor.[38]

The men were apprehensive, as was the rest of the country. Attitudes towards the Japanese ranged from fear, to bitterness, to hatred. In May 1941, most Americans approved of economic pressure against Japan for their war in China, but few supported martial responses.[39] Over the early course of the war the majority of Americans would come to hate the Japanese even more than the Germans, likely through a mixture of incredulity over the surprise attack at Pearl Harbor and a solid dose of racism. Sailors were taught through propaganda videos that they "cannot measure Japanese sense of logic by any Western yardstick," that the Japanese held a "primitive moral code," that Japanese soldiers "led a spartan existence, and become used to the simple rations which be their lot until the day of final victory," and that although small in stature, the "Japanese soldier is expected to compensate for his small size by his fanaticism in battle."[40] There were some truths in these assessments sprinkled with racism, as the Japanese government had certainly fostered a militant culture for decades.

On the other hand, a mix of bravado and racism built the idea that there was no way the Japanese could defeat Americans in a fair fight. Official military training products routinely denigrated the Japanese as inhuman and comical, sometimes displaying them as monkeys. Such depictions tried to deflate the supermen mythos.[41] DB did not reveal much of his thoughts towards the Japanese beyond the use of the term "Japs" that was so common as to hardly have been considered derisive.

By late January, ABDA got its chance to hit the Japanese hard. A fleet of transport ships supporting the invasion and occupation of Balikpapan and its surrounding oil fields was sitting relatively undefended in the harbor. Glassford readied all available surface combatants to attack that fleet. *Boise* was the biggest ship available and would serve as the force's flagship. With them would be the older light cruiser USS *Marblehead*, which was operating with one of its turbines offline and could only make 15 knots, and four ancient destroyers: the *John D. Ford, Pope, Parrott,* and *Paul Jones* (DD-230).[42]

The force set out from Kupang Bay on January 20. As they turned north through the Sape Strait, *Boise*'s crew felt a shudder through the deck plates.[43] Many crewmembers were thrown to the deck.[44] While traveling some of the most poorly charted waters in the world, the ship had struck an unknown pinnacle of rock and coral. The crew acted quickly and professionally to limit the damage by closing off the flooding compartments and ensuring the seaworthiness of the vessel.[45]

A ship striking an unknown object can be a violent, incredibly uncertain, and frightening moment for the crew. Although few *Boise* veterans left behind vivid descriptions of the incident, their thoughts at the time were probably similar to the crews of the U.S. Navy's worst peacetime disaster nineteen years before. On September 8, 1923, a squadron of destroyers ran aground on a rocky California coast. A combination of bad weather, poor navigation, and a tradition of ships "following the leader" resulted in seven ships destroyed on the rocks in a matter of minutes. The skipper of the USS *Young* reported a "terrific shock that knocked him to the floor." The USS *Fuller*'s skipper simply recalled later that the ship "felt a tremor" and quickly lost power due to water flooding the engine rooms.[46]

Historian Morison acquitted Captain Robinson of any fault for the incident. He wrote that the skipper "was not to blame for this accident; Netherlands East Indies waters are as tricky as any in the world, and the charts then available to the United States Navy were based on incomplete surveys."[47] In fact the same day, the U.S. submarine *S-36* ran aground in the Makassar Strait and had to be abandoned, and two weeks later the Dutch lost the destroyer *Van Ghent* in the same fashion.[48] Yet the fact remained that *Boise* was out of action for the upcoming fight. Glassford ordered *Boise* and *Marblehead* to leave the task force and take shelter in the nearby Warorada Bay, where he shifted his flag and *Boise* passed off enough of their fuel to top off *Marblehead*. However, due to the new flagship's limited speed and the fleeting nature of the target at Balikpapan, the destroyers pushed on without the support of either ship's 6-inch guns.[49]

The crew's disappointment was palpable. DB wrote with clear disappointment after "running aground" that "we should have met the Japs in the morning." Instead of taking the fight to the enemy, *Boise* sent divers under the hull to inspect damage.[50] DB described the event as "put in at some bay and sent a diver down to look at the bottom. It is pretty bad so I guess we will have to put in at a yard someplace. Got under way after looking over the damage." What divers found ended their participation in that first, desperate phase of the war as well as Captain Robinson's career.

The damage was significant and included a large gash in the hull over 100 feet long that required a dry dock to properly repair.[51] Glassford's parting orders were for *Boise* to sail to Tjilatjap on the southern coast of Java to find a dry-dock. Creeping along at 13 knots they were at terrible risk from air attack and enemy submarines.[52] *Boise* was a wounded warrior able to crawl and lash out, but not run or fight.

Meanwhile, the intrepid "four-piper" destroyers pushed to Balikpapan. The opportunity to hurt the enemy was still sitting in that bay, and Commander Paul Talbot of the *John D. Ford* was determined to lead the force into the jaws of the tiger. The force wound its way north to deceive enemy aircraft, fighting seas so heavy that the swells broke the windows on the vessel's bridges.[53] At 1930 the fleet decrypted the simple order from Admiral Hart: "Attack!"[54]

Talbot issued simple orders: "Torpedo attack; hold gunfire until the 'fish' are gone; use initiative and prosecute the strike to your utmost." They were to dart in, launch their torpedoes, and then use their own discretion to maximize damage on the enemy fleet sitting quietly at anchor. The ships were challenged by a Japanese destroyer as they approached, but the Japanese did not fire or raise the alarm. At 0246 on the 24th the "cans" sighted the enemy ships highlighted by flames from the recently bombed oil facilities ashore.[55] They could not have asked for a better setup for their attack.

They charged at 27 knots and fired spreads of torpedoes at the anchored ships and a contact off their starboard bow they thought was a destroyer. The initial high-speed attack proved ineffective in all directions. As the ships passed the enemy's northern flank, the *Ford* cranked the wheel to the right for another pass. As *Ford* swung around, *Parrott* fired three more torpedoes that struck home, sending the 3,500-ton transport *Sumanoura Maru* up in a tremendous explosion.[56] Commander Welford Blinn of the *Pope* later claimed that "upon being hit the flames reached a height of over 800 feet and it literally blew to pieces."[57]

As the Americans continued their attack, Japanese commander Admiral Shoji Nishimura misunderstood the threat and led his destroyers away from the battle to search for submarines. The confusion continued as *Pope* struck home with a torpedo attack against the *Tatsukami Maru*. Five minutes later *Pope* and *Parrott* took down the 750-ton torpedo boat *PC-37*. Shortly after, a shot from *Paul Jones* sent the *Kuretake Maru* to the bottom.[58]

Thirty minutes into the battle the Americans were low on torpedoes but not out of fight. Talbot led the column in a sweeping 270° turn to port and back into the fray. Chaos reigned. The cans fired their 5-inch guns and launched the last of their torpedoes at targets on both sides while Japanese gunners fired wildly.[59] Blinn recalled "there is nothing so thrilling or exciting as a night battle" and this fight was certainly proving exciting.[60]

During the melee, the column that had displayed exemplary seamanship in staying together now started to lose sight of each other. They dodged sinking Japanese merchant ships and, in the case of *Ford* and *Pope*, narrowly avoided hitting each other.[61] The trailing two ships, *Parrott* and *Paul Jones*, peeled off to starboard and departed the fight to south. *Pope* tried to follow the leader after their near collision but also lost sight a few minutes later and retired to the south. Talbot pushed his attack close to shore, firing the whole time. At 0347, an hour into the attack, he finally turned *Ford* south to link up with the rest of the destroyers, still firing away and damaging several remaining targets.[62]

The Battle of Balikpapan, sometimes called the Battle of Makassar Strait, was certainly valiant and a tactical victory for the first American surface ships to see battle since 1898. They caught the enemy by surprise, struck hard and fast, and retired with only minimal damage. Still, some historians would later deride the results of the attack since they sunk only four of twelve transports and one of three patrol craft. Worse, Balikpapan still fell to the Japanese a few days later, resulting in a strategic loss for the Allies.[63] While the tangible effects of the attack are undisputed, one should remember that these men entered combat for the first time, hit the enemy, and came home alive. They put aside their fear, applied unproven tactics in a chaotic situation, utilized possibly faulty torpedoes, and pressed home the attack three times.[64] The men fought hard, and although their battle was largely forgotten in the larger events of the war, those men deserve credit for proving that the United States Navy would not back down from a fight. Perhaps their spirit should be remembered more than their results.

The next day, *Boise* limped into Tjilatjap as the *Marblehead* met up with the destroyers to help shepherd them to safer waters. In port the engineers and command staff were busy trying to determine the extent of the damage and what could be done to somehow get the ship back into the fight. The rest of the crew had little to do besides stand watch and man the anti-aircraft guns. Liberty was granted to some of the men, and DB wrote he was "going over and drink a little tonight."[65] The nerves of the crew were frayed from the accident and the slow tension built from weeks of operating under the nose of the enemy. The men were also probably frustrated at again being denied their chance to fight. Young men, particularly those who volunteer for military service, are always chomping at the bit to prove themselves. They want to know how they will perform under the worst of circumstances. Would they hold their positions and fight, or would they succumb to their fears and cower and run? *Boise*'s crew could not yet answer those questions, and their only immediate solace was release into alcohol.

Tjilatjap was nearly unpronounceable to the Americans, and their derision of the backwater port was evident in their preferred, more pronounceable, moniker "Slapjack."[66] Still, liberty was liberty, no matter the location. DB continued a tradition in Tjilatjap that he started in Manila of grabbing menus from places he visited as a souvenir. He and his friends visited the Florida Restaurant, named for the abundant flowers of Java. "You won't believe your mouth," the menu advertised. It also touted selling natural, fresh fruit juice that was healthy and rich in vitamins.[67] The restaurant may have been the highlight of the town. Tjilatjap is mostly remembered as the site of the final, desperate evacuations from Java a few weeks later, but then it was just a small port with limited services and amenities.

Captain Robinson did not get the opportunity to find out how well his men could fight. He was replaced on the 27th by his executive officer, Captain Edward J. "Mike" Moran. As previously noted, it is unlikely that the accident was his fault, yet the ultimate responsibility for a ship lies with the captain alone. He was in charge when it happened, and now the ship was out of action in the most desperate theater of the war. The Navy had to address the situation in some manner, and thus Captain Robinson was recalled to Washington and command passed to Captain Moran.[68]

Moran had a mess on his hands. Hull plates along both sides of the keel were buckled from position 66 through position 89. Rivets were sheered and, worst of all, there were significant sections where a four-foot gap was torn between the keel and the plating.[69] Still, Moran knew the score in the Java Sea. He had the crew spend January 30–31 making temporary repairs to the boilers and filling damaged sections with rocks for ballast, a backbreaking assignment. At the same time, he fought a losing battle against orders to withdraw to Ceylon (modern-day Sri Lanka) for repairs. The final damage report stated, "In consideration of the situation developing in the Java Sea and in the knowledge that the presence of this ship would be of value, the Commanding Officer informed ComTaskFor 5 by dispatch [sic] that BOISE was capable of offensive operations at speeds up to 25 knots in smooth water."[70]

Despite the bravado from Moran and the crew, the brass decided that *Boise* would need more than ad hoc repairs before they could hold their own in a fight. The orders to proceed to Ceylon stood, so on February 2 they set sail for the territorial capital at Colombo. Before departing, they unloaded a good share of their ammunition to be passed to those ships still in the fight. Although the long, slow trip across the Indian Ocean was completed "without incident," DB noted a few exciting moments.

Captain Edward J. "Mike" Moran (right) with an unidentified lieutenant aboard the *Boise* (National Archives: 80-G-36310).

On February 5, they sighted a submarine at 27,000 yards. One of the SOCs launched to investigate, but the sub dove as the plane approached. Somehow, they identified the U-boat as the HMS *Truant*. They observed more of the British fleet on the 7th when they passed the HMS *Enterprise* and an accompanying cruiser, part of the Empire's last efforts to hold Singapore and keep the Japanese away from their colonies in India.[71]

They pulled into the harbor at Colombo on the 9th. DB noted, "I have never seen so many ships at one time. There is easily over a hundred. A lot have Evacuees from Singapore, Hong Kong, etc. English Cruisers *Dorsetshire, Cornwall, Glasgow* and carrier *Hermes* are here."[72] The ship's log recorded that the harbor was packed with over eighty ships awaiting repairs that the local workforce was not trained or equipped to handle. Because of the wait, Colombo proved to be little more than a frustration for Moran. Local officials were adamant that it would be days before *Boise* could be placed in a dry dock, and even after the four days required for that process all they could do was further examine the ship. They could not provide repairs. Colombo was a waste of time, and Moran agreed with British officials that *Boise* would have to continue the journey west to Bombay, India, before anything could be done.[73]

The crew took advantage of the time to explore a city with the strange dichotomy of Sri Lankan history and British colonization. DB spent time ashore as he did on Java, looking for food and drink not available on the ship. The British provided sailors with information to guide their visit. They were urged to remain within a few blocks of the harbor known as the "Fort" where shopping was regulated, money changers were certified, and drinks were expensive but available. It may have also been easier to keep an eye on the troops. Transportation was available to see the area, including rickshaws for

A Curtis SOC-3 "Seagull" of VCS-7 being hoisted from the water after a mission (courtesy William L. Swisher, Lawson Collection, Emil Buehler Naval Aviation Library, National Naval Aviation Museum).

thirty-five cents, and it was suggested that the only thing worth seeing was the residential gardens south of the Fort.[74]

DB and his friends Mague and Oldham explored the Fort whenever they could get away from the ship. The guide mentioned alcohol was expensive in Colombo as everything had to be imported to the island. This was evident from a menu that DB acquired on the 10th from the "Palm Court and Lounge," where prices set in August were not up to snuff, and all drinks with gin had their prices crossed out and then penciled over with a ten-cent upcharge. One wonders if the prices to import gin had risen, or if the presence of all those British ships DB mentioned drove them up. Still, hard alcohol was cheaper than beer, and thus probably the drink of choice for sailors of all nations. The men had large appetites after being cooped up and fed Navy-issued chow. DB put away six eggs and bacon to the tune of seven rupees and fifty cents at the Prince of Wales Hotel on the 12th.[75] Or maybe it was just a little taste of home.

By the 18th everything was arranged between the U.S. Navy and the British government, so the damaged ship set sail. They collected their SOCs as they left the harbor. The planes had been loaned out to help patrol the waters south and west of the island, as the British had only a single PBY aircraft for the job.[76] Airpower was proving critical for the war effort, and even the painfully slow SOCs proved effective in watching for danger. *Boise*'s next destination was Bombay. As they put the isle of Ceylon behind them, everyone desperately hoped they could fix the ship and get into the fight.

Although *Boise* had left the Southwest Pacific, the conclusion of the ABDA story is still linked to the ship. Admiral Karel Doorman's fleet went out February 26 with heavy cruisers *Houston*, HNLMS *De Ruyter,* and HMS *Exeter*; light cruisers HMAS *Perth* and HNLMS *Java*; and some destroyers but no air cover. The *Exeter* manifested everyone's excitement by blasting "A Hunting We Will Go" from the loudspeakers. Their initial search proved fruitless and enemy scout planes found them instead. The next day the exhausted crews were returning to port for refueling and rest when a Dutch scout spotted the enemy. Doorman skipped refueling and put back to sea. The game was afoot.[77]

The battle was joined late in the afternoon when enemy ships were spotted to the northwest. Japanese destroyers launched dozens of long-range torpedoes. *Exeter* was rendered helpless early by long-range shellfire, while Dutch destroyer *Kortenaer* was struck by a torpedo, folded up like a jack-knife, and went under in fifty seconds. The British destroyer *Electra* was sunk by gunfire before the Japanese withdrew around dusk. *Exeter* restored power and retreated with a Dutch destroyer as escort. Four American destroyers also withdrew due to a lack of fuel. The ships were running low on ammunition, having fired far more shells than most planners thought was possible in a single engagement. The lull did not reduce the tension or the danger while Japanese planes tracked them. Just before the fleets found each other again the British destroyer *Jupiter* hit a mine and stopped dead in the water. A Japanese shell hit *De Ruyter*, and then torpedoes began streaking towards the Allies, soon finding *Java*. The resulting explosion was tremendous. *De Ruyter* was also struck. The two ships were crippled, so Doorman ordered his last two surviving ships to leave the doomed vessels to their fate and retreat to fight another day. *Java* sunk in eight minutes, and the admiral aboard *De Ruyter* followed shortly after, never to be seen again.[78]

Both surviving ships were in desperate need of repair, but intelligence reports suggested the last remaining route out of the Java Sea was still open.[79] *Houston* and *Perth* hoped their luck would hold long enough to escape. At dusk on February 28, *Houston* and *Perth* began their run to safety. Hopes were high, but the crews were exhausted. The enemy spotted them near the Sunda Strait, and although they could have run they chose to to fight. *Houston* radioed a last message: "ENEMY FORCES ENGAGED." *Houston* and *Perth* fired everything they had, giving as good as they got. Torpedoes raced across the sea, sometimes finding the Allies and sometimes finding Japanese transports. The two intrepid cruisers literally fought to the death. Survivors were few, and although the Japanese were hurt in the Hail Mary attack, the total invasion and occupation of the Dutch East Indies continued unabated. The last of the ABDA fleet was gone, sunk to the bottom of the sea in a blaze of glory.[80]

The wounds of ABDA ran deep for the men who fought the lost cause in the Java Sea. Scores died as the Japanese relentlessly hunted down the small fleet and sent most of it to the bottom. Many survivors envied the dead as they went on to spend years languishing in POW camps. The men of the *Houston* ended up in hellish POW camps building bridges in Burma, and most did not live to see repatriation.[81]

Of those who survived the war, many harbored ill will and downright hatred for the *Boise* and crew. Despite the significant damage to the ship, some felt they should have stayed and fought to their death as many other ships had done. This would have made little military sense, but for those who have fought and seen their brothers die, rationality is not always what salves their spirits. Still, some survivors wondered what might have happened in late February if *Boise* or *Marblehead* had remained in the battle line. A few months later *Boise* crossed paths with some of the survivors from Java Sea who called the *Boise* the "Reluctant Dragon" and mocked the crew by asking if their current port of Perth, Australia, was safe enough for them.[82] Obviously, this rankled the crew that was itching for a fight with the enemy. Even years later the animosity lingered. The son of one *Boise* veteran ran into a World War II sailor while visiting Yellowstone National Park. The sailor was wearing a jacket that proudly read, "The Forgotten Fleet." The son asked the man about his experience, and when he said that the jacket commemorated his time in the Java Sea, the son told him that his father had been aboard the *Boise* at the time. "Fuck the *Boise*," the man simply said and turned away.[83]

The *Boise* had indeed missed out on the chance for a heroic and fatal last stand. Still, the men were no cowards, and their ship had plenty of fight left. They would need it soon, for Neptune still demanded sacrifices.

3

Recovery and Diversion

INDIA AND THE PACIFIC

It took three days for *Boise* to sail around the Indian subcontinent and pull into harbor at Bombay. The officers and engineers held a conference with the British and Indian naval officers in charge of the shipyard. The good news was that the shipyard had a dry dock large enough for the cruiser that could accommodate the needed hull repairs. The bad news was that the craftsmen in Bombay were hardly more efficient or capable than their Ceylon counterparts. Repairing the *Boise* would require a great deal of technical work on the part of the crew.

DB was less interested in the repair details, or was not privy to them. Instead, he wrote of the popularity of Western vessels anchored in the bay, and their income: "Some natives came alongside and tried to sell things." There is no mention of whether the locals were successful in pedaling their wares, but at least this time the men did not make them dive for coins simply for entertainment. His fascination with famous warships also continued. He noted in his diary that "the old USS *Mississippi* which we sold the Greeks in 1911 is in here."[1] His fascination with naval history aside, it was unlikely that the now–Greek battleship *Kilkis* was present as a Luftwaffe dive-bomber sent it to the bottom of the Aegean Sea in April of 1941.[2] Then again, sailors tend to love a good ghost story, so maybe the crew sighted a World War I era specter!

Due in part to the old sailor aphorism that states anything that can go wrong will, now known as Murphy's Law, the repairs could not begin immediately. They had to wait until early March for a spot in the dry dock. For a week they sat at anchor while every man who could get liberty found their way ashore. On March 1, it was almost time for the *Boise* to move into dry-dock, so their stockpile of 6-inch ammunition was unloaded. The crew kept boxes of 5-inch shells available at each of the anti-aircraft guns.[3] The threat of air attack was ever-present, and this way Moran ensured his ship could fight back in the event of an air raid, even if they were a sitting duck.

Captain Moran's intuition of possible Japanese mischief was not paranoia. The Japanese seemed eager to prove that the war could strike anywhere, even in Bombay. In the late afternoon on the same day they unloaded their ammunition, *Boise* received an emergency message from the U.S. transport ship *President Polk*, which had departed the harbor earlier that day. They reported a submarine that was attempting to follow them. *Boise* launched two SOCs, each armed with two 100-lb bombs. The crews hurried towards the transport as quick as their little engines could carry them. As the planes approached, the *President Polk* reported the submarine dove beneath the surface, possibly after sighting the incoming planes. The aircraft stayed in the area until almost dark, ensuring their quarry stayed submerged and allowing the transport to escape unscathed.[4]

On March 4 repairs finally began, but Murphy reared his head again. Due in part to years of deliberate neglect by the British colonial overseers in training and equipping the Indian docks, the dockworkers did not have the expertise required to repair *Boise*. That along with cultural differences between the Americans and the Indians meant endless headaches for Moran. He wrote in the repair report "the standard of labor at Bombay is low—incomparably low alongside American standards. The machinery is archaic …, and time has little significance."[5] One sailor recalled that the local workers "drove the Old Man (Moran) crazy!" and that he wanted to fire them all until the British officials convinced him that such actions would cause a mutiny.[6]

The entire crew was eager to rejoin the war as quickly as possible and could not tolerate an extended repair job. Worse, they knew combat was nearly assured after they left Bombay, and they could not accept poor workmanship. They needed to be certain that the ship could hold its own in a fight, and hopefully survive the encounter. The solution was for the crew to take an active part in the repairs.

Boise welders, shipfitters, and carpenter's mates enthusiastically jumped into the job. They took the lead from the local contractors, leaving the grunt work of "driving the rivets, drilling and shaping plates and minor welding and caulking" to the local employees. The men worked around the clock in twelve-hour shifts, with the specialists giving up liberty to ensure the job went as quickly as possible.[7]

The crew had other issues to overcome as well. Repair materials were difficult to find in the correct dimensions, if they were available at all. Fresh water was in short supply for everyone at the docks due to an outdated reservoir and piping system in the nearby hills. The crew experienced difficulties in obtaining any number of items, including "monel" (Monel Metal's nickel alloy) stock; rubber goods; lumber; some types of leather goods; all kinds of electrical materials; boiler material; optical material; packing; paper; lubricating oils, greases, and aviation gasoline; all aviation stores; hardware; medical supplies; canned fruits (scarce and very expensive); canned milk and canned vegetables. Commodities such as coffee, rice, and tea were easier to come by, along with bearings, meat products of poor quality, and clothing, with the noted exceptions of shoes and hats.[8]

The Bombay electric grid was not compatible with *Boise*'s 440-volt systems, so the ship had to create its own electricity. The men rigged kerosene-driven pumps on the deck that cycled cooling water through the condensers to ensure nothing overheated. A week later the crew determined that a portable welding machine was needed to maximize welding capacity, so they asked the British. The local officials reported no machines were available in India, so the *Boise*'s First Lieutenant took up the matter and located four machines for sale in the local area. The *Boise* purchased one, and the British Navy acquired the other three, presumably thankful the Americans had accomplished the hard work already.[9]

Moran met with British Rear Admiral Turner, the commander of the Bombay shipyard, on the 9th, informing him that although repairs were progressing, they would not be completed within the allotted three-week timeframe. To Moran's pleasant surprise, Turner had taken a personal interest in getting *Boise* back into the war and replied, "You will complete on time." He made the Americans' repairs top priority, providing resources and cutting through red tape wherever possible.[10]

3. Recovery and Diversion

On Friday the 11th, the employees of the Mazagon Company leading repairs went on strike and the dock filled with angry, shouting men. Moran took no chances, issuing sidearms to his officers and deploying Marines in positions along the deck with machine guns. The show of strength prevented the mob from taking out their frustrations on the *Boise*, and the workers settled their differences with the company in time for the next morning's shift to resume working.[11]

During repairs, there was ample time for crewmembers not involved with welding and similar activities to take liberty. DB's log simply reflected the days the ship sat in dry-dock. Surviving pictures and stories from the period show that he and his friends were able to find or, in some cases, make their own fun.

Bombay was the most alien place yet for the young Americans. Officers reminded the men before going ashore that the local Hindus and Muslims would dress and act differently. The crew responded with surprise at the wondrous Indian city, especially the cows who wandered the streets.[12] Cows are sacred to Hindus and are allowed to go where they please. One sailor noted "babies laying alongside the curb" and flies everywhere.[13]

Pictures show DB and friends smiling in their whites in front of the imperial columns of the Gateway of India arches, the nineteenth-century colonial-style Taj Mahal Palace Hotel, and the Flora Fountain. The men were fascinated by the performance of a local snake charmer. DB enjoyed fresh eggs again and found an opportunity to indulge his love of dancing at the "F. Cornaglia Limited." He preferred jazz, but the establishment's ballroom dancing either scratched his itch or offered a more eclectic music catalogue than advertised.[14]

DB (back row, fifth from left) poses with a group of friends while on liberty in Bombay, India (Fitch Family Private Collection).

The crew's greatest delight came from an afternoon of rickshaw touring. The small vehicle included a bench for two people balanced atop two wheels and was typically pulled by a local holding two long poles. At first the sailors enjoyed being toured around the city, taking in the sights. After a while they became bored, and a sporting mentality took over. The men began paying the locals to race the rickshaws, with the sailors whooping and hollering with delight as both passengers and spectators. Betting naturally took place as they determined the fastest "puller" in Bombay. The men demanded more entertainment so they began to trade positions with the locals. Now the sailors rushed through the streets pulling the rickshaw owners as everyone roared with delight. Everyone, that is, except the local British upper class. Colonial officials and their families began to gather on balconies overlooking the street where the races took place. The looks of pure disdain cast upon the Americans who were taking the place of the common folk was one of the greatest experiences of the war for some of crew. Evidently a local ordinance was soon passed mandating that Allied servicemen could no longer pull rickshaws. The story of "pissing off the Brits" was told and retold by the crew over beers for many years to come.[15]

Work continued unabated through the end of March. The daily log is filled with reports of plate fitting, welding, riveting, and testing. At 0245 on April 2 "the last tank passed its hydrostatic test," and the crew wasted no time. Fifteen minutes later the dry dock was flooded and *Boise* felt water beneath the hull once more. Later that morning they moved to a berth and began taking on oil and aviation gas. Friday the 3rd, they loaded ammunition and other stores and by 1500 were underway for Fremantle, Australia.[16]

In the end, the crew completed what was reportedly "the largest single repair job ever undertaken at Bombay."[17] Moran noted that warped sections of the hull remained, and repairs would ensure "adequate strength and watertightness," but the ship could not "be considered to have received permanent repairs." *Boise* was also treated to a scrub down where the barnacles were scraped off while two coats of British "Red Hand" anti-corrosive paint with an additional coat of "anti-fouling" paint were applied.[18]

The men had performed miracles to get the *Boise* back to sea with limited resources or outside help. They were rightfully proud of themselves and ready to get back to the fight, but the Navy was not ready to return them to combat just yet. En route to Fremantle the Navy passed follow-on orders for the ship to continue to Mare Island Naval Shipyard after Australia to have their repairs inspected by the Navy's experts, install new anti-aircraft weapons, and conduct "other authorized work."[19]

As *Boise* began the trek back to Australia, the great machinery of a world war decided to make use of their current geographic position. On April 4 they received orders to return to Ceylon to escort a convoy of merchant ships bound for Australia. This would free up a British cruiser to pursue more urgent missions.

Yet the war interrupted plans again. The Japanese Imperial Navy sent the largest naval force to date into the Indian Ocean. Two fleets hunted military and merchant vessels alike, with almost no Allied resistance. The main fleet under Admiral Chuichi Nagumo boasted five fleet carriers, four battleships, and an assortment of cruisers and destroyers. The second fleet under Admiral Jisaburo Ozawa consisted of a light carrier and several surface ships. On April 5, Easter Sunday, Nagumo's fleet sunk its teeth into the port at Colombo while *Boise* was still 800 miles away. Japanese planes sunk a destroyer, a merchant ship, and devastated the docks. They also spotted and sunk the

British heavy cruisers *Dorsetshire* and *Cornwall*. Southwest Pacific Command wisely radioed *Boise* on the 6th to remain 700 miles west of the island until the convoy could be formed out of the chaos.[20]

Japanese aviators returned to the island on the 9th, raining death over the port at Trincomalee. They sent numerous merchant ships to the bottom along with smaller British naval vessels. They overwhelmed the older British carrier *Hermes* and the escorting destroyer *Vampire*, sinking both. In between the raids, Ozawa's smaller fleet proved an absolute terror to merchants in the Bay of Bengal, sinking 88,165 tons of shipping on the 6th, the "worst single day loss of the war for Allied shipping," according to historian Richard Frank. Three out of the four vessels DB marveled at upon their arrival in Colombo were gone.[21]

Due to the ongoing chaos in Ceylon, *Boise* was ordered to proceed to Fremantle without the convoy after a day of steaming in circles.[22] They once again avoided the proverbial hangman's noose. Still, the trip to Australia was tense. The ship received word that the Japanese occupied the Christmas Islands southwest of Java. Japanese air raids now reached Australia, threatening northern ports. All these enemy operations threatened the *Boise*'s voyage, not to mention the ever-present threat of submarines. Without a destroyer escort, the ship had no protection from the underwater menaces save for searches by the SOCs. They maintained radio silence and trusted to a brisk pace of 16–18 knots and the vastness of the open ocean to hide them. They arrived in Fremantle on the 16th without being discovered.[23]

They did not stay long. DB noted that their sister ship *Phoenix* was in port and that "the Asiatic Fleet is here." The Asiatic Fleet was officially disbanded but the men were probably happy to see significant American combat power once again. By the 18th they were underway to Melbourne. DB wrote that they "have some wounded from the destroyers that were sunk."[24] Records list only three non-enlisted passengers without mention of their origin or purpose, but if *Boise* was transferring battle casualties it is almost a given that the sailors were provided with new stories, rumors, and perceptions of the war. This was also the first time they saw the terrible wounds that modern warfare can inflict on the human body.[25]

The crew was also informed that their ultimate destination was the United States.[26]

Wider events continued while *Boise* received repairs and began the trek home, and most were in Japan's favor. In the Philippines, the desperate struggle for the Bataan Peninsula ended on April 6 when Major General Edward King surrendered his starved and exhausted troops. MacArthur's stronghold on Corregidor at the mouth of Manila Bay lasted just a few weeks longer, falling on May 6. MacArthur had slipped away earlier, on March 11, aboard a patrol boat to begin a treacherous evacuation to Australia with his family and a few lucky staff members. He arrived safely and vowed to the Filipino people and, perhaps more importantly, the American media: "I shall return."[27]

The incident showed a rare crack in the armor of MacArthur's carefully crafted public image. He was undoubtedly a hero to many Americans, a symbol of continued defiance against the Japanese onslaught. He wanted to stay with his men, and eventually President Roosevelt had to order him to depart because he knew how devastating MacArthur's capture or death would be for the country's morale. Still, some of his men on Bataan took to calling him "Dugout Doug" because they believed he was living in comfort while they starved, fought, and died in the muddy jungle. His evacuation did not help his reputation with those who already doubted his ability or courage.

When MacArthur was awarded the Medal of Honor in the wake of the defeat, some found this to be an outrage.[28] Major General Dwight D. Eisenhower, the man who would soon lead Allied forces in the European Theater of Operations (ETO) and former member of MacArthur's staff in the Philippines, thought the Medal of Honor should have been awarded to General Jonathan Wainwright instead. Eisenhower wrote in his diary that "[Wainwright] did the fighting in the Philippine Islands, another got such glory as the public could find in the operation."[29] DB did not share his thoughts on MacArthur until later in life, but sitting in India he and many of his shipmates probably agreed with much of the country that he remained one of America's best hopes for victory.

The fall of the Philippines left over 20,000 American soldiers and 80,000 of their Filipino allies in the hands of the enemy. Many of these men died in the now infamous Bataan Death March while being forced to walk through seemingly endless jungles. Those who fell due to injuries, dehydration, exhaustion, or hopelessness were typically left for dead or executed by their guards. The survivors were moved to hellish prison camps across the island and the Japanese Empire. Some were required to work for their captors, others fought just to stay alive for a seemingly distant and unlikely day of repatriation or rescue. Many did not survive.[30]

While *Boise* sailed around Australia, there were small rays of hope for the Allies. On April 18, the biggest morale boost of the so-far gloomy Pacific War came from a unit led by the famous and incomparable pilot Lieutenant Colonel James H. Jimmy Doolittle.

Three months earlier, the president demanded to know how the U.S. could "do something" in response to Pearl Harbor. Captain Francis S. Low came up with the idea to launch Army twin-engine bombers from Navy aircraft carriers to strike Japan and then land in friendly territory. Admiral Ernest King was intrigued by the idea and brought it to Army Air Force Commander, General Henry "Hap" Arnold.[31]

Arnold was enthusiastic about the plan despite its obvious risk. He quickly chose Doolittle to lead what he considered a "near suicidal mission" because of Doolittle's astounding aviation career. He had won numerous famous air races, sold aircraft around the world, earned advanced degrees from MIT in the fledgling science of aeronautical engineering, and pioneered flying an airplane by instruments. He was also an inspiring leader.[32]

Doolittle accomplished the near-impossible and trained his men to conduct B-25 bomber takeoffs in the 500 feet provided by a carrier deck. Twenty-four volunteer crews of five men each and their ground crews trained hard under a veil of secrecy. They knew only it was a highly risky mission that promised to directly attack the enemy. The third week of March, the Navy's newest carrier, the USS *Hornet (CV-8)*, was passing through the Panama Canal on the way to the West Coast to host the crazy assortment of Army fliers. The fifteen additional ships needed to escort and protect the *Hornet* were also nearly ready, so word passed to Admiral King who quickly shared it with Arnold. The mission was set in motion with the message: TELL JIMMY TO GET ON HIS HORSE.[33]

The fleet assembled in pieces as it crossed the Pacific. The final two-carrier armada sailed under Vice Admiral William "Bull" Halsey and contained another of *Boise*'s sister ships. The *Nashville* could provide a quick punch against enemy ships and airplanes if needed. By April 13 the fleet sailed toward their destiny in Japanese waters. The plan was to get within 500 miles of Japan and launch the bombers. Unfortunately, this plan was interrupted early on the morning of April 18.[34]

At 0300 the carrier *Enterprise* picked up surface targets at the periphery of their range. At dawn they launched aircraft that confirmed the fleet had struck the outer ring of the Japanese picket, fishing boats with light armament. But it was not the guns that threatened the operation, it was their radios. The ninety-foot Japanese fishing boat *Nitta Maru* nearly missed the opportunity to play hero when a crewman first thought the ships were Japanese carriers! The boat's skipper knew better and quickly sent word to Tokyo of an approaching American fleet.[35]

Halsey knew their cover was blown. He faced a tough decision. He could continue sailing closer to the intended launch point and gamble on the enemy attacking and possibly sinking a significant portion of the American fleet in the Pacific. He could cancel the operation and turn the entire fleet around. Or he could launch Doolittle from their current position 650 miles away from Japan and hope that the Army fliers had the gas to reach their recovery fields in China. After a quick conversation with the fliers, they both decided the opportunity to strike back at Japan was still too good to pass up.

The weather was terrible, and veterans of the operation recalled the ocean swells breaking over the bow of the carrier. Thanks to the high winds and *Hornet*'s speed, the winds blew across the deck at 75 knots, helping all sixteen B-25s lumber into the air. Doolittle led his men in the first plane, and they flew at wavetop levels to hit military targets in and around Tokyo. The story of their flight and the harrowing aftermath is told brilliantly elsewhere but suffice to say the Doolittle Raid achieved surprise and struck at the very heart of the Japanese Empire with little resistance. They faced myriad challenges, and nearly all of them ran out of gas and bailed out of their aircraft later that night over or near China. Some were captured, some escaped thanks to the help of Chinese civilians and eventually Chiang Kai-shek's army. The Japanese paid terrible repercussions on the Chinese along the coast where most of the Americans landed, killing tens of thousands of civilians. All of Doolittle's men, and the Chinese civilians who aided them, are remembered as heroes.[36]

Halsey's task force still had its own part to play. Before the bombers were even in the air, *Nashville* began raining 6-inch shells on the tiny *Nitta Maru* at 0753 at 9,000 yards. The *Enterprise*'s planes next took a crack at the ship, bombing and strafing it while the crew fired back with machine guns and a small cannon. Still the ship defied the Americans. At 0821 *Nashville* opened up again with the big guns after closing the range. Two minutes later the *Nitta Maru* slipped beneath the waves and the cruiser rejoined the fleet.[37]

The fleet fled eastward. At 1409, aircraft detected two "sampan" boats, as the *Nashville* log described them. The ship watched as the planes tried to sink it. Like the *Nitta Maru*, this small vessel proved hard to hit and sink, so at 1422 the cruiser fired the 6-inch guns at 4,500 yards. This time they fired their volleys in time with the waves, thus conserving ammunition and improving their accuracy. A few minutes later the 5-inch guns joined the fight. By 1440 the small boat was sinking. *Nashville* was able to recover five survivors, along with the crew of a downed *Enterprise* aircraft. Navy planes also improved their accuracy and by evening attacked sixteen additional Japanese picket ships and "sank several of them."[38]

Captain Cravon, the *Nashville* skipper, thought there were good and bad lessons for other *Brooklyn*-class cruisers. The ship proved useful as a screening vessel for the larger fleet, although they could have reacted quicker to the *Nitta Maru* if they had pre-approval from Halsey to engage without seeking permission. The bad news was that it took 915 6-inch rounds to sink it. Cravon fully admitted that while the gunnery results "appears ridiculous, and obviously was excessive," there were mitigating factors and ways to improve. He thought the crew performed well with their spotting, point, and control, but that delays in sinking the ship were due to "protection given by the swells, which had a height from crest to trough of about 20 feet; rapid and appreciable vertical movement of the target imparted by the swells; and luck." He also noted that the crew had never practiced gunnery in conditions as rough as those on the 18th. By the second engagement the crew adjusted their firing tactics and achieved results with only 102 6-inch and 65 5-inch rounds fired.[39]

The cruiser community learned important gunnery lessons during the Doolittle Raid, but the world took note of the broader implications. The raid was an incredible boost to the morale of the American people. Headlines around the country heralded the attack, despite the fact that the only source of information at that time was Japanese radio reports. *The New York Times* declared, "Japan Reports Tokyo, Yokohama Bombed by 'Enemy Planes' in Daylight," and the *Los Angeles Times* proclaimed, "Tokyo Bombed: Allied Craft Hit Capital." The *Chicago Tribune* read "Planes Bomb Tokio [sic]!" with a sub-line explaining "Japanese Radio Reveals First Attack; Claim Several Aircraft Shot Down." When a reporter asked President Roosevelt for details about the attack, he coyly replied, "They came from our new secret base at Shangri-la," an entirely mythical location.[40]

While America celebrated, Japan reeled from the attack. Many had not believed their homeland was vulnerable. In a reversal of December 7, 1941, the Japanese military tried desperately to strike back at the Americans. They launched land-based bombers from Japan to find and destroy *Enterprise* and *Hornet*, along with dispatching a squadron of submarines. They sent all three available aircraft carriers in pursuit. But the Americans had launched from much further away than the Japanese anticipated thanks to the B-25 range, and all the Japanese response was for nought.[41]

The Pacific Fleet also celebrated, along with recording several key lessons:

> The raid on TOKYO and vicinity has caused the Japs to search with their air, surface, and submarine units. This search may possibly delay the SW Pac offensive as the RYUKAKU probably is at sea searching—as are air units from the KAOA. It should be noted that (1) this raid ties up important forces for a long time (2) The military damage is small (3) the risk of loosing [sic] a CV is great (4) Bombing of shore objectives in this manner does not altogether agree with Cominch…. The raid does have, however, great public approval. As one result of this raid we see the good work being done by our radio intelligence.[42]

The crew of the *Nashville* rightfully felt immense pride. They were part of history, the first strike on Japanese soil. Their postwar history proudly proclaimed: "The NASHVILLE, on the 'Shangri-La' raid on Tokyo in April, 1942, sank the two ships which first spotted the carrier force moving in on the homeland."[43] They did their part and engaged the enemy, learning valuable lessons for future surface engagements. They were the first *Brooklyn*-class ship to engage the Japanese with their main guns, and the first to approach Japan itself. They would not be the last, and the mission would soon influence *Boise*'s fate.

The *Boise* crew probably heard about Doolittle's Raid during their brief stop in Melbourne. The ship's radio operators routinely copied press reports from the airwaves and passed along that information to the crew, but they may have also caught newsreels and certainly traded rumors with other sailors in port.[44] DB and his friends apparently found a good time as the only American ship in port. He wrote, "Hate to leave even if we are going home. Sure met some swell people really treat you right."[45] Sadly, he did not elaborate on the good times, but we can be fairly certain they enjoyed the drinks and non–Indian food.

They sailed into port at Pago Pago in the Samoan Islands on May 2 and stayed just long enough to take on fuel. DB thought it "a very pretty place." They saw their *Brooklyn*-class sister, *Honolulu*.[46] That crew had received their baptism by fire on the first day of the war. They, along with sisters *Phoenix* and *St. Louis*, had been at Pearl Harbor on December 7. All had fought against the Japanese air attack, but *Honolulu* had the disadvantage of being moored and completely unready to sail. Shortly after the first bombs and torpedoes hit battleship row at 0755, men began to light the boilers and hammered away at the attacking aircraft with anti-aircraft guns while the crew tried desperately to get underway. At 0920 all their boilers were lit, but a 250-lb bomb crashed through the pier fifteen feet from the hull and exploded underwater. The explosion ripped holes in the hull, allowing seawater to rush into several oil tanks. It warped deck plates and a mix of oil and water began to flood several wiring passages and one of the magazines. The wound was not fatal, but it stopped the ship from joining *Phoenix* and *St. Louis* as they sallied forth from the harbor to seek out and punish the Japanese fleet.[47]

For ten days, the ship dashed northeast across the vast blue sea, again without escort.[48] During the trip to San Francisco Moran kept the crew busy, ensuring they did not fall into depression as the war continued without them. The crew conducted daily drills with all major weapons. Several General Quarters drills were run. In each, the men rushed to their individual battle stations and the ship organized itself into three groups. The first was ship control, which included all functions needed to maneuver the vessel, communicate, and detect threats. The second group was damage control. Those men stood by to fight fires, aid the wounded, and conduct hasty repairs to ensure the survivability of the ship.[49]

The final group was gun control: Everyone needed to shoot at the enemy including loading, aiming, and firing the ship's weapons. Under the watchful eye of the gunnery officer, Lieutenant Commander John Laffan, the group drilled hard. At dawn the 6-inch batteries were called to their stations along with everyone else by the General Quarters bugle and call over the intercom: "Man your battle stations."[50] They were given simulated targets. The gun crews practiced and perfected major and minor muscle movements to ensure shells were quickly sent from below decks up to the turrets and loaded, targets were plotted, and the guns were elevated and aimed at the target. The 5-inch gun crews likewise went through the motions, but typically trained their weapons towards the sky in preparation for shooting down Japanese Zeros. The entire process was critical to make sure each man could accomplish his individual task quickly, with no wasted movement, even in the extreme temperatures found below decks as the ship sailed through the tropics. Thanks to the continuous practice, several of the gun crews boasted a Navy-sanctioned *E* on the side of their turret, noting their achievement of "Excellent" performance per the regulations.[51]

They arrived at Mare Island in San Francisco Bay on May 13. They sailed under the Golden Gate Bridge at 1015, a signal to everyone they were back in the United States. For the next three weeks the ship would receive "damage repairs and urgent military alterations." The entire crew was ecstatic when the day after they tied up to the pier, multiple trucks delivered six months' worth of mail and care packages! Some lucky members of the crew were granted leave and allowed to travel home. Two days later the crew received word that the repair and retrofit period would take an extra three weeks. Thanks to the extension, DB was granted seven days of leave starting on June 1.[52]

While DB and the rest of the crew took time to relax, one of the biggest battles of the Pacific War was waged around a small island in the Central Pacific called Midway. On June 4, the U.S. Navy finally got the best of the Japanese. The Japanese sent a fleet backed by their largest aircraft carriers to occupy the tiny island and control its airfield, while another force invaded the Aleutian Islands of Alaska. Thanks to a fantastic piece of intelligence by Captain Joseph Rochefort and his team of cryptographers, the Americans knew the Japanese target and laid a trap with their own carriers. After a wild day of air attacks on the island and each other's fleets, the U.S. sunk four Japanese carriers with the loss of only one American carrier. The battle fundamentally shifted the balance of naval power in the Pacific and opened the door for the Allies to begin chipping away at the Japanese Empire.[53]

Meanwhile, at Mare Island the Navy's engineers signed off on the repairs accomplished in Bombay. The ship received upgraded anti-aircraft defenses. The superstructure now bristled with 20mm cannons that packed considerably more punch than the previous complement of .50 caliber machine guns.[54] More important than the firepower was the installation of new sensors. *Boise* received or upgraded "two different types of radar for AA fire control, two for main battery fire control, one for long-range air search, and one for short range surface search. There was also special equipment for IFF, which was slaved to each of the search radars." IFF stands for "Identify Friend or Foe" and is a system that helps determine whether aircraft are friendly or not. The new SG surface radar was only the fourth set installed in any Navy ship and would provide an incredible ability to find and engage enemy ships beyond the ship's line of sight, but involved a steep learning curve for officers to interpret and utilize its information.[55]

On June 19, the *Boise* pushed back from the dock to help escort a convoy to New Zealand. The crew had three days to test and calibrate new equipment and conduct degaussing and deperming, processes that helped reduce the hull's magnetism and thus reduced the threat from underwater mines.[56] Just before they departed for good the ship's officers and the local Shore Patrol did everything possible to round up *Boise*'s crew. When the ship pushed off, they were short sixty-three men recorded as either Absent On Leave or Absent Without Leave (AWOL). Over fifty were quickly reclassified as deserters. It is hard to say why they did not rejoin the ship. Many were probably delayed for legitimate reasons. Some were likely sick of Navy life, afraid, or some combination of the two and decided it was better to live as fugitives than to live and possibly die under Navy discipline. They risked everything as deserters; the punishment for men convicted could be death.[57]

The crew welcomed 250 new shipmates filling the ranks. *Boise* rejoined the war effort with 995 men onboard. As they passed under the Golden Gate Bridge, many of the sailors surely wondered if they would live to see home shores again.

On June 22, *Boise* led a flock away from the West Coast bound for Auckland, New Zealand. They were charged with ensuring the safety of the USAT *Ericcson*, USS *George F. Elliott*, MS *Klipfontein*, MS *Torrens*, SS *Jupiter*, USS *Pelias*, USS *Barnett*, and the SS *Matsonia*. They would be joined later by the USS *Heywood* and SS *Cape Flattery*.[58] This was a motley assortment of dedicated Navy attack transports, a submarine tender, and converted ocean liners carrying troops and supplies.

Boise kept a careful watch on the surrounding seas with radar and the SOCs. This

3. Recovery and Diversion

kept some of the crew busy, but the rest were susceptible to the tedium of convoy duty. Moran had to ensure the crew did not become complacent, and the answer came via a new arrival, the new Damage Control Officer, Lieutenant Commander Tom Wolverton. He would direct all efforts to keep the *Boise* in the fight if they received damage and ultimately keep it afloat if the enemy got the best of them. The crew needed to be prepared for these contingencies, so Wolverton put the crew through their paces with drills every bit as important as Laffan's gunnery practice. The journalist Frank Morris provided a description of one such event in his book *Pick Out the Biggest*. He described how Wolverton would distribute sealed envelopes to various stations with specific times listing their opening. When the drill commenced, men opened their envelopes and received vague inputs such as a lookout reading "You sight two cruisers, hull down, broad on the port bow." There are no further instructions, and it was up to the crew to work through the problem as Wolverton's messages increase the chaos and pressure. Orders were sent around the ship, sometimes left unanswered because various stations were now manned by simulated dead men. Damage control teams were dispatched around the ship to fight mock fires, and the crew adapted to various systems going offline due to shell damage, bomb strikes, and even simulated torpedo hits. Once Wolverton felt the ship met his objectives for the drill, he gathered members of the crew to review what happened. In this case, hard lessons were learned when a young lieutenant admitted he did not dispatch his men to fight a fire in a neighboring battery where everyone had been killed. Such a mistake could cost more lives, and even the ship.[59]

DB had a different type of lasting experience during the convoy. On June 25 he was called before a Captain's Mast. According to the Naval History and Heritage Command:

> The term "mast" refers to the ceremony that takes place when the captain awards non-judicial punishment for regulation infractions or official recognition for "jobs well done." In the days of sail, ceremonies were held under the mainmast on a regular basis and usually on a Sunday morning just before divine services. Consequently, the ceremony came to be known as "mast" in recognition of the locality of the presentation.[60]

DB was not called in front of Captain Moran for accolades. As he put it, "Went to captains mast … for our little deal in Frisco." While enjoying some liberty in San Francisco, he returned to the ship sixteen and a half hours late, or "absent over leave." Because a disciplined crew was the backbone of the Navy, it took such absences seriously. The meeting with the captain was likely preceded by a less-than-friendly chat with the ship's senior chiefs, where they berated the wayward sailors in a manner that many found worse than meeting the "Old Man" afterward.[61] DB's infraction could have resulted in any one or part of these punishments:

1. Reduction of any rating established by himself.
2. Confinement not exceeding 10 days, unless further confinement is necessary, in the case of a prisoner to be tried by court-martial.
3. Solitary confinement, on bread and water, not exceeding 5 days.
4. Solitary confinement not exceeding 7 days.
5. Deprivation of liberty on shore.
6. Extra duties.[62]

DB's punishment was a restriction to the ship for thirty days. Only he knew if the activities of the day were worth the punishment. The Navy would have to wait and see if it was enough to dissuade future snubs of the regulations.[63]

The monotony continued unabated until mid-day on the 30th. DB wrote, "Contacted submarines at noon. I was in chow line." Lunch interrupted; everyone ran to battle stations. Thankfully, whoever they saw dove without taking a shot at any of the transports or picking a fight with *Boise*.[64]

The trip continued uneventfully. The convoy was rerouted to Wellington, New Zealand, which mattered little to the crew. One crewmember summed up everyone's thoughts on convoy duty with a single word in a diary: "Monotonious [sic]."[65] On the 11th, they saw their charges safely into the harbor or the custody of other warships to continue to Australia. DB remarked, "Some more ships left today and went into Wellington. We did not stop but went through Cook Straits [sic] and started north again for Auckland. The mountains are all snowcapped and pretty cold."[66]

They finally got a break on July 14 when they anchored at Auckland. There was a plethora of opportunities mentioned in the "Haeremai" or "Welcome" guidebook. Sailors could get free cinema tickets, take sightseeing tours, attend dances, religious services, or hit up a handful of lounges and clubs for free. They were also invited to attend rugby matches, hockey games, and horse races. Regardless of what they chose the Kiwis wished them "kia ora" or "good luck," and probably hoped the sailors would not cause too much trouble.[67]

DB continued his habit of recording other warships in the harbor. He spotted a British ship that was something of a celebrity, the HMNZS *Achilles*. He described the ship as "a light cruiser which was in the Graph [sic] Spee Battle," as he and his shipmates certainly knew the *Achilles*'s story.[68]

The German *Graf Spee* was an odd ship with six 11-inch guns, eight 5.9-inch guns, and twenty-one torpedo tubes on a vessel with only a 16,280-ton displacement. It wreaked havoc early in the war, sinking nine British freighters. It was so successful that the British and French combined efforts and formed eight separate groups to hunt for it. On December 13, 1939, the British tracked down the *Graf Spee* with three cruisers. A brief exchange left the HMS *Exeter* and the Germans burning while light cruisers *Achilles* and HMS *Ajax* bracketed the ship with deadly fire. The Germans attempted to hide in the neutral port of Montevideo, but were denied refuge after seventy-two hours. With the light cruisers lurking at the mouth of the harbor, the Germans opted to scuttle their "pocket battleship" rather than risk another battle with *Achilles* and *Ajax*.[69]

The battle proved the value of light cruisers to close with and inflict damage on enemy ships. The meeting in New Zealand certainly invoked an itch by the *Boise* crew to fight in a battle as significant as *Achilles* had. Little did they know their chance for glory, infamy, or both was rapidly approaching.

The Americans were ready to take offensive action against the Japanese later in the summer of 1942. They were going to draw a line to stop the Japanese and start pushing back. The chosen place was Guadalcanal in the far-flung Solomon Islands. The 1st Marine Division was tasked with invading the island and taking control of the under-construction Japanese airfield there. The airfield would then launch American planes to cover further advances into the hilly interior of the island, and finally push the Japanese from the island and eventually back up the island chain to the northwest. The Navy was assigned to transport the Marines while protecting them from Japanese air raids, bombardments from surface ships, and any reinforcements to the island.[70] The entire operation was named Watchtower.

An armada was established with the bulk of available American combat power

3. Recovery and Diversion

in the Pacific, and the landings were set for August 7. The fleet included three aircraft carriers, a battleship, five heavy cruisers, one light cruiser, and three oilers. Another eight cruisers accompanied the amphibious force.[71] It did not include the *Boise*, for fate had another role for them to play. In early July, the commander of Watchtower, Rear Admiral Richmond Kelly "Terrible" Turner, requested that Admiral Nimitz conduct as many diversionary operations as possible coinciding with the fleet buildup and landings. The idea was to draw Japanese attention away from the Solomons, and hopefully get them to divide and distract their fleet to help ensure the Marines could take and hold the Guadalcanal beachhead and airfield. Nimitz decided these efforts would include a bombardment on Japanese positions on Kiska in Alaska, a raid on Makin Island in the Gilbert Islands, bombing raids on Rabaul, Buna, and Wake Island, a raid on shipping near the Japanese islands, and asking the British for an attack in the Indian Ocean.[72] The shipping raid would hopefully invoke the same fear and response that Doolittle sparked in April.

The raid on Japanese home waters required a ship that could act independently from the fleet. It needed to be fast but carry enough fuel for the mission without outside support. It needed enough firepower to hurt the enemy but also fend off superior attacks. It also needed eyes and ears beyond what the crew could see from the topmast, such as a complement of scout aircraft and the latest radar. The mission was practically copied from the *Brooklyn*-class cruiser design requirements.

On July 18, the *Boise* pulled out of the harbor at Auckland. Once safely away from port, Captain Moran opened a set of sealed orders. These orders revealed that *Boise* was assigned the task of being a one-ship fleet. They were finally tasked with taking the fight to the enemy.[73]

The ship first needed to top off stores and reposition. They were ordered to proceed at the inefficient speed of 20 knots or better and to continue without an anti-submarine escort once their assigned destroyer, USS *Barker*, experienced mechanical issues and could not keep pace.[74] On July 22, the *Boise* crossed the International Date Line once more. They received an order that was sent broadly across the Pacific Fleet for men to destroy their diaries, lest any information from a captured sailor reveal anything meaningful to the enemy. DB apparently complied at least in part because he tore half a page from his log. After that he must have decided he met the spirit of the order, as the log continued. He never again removed any information from it.[75]

They pulled into Pearl Harbor on the 25th. The men were struck by the destruction still evident from the Japanese raid that started the war seven months prior. DB wrote that the harbor was "still in pretty bad shape[,] still wreckage lying around." He recorded the battleships *Arizona*, *Oklahoma*, and *Utah* as sunk, and the *California* and the *West Virginia* were undergoing repairs in hopes they could be returned to the fight quickly.[76] Vincent Langelo wrote that the sight was "sickening" and "depressing," yet the men felt galvanized and "more determined than ever to even the score" with the Japanese.[77]

Their stay was just long enough to receive detailed orders and make ready the ship for cruising and combat. By the morning of the 27th, they set sail to conduct gunnery practice while en route to Midway. They again ran at a brisk 22 knots. Meanwhile, another Watchtower diversion was delayed when Task Force 8 encountered bad weather around Kiska and could not bombard the Japanese forces entrenched there.[78] The bad weather was a harbinger of bad luck for the various diversion missions.

Boise pulled into Midway Island on the 29th and observed the aftermath of another infamous battle. DB remarked, "God what a barren place." Other crewmen granted brief liberty on the island noted shell holes around the one-mile island and an overabundance of excrement from the local gooney bird population.[79] The still-functioning airfield may have been crucial for the U.S. war effort, but the island offered little to the men besides an opportunity to top off the fuel bunkers.

On the evening of the 31st they put Midway behind them. The *Boise* now sailed into a black hole with no contact with the outside world. Radio silence was the standing order, and there would be no contact with other Americans or anyone else until the mission was complete. If they ran into trouble, they were on their own.

The crew was finally informed that they were on a top-secret mission that would take them into Japanese waters. DB wrote, "The ship is underway to shell the coast of Japan Wed Night." He was slightly off, but his follow-up entry that "there must be some kind of a move on and we're decoy" proved that the scuttlebutt was either accurate or at least logical. Whatever the specifics of the mission, there were "different expressions on the crew's face today." Seaman John Macomber recalled, "The old man, the skipper, getting on the PA system and saying, 'We are going to raid the Japanese coast on Tuesday evening.' We were all alone. Everybody looked at everybody else and said, 'Is the man crazy?'" Ensign Starnes thought the Navy considered them expendable.[80]

Moran and his officers certainly knew the mission, and the danger. The August 2 log clearly set the score: "In accordance with CINCPAC Operation Plan 37–42 of July 25, 1942 BOISE left MIDWAY July 31, 1942 to conduct a raiding cruise on small enemy patrol vessels off the coast of HONSHU, in order to create an impression that a task force was approaching JAPAN."[81] With any luck, they could repeat *Nashville*'s success of sinking a few picket ships as they sent out a frantic radio message that brought the Japanese fleet rushing towards the cold waters of the northern Pacific Ocean.

On August 2, the ship slowed to 15 knots and conducted continuous zigzag maneuvers at night to avoid Japanese submarines. During the day they launched the SOCs and continued towards Japanese waters via a route that took them well north of Midway and then west towards Asia.[82] Tension was thick. The new gunnery officer, Commander W.C. Butler, Jr., remembered, "We went far north of all the mandated islands and for days it seemed we steamed across and across and not a thing in sight."[83] DB wrote that the entire crew was rushed to General Quarters early that morning when an aircraft was spotted. It turned out to be an American PBY scout aircraft, and everyone relaxed slightly, but the main battery was kept at "Condition II" and ready to fire twenty-four hours a day.[84]

Through the 3rd and 4th, they crept steadily north and west. Although they maintained strict radio silence regarding outgoing transmissions, they received daily updates from CINCPAC. On the 3rd they learned the only other American ship in the region, the submarine *Guardfish*, had been informed of their mission. *Guardfish* may well have been the only other vessel at sea that knew of *Boise*'s mission. The next day they were told to be on the lookout for a pair of Japanese cruisers bound for Alaska, the *Tama* and the *Kiso*.[85] Butler remembered hearing from the ship's intelligence officer they were "light cruisers" and he was confident "we could handle them."[86] A cocky attitude for the crew to think they could handle a fight where they would be outgunned two-to-one, but it shows the eagerness and almost desperation to prove themselves in a fight. It is probably fortunate for everyone the three cruisers did not cross paths.

Late in the afternoon of the 5th, *Boise* reached a position roughly 750 miles east of Tokyo. They had about three hours until sunset, and Moran determined there was not enough time for the ship to continue west and still be able to escape the land-based bombers by dawn the next day if they were discovered. He decided to launch two SOCs to dart westward and seek out the line of picket ships with enough time to return to *Boise* before dark. The ship could then seek out those ships, raise hell by forcing them to send radio signals to the home islands, and then sink them, hopefully using fewer shells than *Nashville* needed.[87]

The ship's navigator briefed the SOC pilots on their position and recovery procedures. At 1541 a pair of 5-inch gun cartridges launched the SOCs down the 60-foot catapult, accelerating them to 60 mph, a speed just fast enough to get airborne.[88] The SOC with tail number 9-C5–5 was flown by Lieutenant J.K. Boal and had ARM2c A.A. "Red" Fletcher manning the radio and machine gun. Aircraft 9-C5–7 was piloted by Lieutenant (j.g.) F.R. "Punchey" Wollenberg accompanied by ARM3c J.S. Petreycik.[89] Meanwhile, the radio room began monitoring as many radio stations out of Japan as possible to learn if the enemy was preparing for an attack.[90] The rest of the crew stood to battle stations.

Each aircraft carried enough fuel for 4.5 hours of flight time. Each also had a "fixed gun" with 500 rounds of ammunition and a "free gun" with 600 rounds, along with two "live bombs," probably 100 lb. bombs like they carried at Bombay, all to defend the aircraft and create mischief if opportunity arose.[91] The weather was cloudy, but still allowed about fifteen miles of visibility. With those conditions, the SOCs would fly about 8–10 miles apart on a parallel track that would hopefully allow them to search an area forty miles wide. They would continue west until they either found the enemy or reached as far as they thought they could with the day's weather conditions and still return to the ship by 1900.[92]

As the planes trundled straight west, *Boise* stopped zig-zag maneuvers and accelerated to 25 knots in the same direction, like a bird dog on a scent. At 1655 the mission struck pay dirt. All Japanese broadcasts suddenly went off the air. This was a pretty clear sign that either the SOCs or the ship itself had been spotted.[93] Most of the crew could do nothing but stand nervously at their stations. Those who could see the ocean certainly strained their eyes for any indication of a threat. Those below decks could only monitor their instruments, clutch their equipment, or mentally rehearse their actions in case of an attack. There was nothing to do but wait.

At 1731 the planes broke radio silence to ask each other if they had seen anything. They had not and were now approximately 564 miles from Tokyo. A few minutes later the SOCs radioed *Boise* to inform them that they had reached the furthest extent of their patrol leg and were returning to the ship. The aircraft turned east, but the process of recovery began to grow complicated.[94]

Thirty minutes later *Boise* overheard chatter between the aircraft. One pilot asked the other, "Can you see me all right?" The disconcerting reply was "Negative." Without visual contact between the two, they could not support each other and, worse, now ran the risk of colliding in the gathering darkness.[95]

The men in the *Boise* radio room overheard the two pilots as they discussed their deteriorating situation and logged the exchange by time and aircraft tail number:

1808	Wollenberg:	"CAN'T SEE YOU."
	Wollenberg:	"CAN YOU SEE ME? I AM FLYING DOWN WIND."
	Boal:	"I AM FLYING (unreadable). I WILL CLIMB."
1810	Wollenberg:	"I STILL CAN NOT SEE YOU. ARE YOU UPWIND FROM ME?"
	Boal:	"CAN YOU GET BACK TO SHIP?"
	Wollenberg:	"AFFIRMATIVE, WHAT IS YOUR POSITION?"
	Boal:	"RETURN TO SHIP. WILL GIVE YOU POSITION IN A MINUTE."

The two aircraft now tried to separate themselves vertically, standard procedure to help avoid a midair collision. They still could not see each other and hoped they could reconnect en route or at the *Boise*. The next series of transmissions show their growing apprehension.

1812	Wollenberg:	"ARE YOU ON WATER? I CANNOT FIND YOU. ARE YOU REMAINING IN THIS VICINITY?"
1813	Wollenberg:	"WHAT IS YOUR POSITION? CAN YOU SEE ME?"
	Wollenberg:	"CAN YOU SEE ME? WHAT IS YOUR POSITION FROM ME?"
	Boal:	"I DO NOT KNOW. I SHOULD BE SOUTH OF YOU. I CANNOT SEE YOU."
	Wollenberg:	"WHAT WAS YOUR COURSE FOR LAST 10 MINUTES?"
	Boal:	"CIRCLING 5 DEGREES STEPPED INTO WIND."
	Wollenberg:	"IS THERE ANYTHING WRONG WITH YOUR ENGINE?"
	Boal:	"NOTHING. GO BACK TO SHIP."
	Wollenberg:	"WILCO."
1815	Boal:	"I AM LEAVING FOR SHIP."
	Wollenberg:	"I AM RETURNING TO SHIP."

By this point it was clear that Wollenberg and Boal had both made navigation errors, probably caused by a combination of stress and miscalculation amplified by the limited visibility from rain squalls in the area. *Boise* also did not see either aircraft on radar, suggesting that the navigation errors were serious and probably compounding. At 1829 *Boise* paused the westward run to recover their third SOC which had launched later and was conducting anti-submarine patrols closer to the ship. By 1842 they had tucked away that aircraft and resumed a straight west course at 20 knots.[96]

By 1847, everyone's concern was growing. No one wanted to remain in close proximity to Japan longer than needed now that the enemy knew they were in the area.

1847	Wollenberg:	"I AM AT 1845 POSITION AND NOT IN SIGHT OF SHIP. AM BEGINNING TO MAKE FOR HER."
1853	Boal:	"7 (Wollenberg's aircraft) LOST WANTS BEARING."
1854	Wollenberg:	"CAN YOU GIVE ME BEARING?"

The problems were cascading, and the pilots and *Boise* initiated their "lost plane procedure" that called for the ship to broadcast a radio signal on a specified frequency that the SOCs could then follow back to the ship. Unfortunately, for the next thirty minutes neither Wollenberg or Boal could pick up the signal with their equipment. The men aboard *Boise* were confident their systems were functioning properly, as the third aircraft now safely aboard was able to monitor the signal with the device installed in their plane. No one was sure why the two aircraft aloft were having difficulties.[97]

At 1900 *Boise* reached the designated rendezvous point and reversed course to 090°, straight east. It was time to start distancing themselves from Japan. Onboard the ship the navigator determined that the SOCs had probably already passed *Boise*. At 1915 the sun sank below the horizon, and the crew prepared for a night aircraft recovery. At 1935 one of the pilots again asked for the homing signal. Moran complied, and made a calculated risk by ordering the 36-inch searchlights turned on to help the pilots find home. Both the lights and the invisible radio waves had a range of twenty-five miles. At 1838 everyone's spirits rose when Boal radioed "BOTH PLANES IN COMPANY NOW" and again asked for the homing beacon. A few minutes later Boal told the ship that he was dropping his bombs, possibly to decrease aircraft weight and eliminate the chances of an accidental explosion when they landed in the dark. At 1946 panic rose when a lookout reported five aircraft flying overhead. Obviously, that many planes could only be an enemy patrol hunting for them, but the radar did not confirm the report, and everyone breathed a sigh of relief as they realized the report was false.[98]

Agonizing minutes ticked by and at 1947 the ship observed a flash of light bearing 255° from the ship. Although the position was behind them, the conclusion was that the light came from the jettisoned bombs exploding and the searchlights were pointed in that direction. Yet the airmen could still not see the ship or its lights. At 1952, Boal radioed "HAVE FORTY MINUTES GAS LEFT. AM LANDING." Once safely on the water, he passed "LAT 43 MIN LONG 48 MIN." The position was two miles west of their originally estimated rendezvous point. With that information combined with the twenty-five-mile range of both the radar and the searchlights, *Boise* determined that the two aircraft were still at least twenty miles away from the ship, bobbing on the dark ocean.[99]

Moran now faced a gut-wrenching decision. His men were lost in the dark in the middle of the world's largest ocean, and the enemy knew they were in the area. The Japanese could be heard on the same radio frequencies the aircrew were using. He could turn his ship around and risk a thousand lives and the ship itself to continue the search for the missing airmen. Or he could continue his course and speed to ensure *Boise* escaped the range of enemy bombers by daylight. There is perhaps no greater leadership challenge than to decide the fate of men under your command. He made the decision to continue east. He knew continuing their search was a dubious task at best, only knowing their approximate direction and distance. The ship could search all night and still likely not find the unfortunate sailors. Worse, at sunup they would be within range of land-based Japanese bombers, and the next report from the lookouts could be the real thing.[100]

DB recalled the evening's actions and Moran's decision as "we sent [the aircraft] seven different frequencies and even turned on our searchlights but no planes. We finally turned at 10:30 p.m. and started getting the hell out of there at 30 knots. We went into 427 miles."[101] Although his recorded times and distances differ from the ship's log, his sentiment certainly reflects the desperation of the crew to recover their shipmates. His recollection of "getting the hell out of there" also indicates the apprehension and even fear of operating in enemy waters now that the Japanese knew of their existence.

The crew remained at General Quarters until the following morning. They took solace at the time that the Japanese knew where the SOCs were located and a search would recover the men the next morning. Although no one wanted to leave their comrades behind as prisoners of war (POWs), it was better than their deaths or the loss of the *Boise*. Admiral Nimitz's files suggest the Japanese recovered one of the SOCs four days later, but there was no mention of any of either aircrew.[102] Their fate is known only to themselves and the sea. Lieutenant Boal, Lieutenant Wollenberg, ARM2c Fletcher, and ARM3c Petreycik were *Boise*'s first combat losses of the war. They would not be the last.[103]

The return trip to Pearl Harbor was uneventful. The ship sailed on in a melancholy, but on August 8 they received word that their losses may have had an impact on the wider war. They received a dispatch from CINCPAC stating, "Believed JAPANESE Patrol line withdrawn about 7th." They responded with the message "ARRIVING OFF PEARL TEN AUGUST X MISSION COMPLETED."[104]

Operation Watchtower was undertaken successfully on August 7, 1942, even though the diversionary missions accomplished little. The British did little in the Indian Ocean, as they had desperately few resources available.[105] They could do little more than "hold the line" and try to repel Japanese incursions. In the end they conducted a minor radio deception campaign backed up by the movement of a few ships, neither of which seems to have made much impact on Japanese deployments.[106]

The Kiska raid was little short of disaster. Task Force 8, consisting of heavy cruisers *Indianapolis* and *Louisville* along with three *Brooklyn*-class light cruisers, *Honolulu*, *Nashville*, and *St. Louis*, was initially prevented from bombarding the enemy-controlled harbor on July 27 due to heavy fog.[107] They tried again on the 29th, again in poor weather, but this time several of the support ships collided in the low visibility. Task Force 8 had no choice but to withdraw and sort out the mess. On August 7, many hours after the commencement of Watchtower due to time zone differences, the ships finally bombarded the harbor. The operation was too late to withdraw any Japanese forces from the South Pacific, and the damage to the Japanese was minimal. Still, the Navy made note of the ability of the light cruisers to produce a high volume of effective fire during the limited periods of good visibility, a key finding for future operations.[108]

Kiska was bad, but Makin was worse. The raid did not take place until ten days after Guadalcanal. It was the first time submarines were used to deliver Marines into battle, and although 222 of them made it ashore undetected they failed to accomplish anything of significance. When they tried to depart in the afternoon, several of the small motor boats malfunctioned, stranding three quarters of the men. They boldly attacked the remaining Japanese forces the next morning, but twelve men were left behind when the force managed to leave. Those men were eventually captured and executed when the Japanese retook the island.[109]

Historian Richard Frank remarked in his seminal work on Guadalcanal that *Boise*'s raid was the only diversion that pulled Japanese military resources away from the Solomon Islands. He noted that radio intercepts from the same time period "suggested the commander of Carrier Division 2 decided to send some aircraft to Marcus Island," a tiny speck of land 800 miles east of Iwo Jima and over 1,100 miles southeast of Tokyo.[110] Frank may have underplayed the Japanese response, though. In the wake of the raid, the Japanese Combined Fleet Chief of Staff, Admiral Matome Ugaki, wrote in his diary on August 12 that his search planes found and strafed one of the floating SOCs. His forces also supposedly sighted another American plane flying in the vicinity. He continued, "as the existence of an enemy was thus confirmed, we issued an operational order to be on the alert. Furthermore, we also ordered a rapid transfer of the Second CVL Division's planes to the east, a sortie of the available submarines of the First Submarine Squadron, and also dispatched the Second Fleet, sailing off Shikoku this morning, to the east of Chichi Jima."[111] This was less than the three aircraft carrier response the Americans recorded, but still suggests the Japanese were significantly worried about another Doolittle-level raid on the home islands.[112] It is difficult to equate men's lives with a reaction by the enemy, but one would hope that the Combined Fleet's concern and reaction meant that *Boise*'s airmen were not lost in vain. Still, the loss of their shipmates haunted much of the crew long after the war. One sailor simply remembered, "I don't think anyone thought that we would get back from that one."[113]

4

Hell at Night

Guadalcanal

Operation Watchtower got off to an encouraging start on August 7, 1942. The landing at Guadalcanal was virtually unopposed, and the Marines easily captured the unfinished airfield. By evening the 1st Marine Division had over 11,000 men ashore along with their equipment. The defenders on neighboring Tulagi and smaller islands put up a stiffer defense but effectively folded by the following afternoon. The invasion caught the Japanese by surprise, and they had no surface ships in the area to repel the landings. They mounted numerous air attacks on the 7th and 8th against the ships and beaches but succeeded in sinking only the transport *George F. Elliot* (AP-13) and severely damaging the American destroyer *Jarvis* (DD-393). The Marines now owned what one knowledgeable Australian had referred to as a "bloody, stinking hole."[1]

The Japanese were not giving up Guadalcanal without a fight. With the notable exceptions of the battles at Midway and Coral Sea, the Japanese had continuously defeated the Allies across half the globe, and they had no intention of ceasing their victorious march. The island and its airstrip were crucial for their efforts to cut the supply lines between the U.S. and Australia. Despite a message sent to the Emperor of Japan stating only 2,000 troops landed to conduct a simple raid and it was "nothing worthy of Your Majesty's attention," the Japanese rallied quickly to respond.[2] On August 7 and 8, they gathered all their surface ships in the region and advanced towards the Americans.

The IJN was the undisputed champion of night fighting, and their response would play to that strength. They had focused on perfecting night attacks as far back as the 1922 Naval Treaty that limited Japan to a smaller navy than the United States and Great Britain. The Japanese developed the tactics and technology necessary to attack their foes at night, a tricky endeavor in the days before radar and night vision devices. They planned to whittle away a larger navy with harrowing and destructive torpedo attacks under the cover of darkness. Then they could close and finish off any confused enemy in a decisive attack the next day. They trained relentlessly through the 1920s and 30s to achieve their proficiency. Sailors joked that their weeks "contained two Fridays and two Mondays" but never a break for the weekend. So far their training had paid off and night attacks had proven ruthlessly effective. Now at Guadalcanal they were ready to destroy the Americans with the same deadly night attacks they dealt to Admiral Doorman in the Java Sea.[3]

On the 7th, Allied pilots spotted the Japanese response sailing towards Guadalcanal. Reports from Allied submarines also noted that the enemy was advancing and

4. Hell at Night

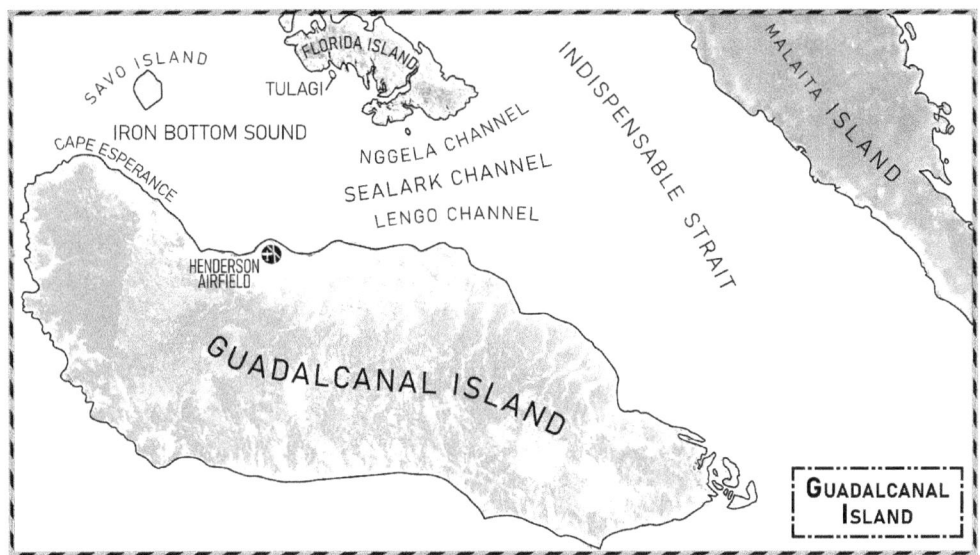

Some of the most important naval battles in the Pacific theater were fought near Guadalcanal while the Marines and U.S. Army fought to maintain Henderson Airfield and eventually push the Japanese off the island.

doing so in a hurry. Unfortunately, they could provide only inaccurate identification of the various ships and no one knew Japanese intentions with any certainty.[4]

The next day another Allied plane spied the flotilla. The report erroneously noted "two seaplane tenders" as part of the formation. This led the Americans to expect an air attack the next day. The fleet had a single ship, the cruiser USS *San Juan* (CL-54), equipped with the new SG radar that was much more capable of detecting marauding Japanese ships at a distance than previous radar systems. They were stationed with the easternmost force looking away from Rabaul. With darkness falling, sailors across the fleet were "dog-tired after two days of incessant action and excitement," and their commanding officers were nearly dead on their feet. The consensus among the invasion's leadership was that an enemy attack was unlikely until the next morning.[5]

The Allied assumptions proved disastrously wrong. Just after midnight, Vice Admiral Gunichi Mikawa delivered the devastating counterstroke the Japanese Imperial Navy had trained for years to employ. From the bridge of the heavy cruiser *Chokai* he led his force tight against the shore of Savo Island to mask their approach. Behind him trailed four more heavy cruisers, two light cruisers, and a destroyer. The twelve-square-mile volcanic island was northwest of the landing beaches and served as the dividing point between the Allied Northern and Southern naval forces.[6]

Mikawa slid past the American picket ship using a combination of darkness, rain, and luck.[7] Shortly before midnight the Allied picket ships spotted Mikawa's spotter planes on radar and raised the alarm, but the Allies failed to counter them. The enemy unleashed several salvos of Type 93 "Long Lance" torpedoes at the still unaware American ships. Five minutes later a destroyer finally sighted Mikawa and frantically called out the enemy's position.

HMAS *Canberra* was the first to suffer Japanese wrath that night. It took two torpedoes and two dozen shells that put the warship out of action. The flying column of

Japanese ships peppered the destroyer *Patterson* (DD-392) until it was burning but did not slacken their pace. A torpedo found the cruiser USS *Chicago* (CA-29) before they were even in the fight. The ship was wounded, but at least managed to return fire. *Chicago*'s skipper then miscalculated the enemy's intentions and steamed in the wrong direction, taking them out of the fight. Worse, he failed to radio any sort of warning to the Northern Force.[8]

Mikawa swung north. *Chokai* fired torpedoes at the next group of surprised American cruisers and lit up the heavy cruiser USS *Astoria* (CA-34) with its searchlights. The two traded gunfire and each scored hits, but the duel was a lost cause for the Americans as fires aboard *Astoria* provided a perfect aim point for the enemy. *Astoria* succumbed to its wounds and settled to the bottom around noon.[9]

A similar situation occurred between heavy cruiser *Aoba* and the American heavy cruiser *Quincy* (CA-39). *Aoba* caught them by surprise and identified them with searchlights before firing. Shellfire set one of the float planes ablaze and again allowed the Japanese to see their target. Additional shells struck the ship as a torpedo ripped open the port side. The captain and much of the bridge crew were killed by shellfire. Survivors jumped overboard and watched their home sink beneath the waves.[10]

The story aboard USS *Vincennes* (CA-44) at the lead of the Northern column echoed their companions. Confusion was the order of the day, but they did strike blood against *Aoba*'s sister ship *Kinugasa* with well-aimed gunfire. Then a shell started a fire that lit up *Vincennes*. The Japanese fired on them from both sides and multiple torpedoes ripped holes in the hull. Mikawa escaped with his force to the north while the doomed *Vincennes* sank.[11]

The Battle of Savo Island was a disaster for the Allies. One Japanese officer noted after the war that "Mikawa achieved one of the most brilliant surface victories of the war."[12] The losses were so bad that the U.S. Navy was forced to cede control of the waters around Guadalcanal to the Japanese. The surviving ships withdrew with much of the Marine's supplies in their holds. In the eyes of thousands of Marines, the Navy abandoned them without support.[13] The Japanese press extolled their victory: "seventeen enemy war vessels are known to have been sent to the bottom. As for the enemy transport ships, 11 of them have thus far been sunk." They further denigrated the Americans, claiming "the fact that the enemy was caught napping … [and] verifies once again there is a world of a difference between the superior strategy employed by the Japanese Forces and that of the enemy."[14]

There was a silver lining to the horrific losses. While the Japanese succeeded in devastating the Allied naval combat power at Guadalcanal, they did not press the attack into the assembled transport ships. Contemporary Japanese naval theory suggested the entire campaign was decided in their favor after such a "decisive battle." The Americans saw things differently and would not truly abandon the Marines to annihilation. One scholar noted that "it probably would have been worth the sacrifice of every ship in Mikawa's squadron to destroy the American invasion transports that night," and that they had missed their "first—and probably best—chance … to win the campaign."[15] The survival of those transport ships meant there was still a chance to resupply and reinforce the Marines now battling in the jungles and hills.

The battle gave the waters north of Guadalcanal the macabre nickname "Ironbottom Sound" due to the volume of sunken ships on the seafloor. The Allies lost four heavy cruisers that night. Another heavy cruiser was severely damaged along with two destroyers.[16] Admiral King called it "the blackest day of the whole war." Over a thousand Allied sailors were killed that night.[17] The disaster was so bad that the U.S. Navy concealed their losses from the public to ensure the Japanese did not learn the full magnitude of the slaughter.[18]

The Marines were in for the fight of their lives. They needed to defend against the Japanese Army pressing on all sides, husband their supplies while praying for more, and complete the airfield as soon as possible.[19] Meanwhile, the Navy had to figure out how they could regain the upper hand.

During the early days of the Guadalcanal campaign, *Boise* was docked at Pearl Harbor for minor repairs and refit after their raid into Japanese waters. They arrived on the evening of August 9, and DB noted on the 14th that "all the old battle ships of the Pacific Fleet came in today[,] all but the *Nevada*. She is in Bremerton. Seven came in all together. The *Hornet* is also here. *Colorado, Maryland, Tennessee, Idaho, New Mexico, Mississippi*, and *Pennsylvania*.—The *W. Virginia, California,* under repair. *Arizona* and *Oklahoma* on bottom." *Boise* was among the giants, but they were not destined for action with battleships yet. The following day they departed for the Southwest Pacific once more at the head of a small convoy. They were bound for Fiji, which was a staging area for the ongoing fight in the Solomon Islands.[20]

The convoy made slow but steady progress across the Pacific. The log noted communications regarding the routine movement of friendly aircraft. Everyone was taking extra care to ensure there was no misidentification that could result in American ships and planes exchanging fire. DB recorded they saw two Navy PBY aircraft on the 20th. On the 23rd *Boise* received updated orders to drop a portion of their flock at Fiji and continue with the rest to Efate. DB's ship spotting noted the escort carrier USS *Long Island* and their sister ship *Helena* (CL-50).[21]

Meanwhile, the Japanese and U.S. navies conducted resupply missions to their forces on Guadalcanal while naval and air forces traded jabs. The Japanese resupplies were so regular that some Americans dubbed the effort the "Tokyo Express." They also repeatedly bombarded the newly completed Henderson Airfield, code-named Cactus, and nearby Marines. American efforts to keep the Marines armed and fed were infrequent, and sometimes destroyers threw barrels of supplies overboard during the night to drift to the Marines on the tide.[22] The Allied strategic picture was bleak after the withdrawal of half the American fleet carriers from the region. *Enterprise* (CV-6) was damaged by enemy bombs during the Battle of the Eastern Solomons and *Saratoga* (CV-3) took a nonfatal hit from a torpedo fired by submarine *I-26* soon after. Luckily both were able to transfer their surviving aircraft and pilots to the embattled Cactus and other airfields in the region.[23] The loss of these ships, although temporary, meant the heavy lifting of Guadalcanal's defense would shift to surface ships and land-based airpower.

Aboard *Boise* everyone was ready to get into the fight, but they remained at anchor until September 6, when they repositioned to another small island, Espiritu Santo. They again waited for orders.[24] Because the crew had little to do, liberty was granted to explore the tropical island. One crewmember recalled touring the local plantations and impromptu swim sessions in the tropical waters. He mentioned nightly movies, and how many of the men dragged their mattresses on deck to sleep under the stars, just to be chased back below-decks by a chilly evening breeze.[25]

On September 14, they finally received orders to be a part of a task force bringing additional Marines to Guadalcanal along with the heavy cruiser USS *Minneapolis*

(CA-36) and the HMNZS *Leander*, a sister ship of the *Achilles*. Several destroyers and minesweepers rounded out the escort force protecting six transport ships carrying over 4,100 men of the 7th Marine Regiment. Together the convoy would constitute Task Force 65 (TF-65) under command of Admiral Turner aboard the transport ship *McCawley* (APA-4).[26]

The landing site was located along the north coast and east of the airfield. The escort ships were responsible for "screen[ing] transport and landing forces against enemy surface, air[,] and submarine attack." DB captured the crew's excitement simply as "the word was passed 'We are heading north to meet the boys.'"[27]

Boise pulled out of the harbor and joined the column of ships heading towards Guadalcanal. They shook off any rust in either their procedures or equipment by conducting "various gunnery and tactical exercises" throughout the afternoon and evening.[28] The crew almost certainly did not mind a day filled with preparations for battle.

On the 15th, the warships met up with their transports and continued north. The 7th Marines were badly needed on Guadalcanal and the task force was heading in that direction. At least until shortly after sundown, when TF-65 turned back to the south. DB astutely noted that "something went wrong we turned around and went south."[29]

Something had indeed gone wrong for the Americans. TF-65 was only one element of ongoing operations supporting the Solomons. Approximately 100 miles west sailed Task Force 61 consisting of America's two fleet carriers in the South Pacific. TF-61 was conducting operations to protect the transports from Japanese air attack.[30] The USS *Wasp* (CV-7) and USS *Hornet* (CV-8) sailed five miles apart with their various escorts. Their scouts reported significant Japanese naval and air activity around Guadalcanal. A single H6K "Mavis" bomber sighted the carriers before American planes shot it down. Additionally, American airpower sighted "3 BB (battleships), 4 CA (heavy cruisers), 4 DD (destroyers)" within 300 miles of Guadalcanal.[31] This information flowed to Admiral Turner, and according to Morison, "Turner felt certain of an ugly reception if he kept going." He could not risk the loss of the Marines before they even hit the beach. Turner's logbook recorded "all factors of situation caused decision on the part of CTF-65 temporarily to withdraw in hopes of more favorable opportunity for reinforcement...." He decided the convoy would continue north until sundown to deceive the Japanese and then turn to the south and wait for an opening to sneak the Marines onto Cactus.[32]

Disaster struck. Around 1420, the *Wasp* was sighted by Japanese submarine *I-19*, who fired a spread of torpedoes that blew gaping holes in *Wasp*'s hull. The explosions spawned infernos that raged uncontrollably thanks to ample aviation fuel and ordnance. The crew fought valiantly for their vessel, but by 1520 the word was passed to abandon ship.[33]

The burning ship attracted additional unwanted attention. Japanese submarine *I-15* was also in the area and honed in on the burning *Wasp*. They entered the fray, firing three torpedoes at *Hornet*. Flag and radio signals flew from ship to ship to warn of deadly "fish." The second carrier was spared, but one torpedo found the new battleship *North Carolina* (BB-55) and tore a hole thirty-two feet wide and eighteen feet tall in the bow. Despite the damage, the remarkable design of the latest generation of battleships allowed the ship to survive the injury and keep station with the fleet. The destroyer USS *O'Brien* (DD-415) dodged the second torpedo, but the third struck home. Luckily for everyone onboard there was no fire, and the destroyer was able to withdraw.[34]

4. Hell at Night

The loss of *Wasp* greatly impacted the strategic picture. The U.S. now had only a single carrier left in the region, while Japan retained two fleet and several smaller carriers. Aboard the *Boise* the crew almost certainly knew of the losses. If they missed the radio chatter between the ships, they likely heard from Radio Berlin that "enemy 22,000-ton carrier has been sunk."[35] The turn to the south along with rumors involving lost American ships had the crew wondering what was in store for them.

The task force sailed south most of the 16th hoping to evade Japanese aircraft and submarines. Admiral Turner was faced with a terrible choice of life and death. Should he send the convoy to Guadalcanal now that their air cover was cut in half due the loss of the *Wasp*? Or should he pull back and regroup, delaying the arrival of the 7th Marines to their beleaguered colleagues? Either choice gambled thousands of lives.

At 1800 Turner hedged his bet and pointed Task Force 65 back to the north. His staff log noted "the strategical situation is doubtful. Practically no plane contacts today and practically no information of enemy."[36] He hoped the lack of enemy sightings meant he had an opportunity to get the Marines ashore.

Shortly after their turn, the convoy spotted a submarine off the left flank. The majority of ships made a hard 45° turn to the right to put distance between themselves and the threat while also pointing their sterns towards any possible torpedoes to decrease their cross section. One of the destroyers charged towards the contact to drop depth charges, or "ash cans" as DB called them, driving the submarine away.[37]

DB noted they did not land any troops, and "we went south all day but changed course to 010 [degrees] North East at 6:00 p.m. We are going to try to take the island tomorrow the 17. The Japs know we're here so will probably have a good scrap." Journalist Frank Morris explained in the vernacular of the time how the *Boise* was finally conducting a mission the crew felt was worth their time and effort. "This was more like it. Captain Moran and the *Boise* men could sniff trouble now—Jap trouble."[38]

The next day brought hazy weather that helped hide the ships. At 1700 the fleet rearranged itself. The cruisers formed a column with *Minneapolis* in the lead, *Boise* 600 yards astern, and HMNZS *Leander* another 600 yards behind. Following them by another 12,000 yards came the transports, while the destroyers pushed ahead and to the flanks of the task force. At 2100 *Boise*'s men stood to extended precautionary General Quarters. DB recorded, "We are going in tomorrow at 5:00 a.m. The transports will follow at 6:00 a.m. We are to land troops at any cost."[39]

By midnight on the 17th the decision was final: They were making a run to Cactus. Hazy conditions made the jobs of skippers, quartermasters, and watchmen more difficult as the fleet took their positions. The latest intelligence reports noted a fleet of Japanese reinforcements was a mere 250 miles west of Guadalcanal. The race was on.[40]

Before dawn, the task force crept through the Lengo Channel. The transports assembled off the coast, north of the village of Honiara. *Boise* and the other escorts established a blocking position to the west to intercept any enemy ships. Shortly before 0600 the Marines were moving from the debarkation line and hitting the beach to reinforce their comrades. Morison described it as "the most orderly fashion of any American debarkation to date."[41]

The Japanese navy was out of position and failed to mount any sea or air attacks on Turner's forces. Japanese ground forces were also unable to deter the landings. In fact, to the delight of the Marines who had endured shelling from marauding Japanese ships over the previous weeks, the morning calm was shattered by U.S. destroyers sailing up and down the beach firing their 5-inch guns at Japanese positions in the jungle.[42]

There was a brief scare when an aircraft approached the fleet from the north. Fearing an enemy scout or, worse, an enemy bomber, *Boise*'s anti-aircraft machine guns opened up. Keener eyes and cooler heads quickly intervened when the aircraft was identified as friendly. The gun crews were ordered to cease fire, but the aircraft was lost to friendly fire.[43]

The entire Task Force steamed away from the beaches that evening after successfully landing over 4,000 troops with their weapons, vehicles, and ammunition. DB enthusiastically recorded the event, writing, "Landed men at 0600 on Guadalcanal. Had all men ashore by 2:00 p.m. Then started on supplies. We landed 15,000 marines." While his estimate of troops better reflected the total Marines on the island at the time, his excitement was not misplaced.[44] The Americans pulled off an important mission that allowed the continuation of the campaign.

Task Force 65 steamed south for the next two days before dissolving. The men of the *Boise* had time to reflect. By all accounts they performed their role effectively, and the successful delivery of the 7th Marines added heft to the airstrip's defenses. A relatively secure airfield at Cactus partially offset the loss of the *Wasp*. Yet a feeling of malaise accompanied any sense of satisfaction. DB noted that despite thirty-three hours at General Quarters, they never lost a man. But they did shoot down a friendly aircraft. On the 20th DB wrote that they sailed past the remaining ships of TF-61, noting the *North Carolina*, several cruisers, and eighteen destroyers. He misidentified the surviving *Hornet* as the *Wasp* but was still awed at the sight of American combat power.[45]

As the *Boise* pulled into Espiritu Santo on the 21st the U.S. Navy in the South Pacific was in dire straits.[46] They had only a single aircraft carrier in the region. The Marine position was tenuous. One CINCPAC report noted "our surface forces in the South Pacific have done nothing the past 30 days to prevent or interrupt these night landings and shellings of Marine positions."[47] Something had to be done to better secure the island, and with the serious shortage of naval airpower this meant that America's surface ships would need to fill that role.

The *Boise* log for the remainder of September was pretty dull. It noted an organizational change that placed the ship under Rear Admiral Norman Scott's Task Force 64 (TF-64) and a lot of time at anchor. One night they conducted a gunnery exercise where confusion caused the destroyer *Farragut* to hit the cruiser *San Francisco*, causing heavy damage to the destroyer. The incident lasted less than two minutes but proved that the danger of night fighting was not limited to the enemy.[48]

The next morning *Boise* was dispatched on a solo mission to locate a PBY aircraft that had been forced to land due to low fuel, which provided a karmic opportunity to redeem themselves for the loss of their SOC crews two months prior. At 0811 *Boise*'s sharp-eyed watchmen spotted the PBY "Miss Bee Have." The aircraft had drifted thirty miles from its original position. As the ship drew closer, the mission became personal for DB when he was ordered to assist the refueling effort. He was part of the small team launched in one the ship's whaleboats to rendezvous with the aircraft. The whaleboats were "light, double-ended, open boats with high bows and sterns ... and [were] particularly well adapted for use at sea, as lifeboats, or for any other service for which boats are necessary." The boat could hold around a dozen sailors but provided a rather miserable ride during heavy seas. DB wrote, "We went in the water, plenty rough." Despite the waves, DB and his companions helped maneuver the PBY into position at *Boise*'s stern. The cruiser shared enough aviation gas to get the PBY home, and the crew used the smooth wake behind the ship to take off at 1017.[49] The crew was certainly pleased to help American airmen avoid the fate of their SOC brothers.

Boise spent the next week at anchor in Espiritu Santo. Boredom reigned. On October 7, the task force was bound for the southern side of Guadalcanal and future operations to protect the Marines. The Japanese were undertaking a massive effort to reinforce their units on the island in anticipation of a major offensive. Their Tokyo Express was scheduled to land 22,200 soldiers over the next week.[50]

DB wrote on the 8th they "left Santos with *Frisco*, *Helena*, *Salt Lake City*, and some cans. We are going to catch the ships that have been landing troops there." The same day *Boise*, *Salt Lake City* (CA-25), and *San Francisco* took turns using each other as simulated targets, firing salvos from their main guns to the sterns of their sisters.[51] None of them could know the next time their guns fired, it would be for real.

On the morning of the 10th, Task Group 64.2 took their position on the foremost edge of the Allied shield at Guadalcanal. Admiral Scott commanded the unit from the bridge of the *San Francisco*. The cruisers were joined by the *Helena* and began patrolling northwest of the island, guarding the same channel between Cape Esperance and Savo Island that Admiral Mikawa used to humiliate the Allies. The tension was felt in the pit of every stomach, but the Japanese did not arrive that night. DB noted with an air of weighted disappointment that "we went in but didn't find anything. Will go back in tomorrow night." Another sailor recorded his anxiety as "I hope we do not keep this up so much longer this getting ready for battle and then not have it is hard on the nerves[,] sorta builds you up to a big let down." Captain Moran called the night's efforts a "dummy run."[52]

The 11th started as inconspicuously as any other day in the war zone. By noon the sky was partly overcast and a steady breeze blew from the southeast creating "moderate" seas with white-capped waves roughly ten feet high. Those conditions would persist long into the night.[53] One sailor added that the sweet smell of honeysuckle wafted from nearby islands, something he described as "very strange, very tropical."[54] *Boise*'s day started with routine duties. Those above deck could look fore and aft at Scott's small fleet, and to the southeast catch glimpses of Guadalcanal and Savo Island. The ships were arranged in a column. Out front was a vanguard of destroyers including the *Farenholt* (DD-491), *Duncan* (DD-485), and *Laffey* (DD-459). At the center of the line Scott led from the *San Francisco* with its 8-inch guns, then *Boise*, followed by the heavy cruiser *Salt Lake City*. In the trail position was *Helena* with the same complement of Mk-16 6-inch guns as *Boise*. Bringing up the rear were tin cans *Buchanan* (DD-484) and *McCalla* (DD-488). Everyone was sailing on a generally southern course. Around 0920 the fleet received orders to "attack against Japanese force of 2 CL (light cruisers) and 6 DD (destroyers) standing toward Guadalcanal Island from the northwest." Scott swung his ships around and proceeded north.[55] This was it.

The afternoon passed slowly for the men. They knew they were standing in the way of the Japanese, but few of the sailors understood what was bearing down on them. DB, with his battle station on the bridge, was one of the few exceptions. He was able to record a remarkable account of the unfolding events from the position of someone who was hearing the inputs from around the ship, the outgoing orders, and the consequences of *Boise*'s actions.

His first entry for the day read, "We started in at 4:00 p.m. at 25 knots. We should meet them shortly after ten. Our PBY's have been giving their position to us."[56] Indeed, the logs of both the *Boise* and *San Francisco* report that Scott shared his battle plan and intentions with the task group. The engine rooms increased speed while the helmsmen continued to drive their ships northward. Around 1800 the ships went to General Quarters while captains informed their crews they would soon be meeting the enemy.[57]

At 2200 the enemy had still not arrived to Scott's well-prepared dance, so he ordered the scout planes launched. *Boise* launched aircraft 9-CS-6 with Lieutenant (j.g.) R.C. Bartlett at the controls. His orders were "to search area of probable contact, scout tactically on locating enemy," and then to recover and land at American-held Tulagi. *San Francisco* also successfully sent an aircraft aloft, but tragedy and miscommunication limited the full potential of Scott's eyes in the sky. *Helena* did not properly receive the order to launch and instead dumped their aircraft over the side to reduce the danger of fire in the upcoming battle. *Salt Lake City* hurled aircraft OS-15 into the air from their starboard catapult when the aircraft abruptly burst into flames and crashed into the sea, taking Lieutenant W.J. Tate and ARM1c O.W. Morgan to watery graves. Observers believed one of the flares intended to mark Japanese ships lit prematurely, resulting in the first deaths of the night. DB wrote, "We kept going couldn't stop, too much at stake."[58]

The burning plane nearly gave the game away. Lookouts serving under Rear Admiral Aritomo Goto spotted the glare of the burning wreckage, but the admiral failed to appreciate the significance and continued his southeasterly course.[59] Murphy's Law struck Goto thirty minutes later when Japanese submarine *I-26* spotted the Americans, but their warning failed to reach him before the battle.[60]

Over the next ninety minutes, the tension bourgeoned. According to the assistant gunnery officer standing on the open bridge with Moran, the night was "perfectly dark," with clouds blocking the stars and no moon.[61] Reports of the enemy fleet trickled in, and Scott maneuvered his force to meet the enemy. At 2250 *San Francisco*'s plane reported "one large, two small vessels, one six miles from Savo off northern beach of Guadalcanal will investigate closer."[62] No one was certain whether these ships were friendly or not, nor whether they were the quarry Scott sought. At 2335 the column swung to the southwest. Due to the difficulty of keeping track of blacked-out ships in the inky darkness, the leading cruiser turned earlier than expected. Moran made a snap decision to follow the leader, which kept the big guns of the cruisers together but meant the leading destroyers were now out of position to either lead or screen their larger comrades.[63] The TF-64 plan was experiencing early difficulties, but the enemy still did not know they were there.

Meanwhile, *Boise*'s SOC was forced to land away from the cruisers due to engine problems. This severely limited the Americans' ability to find, follow, and illuminate the Japanese.[64] At 2325 *Helena*'s new SG radar identified a Japanese force separate from the one reported by aircraft. *Boise*'s radar operators spotted the enemy a few minutes later with their own SG equipment. While the navigator confirmed they were not misidentifying an island as an enemy contact, the picture became clearer and the crew informed Moran, "Radar Contact, 5 ships bearing 065 degrees (295 degrees True), range 13,300." The plot looked like a T with a row of three contacts in a line leading away from *Boise* and another contact flanked each side of the leader.[65] *Boise* made ready for combat. They set condition "Affirm," activated their tracking radars, and loaded the guns.[66]

Boise and *Helena* were both tracking the enemy with their advanced SG radars. Unfortunately, neither ship immediately passed on the information to Scott aboard the *San Francisco*. His ship had the older SC radar which he feared the Japanese could detect and therefore forbid its activation.[67] When the radar contact reports finally reached him, he was uncertain whether they referred to the enemy or his own destroyers now charging back towards the cruiser column. To make matters worse, the skipper of the *Duncan* had picked up the Japanese fleet with his own FCR and was charging towards the threat to fulfill Scott's order to open fire as soon as they identified the enemy.[68]

The enemy continued to close range, but everyone held their fire. Perhaps the most nervous members of the fleet were the radar operators who counted down the distance to their foe, anxiously wondering if they were going to fire before the Japanese or not. The ranges clicked down. 10,000 yards. 9,000 yards. 8,000 yards.

Still no word to fire.

7,000 yards. 6,000 yards. 5,000 yards....

The enemy was now visible to the naked eye from several positions across the task force. Still Scott did not give the order to fire.[69] The skipper of the *Helena* could not take it anymore and radioed Scott for permission to fire. Now the confusion of the situation caused a mistake in the American's favor. The radio exchange was short and poorly worded. The *Helena* sent the message "Interrogatory Roger" to Scott. The message used the code words asking "permission to fire?" However, Scott replied to his radioman "roger," which also means acknowledgment of a message. Captain Hoover of the *Helena* asked a second time and received the same reply. That was enough for Hoover, his eager gunners, and the rest of the fleet. *Helena* fired the main guns at 2346.

Like a switch being thrown, the line of cruisers followed suit, launching lethal salvos from their guns to slay the Japanese fleet. Goto's task force was taken completely by surprise. Steel flew, and men died.

Aboard *Boise*, in the seconds before the barrage, the gunnery officer asked Captain Moran which ship they should target. He uttered the laconic but logical instructions that immortalized him and his crew: "Pick out the biggest one and fire."[70] Months of anxiety were washed away as the crew performed their duties to win this contest. DB and everyone else pushed their fear down deep. *Boise* thundered as every one of the main guns and starboard secondary batteries opened fire. The flashes from the main guns were bright enough to temporarily blind everyone on the bridge, including Moran.[71]

The biggest was the heavy cruiser leading the Japanese, initially identified as *Nati*-class. At a range of roughly 4,500 yards, the initial shots would have been relatively easy even without radar and machines running the gunner's calculations.[72] DB gleefully described the first salvo as occurring at "about 2½ miles couldn't miss. We took them by complete surprise."[73] He was absolutely correct. The first salvo straddled the target and *Boise* observed multiple hits. They adjusted fire "up 100," a slight elevation to the main guns, and continued to hammer the cruiser.[74] *Salt Lake City* added 8-inch shells to the same target and they left it burning.[75] Moran proudly recalled later that they "poured about 340 six-inch into the heavy cruiser and after two and a half minutes he was in a bad way and four minutes time from the opening fire he broke in two and sank with the screws still turning over...."[76] The signal officer, Davis, remarked, "She looked just like an automobile going over the brow of a hill," and other men reported the ship never even trained its guns on the Americans.[77]

The men on the 5-inch secondary batteries were not about to miss out on the action. The smaller cannons engaged a ship believed to be a destroyer to the left of their big sisters' target. The FCR spotted splashes on both sides of the target, suggesting several rounds were striking home. By 2350 they could no longer see the destroyer and they ceased firing after two minutes. Petty Officer Garnett Moneymaker was manning a searchlight high above the deck and recalled "the red tracers on the shells make them look like they are floating through the air." Spotters quickly reported this target as sunk. Not a bad start for the little guns.

Boise was producing an astounding rate of fire. Rather than rely on salvos fired from all the 6-inch guns at once, individual turrets and guns were firing as quickly as they could load the breaches.[78] The Mk-16 guns were proving to be a fine investment for the U.S. Navy's light cruisers. Moneymaker claimed from his perch that "we put out about 200 shells in the same time that the other ships put out three salvos. They are firing by salvo and we are rapid firing."[79] While this comment may well be bravado, it certainly speaks to the violence *Boise* was unleashing.

Two targets were gone from the radar screens and lost to the sea and darkness. But this was no time for the crew to rest on their laurels. *Boise* was now in something akin to a barfight, where friend and foe were quickly mixing and everyone was out for blood. At 2350 *Boise* shifted their full weight to a new target. This one was near the location of the first destroyer that the secondary batteries had decimated. Fifteen main guns and four 5-inch guns poured their wrath into the new target. It took less than two minutes before this third target was burning and also disappeared from the radar scopes. The fire from *Boise* and the other cruisers was so intense nearby ships thought it looked like machine-gun fire.[80]

Throughout the ship men were kept abreast of the situation by a near-continuous description of the battle over the ship's PA system.[81] Hundreds of men who could not see beyond their particular few feet of deck, machinery, or equipment knew the score. Some men certainly cheered while others simply dug deeper to maximize individual efforts that would ensure the continued destruction of the hated Japanese. They had every right to feel pride. There was no doubt anymore that they could fight as well as anyone, and the *Boise* was no longer the "Reluctant Dragon."

Wolverton took it upon himself to serve as the ship's announcer and broadcast updates to the crew. He also tried to break the tension in his own compartment with an oft-repeated story. Remembering a time before the war when he took his four-year-old to an amusement park and the boy succumbed to terror at the top of a roller coaster, Wolverton repeated his son's words to his men in a high-pitched squeak: "Daddy—I want to go home now!" The moment of ridiculous levity in the face of mortal peril helped many of the men conquer their own fear and focus on the task at hand.[82]

Boise swung attention to a fourth target when an urgent call came from Admiral Scott to "cease firing, all ships." Moran kept his gunners in action, later recalling "at this time, the *Boise* was the only ship firing as our own destroyers were coming up in between the lines in preparation for a torpedo attack. But our information by radar was so good that we continued to fire." He even claimed for most of the next six minutes they were the only ship firing on the enemy.[83] Scott later lamented, "In fact [the fire] never did completely stop" and continued to fear his ships were shooting at each other, but Moran clearly saw the situation differently.[84] His current target quickly spouted flames and spotters described the ship as "a two-stacked cruiser, unmistakably Japanese, with trunked forward stack and latticed tripod mainmast close to the after stack."[85] *Boise* had its teeth sunk into prey and was not about to let go.

Scott had "crossed the T" of his enemy, a naval tactic which allowed his ships to utilize all their main guns while his adversary could only fire their forward batteries.

Admiral Goto quickly recognized this fact and ordered his ships to perform a 180° turn to escape the trap. At the same time, his ships began returning fire with every gun that could track an American ship. *Boise*'s rapid and continuous gunfire meant plenty of bright flashes from the barrels to mark its position for enemy gunners. Their aggression and tenacity now made them an excellent target.[86]

War can be one of the most exhilarating experiences a man can undergo, especially when on the winning side. War can also be the most traumatic of human experiences, especially when the enemy's will and steel find a man and his friends. DB and everyone else were living high with the former emotion for the first few glorious minutes of fighting, but trauma, fear, and pain were knocking on their door.

Between 2353 and 2357 *Boise* received a tutorial on the receiving end of war. The log noted that "whistling of projectiles overhead was observed" followed by rounds that straddled the ship on both sides, sending up splashes of water tall enough to soak men in positions high above the deck. Then the enemy found the range. The first hit came at 2354 near the forward mess hall. It dented the armor and cut their degaussing cable, but the damage was minimal.[87]

Boise continued firing as the next enemy rounds hit them right in the middle of the ship. A smaller shell hit near "A.A. gun #3" causing some damage and a handful of minor casualties among the gunners and a few men with the misfortune of moving through a nearby passageway. Another couple of shells seemed to be rebukes aimed directly at Moran when they penetrated his cabin and started a fire. He responded wryly to the report, "tell the gentlemen I'm sorry I wasn't at home."[88] The #1 5-inch battery also lost power and communication. These were glancing blows at best and did little to dampen the fighting spirit of the men or the effectiveness of the ship. A chief bos'n mate in the #1 fire director responded to the incoming rounds almost in surprise, "Say[,] those sons of bitches are shooting back at us!" At 2357 *Boise*'s bite proved bigger than their opponent's when the adversary ship was rocked by a series of violent explosions and "she was not seen again." *Boise* ceased firing and hungrily looked for another target.[89]

While this latest duel was taking place, Scott shifted his task force column to the west. *Boise* followed the leader to the new heading of 300° without any signal from the flagship. The other cruisers also turned west and along with their destroyers continued pouring fire into the burning Japanese ships. Moran later recalled engaging three separate targets during this confusion.[90] At midnight Scott ordered his forces to cease fire, and this time most of his men followed orders. Scott quickly put order to his force through brief light signals that identified the friendly vessels. He then readied the force to pursue and finish off the enemy.[91] DB's situational awareness was off in his description of the circumstances at midnight, but his sentiment was spot-on when he wrote, "They couldn't run we had them trapped in a cove, all they could do was fight or die."[92]

The enemy was taking a pounding but was still determined to hurt the Americans wherever possible. They may not have been as trapped as DB thought, and fleeing was certainly an option, but they also had plenty of fight left. As the Americans cleaned up their column for the pursuit, at least one Japanese ship launched torpedoes at their pursuers. They were likely the dreaded "Long Lances" that caused so much destruction in August.

At 0006 *Boise*'s spotters reported a torpedo wake. Moran ordered the quartermaster to input hard right rudder, jarring the ship to starboard. The violent maneuvering knocked many men to the deck. Some even thought the ship was sinking.[93] Luckily the torpedo slid past the port side of the ship just in time for the men to spot a second torpedo wake that missed the stern of the ship by only thirty yards. Quick decision-making by Moran and exquisite execution by the crew saved the ship. The entire crew, but especially the most vulnerable men belowdecks, breathed a sigh of relief as the ship rejoined the cruiser column.[94]

More good news arrived when the repair parties reported the fire in the captain's cabin was extinguished. Men from the adjacent 5-inch gun crews had assisted and were now back at their positions ready to fight. They did not have to wait long as the radar found another target to their starboard. The guns opened up again at 0009 with the aid of the ship's searchlights. Moran decided his gunners needed the visual light to keep the pressure on the enemy because the radar screens were now a jumbled mess of ships and geysers from the cruiser's shells. One of the men in the radio room remembered the lights were so bright that "I could have read a newspaper." DB wrote, "we started firing again this time at 2300 yards. A little more than a mile. We kept firing this time till they were all sunk or going under." *Boise*'s fire was again murderous, but there is an old military maxim that began to apply to the fight. It states that tracer bullets work both ways, meaning that the brightly burning projectiles do not just help a gunner find a target, they help the enemy find the shooter. The same is true for searchlights, and the highly skilled Japanese gunners of multiple ships now had an incredible view of the *Boise* thanks to the lights.[95]

Boise's current opponent took a beating and burst into flames, but this duel was destined to be more even than the previous. The ship fired back and landed at least four hits on *Boise*. Explosions rocked Moran and his men. Worse was the emergence of a new threat. A previously unidentified Japanese ship appeared out of the dark off *Boise*'s starboard bow. This threat was identified as a heavy cruiser none of the Americans were currently tracking or engaging, and they locked their 8-inch guns onto *Boise*'s searchlights to unleash hell. As Morison later wrote in the Navy's official account of the battle: "For three minutes *Boise* was given a demonstration of accurate Japanese gunnery."[96]

The first few rounds straddled the ship. Then the gunners found their mark at 0010. An 8-inch shell hit the barbette of Turret 1.[97] It was embedded in the thick armor designed to protect the turret with its nose exposed to the gun crew. The Japanese fuse failed to explode immediately, providing a brief opportunity for exodus. Lieutenant William "Beaverhead" Thomas knew the 250-pound shell was a literal time bomb and ordered everyone out of the small escape hatch. He stood his post while his men evacuated and picked up the phone to inform the bridge "the fuse hasn't gone off yet. I can still hear it spluttering...."[98] He never finished the sentence. The fuse finally did its job by detonating the high explosives inside the turret. Thomas's quick and selfless actions saved eleven of his men. The rest perished with him in a fiery explosion that cracked the main deck. The holes in the deck allowed lethal gases to escape the turret. The combination of gases and pressure knocked a nearby repair team "out of commission," killing five of their members.[99]

The second shell to strike home did so along the ship's starboard side. It penetrated the hull below the armor sheeting and exploded in the magazine that fed Turrets 1 and 2.[100] The shell was a specially designed "diving shell" meant to maintain its ballistic properties after hitting the water and strike ships along their lightly armored bellies.[101] This allowed it to rip a hole in the hull nine feet below the waterline. The blast killed everyone in the vicinity. Flames leapt in every direction. Men above the main deck observed flames pouring through openings in the two forwardmost turrets. The crew of Turret 2 never had a chance. The pressure, heat, and gases killed the men instantaneously at their stations. The hellfire burned some of the men who had just escaped Turret 1. Solid engineering and proper procedures ensuring hatches were closed between compartments contained the fire in the vicinity of Turret 3 and forward. Still, most of the men in the area, with the exception of those in the Turret 3 handling room, were killed.[102]

Further fire or another explosion in the magazine threatened to break the ship in two. Wolverton ordered his men to flood the forward magazines, but there was no reply from his men in that part of the ship. The explosion cut the communications, and everyone nearby was dead. Survivors from other parts of the ship were unable to reach the remote-control flooding panel and valves. This would have been the end of *Boise* had the 8-inch shell and its explosion not also provided the means for salvation. The gaping hole below the waterline allowed enough water to pour in to smother the flames and soak the remaining gunpowder.[103]

High above the deck, Moneymaker exhibited the sentiment of much of the crew during those helpless moments of terror. He explained what it was like to be on the receiving end of such deadly fire: "Can't say just how I feel but I am definitely scared, but I can still do all that I am supposed to do. Just feel sorta small." Despite feeling small, he continued to do his duty. The fighting knocked out both of his searchlights. Whether they would be needed again or not was outside his control, so he sprang into action to replace damaged components "the fastest that I ever moved."[104]

The next shot that the Japanese landed hit Turret 3.[105] In a matter of seconds, *Boise* went from a conquering hero firing fifteen 6-inch guns to a wounded animal missing half its claws. The repeated blows again dropped men to the deck. As the men on the bridge recovered, Moran ordered the quartermaster to input full left rudder and accelerate to flank speed. The front of his ship was ablaze and the intrepid light cruiser was outmatched.[106] They needed to get away, or at least turn so their aft turrets could continue fighting.

Turret 3 was saved from an explosion like the ones that killed their forward comrades. Instead, the shell "detonated against the faceplate under the left gun…. Fragments scored the slide cylinders of all turret #3 guns to a depth of ½"; the main deck under the hit was ruptured at its boundary with the turret; and the plating of the forward superstructure was extensively punctured." The blast also damaged the nearby 5-inch battery and the forward fire directors. Their turret filled with fire, but the men continued to fight. Despite the noxious fumes filling their lungs and obscuring their vision, the men managed to get off two more rounds per gun. After those determined rounds the gun captain decided his equipment was too damaged to continue fighting. There was also no way to easily get any more ammunition with the loss of the forward magazines.[107]

Two more significant hits shook the *Boise* in short succession. They were 5-inch shells from the target *Boise* had lit up by searchlight. Both rounds punched through the starboard hull close together and passed entirely through the ship without exploding. These hits were relatively minor considering the fires raging elsewhere, but they did manage to destroy the library, carry away several of the Marine's clothing lockers, and cut a heating system manifold near sick bay that poured steam into the compartment and hindered damage control.[108]

Seconds later another pair of 5-inch shells added fresh holes to *Boise*'s battered hull. These added to the flooding of forward compartments. The hits "appeared particularly heavy to the personnel below decks aft, giving a 'wave motion' to the entire hull" which led many to believe they had been hit by a torpedo.[109] One shell struck Joseph Fenton's compartment. His damage control team pushed out as water rushed in, only to be ordered back in by a chief to plug the holes with mattresses. Just below them the hits plunged the engine room into darkness. Frederick Klemm recalled "just a real bad sound," of the shell skipping off the thick steel deck above their heads. He later admitted his fright, but chuckled because "the engineering officer was scareder[sic] than I was, he was holding my hand!"[110]

In the aft portions of the ship one sailor loading shells into the guns of Turret 4 battled his own fear to keep *Boise* in the fight long enough to escape. William Mulvey shared with an interviewer after the war his memory of those few minutes. He described hearing "Turret one's been hit, all men killed. Turret two's been hit, all men killed," then a few moments later, "Turret three's been hit, and I'm in Turret four! So we're hustling, keeping those bullets going up."[111] *Boise* continued to fire from the aft turrets in a desperate attempt to keep the hungry enemy at bay.

Before the Japanese could punch Mulvey's ticket and take out all of *Boise*'s guns, a hulking mass sailed into view between them and the enemy. Like an avenging angel, *Salt Lake City* charged between *Boise* and their foes. The move was a strange mix of courage and foolishness on the part of the *Salt Lake City* captain that can only be found in the chaos of war. The ship had observed *Boise* "haul out of column to port with fire blazing around her forward turrets, but notwithstanding maintaining a most heavy volume of fire from the after turrets."[112] The larger cruiser put itself on the line and acted as a literal shield for *Boise*. Their 8-inch guns thundered at the heavy cruiser. After the first salvo the enemy guns went silent, but this did not satisfy the *Salt Lake City*. It put four more salvos from the main guns into the cruiser until "she was seen to sink." With their reckless act of salvation and vengeance complete, *Salt Lake City* continued after the enemy.[113] DB described the events as "we were hit by 5 eight and four 5 inch shells. One got our forward magazine and set us on fire, then the *Salt Lake City* moved in front of us. She took our fire getting three hits before she polished off the big Jap of the *Mogami*-class. She saved the day for us."[114]

It was now 0012. *Boise* had endured "twenty-seven minutes of hell."[115] The aft and starboard batteries fired a few more rounds until they lost the range of any targets. Crewmembers looking aft were treated to the explosion of the cruiser *Salt Lake City* tangled with.[116]

The view forward was considerably worse. "Smoke, debris, hot water, and sparks flew up well above the level of the forward directors and seriously obscured visibility from Batt I…."[117] *Boise*'s bow was low in the water thanks to the flooding, and they listed to starboard. Damage reports poured in from around the ship, and any one of the issues could slip the ship beneath the waves for good. The ship's log succinctly listed the major problems as of 0013:

> Forward turrets were all out of action. Forward 6" magazines and handling rooms were all flooded. Turrets #1 and #2 were burning fiercely, and casualties to personnel in battle stations forward of superstructure were in the neighborhood of 75 per cent [sic]. The topside fires still made the ship visible for miles. Flooding was in progress from last hit.[118]

4. Hell at Night

The entire crew faced the incredibly difficult challenge of shifting from battling the enemy to fighting for their survival. On the bridge and in the map room, the crew, including DB, scrambled to steer a safe course to the southwest away from the battle that would also keep them away from new dangers. No one wanted a repeat of the 1942 hidden reef incident, and everyone prayed that there were no additional enemy ships near enough to resume the fight.[119] They still had full power for the engines, so even if their ability to fight was limited they could run and maneuver.[120]

The ship suffered from two types of potentially fatal wounds. The first was flooding. The water that poured into the hull extinguished the initial fire below deck and prevented a catastrophic explosion, but now that water threatened to sink the vessel. The damage control parties did what they could to halt the spread of the water. They plugged holes with bedding backed up with shoring. They also rigged submersible pumps and were able to keep the ship afloat.[121]

Others battled the flames that threatened to consume them from within. In only five minutes the exceptionally trained crew had the fires on the forecastle extinguished. The burning turrets proved more challenging. Atop Turret 2 was a collection of brightly burning lifejackets. An unknown sailor climbed the scorching turret to cut them away before the fiery material could detach and start additional fires.[122] This was just one of many anonymous acts of bravery that evening.

Firemen quickly tackled the flames in Turret 1. Lieutenant Thomas's order to evacuate now helped save more than his crew. The open hatch provided the perfect access point for the hoses. The firemen's water quickly doused the danger there.

Turret 2 proved much more difficult. First the men needed to defeat the external flames and gain access to the interior. As they set about this task, a gunner's mate stationed below decks named Ed Tyndal arrived at the scene. He was adamant that they let him enter the turret to rescue survivors, including his younger brother Bill. He begged and pleaded with the damage control party to let him enter the inferno. The men held the bereaved sibling back. They knew there was no possibility of survivors inside that kiln.[123]

The external flames of Turret 2 were smothered quickly. When the crews reached the escape hatch, they found it jammed shut. No one could find a way to pry it open. It may have been blocked by the corpses of their crewmates. In the meantime, the firemen pressed their hose nozzles to the small case-ejection slots. These small openings provided a space to push expended shell casings out of the turret during battle. They were not large enough to see what effect the water was having on the flames, but it certainly could not hurt. The indirect method took nearly an hour to extinguish the blaze.[124]

The fires were not the final threat from the turrets. It was impossible to know whether the guns of Turret 2 were "hot" or not, meaning the crew did not know if there were live shells loaded into the guns. Someone had to access the turret and ensure the guns did not inadvertently fire. That situation could result in the gun blowing itself to pieces and reigniting the fires that so recently threatened the ship. Eventually the crew pried open the access hatch to Turret 2 and a gunner was able to enter the black hellscape. He cut the electrical lines to the guns along with other measures to prevent disaster. While inside he also glimpsed the charred remains of his shipmates. He reported with pride that all of them were still at their stations.[125]

Men who could be spared from their battle stations and the repair teams provided basic first aid to the wounded. They carried the worst cases to the makeshift sick bay, a space that itself had been peppered by shell fragments. Many men harbored small injuries but their pride and determination would not allow them to leave their posts for treatment. Moneymaker caught a piece of shrapnel just below his right eye, while his shipmate manning the neighboring Spotlight 3 was struck with a piece in the ankle. Neither even considered leaving their stations.[126]

Where the wounded could not be evacuated, they were likely propped against bulkheads to aid breathing, or laid flat with their feet elevated to treat for shock per Navy first aid training.[127] The sick bay was unusable thanks to the steam and sloshing floodwater. Wounded men were instead taken to an impromptu aid station set up near the chief petty officer quarters. That position was also rendered unusable during the fight to save the ship, and the medical officer "performed the bulk of his operating in the galley, bakeshop, and vegetable locker."[128] The number of wounded was relatively small considering the violence *Boise* experienced during the battle. Many men thought it a mercy that most of their fallen comrades had died instantly.[129]

Below the forward turrets, most men were killed quickly, but the crew still conducted an exhaustive search for survivors. Men wore respirators for the smoke and fumes and slowly combed through the wreckage. Their flashlights poked dim holes in the darkness because Wolverton had cut power to all forward compartments to prevent electrical shorts from starting another fire. Their efforts provided salvation for a handful of men still breathing.[130]

Marine Sergeant Berry Perry sadly demonstrated the multitudes of ways men could die in combat. He survived the battle, and the next day was observed drinking a cup of coffee when he said to his comrades, "I feel a little sick, I think I'll go lay down." He died in his bunk shortly after without a visible scar. He had inhaled poisonous gas during the battle, and according to a friend "the gas turned to liquid in his lungs."[131]

Separate from the physically wounded were some men who could not mentally process the events of the previous hours. Moneymaker wrote of two such cases: "Mr. Clark is batty. One kid is paralized [*sic*] from shock. He can talk but can't feel, move or eat."[132] Such reactions are common in all wars, and many people recover quickly and return to duty. The entire crew suffered various levels of psychological injury; these men were just the first to openly display the symptoms.

On top of flooding, fires, deaths, and injuries, *Boise* lost external communication during the battle. Shellfire had wrecked the power cables for the TBS-50 radio.[133] This meant Moran could not inform Admiral Scott or anyone else they were leaving the column or of their condition. The last the task force knew, *Boise* had sailed west while burning. The ship's successful efforts to quell the flames and then to work under impressive light discipline now worked against them. Everyone assumed *Boise* had succumbed to its injuries. Scott broke off further enemy pursuit around 0020 and tried to gather his disparate forces in case of a second round.[134] He ordered the commander of his destroyers to "detail one of your boys to stand by *Boise*." They only had a rough idea of where the cruiser may have sunk, and they feared a difficult search for any survivors. Scott mentioned in his initial battle report to his superiors that "*Boise* burning badly when last seen."[135]

Boise was anything but sunk. By 0230 the most pressing concerns were addressed, and Moran felt they were ready to rejoin the task force. And why not? Despite their damage and losses, they could still maintain a respectable speed, although high speeds threatened the temporary hull repairs. They could also still contribute six 6-inch guns and their secondary batteries to any fight if the Japanese wanted to reengage. Besides, they were a lot safer in a group with their comrades than they were sailing alone and vulnerable.

4. Hell at Night

Their spirits were further raised when they recovered the wayward Lieutenant Bartlett and his stranded SOC. He was not to share the fate of his comrades off Japan, and once aboard the ship gave a hair-raising report worthy of the ship's experience that night. He informed Moran that "3 Japanese warships passed his plane close aboard on course about 320, at a speed about 18 knots. The ships, which passed him at distance of less than 300 yards, appeared to be a small cruiser similar to YUBARI, the ITUKUSIMA, and a destroyer, possibly of the HATUHARU class." They considered the *Itukusima* identification "particularly definite."[136] Bartlett was certainly susceptible to the confusion of the night, but it is undeniable that he witnessed enemy ships pass his position. This led credence to the growing idea that there was at least one additional Japanese force in the area that may or may not have included the heavy cruiser that surprised and pummeled *Boise*. Bartlett was also incredibly lucky he was not spotted while floating on the waves, or he most assuredly would have attracted attention of the steel variety from the passing Japanese.

The ship now needed to rejoin the rest of the task force. Radar picked up a group of ships that should be their comrades, but the fleet did not possess any systems to identify each other with radar. That capability would come later in the war. Therefore, since neither *Boise* nor Scott's force knew if there was still a Japanese fleet in the area, the possibility of friendly fire during any rejoin maneuver was high. *Boise* double-checked every functioning gun to ensure it was loaded. The crew was an extreme mix of exhaustion, fear, adrenaline, and anger unique to combat. They wanted to survive the night, but they also wanted revenge. Commander Butler recalled, "No one was in the mood for not shooting." Thankfully, as the ship approached the rest of the Americans, everyone in Scott's force held their fire and *Boise* was positively identified through signals.[137]

At 0245 *Boise* rejoined Scott and the others. Thousands of men breathed a sigh of relief that the ship was not lost. Still, dawn was several hours away and threats could be prowling anywhere. Scott resumed his patrol, cruising southeast at 20 knots while his ships tended their wounds.[138]

In the wake of the battle, the men of the *Boise* came to terms with the dichotomy of triumph and loss. They had been a significant force in the rout of a Japanese task force. They had redeemed any honor they may have lost from running aground ten months earlier. They had upheld the honor of the U.S. Navy and avenged the losses at Savo Island. But they had paid a terrible toll. One hundred seven of their own were dead, and 35 more brought Purple Hearts home along with their severe wounds.[139]

During the battle *Boise* contributed more than its fair share to the action. DB recorded the shot count for each of the turrets. He listed[140]:

Location	Rounds Fired
Turret 1	99
Turret 2	103
Turret 3	111
Turret 4	139
Turret 5	156
5-inch Batteries (combined)	823

This accounting is logical and similar to the estimates given by Moran after the battle. The ship's log admits that due to the destruction of the forward magazine it is impossible to account for every round fired that evening. Every gun that could face the enemy had plenty of work, regardless of the exact amount of ammunition expended. The aft turrets fired more than the forward guns simply because they survived and kept firing as *Boise* escaped. Moran later praised his gunners for their "unparalleled" excellence in fire discipline, either forgetting or overlooking the moments of trigger-happiness that ultimately kept many of the Japanese on their back foot throughout the engagement.[141]

Thanks to the prodigious output of shells and the numerous explosions on enemy ships observed throughout the evening, the men believed strongly they had inflicted incredible damage on the enemy. DB wrote, "The *Boise* was credited with a heavy cruiser of the *Nachi* class and three destroyers. Also helped sink two others. One *Mogami* and one older four stack type." Moran told a Navy intelligence officer a few months later that "the actual score for the night was four cruisers sunk and at least five destroyers. We lost the *Duncan*."[142] Shortly after the battle Moran ordered the silhouettes of six Japanese ships painted on the bridge. The report to Admiral Nimitz in Hawaii after the battle estimated "one cruiser sunk, one cruiser damaged, four destroyers sunk or damaged, small

Sailor W.R. Martin shows off the Japanese trophy flags painted on the pilothouse as a scoreboard of enemy ships claimed sunk in the Battle of Cape Esperance. The six Japanese ships (two heavy cruisers, a light cruiser and three destroyers) greatly overstated the actual enemy losses, which were one heavy cruiser (*Furutaka*) and one destroyer (*Fubuki*) sunk and one heavy cruiser (*Aoba*) badly damaged (National Archives: 80-G-36299).

transport probably sunk."[143] The *Boise*'s after-action report also estimated that they had killed between two and three thousand Japanese sailors.[144]

The task force believed upon review that they had faced three separate Japanese forces that evening. The first group was the force they tangled with and dealt significant damage. They estimated that group consisted of three cruisers and three destroyers. The second group was of unknown size but contained *Boise*'s heavy cruiser nemesis. The Americans believed that group arrived at the tail end of the battle and departed rather than risk further losses. The third group was the force that *San Francisco*'s scout plane observed before the battle and later passed Lieutenant Bartlett's floating plane. That force was responsible for landing Japanese troops on Guadalcanal.[145]

In reality the official "score" was inflated, but not intentionally so. The overall composition of Japanese forces was also an overestimate. The inaccuracies reflect the confusion that surrounds combat, especially at night. Admiral Scott and his task force had actually fought fewer Japanese ships that night than they claimed to have sunk. Admiral Goto had led the three heavy cruisers *Aoba*, *Kinugasa*, and *Furutaka* into battle. The lead cruiser was flanked by a pair of destroyers, *Hatsuyuki* and *Fubuki*, resulting in a T formation. Goto's group was overmatched in both ships and guns. A second force known as the Relief Group of two seaplane tenders and seven destroyers managed to land troops, supplies, and equipment on Guadalcanal. The third force did not exist, but was instead a case of misidentification and confusion from the battle that became known as the Battle of Cape Esperance. Modern historians think the ship that inflicted so much pain on *Boise* was likely the *Kinugasa*, who had somehow avoided the initial American onslaught and was basically undamaged when it fired on the *Boise*.[146]

The Japanese certainly suffered during their clash with the Americans. The destroyer on their right wing, the *Fubuki*, was sunk early in the battle when the ships tried to turn and flee. The cruiser *Furutaka* took incredible damage and sunk at 0248. The flagship *Aoba* also suffered tremendous damage from the American guns. Admiral Goto was killed on the bridge in the opening minutes of the engagement, a significant blow to Japanese cohesion. The ship survived the encounter but was battered. *Kinugasa* and *Hatsuyuki* both sailed away mostly unscathed. American aircraft also managed to sink two of the Relief Group destroyers the next day as they withdrew up the Slot.[147] It would not be until after the war that the Americans learned the truth of the night.

On the American side the losses were lighter, but not insignificant. Besides the damage to *Boise*, the other cruisers also took several hits. *Helena* was the best off and received little damage. *Duncan* was sunk during its solo run against the Japanese left flank. The survivors contended with sharks during the night that were later fought off with rifle fire from *McCalla* sailors. The effort was highly successful and 195 men were recovered, but they lost 48 of their brothers.[148] They likewise tried to save Japanese survivors from the sea, but most refused rescue from their sworn enemies and eventually succumbed to the elements.[149]

The fate of the *Farenholt* justified Scott's concerns of misidentification. The small destroyer took several hits around the same time *Duncan* went down. Shells peppered the superstructure and tore a hole in the hull above the waterline. That hit also cut communications, and escaping steam forced sailors to abandon several compartments below decks, crippling the ship's ability to fight. When the crew analyzed the damage after the battle, they determined it was caused by 6-inch shells like those fired by the American light cruisers. More damning was the location of the damage. The hits were on the port

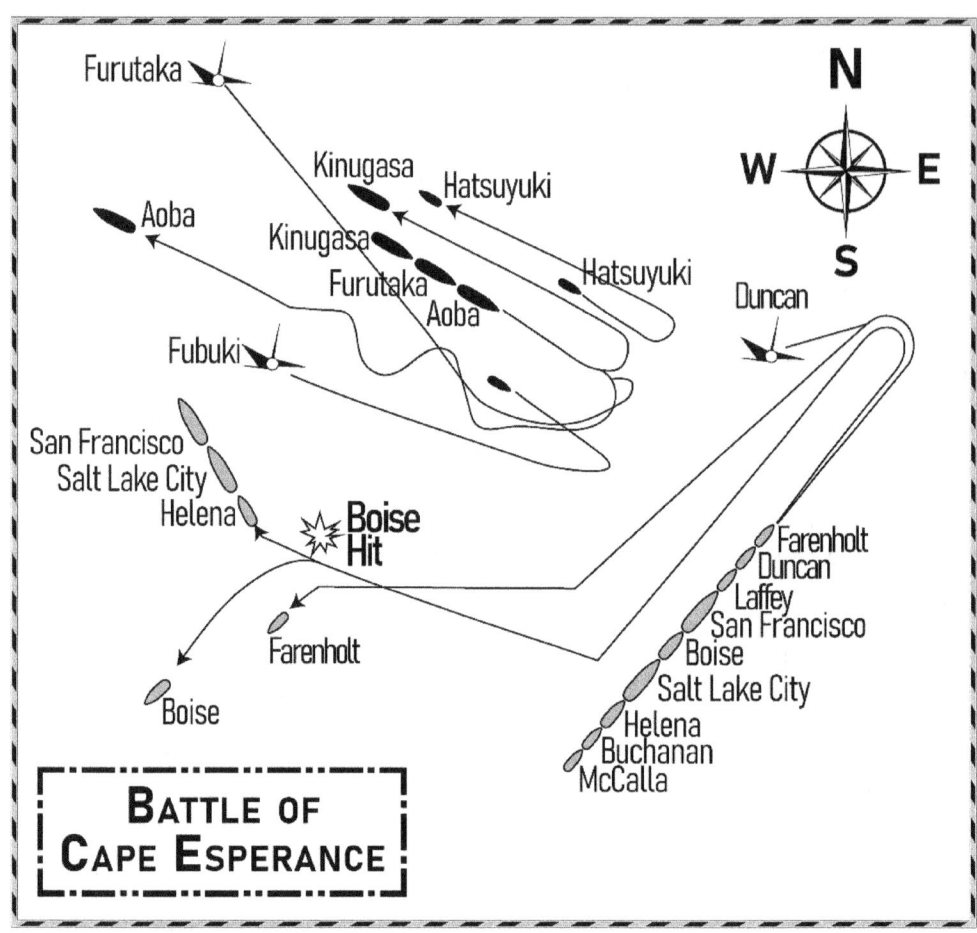

The Battle of Cape Esperance was fought off the northeast corner of Guadalcanal on the night of October 11–12, 1942. *Boise* **was granted much of the credit for the victory, but the crew and ship paid a steep price for their notoriety.**

side of the ship, the side facing Scott's cruiser line. The damage was almost certainly the result of "friendly fire."[150] Three men died and another thirty-four were injured.[151]

Most Americans saw the battle as a resounding success. They had sunk more tonnage than they had lost, and that was cause for celebration. The Navy declared it a "one-sided" and "conclusive" victory thanks to surprise, good judgment on behalf of the American skippers, and excellent gunnery.[152] Morison described the battle as having given "the tired Americans a heartening victory and the proud Japanese a sound spanking."[153]

Individual acts of heroism aboard the *Boise* were countless. The executive officer, Commander B.K. Culver, described a few notable occurrences in his official report. The account is short on details but alludes to incredibly brave actions where men battled the elements of a burning ship and their own fear to save others. His narrative is worth recounting in whole as a testament to individual valor, as well as a tribute to all the acts that were not witnessed or recorded:

It is recommended that special commendation be given Ensign DUNCAN for his leadership and his disregard for personal safety in connection with fighting of fires in turrets one and two; to Carpenter KELLEY for his work for taking charge of the repair work forward after the officer in charge and most of the forward repair parties had been killed; for directing the rescue of certain men on the second deck who had been overcome by gas; for his part in the rescue of BINDER, A.D. SF2c, U.S. Navy from the pump room forward. He also directed shoring operations on bulkhead twenty-three on the third deck and was of invaluable assistance to the Executive Officer during the entire period following the action. DONAHUE, P.A. BM1C, US Navy, is commended for his part in the rescue of BINDER, A.D. SF2c, US Navy from the pump room. DONAHUE descended into the trunk half full of water, released the scuttle, secured a line to the wheel and assisted Mr. KELLEY in raising the scuttle against the water pressure. Mr. Kelley then reached down and pulled BINDER from the trunk. RALSTON, C.T. BM2c, US Navy, is to be particularly commended for his leadership, initiative and the speed with which he translated an order into action.[154]

Admiral Scott received the Medal of Honor in part for his actions that night.[155] Many of his contemporaries drew strong tactical conclusions from his actions and tried to emulate them in later battles.[156] Aboard the *Boise*, nine officers and four enlisted personnel were awarded the Navy Cross, including Moran. Ensign Duncan and BMC1 Donahue were both awarded the medal based in part on the XO's recommendation. Three others were awarded posthumously to the families of Lieutenant (j.g.) William Thomas, Lieutenant (j.g.) Milo Evarts, and GM1c Mino Poole. Lieutenant Commander Wolverton received the Silver Star for his actions, and another six personnel were recommended for the medal but there is no record of receipt.[157] Regarding the rest of the crew, an old military aphorism certainly applied to the battle: Many men earned medals that night. Some of them were even awarded.

The Japanese saw the outcome of the battle, which they called the Second Battle of Savo Island, differently. At least one officer recalled the battle as a victory because Goto succeeded in getting Allied forces to withdraw from Ironbottom Sound. This cleared the way for Japanese battleships *Kongo* and *Haruna* to sail along the northern Guadalcanal coast on October 13 and punish the Marines at Henderson Airfield unopposed. Cruisers *Chokai* and *Kinugasa* provided an encore the following night.[158]

However, one surviving Japanese commander saw the night as a personal failure. Captain Kikunori Kijima commanded Cruiser Division 6 under Admiral Goto. During a post-war interrogation he called the opening salvos a "surprise attack." Even though he told the dying admiral that they sunk two American cruisers in the exchange, he ultimately "failed in this task and was relieved as soon as we arrived at Rabaul."[159]

Modern historians tend to agree with the Japanese when considering the strategic impacts. Although the Americans fought bravely and effectively, the battle failed to stop the Tokyo Express reinforcement, resulting in additional desperate battles for the Marines. The Americans did not inflict nearly the damage on the Japanese fleet that they thought and had to withdraw their surface fleet from the area, which allowed the Japanese to continue attacking the Marines with naval bombardment. The battle simply arranged the chess board for the next major naval battle off Guadalcanal.

These arguments do not diminish the moral victory felt by DB, the *Boise*, and everyone else present the night of October 11. The action that night mattered deeply to those men, and the win defined many of them for the rest of their lives. Furthermore, the American people needed the win. It may seem cynical to celebrate a victory beyond its merits, but propaganda abounded on all sides of World War II and was critical to morale at home. People needed inspiration to continue producing, sacrificing, and supporting the fight. The Battle of Cape Esperance provided a much-needed win, and the men of the *Boise* would soon be lavished with praise for their part.

For DB, the morning of October 12 brought him face-to-face with mortality. With the fires quenched, the crew now had to deal with their fallen shipmates. DB wrote that they "worked all day getting our dead men out of turrets and other places." He later elaborated on that grimmest of duties. Early that morning he was assigned by a chief petty officer to remove the bodies from one of the scorched turrets. The air inside the turret was stagnant and hot from the South Pacific air and residual heat of the metal. Everything was various shades of black, and the men's flashlights cast otherworldly shadows through the lingering smoke. The stench of burnt flesh and the sight of horribly misshapen bodies overpowered the men. DB ran from the turret to vomit. As he tried to process this nearly literal scene from Dante's hell, he felt a firm but comforting hand on his shoulder as he struggled back to his feet. The hand turned him around and DB saw the chief who had assigned him, who looked him in the eye and offered the only encouragement he could. He said, "Don't worry, they can't hurt you. They're your brothers." DB reconsidered the task at hand and found the courage to help his fallen friends.[160]

No matter how one saw the battle in a strategic sense, the crew of the *Boise* sailed away with heavy hearts. So many friends, crewmates, and brothers had been lost. Everyone felt the loss, and the physical damage was a daily reminder of the human cost of the war.

Captain Moran bore the awful burden of writing to the families of his fallen men. One of the fallen was Robert Tripp of Ashby, Minnesota. He had come aboard only seven months earlier.[161] Tripp was killed in action on that hellish night, so Captain Moran wrote the following condolence letter to his mother. It serves as a testament to the sacrifice of all the lost men of the *Boise* and the sorrow of the survivors.[162]

Dear Mrs. Tripp:

I am sorry I have been unable to write sooner to tell you of my deep sympathy in the death of your son, Robert, in action, on board the Boise.

He was a fine, decent, intelligent young man, and was liked and admired by his shipmates. His temperate habits (he never smoked nor drank) and his true devotion to his family and to the "girl back home" he loved, won his shipmates' respect and admiration.

He died, heroically, at his battle station, during our action with the enemy on the night of October 11th. The battle took place near the island of Guadalcanal, in the Solomons. I know you will be thankful to know that his death was instant, and that he suffered no pain.

May the knowledge of his heroic death, and your pride in his self-sacrifice for his flag and country, help you in the deep sorrow of your loss.

Very sincerely yours,

E. J. MORAN

Captain, US Navy,
Commanding USS Boise

Interlude
Home—Philadelphia

Admiral Scott departed the Guadalcanal area for Espiritu Santo on October 12 with TF-64.[1] They were battered, but not defeated. Men across the task force battled mixed emotions that ranged from elation to profound grief, all overshadowed by exhaustion.

At 1230 on the 13th, *Boise* momentarily broke from the formation just off Espiritu Santo. Moran called all hands to the deck for a funeral service. Sixty-seven of their brothers had been recovered and were now committed to the deep. The men stood at attention while their hearts welled with emotion. DB wrote, "We buried 68[,] others still trapped in the flooded magazine. The water was calm and a lump formed in my throat. When taps was blew tears ran down my cheeks. I wasn't the only one." The heavy cruiser USS *Chester* greeted *Boise* as they pulled into port. In a show of respect to the battle and the fallen, the crew lined the rails and offered their own salute.[2]

Boise's war was on hold. They needed extensive repairs, and the unique construction of the turrets alone meant replacement parts could not simply be rushed to the South Pacific. The experience with the various dry-dock facilities made it clear finding qualified personnel and equipment in Asia or even Australia to get them operational again was unlikely. The shipyards back home were the only viable option.

Work parties continued to recover the remains of the fallen. On the 15th, the ship held funeral services for nineteen more men in a cemetery on Espiritu Santo. DB complained that "the[y] were beginning to smell." Moneymaker wrote that the odor of death was enough to prevent sleep. These were not derogatory statements, but rather an acknowledgment of one of the simple and horrible facts of war that the newspapers typically gloss over. DB noted the dead sailors still not recovered: "We still have 25 more in the magazines."[3]

The 15th was also the day for the Cape Esperance task force to part ways. DB watched as "the *Helena*, *Frisco* and *Chester* got underway. The Japs have a large force steaming south." He recorded that afternoon that "us, the *Salt Lake City*, and some cans got underway for New Caldonia [sic]. All are damaged. As we were leaving the *Washington* and *Atlanta* came in for fuel."[4] For many men who had just experienced battle for the first time, it probably felt like time should have stopped. The battle for Guadalcanal would continue for months no matter how they felt. But without the *Boise*.

The long road home started with a trip to Noumea in New Caledonia. The battered ships tried to proceed at 20 knots, but Moran requested they slow back to 15. Any faster stressed the temporary bulkheads keeping the sea out.[5] Once in port, they pulled alongside the USS *Argonne*. The two ships kept each other company for several days while *Boise* sailors continued to assess damage.

On October 18, DB was again tasked to remove the dead. "Got the rest of our dead out. They were really in bad shape. Had been in the magazine 6½ days. They smelled terribly and had started to decompose. Got 23 out today." Those men were laid to rest the following day in another cemetery far from home.[6]

They remained in port until the 24th. They said goodbye to *Salt Lake City* before then. DB and every one of his crewmates owed them a debt of gratitude for their brave foray between the burning *Boise* and the Japanese cruiser.[7]

They were bound for Tutuila in American Samoa, better known as Pago Pago to the crew, where they had stopped in May. The ship needed to load additional ballast to safely journey home. According to DB "a half million dollars worth" of nickel was readied for them.[8] The trip was slow. *Boise* made about 17 knots, but at least had the *Argonne* for company on the trip. Extra eyes spotting for enemy submarines never hurt. By the 26th they worked up to sustaining 20 knots. They crossed the International Date Line and received updated orders. The Vice Chief of Naval Operations informed them that "to relieve work load on West Coast and expedite completion, *Boise* assigned availability PHILADELPHIA."[9] That meant a trip through the Panama Canal and duties on the East Coast for the first time in the war.

They arrived in Pago Pago on the 27th. "Hasn't changed much except for some new docks. Awfully hot," according to DB. They remained in port just long enough to refuel and load their ballast before setting off for Bora Bora.[10] By the 30th they were far from the front lines and anchored in a tropical paradise.

DB wrote of the island "a pretty place, not very far from Tahaiti [sic]."[11] He also delighted in taking in a movie at the Army base, the Abbott and Costello flick *Hold That Ghost*. It seemed a welcome distraction.[12] The feature film may also have been accompanied by one of the new weekly newsreels put out by the Office of War Information. President Roosevelt authorized the program in 1942 and it became a ubiquitous form of war information for domestic and foreign audiences.[13] The crew probably did not care what movie was shown thanks to the paucity of shipboard entertainment. Sailors have long complained of the monotony of shipboard life, and after a time of significant loss distractions were particularly welcome.

The following morning the ship departed. There was little to see except the vastness of the Pacific Ocean and their escort destroyer USS *Warrington* (DD-383).[14] The pace of duties was slow and relaxed compared to the constant stress of their time in the South Pacific. They arrived at Balboa to enter the Panama Canal on the 13th.

The Panama Canal is one of the greatest marvels of human engineering ever accomplished. The shortcut across the Western Hemisphere continents through the hills of central Panama cut the sailing distance from New York to San Francisco by 8,000 miles.[15] The reduction was critical for the U.S. Navy during wartime, facilitating the rapid transfer of ships between the Atlantic and Pacific theaters. The shortcut also saved millions of dollars in fuel costs.

According to a Navy report written just before the route opened, a series of three locks lift ships from sea level to Lake Gatun, roughly eighty-five feet above sea level. Each lock either pumps in or drains water until the ship is at an equal level with the next step and then giant doors open to allow the ship to pass. The locks provide enough space for ships up to 1,000 feet long and 110 feet wide. After ascending to Lake Gatun, ships sail across the lake, which is kept at a proper depth thanks to a giant dam. At the far end, ships descend via three more locks to sea level on the other side. The roughly fifty-mile journey was expected to take ships approximately 10–12 hours, three of which were spent in the locks.[16]

Thanks to the war the banks of the canal bristled with guns and barrage balloons. Bomber and reconnaissance planes buzzed from nearby airfields searching for the enemy above and below the surface. Radar waves also crisscrossed the airspace in a constant vigil designed to avoid another Pearl Harbor. The Navy feared a Japanese carrier raid from the Pacific side that in a worst-case scenario would cripple the war effort by damaging the locks beyond use. On the Caribbean side the threat came from dreaded German U-boats. These were less of a danger to the physical infrastructure of the canal than they were a bane of every ship captain. Just three U-boats near Panama sank fifteen ships the previous June and July. The sector had been quiet since then, but the underwater menaces had claimed another sixteen ships in October in the Caribbean sectors *Boise* needed to pass through.[17]

While *Boise* transited, the ship came across the new battleship *Indiana* (BB-58) and the USS *Columbia* (CL-56). The *Columbia* was one of the new *Cleveland*-class light cruisers commissioned during the war. Although newer, the class had fewer 6-inch guns than *Boise* but were better able to handle the growing threat of enemy airplanes thanks to their increased AA batteries.[18] Both ships demonstrated the power of American industry that was beginning to flow into the war against Japan.

It took the ship about seven and a half hours to pass from the first lock on the Pacific side to Colon on the north side where they docked to take on fuel. For the first time in the war, they reported to the commander of the Atlantic Fleet. They certainly were not ready for combat duties, but the change would have ramifications for the ship's future.[19]

Boise would not depart until the following day, so some of the crew, including DB, got to go ashore on the Atlantic side of the passage and explore the streets of Colon and neighboring Spanish colonial-era forts.[20] However, it is most likely that DB and his friends went in search of bars and cheap alcohol.

Boise departed on the final leg home on November 14. To help ward off any lurking submarines they were escorted by the destroyer *Champlin* (DD-601), but something larger than *Champlin*'s depth charges helped clear the way of German threats.[21] On November 8, the U.S. Army entered the fight against the Nazis, Italians, and Vichy French troops with Operation Torch. Over 100,000 troops, three quarters of them American, invaded North Africa across Morocco and Algeria.[22] The U.S. Army history of operations in the Caribbean believed that Torch drew the majority of German submarines to the Atlantic sea-lanes and the coast of North Africa in hunt of Allied supply ships. If true, it greatly reduced the threat to *Boise*.[23]

The trip was completely uneventful thanks to the shadow of American airpower, the stout *Champlin*, and the giant distraction of Operation Torch. On the 19th *Boise* tied up alongside Pier 4 in Philadelphia. It was one year and a day from when they had departed Pearl Harbor for the Philippines.[24]

Many years after the war *Boise* survivors recalled the day:

> Patch-work covered a gaping hole in her hull, her tall mast was scorched by flame, great blisters of paint bulged from her superstructure. Hundreds of fragments had scarred and pocked her but she moved proud and unfaltering through the early morning haze. River boats tooted their greeting, sailors swarmed over the decks of adjoining ships to wave and

yell at her, thousands of workmen set up a cheer as she moved ever so slowly into her berth. As the first mooring line reached the pier, a navy band played "Hold That Tiger" for a tiger she was.[25]

The crew welcomed Chief of Naval Operations Admiral Ernest King aboard less than an hour after arrival.[26] He was but the first of many dignitaries to pay respects to the ship and crew. America at the time was hungry for heroes. People had celebrated the victory of Midway, but much of the war in the Pacific was censored. *Boise* certainly earned significant credit for a big win over the Japanese. Unjustly, though, they received more than their share thanks to the Navy's policy of limiting information for security reasons. The general public did not know of the bravery of anyone else from Scott's task force, so the media and the people heaped praise on the known ship. *Boise* and the crew were avatars for every ship and sailor. The public wanted to celebrate, so they celebrated them.[27]

DB lamented the attention. He wrote, "We made headlines all over the country. The newspaper men flocked aboard and practally [*sic*] drove us crazy with questions."[28] The novelty wore off quickly for the men who were still grieving the loss of their friends and wrestling with the good and bad memories from the battle. The press only presented the good side. One sailor described the attention as a "big gooey spill in the papers."[29] Portions of headlines recorded by veterans lauded:

Captain Edward J. Moran (left) escorts Admiral Ernest J. King, Commander in Chief U.S. Fleet and Chief of Naval Operations, on an inspection of the ship and crew at the Philadelphia Navy Yard, 20 November 1942. Walking behind them is Rear Admiral A.E. Watson, Commandant 4th Naval District (National Archives: 80-G-40066).

BOISE BECAME "BLACK PHANTOM" OF TOKIO; "SUNK" FOUR TIMES....
"ONE-SHIP FLEET!": FLEET'S "FIGHTINGEST" CREW MANNED BOISE BLASTED....
"LOST" CRUISER ARRIVES HERE....
CRUISER "BOISE" IN PHILADELPHIA; SHE'LL FIGHT AGAIN, BUT SIX JAPS WON'T[30]

The president of the city of Boise Chamber of Commerce lauded the "one-ship fleet" and presented the crew with a plaque from the city. They would eventually raise three million dollars in war bonds for repairs as well. On November 30, *Time* magazine ran an article titled "They, Too, Were Expendable" with a picture of Moran shaking hands with Admiral King.[31]

Meanwhile, men on both sides continued to die at Guadalcanal. They died on the land, in the air, and in the unforgiving water. Across Eastern Europe the Russians and Germans fought a titanic battle. The battle of Stalingrad raged, with millions of soldiers fighting at what would become the high-water mark of the Nazi Empire. The British were now joined by American forces in North Africa to push back German and Italian forces. The Japanese were still pressing to conquer China while the latter's forces held on by a shoestring. The truly world war was also bleeding lives in New Guinea, Burma, the North Atlantic, the skies over Europe, and elsewhere. Against this backdrop the *Boise* men had the chance to catch their breath, grieve, and celebrate their own lives. It was an opportunity that millions of people around the globe would have gladly killed for.

In Philadelphia, *Boise*'s crew salivated at the chance for leave. There was family to visit, sweethearts to hold, and memories to purge. DB left Philadelphia on December 10. He had twenty days to do as he pleased.[32] He secured a train ticket to Salt Lake City and returned to his family and the city of his rambunctious youth.

His time with his family was brief. After his arrival he jumped in the family car for a drive with his father. Shortly after leaving the house, DB pulled into a state-owned liquor store, the only place someone could purchase alcohol. He went inside and purchased two bottles of whiskey, which was the maximum allowed by law. DB then drove to the next store and did the same. At the third stop his father, himself no stranger to shirking the law, angrily chastised DB. He realized DB was stockpiling whiskey, which was against Utah law. He shouted, "You can't do that! They'll arrest you!" At that point the hard-eyed veteran did not care about local laws. He laconically answered, "What are they going to do, put me in jail?" Men who have experienced the horrors of war are often disconnected from those who have not, and DB was no exception. His demons were far scarier than the local constabulary, but he did not intend to spend his leave in the company of either.[33]

DB and his father made a few more stops for alcohol. Eventually DB was satisfied with his hoard of whiskey bottles. He had no intention of bringing it home and drinking socially with his family. He longed for solitude. He instead went to his Uncle Dick and arranged to take a mule train into the mountains. He spent nearly two weeks blazing trails through the early winter conditions, guiding his mules with bags full of supplies and milk cans carrying small "fry" trout to seed mountain lakes. DB used nature, manual labor, and whiskey to try and reconcile all he had lived through. Like so many of his generation, he used alcohol-induced sleep to keep the demons at bay each night. Hangovers were easier to deal with than memories of constant fear and uncertainty, the thunder of gunfire, and the smell of friends' burnt flesh.[34]

DB returned to the *Boise* just in time to stand watch on New Year's Eve. Nothing from the next three months was important enough to him to record in his diary.[35] Instead, his time with his crewmates in Philadelphia is recorded through mementos.

The adoration poured upon *Boise*'s crew came with plenty of social opportunities. While dockworkers crawled over the ship replacing damaged components, the crew crawled through the neighborhoods of Philadelphia. The Philadelphia jazz scene was thriving in early 1943, and some argued it rivaled that of New York and even New Orleans. DB may have had a chance to see the iconic Dizzy Gillespie who was playing in the city.[36] DB and his friends frequented the local jazz establishments, and particularly enjoyed the Open Door Café where they were regulars and known by the band. Jack of the "Jerry and Jack Delmar" band that played the Open Door sent DB a postcard a few months after the ship departed. The front showed a picture of the band and on the back was scrawled the first few bars of "Can't Get Started," a slow and sultry tune later covered by everyone from Ella Fitzgerald to Frank Sinatra. Below the music Jack extolled "may this remind you of a few happy times and regards to the rest of the boys."[37]

There were also more formal celebrations for the men. On February 11 the Philadelphia Navy Yard Development Association sponsored a "Reception" for the crew at the prestigious Broadwood Hotel Ball Room.[38] On March 5 the crew again celebrated with a "Ship's Dance" at the upscale Benjamin Franklin Hotel, just three blocks from Independence Hall.[39] The men reveled in these chances to live life to the fullest and overshadowed their fear and doubts from Guadalcanal with music, dancing, strong drinks, and the company of Philadelphia's finest ladies.

The public demanded more of their heroes than just drinking and dancing. Much of the crew was idle during the repairs, so many were tasked with speaking engagements around the area to promote the Allied cause. The U.S. government knew that they needed to maintain public support for the war and sending "heroes" into the community was good for morale, support, and recruitment.[40]

While officers and chiefs spread the *Boise* story in pursuit of recruits, war bonds, and public good will, the rest of the crew continued duties while the ship remained tied up to the Philadelphia pier through mid–March.[41] The ship log from February provided a litany of routine reports from the various departments, daily crew musters at 0840, the administrivia of men reporting to and departing from the ship, and mess deliveries. Each delivery required an officer to conduct an inspection of the quantity and quality of the incoming food. It was definitely a perk for the officers to inspect the more delectable foods including ice cream and fresh fruit. Then again, Lt (j.g.) R.A. Griffin got the task to inspect 200 pounds of cabbage and 500 pounds of onions on February 12, thus proving that not all duties are desirable, even for officers.[42]

Many of the log entries dealt with the constant problem of sailors going AWOL or getting into other trouble while ashore. Absenteeism was the main problem, but several offenses must have kept the officers shaking their heads. These included one sailor drunk on duty using obscene language towards an officer, another found with stolen clothing, and a third delivered by shore patrol after twenty-two days AWOL, although punishment could be administered for returning as little as fifteen minutes late![43]

Some of the ship's veterans were reassigned to other ships. The Navy spread their combat experience around to prevent idleness and improve the readiness and capabilities of the burgeoning fleet. New crewmembers reported aboard with their records and personal "bags and hammocks."[44] Other men came and went to advanced training. Some required additional training to fill positions of greater responsibility, while others trained on new ship systems like the 40mm anti-aircraft guns. Each sailor was needed at the top of their game as the repairs neared completion in March.

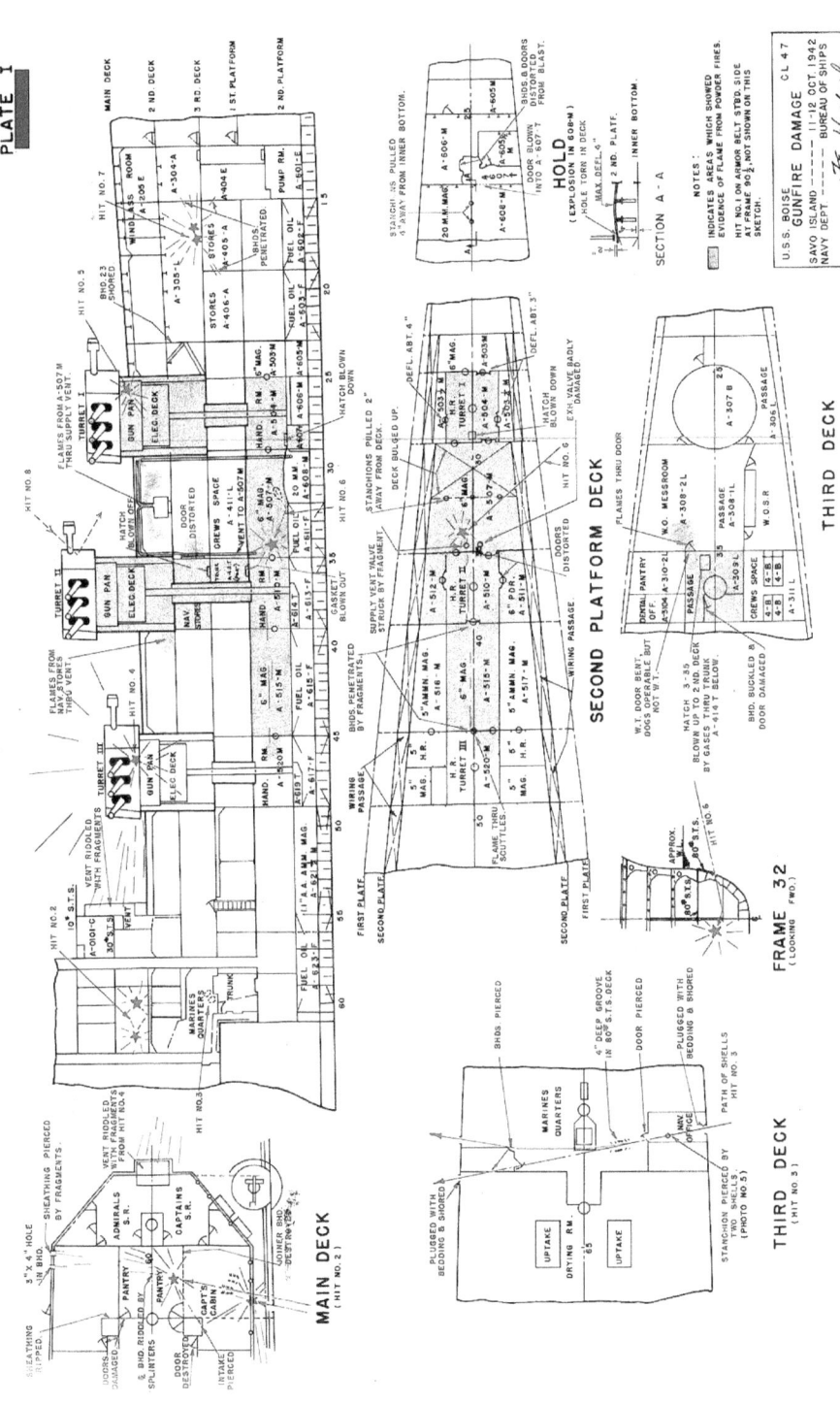

This diagram from the official damage report shows the extent of the damage *Boise* incurred at the Battle of Cape Esperance (Naval History and Heritage Command: Plate 1 War Damage Report no 24. U.S.S. Boise CL47).

Boise was so damaged that many engineers were surprised it stayed afloat after the punishing beating by the Japanese. The Navy wanted it repaired and back in action as quickly as possible. They also wanted to investigate what design features worked and which ones did not so they could incorporate the findings into new warships. *Boise* was about to become a case study for modern warfare.

One of the first things the engineers noted was that *Boise* was a truly lucky ship. Despite the damage, it stayed afloat. The *Quincy* and *Astoria* had each suffered hits from 8-inch shells to their turrets in the Battle of Savo Island with catastrophic results. *Quincy*'s Turret 2 was completely gutted and left "burning so violently that some observers thought the ship had blown up." *Astoria* had the misfortune to be hit with an armor-piercing shell that completely defeated the barbette armor. The resulting explosion and fire hastened the ship's demise due to an explosion in the 5-inch gun magazine. What made *Boise* so lucky when their turrets were hit? In part it was the enemy ammunition. The shell that hit Turret 3 was flat-nosed and only able to punch through about four inches of armor, leaving *Boise* two inches of steel to spare. Additionally, the Navy's Bureau of Ships (BuShips) recognized that *Boise*'s "Class A" faceplate had a "hard surface to break up armor-piercing shells" that *Astoria*'s "Class B" faceplate lacked. The circumstances possibly saved the ship, although the men of Turret 1 lost their lives due to their barbette's failure to stop that particular shell.[45]

Seaman First Class Charles Olinger points out shell fragment damage to the ventilation trunk on the front of the superstructure, just above the main deck (National Archives: 80-G-36296).

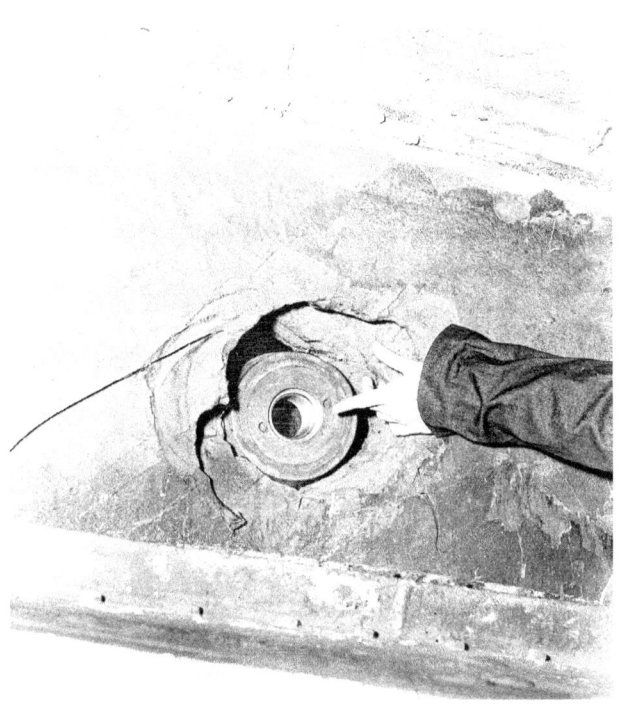

The remains of an 8-inch shell lodged in barbette #1 after the Battle of Cape Esperance (Official USN photo found in Fitch Family Private Collection).

BuShips also concurred that the extensive flooding from the hits to *Boise*'s hull saved them. The engineers were amazed that a hit and subsequent fire in the magazines did not sink the ship. They were also surprised at the performance of the Japanese shells. They had previously thought that a shell would have needed to be fired from a considerably further distance than happened at Cape Esperance to penetrate the hull nine feet underwater. *Boise*'s survival helped them surmise that the Japanese were using a new type of shell specifically designed to punch holes in ships below their armor belts.[46]

The repairs took months and were not limited to patching holes from the battle. The Navy wanted *Boise* back in action in an improved state. BuShips had been examining battle damage from across the fleet in both theaters, as well as analyzing after-action reports from skippers and engineers to determine how to make the U.S. Navy more lethal and more survivable. One of the greatest concerns of the time was the threat posed by enemy aircraft. *Boise* had not yet come under intense aerial bombardment, but the war showed it was a preferred aspect of naval warfare by all combatants.

To improve their ability to defend against enemy aircraft and bombs, ships required better methods to spot and track incoming aircraft. The first step was to improve visibility for the ship's spotters and leadership. *Boise*'s conning tower was removed and in its place DB and his fellow quartermasters were given a splinter-proof compartment to operate the ship beneath a new open "fighting bridge." An air defense battle station was added just behind the open bridge, and another one was set up in the aft superstructure. To accommodate the new spaces, the foremast was pushed back seven feet, giving everyone a better view of the sky.[47]

Just seeing enemy aircraft obviously was not enough to give *Boise* a fighting chance. They could always maneuver, but shooting down the enemy was a much more practical and satisfying response. Fierce battles between Japanese planes and Allied surface ships had demonstrated that 5-inch and .50 caliber machine guns were insufficient, so the Navy was adding 20mm and 40mm anti-aircraft guns to their ships as quickly as possible. This was *Boise*'s opportunity to add both. By the end of the refit, the ship bristled with new armament including twenty-eight single-barrel 20mm guns and four quad-barreled 40mm gun turrets on each side amidships. The added weight to the top of the ship made *Boise* more unstable than before, but the addition of several tons of anti-aircraft ammunition helped provide balance.[48]

The ship already had the advanced SG surface radar from the previous overhaul, so still boasted one of the best surface radars in the fleet. Yet radar technology and the systems to guide guns onto a target were rapidly advancing. To assist the burgeoning anti-aircraft capability, *Boise* received new FCRs, including two Mk-57 blind-firing directors and two Mk-63 directors. The new systems would soon be put to the test.[49]

Boise also received a new complement of SOC Seagull scout planes. These included two of the most advanced versions of the aircraft, the SO3C-1. The rest of the hangar was filled with older model SOCs.[50]

On Wednesday, February 10, the ship said goodbye to Captain Moran in a simple change of command ceremony. He was bound for temporary duty in Washington, D.C., with the Chief of Naval Operations. Following that he was destined for the position of Navy Postal Coordinator–Pacific Coast in San Francisco. It was a decidedly unglamorous position for a man who now had one of the most battle-hardened reputations of any skipper in the U.S. Navy, but provided him a well-earned rest. Commander Burnett Culver assumed temporary command of the ship.[51]

Captain Leo Hewlett Thebaud reported aboard on the 23rd and assumed command for the ship's next chapter.[52] Thebaud was a highly experienced officer. He had twenty-nine years of service under his belt including time aboard cruisers and battleships. He was coming from a shore assignment, but he already had combat experience from World War I where he earned the Navy Cross for actions as the captain of the destroyer USS *Paul Jones*. Thebaud had not spent World War II entirely behind a desk either. He had commanded destroyer squadrons and convoy task forces since before the U.S. entered the war until his brief hiatus at the Bureau of Naval Personnel.[53] The men of the *Boise* may have lost a fighting captain, but their new skipper certainly had the pedigree of a man who could lead them into trouble and successfully see them through the challenge.

His vessel finally left the pier February 19, albeit for a short time. The ship repositioned to a nearby dry dock, assisted by seven yard-tugs for the quick forty-five-minute journey.[54] Thebaud's job was to oversee final repairs and get the ship and its veteran crew back into the war.

They spent several more weeks in dry-dock putting the finishing touches on repairs and installing the new systems. There is no record of the ship log from March 1943, so daily details are sparse. By March 19 *Boise* was finally ready to get underway. DB wrote, "have been here 4 months to the day. Tied up at the degaussing pier—pier 46 Philedelphia [sic], Pa." The following morning, they cast off and cruised down the Delaware River to test the new anti-mine gear in the Delaware Bay. According to DB the ship arrived in Norfolk, Virginia, on the 25th, and departed the following day "for our trial run and firing practice."[55]

April proved a month of testing, training, and boredom. The ship was back at sea, but the men needed to work together to become a fine-tuned fighting machine once again. The new sailors needed to learn their jobs and equipment, and the veterans needed to ensure the newbies would fight and avoid panic when the time came. The SOCs towed banners for the anti-aircraft gunners. The main guns thundered once more in anticipation of future fights. They all had a lot to live up to, and it seems that the main guns in the rebuilt and refurbished forward turrets functioned without a hitch. On the

7th they increased the difficulty by reacting to "surprise" targets. This was the best possible training to get ready for the same types of threats they faced at Cape Esperance.[56]

On the 9th it was time for *Boise* and the men to prove they were ready once again for combat. Rear Admiral L.A. Davidson, the commander of Cruiser Division 8, came aboard along with the captain of the USS *Philadelphia* to conduct the "Annual Military Inspection." The *Philadelphia* was another *Brooklyn*-class cruiser and Captain Hendron was the perfect expert to judge *Boise*'s readiness.[57] Inspections are the second most stressful experiences in the military, right behind combat. Thebaud's job was on the line, as were the jobs and reputations of his subordinate officers. The stress and drive for perfection, or at least a passing score, flowed down on the enlisted men like a typhoon. The men of each department were driven to their utmost. Their pride was certainly on the line, but so were possible promotions and future liberties. At the very least, a poor performance would mean additional training and time at sea instead of American port calls with good food, alcohol, and women.

They hoisted anchor in the inky blackness of the morning and wound their way through the submarine nets. By 0800 the ship was in the open sea off the coast of Virginia and the inspection drills began at 0812. First up were the various functions that brought men away from the ship. They "called away" the party that would board another ship, followed by the "prize crew" that would take control of and sail a captured vessel. They were followed by a "fire and rescue" party and then a plane salvage party. At 0950 it was time for the entire crew to participate and they were called to General Quarters. The crew was given a "battle problem" reminiscent of those the crew practiced before Guadalcanal. They maneuvered the ship, adjusted speeds, and simulated reacting to an enemy attack. They also worked their way through simulated damage control, an event that certainly opened old wounds for the men who fought in October.[58]

Next up the men below decks got to prove their engines were up to snuff. They poured on the speed as the ship accelerated to 30 knots and ran at full power. Not only did they test the engines, they also proved that the Philadelphia Naval Yard had properly repaired the hull damage. Everything functioned as expected, so the men were rewarded with an abandon ship drill. At 1203 the inspection was completed. The ship continued up the Delaware River once again and tied up alongside the pier in Philadelphia, where they bid farewell to the admiral and Captain Hendron.[59] The ship, captain, and crew apparently passed as there were no major changes in the muster rolls. *Boise* would soon find itself sent back into harm's way.

The log had no details for the next ten days, but there was a significant event for DB. His best friend S1c Charles Oldham was reassigned. The two had been together since before the war and appeared in the few pictures DB kept later in life.[60] It is never easy to part ways with a friend, but it is doubly hard to say goodbye to someone you went through battle with. It is even worse when you know one of you is going back into the fight, and the other is not. Goodbyes during World War II had a significant chance of being permanent. Hopefully in the quiet days in Philadelphia they got the chance to have a few drinks together.

Boise left Philadelphia a few days later for more of the same. DB wrote, "Left Norfolk went out in Chesepeake [sic] Bay for operations. Operating in and out of Norfolk, and firing, and practice in general in Chesepeake [sic] Bay."[61] They were clearly getting ready to return to the war, but no one knew which fight they would join. The Pacific Fleet was still battling in the Solomon Islands, raiding the flanks of the Japanese Empire, and helping push the Japanese out of their perches in Papua New Guinea. Meanwhile, convoys across the Atlantic required escorts to Great Britain as well as North Africa. Everyone knew that further pushes against Italy and Germany were coming, and those operations would require naval support as well. *Boise* could be used anywhere and was needed everywhere.

Yet May just brought more training. Their drills were quickly becoming more complicated and intense. On the 15th they began training with their sister ships *Philadelphia* and *Savannah*. They practiced coordinating their fire on targets spotted by the SOCs to deliver massive bombardments on a single enemy while moving in formation. It was highly reminiscent of their battle at Guadalcanal. A few days later they started working with the significantly smaller motor torpedo boats. These boats are better known by their "PT" nomenclature, short for Patrol Torpedo. The roughly eighty-foot wooden vessels were designed to dart quickly towards larger surface ships, launch torpedoes, and then escape again before larger vessels could react, although they proved adept at many missions including raiding, reconnaissance, and rescuing downed airmen. The arguably most famous PT boat of the war, *PT-109*, was commanded by the future president John F. Kennedy.[62] During the drills the vessels would work together to swarm and overwhelm enemy ships. In a few of the night drills *Boise* fired illumination flares for the agile vessels while they maneuvered towards their prey.[63]

After a few days, they retired to port in Norfolk for five days of "limited availability." Presumably the crew was given liberty in advance of an upcoming operation. *Boise* and the crew were ready. The question on DB's and everyone else's mind was where and when they would get back into the fight.

Moneymaker, now a petty officer, jotted a few lines of a poem while *Boise* faced the unknown, perfectly summing up the thoughts and tense anticipation of his crewmates:

> I Live and know not how long
> I travel and know not whither
> I die and know [not?] when
> Strange that I am so cheerful.[64]

5

Covering Fire

Sicily and Italy

The wind howled and the sea rolled. *Boise* and the crew stood firm, unperturbed by the waves that rocked the flock of smaller ships and boats assembled to the west. The men aboard those smaller vessels were drenched in seawater, and many were sick to their stomachs from the rough weather and tense nerves.[1] Four miles in front of them stood the first European coast America would assault during World War II. Operation Husky, the invasion of Sicily, was underway.

The men of the *Boise* sailed back into battle with considerably more confidence than the soldiers in the landing craft. After Guadalcanal, they were veterans of Hell. The survivors had seen the worst horrors conjured by the gods of war, and they were ready to enter the breach once more. DB wrote before the battle, "I believe we will take 'em with no strain."[2]

Along with confidence earned through battle, the *Boise* enjoyed more support than they could have imagined only a year earlier. The British Royal Navy had fought for years to wrestle control of the Mediterranean Sea from German, Italian, and French fleets. By the summer of 1943, they were largely incapable of resisting Allied naval action. Allied aircraft also pounded airfields around Sicily for weeks before the invasion. The pilots cratered runways, destroyed fuel and ammunition dumps, and endlessly hounded enemy planes on the ground and in the air, forcing the enemy to disperse their surviving aircraft and limiting their ability to mass their air forces to resist landings.[3] Now the Allies had a fleet that could dominate the Mediterranean. The Americans and British sortied 2,950 vessels including submarines, transports, destroyers, cruisers, battleships, and carriers to take the fight to European soil. Over 1,700 of those were various type of landing craft needed to get the fighting men ashore.[4]

The enemy in Sicily was a hodgepodge of combat veterans and unbloodied garrison troops who had a mix of weaponry ranging from antiquated World War I rifles to the most modern of German tanks, the dreaded Tiger. At Gela in *Boise*'s landing sector, the beaches were held by troops of limited ability and their positions were tenuous. Local workers had been hard at work building pillboxes, gun emplacements, and other defensive works, but had achieved mixed results. Time was limited and materials scarce. The concrete was of poor quality and reinforced with whatever metal was on hand. Instead of the rebar that German positions relied on in Normandy, many Sicilian defenses were constructed with rusted barbed wire from the neighboring fields.[5] Worse, some positions were merely decoys and mock-ups, some reportedly made of cardboard.[6]

Boise participated in the invasion of Sicily and mainland Italy in 1943. The crew also visited ports across North Africa during the campaign.

The defenders were not toothless. Four divisions were positioned to respond to an attack along Italy's south coast. Two were Italian infantry divisions that may or may not put up a fight against the U.S. Army. These men manned the beach defenses. Behind them were two divisions with more fire in their bellies. The Italian Livorno Division consisted of veterans from the French campaign. The unit was not elite, but the men knew how to fight and were capable of disrupting Allied plans.[7] The final division posed the biggest challenge. Many planners considered the German Hermann Goering (HG) Division to be a "crack" unit with the training, equipment, and drive to put up a significant fight. The unit was a mix of African veterans and green troops. The HG fielded some of the finest tanks in the German army, including Mark III, Mark IV, and the behemoth Tiger.[8] Infantry battalions accompanied the tanks. The HG commander, Major General Paul Conrath, was a veteran of the Eastern Front.[9]

The Allies were about to tackle their toughest challenge yet, and *Boise* was integral to the plan.

A few weeks before Husky, *Boise* departed Norfolk with sister ships *Philadelphia*, *Birmingham*, eighteen transports, and twenty-four destroyers on June 8, 1943. DB was pretty sure "something big coming up," and the scuttlebutt was that Gibraltar was their destination. On the 17th, DB noted they were part of Task Group 65.7 and their destination was Mers-el-Kebir in western Algeria. Two days later they passed Gibraltar as predicted, and DB noted, "god what a rock."[10]

They arrived in the Mediterranean on the 21st and joined the U.S. 8th Fleet, but their reputation preceded them. Rear Admiral John Hall, the commander of Task Force 81, enthusiastically welcomed the combat veterans with a message stating "AMPHINAW PROUDLY WELCOME CAPTAIN, OFFICERS AND CREW OF SHIP ALREADY FOUND STRONG IN BATTLE." Not to be outdone, another *Brooklyn*-class ship, the *Savannah*, signaled "GREETINGS AND SALUTATIONS. WE'RE GLAD TO HAVE YOU WITH US."[11] These were powerful words of encouragement from fellow sailors who were no strangers to battle themselves.

The following few days the *Boise* and their wards readied for the first major Allied invasion of Europe. They helped pre-position troops across the North African coast and participated in practice operations for the landing craft and troops. By July 6, Captain Thebaud passed word to the crew that it was time for the *Boise* to get back into the war. They were to "cruise around for a few days with the S. [*Savannah*] and P. [*Philadelphia*] and some cans looking for trouble. Then we will meet our transports and land troops on Sicily."[12]

The ship and the rest of the Covering Task Force departed Algiers around 1800 local time towards the northeast at 15 knots. By midnight they steamed east, looking for the trouble that the captain alluded to. For the next two days *Boise* maintained its place as third of three cruisers behind *Philadelphia* and *Savannah*. They continued a generally eastward journey past the southern coast of Sicily, occasionally coming to General Quarters to repel air attacks. On July 8, the *Boise* fired its guns in anger for the first time since Guadalcanal, although it was only to sink a suspected sea mine.[13]

On July 9 the wind howled and storm clouds loomed from Algeria to Sicily, but the invasion ships set their course. Conditions worsened as the fleet approached their invasion positions and soldiers readied themselves and their equipment on the decks and in the holds of hundreds of landing craft and ships for Operation Husky.

The first major invasion of Europe had been under consideration for months, even years. While the highest echelons of the United States government had pushed for a direct crossing of the English Channel, cooler and wiser heads from Great Britain, led by the indomitable Prime Minister Winston Churchill, pushed for an invasion in an easier area than northwestern France.[14] A raid on Dieppe, France, almost a year earlier had ended disastrously, with much of the invading force killed or captured. The British half of the Alliance figured that an invasion of southern Europe could push Italy out of the war, support the Soviet Union by drawing away troops and resources from the Eastern Front, and ultimately help the Allied nations learn to work together before an invasion of France.[15]

Several locations were discussed for the invasion but they eventually decided on Sicily, the often-conquered island off the "toe" of Italy. The island was within range of Allied airpower, and planners were reasonably certain they could keep the invasion sea-lanes free of enemy ships and submarines. The plan called for British forces under the legendary Field Marshal Bernard Montgomery to land near the ancient city Syracuse and fight their way to the northeast tip of the island at Messina. Meanwhile, American forces under Lieutenant General George S. Patton would land on beaches along the southern Sicilian coast.[16]

The U.S. area was divided into three landing sectors focusing on the towns of Licata, Gela, and Scoglitti. They were code-named JOSS, DIME, and CENT, respectively.[17] *Boise* was assigned to the center DIME sector and ordered to protect the landing fleet and the men of the 1st Infantry Division and their supporting units, including a Ranger Battalion led by Lieutenant Colonel William O. Darby.[18] The most important objective of DIME sector was the Ponte Olivo Airfield. Also a part of *Boise*'s flock was the attack transport ship USS *Monrovia* (APA-31). *Monrovia* was a brand-new vessel outfitted as Vice Admiral Henry Hewitt's flagship for the entire Western Naval Task Force. Patton and his staff also berthed aboard the *Monrovia*, meaning the top minds of the American half of the invasion sailed under *Boise*'s protection.[19]

The ocean south of Gela in the DIME sector was broken into three sections to deconflict the landing ships from the warships sent to cover their approach. *Boise* drew an assignment in Gunfire Support Area Number 2 on the eastern side of the landing sector. They were accompanied by two tin cans, the *Jeffers* and *Stanton*.[20]

An amphibious landing the size of Husky required significant support from warships to cover the beaches and to protect the landing ships from enemy boats, ships, submarines, and aircraft. The U.S. Navy of 1943 was still stretched thin. Husky would be conducted without U.S. aircraft carriers, battleships, or even heavy cruisers. The biggest dogs in the fight would be the 6-inch guns of the light cruisers.[21]

As the naval armada moved into position under the cover of darkness, the skies of Sicily filled with Allied aircraft. Bombers decimated airfields, ports, railroad junctions, and even cities. Allied pilots struck anything that could hinder the invasion. DB noted as *Boise* approached the coast that "Flying Fortresses had bombed the city of Gela before we got here. It is burning like hell." A crewmate wrote "One thing that helped the morale was the large flights of bombers were going over to lay some eggs for Il Duce."[22]

DB also saw swarms of cargo planes flying over the fleet. The planes were filled with paratroopers who were supposed to secure key terrain in front of the landing beaches. The plan was to stop the enemy from mounting a counterattack when the beaches were most vulnerable. In the DIME sector, this meant holding high terrain for general observation and crucial road junctions that responding German and Italian tanks could use. The key point in the sector was a Y-intersection northeast of Gela.[23]

5. Covering Fire

At 0200 the landing craft started their run on the beach.[24] Out front were Darby's Rangers. Darby made a name for himself with daring operations in North Africa and was the perfect man to lead the bold opening to the Sicilian campaign. Their mission was to secure Gela's small jetty, a critical objective for the DIME sector, and then the town itself. Unfortunately, Italian troops heard the assault craft approaching and set off dozens of explosive charges attached to the jetty in a blinding flash seen across the task force.[25] Any chance of using it for the landing operation was gone. The Rangers pressed on unperturbed. Adjusting their landing point to the east of town, they hit the beach around 0245 and pushed to their second objective.[26]

Boise continued to steam in zigzag patterns around the assigned position on the invasion's right flank along with *Jeffers*. The men on the bridge took note of a searchlight that was harassing the landing craft, highlighting their positions for enemy gunners. The *Boise* gunners plotted the searchlight position and vowed to destroy it the next time it illuminated.[27]

Just before 0400, as darkness began its slow fade into dawn, the two warships opened fire. Their initial targets were prearranged and consisted of pillboxes, shore batteries, and anti-aircraft guns. Five minutes later, they eliminated the annoying searchlight.[28] *Boise* worked methodically with all the big guns. According to Butler, the *Boise* alternated fire from each turret every 5–15 minutes until sunrise. The newly repaired Turrets 1 and 2 sent the first wave of shells towards the enemy without any issues, demonstrating to the world that *Boise* was back. The crew eased into the fight, launching a total of seven volleys of three shells each at the enemy over the next two hours.[29]

By 0600 the battle ashore was progressing well. The Rangers secured Gela after several hours of bitter street fighting.[30] The 1st Infantry Division was unloading as quickly as possible, but the coastline was dotted with false beaches and sand bars that made the landing crafts' jobs difficult. The soft sand made unloading tanks and heavy artillery

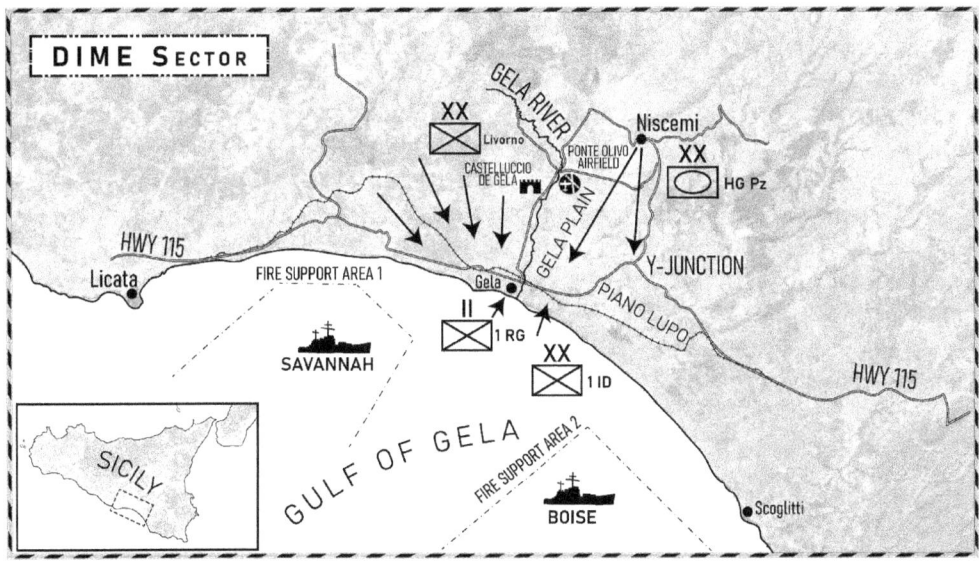

Boise supported troops ashore in the DIME Sector of Sicily. Their gunfire proved crucial in repelling German and Italian counter-attacks.

particularly difficult. Thankfully, the soldiers landing near Gela encountered little enemy resistance thanks to the hard fighting of the Rangers and naval shells.[31]

Boise readied the next arrow in the quiver. Two crews stepped to their SOCs ready on the stern catapults and prepared for launch. Lieutenant (j.g.) Cyril Lewis and his radio operator catapulted from the ship and flew south of the fleet to gain altitude without drawing any friendly fire. He climbed to 4,000 feet and flew a course along the beach in DIME's eastern sector. Finding the area surprisingly peaceful, Lewis pushed inland and tried to identify some of the precoordinated targets on his maps, but found the maps of particularly poor quality. He quickly switched to photos overlaid with a target grid to orient himself. Just as he started to identify enemy positions, all hell broke loose.[32]

The quiet flight was loudly interrupted by anti-aircraft fire that bracketed the little airplane between ominous black clouds of death pilots called flak. Lewis pushed the nose of the little aircraft forward and dove towards the earth, doing everything possible to interrupt the AA gun's firing solution. He weaved left and right, trying to remain unpredictable, and pushed the tiny engine to its limits. Flak clouds erupted around and behind him as he neared the relative safety of the coastline. As the enemy fire trailed off, he had a new problem. The engine was failing.[33]

Lewis had noted on takeoff that this particular aircraft, serial number 0S2N, had an engine that "ran hot" and had a particularly hard time climbing. Now that same engine was icing up and dying. He could not use the engine's built-in heating system to melt the ice because of the already high temperatures in the cylinder. So he did the only thing he could and tried to get as close to the *Boise*, and as far away from the enemy, as he could. The plane glided slowly with the engine sputtering. It would start and stop unexpectedly, until suddenly at 3,000 feet the motor caught and remained in operation. Lewis knew that the *Boise*'s big guns were essentially blind without him spotting targets, so he made a courageous decision and turned his aircraft back towards the coast and into harm's way, engine troubles be damned.[34]

Below Lewis the soldiers of the 1st Infantry Division were flooding ashore. Thanks to Darby's attack and cover from the Navy, the landings were largely unopposed by enemy fire. One soldier still afloat with the reserve force noted the sight of the big shells streaking towards the shore in the semidarkness. Lieutenant Frank Johnson later wrote, "The rising sky of dawn reveals the level, hazy plain of Gela, partially obscured by smoke, dust, and flaming bursts of shell fire." He described the shells themselves: "Some are solid flame, some intermittent, but all are dynamic and graceful as they lace the sky."[35]

For the sailors still on the water, the Sicilian beaches stretched across the horizon, and small peaks poked up into the morning sun. The sight proved less than inspiring to many of the Americans as they gazed upon Europe for the first time. The famed reporter Ernie Pyle observed the invasion from the deck of the *USS Biscayne* and painted a drab picture of the coast off Licata ten miles to the west of the *Boise*. He recorded:

> When we got our first look at Sicily, we were all disappointed. I for one had always romanticized it in my mind as a lush, green, picturesque island…. Instead, the south coast of Sicily seemed to us a drab, light brown country, and there weren't many trees. The fields of grain had been harvested and they were dry and naked and dusty. The villages were gray and indistinguishable at a distance from the rest of the country. Water was extremely scarce. On the hillsides a half mile or so back of the beach grass fires-started by the shells of our gunboats-burned smokily [sic].[36]

The sights may have been uninspiring, but luckily for the invading forces the initial defenses were equally dull. The enemy on the beaches essentially evaporated as U.S. infantry and engineers scrambled ashore. The men moved quickly to secure the beaches and make ready for follow-on troops and equipment. Troops crept cautiously over Highway 115 and the railroad that ran east of Gela. The road continued on to Piano Lupo where paratroopers under Colonel James Gavin roamed after their transports scattered them across southern Sicily during their night drop. One of Gavin's most trusted subordinates, Lieutenant Colonel Arthur "Hard Nose" Gorman, collected as many men as possible and prepared to attack bunkers around the Y-junction known as "Objective Y." There a road branched from Highway 115 going north to the small village of Niscemi. The position was a vital linkage between the DIME and CENT beachheads, as it was the only road through the hills separating the two sectors that tanks could traverse. The north-running road led to Niscemi and then to Caltagirone, the new home base of the HG Division.

Gorman's men were up against a series of concrete bunkers that provided deadly interlocking fire from multiple directions into Objective Y. The paratroopers were experts at attacking such positions, as they had proven all morning, but such attacks were always susceptible to high casualties. The pillboxes were squat, cylindrical masses sprouting along the surrounding hills like deadly mushrooms filled with riflemen, machineguns, and small artillery pieces. Even if they were constructed with poor materials, they were formidable to the lightly armed paratroopers.[37]

Before ordering his men to advance into the teeth of the enemy, Gorman tried to call in fire support from the Navy. One of the SOCs appeared overhead shortly after first light, but the paratroopers watched with horror as it was pounced upon by a German fighter and shot down before Gorman could relay his request to *Boise*. Still, Gorman thought the mere threat of the *Boise* might be enough to win the day. He sent an Italian prisoner over to one of the bunkers with an ultimatum: Surrender or suffer the wrath of the Navy's big guns! The Italians had no idea that without the SOC overhead, Gorman could not communicate with *Boise* or anyone else, and quickly surrendered their positions without a fight.[38]

To the north of Objective Y, General Conrath was faced with difficult decisions. The unit was in a good position to counterattack the American landings in the south and, sitting twenty-five miles inland, was out of range of the American naval guns. However, his single division was up against at least two American divisions and support units. Worse, Gavin's roving paratroopers were cutting communications and providing a confusing idea of how big the invasion was and where it was focused. Conrath could not coordinate with his Italian allies or his headquarters.[39] Still, it was his division's job to repel the Americans, so he decided to split his forces into two columns to push the Americans back into the sea at Scoglitti and Gela.

The men near Gela were spared the massive Tigers, but were in the path of Conrath's smaller Mark III and IV panzers. The attack also included support from the division's reconnaissance company, artillerymen, and engineers. The bulk of the unit's infantry pushed east with the Tiger tanks towards CENT sector.[40]

At 0830 Lewis spotted the scattered tanks from the air and radioed enemy positions to *Boise*, who let loose with nine rounds of 6-inch shells, repelling the counterattack at Objective Y. While the shelling was accurate, some German elements were able to withdraw back to Niscemi. Lewis passed accurate coordinates to his ship, but the target description was either lost or distorted, resulting in a minimal number of shells. The chance to destroy even more enemy tanks was missed, and Captain Thebaud later recalled, "Had we only known what we were shooting at, we would have cut loose with the whole 15-gun battery!"[41]

The hodgepodge HG force made little progress. The scattered paratroopers harassed the tanks and their supporting units every step of the way from their starting point at Niscemi to the Y-junction held by Gavin. The disciplined American troops held elevated positions and directed machine gun and mortar fire into the advancing Germans.[42] The combination of professional and violent actions from the paratroopers with the accuracy of *Boise*'s 6-inch guns handily carried the day against the HG's western column.

To the southwest of the Y-junction, Major General John Lucas, a key subordinate of Patton's, came ashore just east of Gela at 0730. Although not directly in the chain of command, he quickly pushed the soldiers on the beach to move out and link up with the neighboring beaches and the paratroopers to their north. Along with connecting the various beachheads, it was time to take the fight directly to the enemy. But Lucas was concerned that the troops were impeded because the Air Force was not properly supporting the ground troops. He had complained to Patton before the operation, and now his concerns seemed realized.[43] He wanted regular coverage over his beach to chase off marauding Messerschmitts, spot targets for his artillery, and bomb any troops that dared to stand in the way of the American advance. While it is probable that Lucas and Patton, along with many other ground commanders, did not understand the broader air plan for the operation, they apparently did themselves no favors either.

Before the invasion, a group of British and American airmen developed new radio equipment for troops to talk directly to aircraft, along with a simple handbook on how to use the equipment with the entertaining but slightly insulting title of "The Child's Guide to Triphibious Operations." The equipment and manual could have saved significant anxiety and lives if employed properly. Patton decided to leave the equipment in North Africa. According to Major General Harold Grant, one of the airmen who developed the equipment and a friend of Patton's:

> They were old hospital vehicles, ambulance types, that they put communications gear in but which were the ground stations for the Air Corps to talk to to support the armored force. [Patton] saw them being loaded, and he said "Throw 'em out; I want more tanks." So they were thrown out and more tanks were put aboard.

With a little bit of embellishment, Grant explained the repercussions of abandoning the best means to talk directly with pilots:

> Yet when [Patton] landed and the gates on the bow of the LSTs [Landing Ship, Tank] were lowered, a German panzer division was sitting right behind the dunes and just shot into the front of it and shot the hell out of his tanks, and he couldn't call for help because he'd thrown his communications away.

Grant later described how the Army then had to rely on the Navy to repel the German tanks.[44]

The HG Division was not the only threat to Gela that morning. The Italian Livorno Division also threatened the sector. Lack of respect between German and Italian military leadership resulted in extreme difficulty for the armies to plan and fight together. The campaign targeting lines of communication only made matters worse. The Livorno

Division went into battle with little knowledge of or coordination with the HG Division a few miles east.[45]

The Livorno consisted of mostly infantry and Renault 35 light tanks. The small, armored vehicles were captured by the Germans in France in 1940, and later passed to the Italians because they had no use for the underpowered 37mm gun.[46] The Livorno was harassed by Allied airpower all day as it moved into a line just north of a plain of wheat fields stretching from the foothills to Gela and the sea. Near the center of the Livorno line stood the ruins of a Norman-era castle, Castelluccio di Gela, sitting on a hilltop. From the top, Italian commanders could see across the open ground for miles in all directions, making it the perfect vantage point to direct troop movements and artillery fire. They could also see the American armada that dominated the sea beyond the town.

As the bulk of the infantry struggled to reach their positions, the Livorno sent a contingent of its Renault 35s and limited infantry support streaking across the plain to dislodge the Rangers from Gela. This left the Italians vulnerable to the same hell the *Boise* dealt the HG Division further east. On the western arm of the DIME force, a U.S. Army shore fire control party requested support from the destroyer *Shubrick*, who opened up with 5-inch guns, destroying several tanks and killing or scattering the infantry. Still, several Renaults found their way into Gela, forcing the Rangers to stalk them through the narrow streets where the naval guns were ineffective.[47] The enemy was starting to learn the hard lesson that the only way to avoid Allied air and sea power was to get so close to the American infantry they did not dare use their heavier weapons.

The morning was not entirely a victory for the Allies. While the men on the ground fought hard to achieve their various objectives, the Luftwaffe and Italian Air Forces struck back. Lieutenant Lewis barely had time to celebrate the devastating results the *Boise* dealt to the HG tanks near Objective Y before conducting a low-altitude sweep of the area to find more tanks. He swooped as low as 1,000 feet, low enough for every German with a rifle to take shots at his SOC, when a pair of Me-109Fs dove out of the sky with every intention of sending Lewis and Lieutenant Harding, flying the other *Boise* SOC, into early graves. Both pilots dove even lower and the Germans somehow missed the pair as they ran for the beach and the protection of their own AA guns.[48]

This aerial attack was the first of many for Operation Husky. *Boise*'s SOCs continued to return to the area south of Niscemi to spot tanks for the 6-inch guns, only to be chased off by the more advanced fighter planes. Lewis provided a jarring recounting of narrowly avoiding death from above, summarized here:

> I was approximately five miles inland at 6,000 feet. AA fire had forced me up. The fighters made high overhead runs from my stern. Turning towards them as they dove I could keep them in sight and just before I judged they would open fire I faked one way and turned sharply the other continuing my dive. They both fired long bursts but missed. They dove below me and came up in my blind spot. When the first plane was where I figured he would open fire, I pulled the plane into a right split S. Tracers went past me, and I felt explosive shells hit the plane. The second plane's tracers were much closer. I came out of the dive at about 700 feet and rolled over, looking for the fighters. As I was nearly to the coastline they withdrew. I called the ship, reporting the plane damaged. They told me to return which I did after unloading my bombs on a place being shelled.[49]

Six SOCs in total were shot down that day, severely limiting the Navy's ability to provide fire support. The crews of those planes likely would have agreed with Lewis's assessment that "it is my opinion that that cruiser seaplanes now in use are not suitable for such duties even if given fighter protections...."[50] The old planes just were not fast or maneuverable enough to survive dogfights.

The Luftwaffe was not content to just blind the ships and their guns by taking out spotters, they wanted to sink them to the bottom. This was the first time *Boise* had found itself under air attack, and the effect must have been sobering, especially for those who had not experienced the hellish night off Guadalcanal. DB recorded rather nonchalantly as only a veteran can that "we had a few air attacks during day. One LST got hit."[51] At 1025, four unidentified aircraft approached the ship directly off the bow. *Boise* responded with fire from the 20mm and 40mm guns from both sides of the ship, adding different pitches to the warship's martial cacophony. Still, the ship was undamaged and the crew undeterred. Only ten minutes later they sent another volley of steel at the German tanks.[52]

Other ships were less lucky. The destroyer *Maddox* was sunk by a Stuka bomber just before sunrise with over two-hundred men killed. Another enemy bomb found *LST-313* later in the day. No one was killed, but the troops lost a significant amount of their anti-tank weapons.[53]

On board *Boise*, the crew kept up a steady rate of fire in support of the Army. They proved crucial in breaking up the German counterattack from Niscemi, striking targets recorded as "pass in hills," mortars, guns, and multiple tanks.[54] At 1530 they destroyed a pesky anti-aircraft position, and did not engage any more ground targets that day. The AA gunners stayed alert, firing a few times to help the SOCs escape enemy fighters. By evening *Boise* withdrew from the beaches. The AA gunners stayed on alert. The ship took up a blocking position between the landing ships and the sea, changing course and speed throughout the night to deter submarine attacks.[55]

General Eisenhower relayed to Allied leadership in both Britain and America that "so far, the operation has proceeded almost exactly according to plan."[56] Patton, however, had serious concerns over the DIME sector. Paratroopers were still scattered and, due to the loss of the Gela pier, offloading of heavy tanks and artillery was slow. He wanted efforts doubled to put his reserve forces ashore.[57]

Sunday, July 11, General Quarters sounded at 0451, a full hour before sunrise. The Luftwaffe waited until almost 0700 to try and cripple the landing effort. DB reported thirty-four bombers attacked DIME force that morning.[58] The ship's log stated a stick of three German bombs missed *Boise* off the port bow by 200 yards. The same attack managed to hit the troop ship *Barnett* killing 7, but the ship stayed afloat.[59]

On shore, Conrath received significant pressure from his superiors during the night to push the Americans back into the sea. He concluded such a task was impossible with the forces under his command, but a determined attack by the HG Division could still bottle up the enemy on the beachhead. Frantic planning with his Italian allies resulted in a plan for the HG and Livorno Divisions to attack Gela along three axes. The coordinated attack was set for 0600, and a portion of Conrath's tanks were instructed to charge across the open plain north of Gela rather than fight down the winding and constricted road from Niscemi. The plain was ideal for the tanks as they had room to maneuver, clear lines of sight into town, and level terrain where they could operate at high speeds. It would also allow individual tanks to disperse, making them more difficult targets for naval gunnery. This was the type of terrain German tanks had dominated since the beginning of the war. The infantry would have a tougher time crossing half a mile of flat, empty fields completely exposed to American fire. Worse, during the night the Americans set up blocking positions halfway across the plain. Italian troops could only hope their own artillery would provide enough cover for them to make the dash to Gela.[60]

Six columns of German and Italian troops would attack towards the coast. Five would converge on Gela. Four columns of Italian infantry would attack from the west and north, while Conrath's tanks would attack across the plain and down the road from Niscemi.[61] All advances would occur within the range of naval guns.

The reality of the counterattack at Gela was messier than the plan. There was no coordination between the columns due in part to a lack of radios. The center Italian column, a battalion under the command of Lieutenant Colonel Dante Ugo Leonardi waited for friendly artillery that failed to materialize, and finally moved out around 0630 under the limited cover of their mortars and machine guns. The infantry columns to the west of Gela likewise started forward haphazardly and without significant support. Conrath unleashed his tanks about 0615, again without coordination with his Italian allies.[62]

The separate advances initially made progress. The counterattack was aided by the combined arms effort brought on by the air attack against the fleet, keeping them busy maneuvering and firing at the sky instead of the beaches. Leonardi's men pushed the Americans off their advanced line and pressed towards Gela. Around 0800 his promised artillery support finally arrived, hammering American positions in concussions and flames, proving that late is better than never. Conrath's tanks likewise forced the paratroopers and 1st Infantry grunts back under the weight of German steel. The Americans fought bravely with small arms and bazookas, but with limited artillery support from the beach they were hard-pressed and forced to give ground back to the Germans.[63] The need for the Navy grew by the minute.

Something besides the air attacks was keeping the Navy from helping their terrestrial brothers. Part of the delay was the lack of spotters. Due to insufficient air cover and the walloping the SOCs took the day prior, none would launch on the 11th. Without eyes in the sky, the ships relied on naval observers embedded with the infantry to relay targets. Strangely, no such calls were made during the first ninety minutes of the counterattack. The battle's official report suggests the observers could not reliably fix targets due to areas of the dry Gela Plain burning from the ongoing battle.[64]

By 0800 *Boise* and the other ships were in position, still awaiting requests for their guns. They waited along with the troops ashore for friendly air cover that never materialized due to poor weather that grounded planes in Malta. Once everyone was certain the Air Force was not coming, *Boise* finally got to work.[65]

At 0810 targets raced across the airwaves and *Boise* thundered once more to make the enemy infantry's lives pure hell. Leonardi's men, who had paid with blood to cross the barren Gela Plain, were not yet to the first row of houses when the earth erupted around them like mini-volcanoes. *Boise* and *Savannah* began to pound the plain, forcing the infantry to dive for nonexistent cover and desperately try to creep forward towards Gela.

Despite the increasing naval fire, Conrath's tanks made significantly more progress. The panzers streaked onto the plain and threatened the landing beaches east of the city. The 1st Division was hard-pressed. At 0640 Brigadier General Theodore Roosevelt, Jr., son of the former president and the assistant division commander, relayed the scene to his boss, Major General Terry Allen. "Terry—look! The situation is not very comfortable out here … 3rd Battalion has been penetrated…. No antitank protection. If we could get that company of medium tanks it sure would help." The numerous sandbars and channels, along with mines, made getting anything to the beach a nightmare. Perhaps worse for the men facing panzers was they had few antitank guns since most had sunk the prior evening with *LST-313*.[66]

In Gela, General Patton himself entered the fray around 0900 now that his men had a solid grip on the beach. After arriving in town, he decided to meet with Darby on top of a tall building in eastern Gela to observe the advancing enemy. When he saw how close the enemy tanks were approaching, he yelled at an ensign assigned to one of the shore parties. The ensign asked if he could help the general with something, when Patton responded with trademark color, "Sure, if you can connect with your ---- ---- [God damn] Navy, tell them for ----- [fuck] sake to drop some shellfire on that road." The unnamed ensign was able to reach *Boise*, who quickly responded with multiple salvos. Patton then growled to the ensign and assembled Rangers "kill every one of the goddamn bastards." *Boise* happily obliged the general's command with thirty-eight rounds from the big guns, devastating the tanks. *Boise* also earned Patton's respect and made him a believer in naval support for his army.[67]

Despite naval support, Gela was completely cut off from the landing beaches. Soldiers scrambled to meet the tanks among the sand dunes, and even the Navy stevedores were ordered to grab rifles and rush forward to join the fight. By 1100 German tanks were too close for the Navy to engage without the risk of hitting Americans. The fight at the beach was in the hands of the grunts.[68]

At sea, the men of the *Boise* and the other warships calmly plied their trade to turn back the other arms of the counterattack. In a little over an hour starting at 1040 the *Boise* fired seventy-eight shells from the big guns at individual tanks and grid coordinates relating to the German offensive.[69] The logs include a laundry list of targets including tanks, crossroads, anti-aircraft batteries, field guns, and even a bridge. The fire was particularly useful against the tank column from Niscemi again threatening the Y-junction. As the infantry was forced to withdraw, it was their fire that halted the advance.[70]

The fight at the beach reached a peak around 1100 as panzers crossed Highway 115 and began firing into supply dumps and landing craft from only 2,000 yards away. To make matters worse, German artillery fire closed several of the beaches to reinforcements. The situation led to a confident message from the HG Division to their headquarters that "pressure by the Hermann Goering Division [has] forced the enemy to re-embark temporarily." The message proved premature, as the Americans were not falling back into the sea. While the infantry kept the Germans occupied, the professionalism of the U.S. Navy beachmasters paid off when the 32nd Field Artillery Battalion arrived ashore under fire, immediately set up their guns, and began firing at the enemy tanks. They were quickly joined by four Sherman tanks and a newly arrived antitank company. By lunch, the counterattack was out of steam and the Germans began withdrawing while Major General Allen's men hounded them back across the plain.[71]

To the west, naval shellfire decimated the attacking Italian infantry as they crossed the open fields, and the Rangers added as much pain as possible with their mortars, machine guns, and captured Italian artillery pieces. By 1130, Patton observed that "the Italian advance seemed to stick…." The Rangers capitalized on the arrival of Shermans, pursuing the survivors as they desperately fled for the mountains. The Livorno Division was rendered ineffective as a combat unit after suffering over 50 percent casualties.[72]

Air attacks continued through the day. At 1113 a pair of Me-210 attack planes tried their luck on the cruiser. Approaching at high altitude they flew straight into the teeth of *Boise*'s AA guns. The sky erupted around the Germans, but they held their course above the rapidly jinking cruiser and released their bombs, missing by a mere 200 yards to port.[73]

At 1545, the DIME fleet was surprised by another high-altitude attack. Thirty-two Junker 88 bombers capitalized on the lack of Allied air cover and rained bombs upon the U.S. ships from 16,000 feet, trying to saturate the area with explosives rather than target an individual ship. *Boise* sped up to 25 knots and "commenced maneuvering on radical courses." The maneuvers worked, but barely. One struck so close it "drenched [the] fantail." Undeterred, *Boise* quickly switched from firing anti-aircraft guns back to shooting tanks.[74]

Not everyone was so lucky. One of the landing ships, the Liberty ship *Robert Rowen*, received three bombs that set fire to a cargo hold full of ammunition.[75] The fleet only downed one of the attacking aircraft in reply. Thankfully, and rarely for World War II naval conflict, all crew and passengers escaped before the ship went up in a spectacular fireball.[76]

The HG Division withdrew back towards Niscemi. The trip proved arduous to the German men who had strained against American firepower all morning. The panzers and their crews were desperate to get beyond the range of those 6-inch guns. As they fled back to the haven of Sicily's mountains, *Boise* called once more.

Thebaud wanted to ensure maximum destruction. He ordered the ship closer to shore to continue harassing the enemy. They risked maneuvering into shallow waters to increase their range. To prevent a catastrophic grounding, sailors known as leadsmen took continuous depth measurements with chains to ensure the ship would not run aground.[77] The method would have been familiar to Mississippi river boats a century earlier, but here the bold seamanship allowed *Boise* to accurately and effectively hit targets ten miles inland. Shore fire control parties happily relayed that "the 6 [inch] HC [high-capacity] projectile with the Mk. 29 fuze [sic] rips the tanks apart."[78] Not reflected in the report was the confusion, destruction, and death *Boise*'s fire caused to the many HG members not encased in armor.

Twilight fell across the beaches and smoke whispered into the air from the waterline, through the town, and across the Gela Plain and into the surrounding hills. General Allen's men pressed into the darkness to seek out the enemy and reclaim all the territory the enemy temporarily denied them that day. The transports continued to land men and equipment on DIME's beaches as the cruisers and destroyers withdrew to deeper water for the night.

The crew settled in for rest, but many remained at their posts. The ship cruised at 15 knots to screen the ongoing landing operations. Mess cooks and their attendants did their best to get hot chow to everyone onboard, and sailors strained their eyes on radar scopes and into the darkness to spot threats. Those threats became all too real around 2155 when enemy aircraft embarked on the time-honored tradition of denying your enemy any rest. Aircraft began dropping flares and continued through the night. *Boise* was forced to respond by increasing speed and maneuvering erratically to ensure they were as difficult a target as possible. Around midnight *Boise*'s luck nearly ran out when the ship was bracketed with flares and four bombs exploded directly in front of them at a thousand yards. All ships in the area increased their AA fire at the unseen aircraft, reducing the likelihood of sleep for even the drowsiest of crewmembers.[79]

Tragedy struck shortly after. The skies were clear and the darkness was lit by a quarter moon, providing minimal illumination to the pilots of 144 American transport planes carrying the 504th Parachute Infantry Regiment (PIR) of General Gavin's 82nd Airborne Division. Gavin worried that his men would be in severe danger if they dropped on the evening of the 11th and thought they should be held for future drops further into Sicily. He was overruled by Patton, who wanted the potent combat power and spirit of the paratroopers on the ground, not sitting at airfields in Africa.[80]

The planes had the misfortune of following the German air raid on the DIME sector by mere minutes. The Gulf of Gela below was packed with men manning anti-aircraft guns, and they all had itchy trigger fingers. Despite the multiple assurances Gavin received that the Navy and Army AA units would not fire on his men, the chaos of the previous day and evening meant there was little fire discipline from the anxious gunners. Communication between the services broke down at the worst moment. As the aircraft entered the prearranged lane for them to approach the beach and parachute into the landing zone near Gela all hell broke loose. Gunners and commanders alike misidentified the American transports and no one was able to stop the melee.[81]

The drop was an absolute disaster and tragedy. Twenty-three transports never returned to their home bases, and 37 were badly damaged. The 504th suffered 229 casualties that night with 81 dead, 132 wounded, and 16 missing before ever joining the fight.[82]

The night ended for *Boise* at 0451 when the crew returned to General Quarters. The sun rose an hour later, and by 0613 the gunners were hard at work sending rounds from Turret 1 at tanks and AA batteries. During these attacks, they had the honor of demonstrating their craft to General Eisenhower when he sailed into the DIME sector to observe the landing operations.[83] He noted soon after in a letter to Army Chief of Staff General George C. Marshall, "I must say the sight of hundreds of vessels, with landing craft everywhere, operating along the shoreline from Licata on the eastward, was unforgettable."[84]

Around the same time, *Savannah* put an end to the enemy's key observation point at Castelluccio di Gela. Several shells slammed into the ancient walls, crumbling half the structure in a heap of broken stone and shattered stained glass. Infantry quickly followed the shells and surrounded the castle, forcing the survivors to surrender.[85] A few hours later, the 1st Infantry Division overran the Ponte Olivo airstrip, the primary objective of the DIME sector. A British Royal Air Force fighter wing would occupy and start using the strip the next day.[86]

Boise fired hundreds of shells at tanks and infantry far in the hills as the Army pressed ever onward. Effective air cover kept the vast majority of enemy aircraft from approaching DIME. Only a single air attack was able to reach DIME that day, and *Boise*'s anti-aircraft gunners drew blood by downing one of them. Shore-based anti-aircraft guns knocked out two more.[87] Killing at extreme distances was becoming routine, and *Boise* was every bit as good at shooting German tanks as they were at shooting Japanese ships.

The reality of modern warfare struck home when around dusk *LCT-215* came alongside the ship to transfer wounded troops and prisoners. DB noted that there were twelve Americans and four Germans, and that "we put them in sick bay and fixed them up." Five more wounded soldiers were brought aboard after dark. The sight of bullet and shrapnel wounds must have been jolting to some of the crew who had not been at Guadalcanal.[88]

By the 13th, the fighting had moved inland beyond *Boise*'s ability to support. Life aboard ship took on a different routine as the crew stayed alert for air and sea threats to the ongoing landing operations. Wounded personnel and POWs were transferred to other ships, and *Boise* passed 20mm ammunition to nearby ships to ensure everyone was well prepared to defeat air attacks. The following day they received orders to join up with *Savannah* and *Brooklyn*, along with several destroyers, and return to Algiers, Algeria.[89]

The crew took a collective breath after the massive bombardments they had dealt the enemy. Officers of the ship and higher commands reflected, trying to parse critical lessons for future operations. It was clear to everyone that on-call fire support from the Navy was an incredibly potent weapon. General Allen's commander of divisional artillery, Brigadier General Clift Andrus, praised the DIME force ships:

> We have handled the fire support of the ships in exactly the same manner that we handled reinforcing artillery of our own. At no time has the Navy hesitated to do anything requested, and their answers to calls for fire have invariably been in the form of remarkably accurate fire delivered in surprisingly short time.
> First Division Artillery recognizes superior gunnery when it sees it, and we are unanimously stating that the support rendered by Admiral Hall's command has been more than we could have expected even from the United States Navy.[90]

Patton concurred and added in his own notes for the campaign, "In daytime, Navy gunfire support is of immeasurable value, and the means now developed by the Navy for putting it on are extremely efficient."[91] Conrath admitted to the effectiveness of the gunfire indirectly when he issued orders to his commanders to rally the troops. They were told to stop their men from "spreading discouraging rumors, throwing away supplies and equipment, and 'running to the rear hysterically crying.'"[92] Eisenhower also agreed with these assessments, and his opinion ensured the continued use of Navy guns to support the Army in future operations. He wrote in a dispatch:

> So devastating in its effectiveness as to dispose finally of any doubts that naval guns are suitable for shore bombardment.... The fire power of vessels assigned to gunfire support exceeded that of the artillery landed in the assaults, and the mobility of the ships permitted a greater concentration of fire than artillery could achieve in the initial stages.[93]

Even the enemy acknowledged the devastating effectiveness of naval gunnery. After the war, Samuel Morison conducted extensive research into captured enemy documents. He noted in Sicily that "frequently, in Italian and German sources, we find that this ferocious and devastating intervention of the Allied Navies was the crucial factor that forced Axis ground forces to retire."[94]

Boise's Shore Bombardment Report for the battle echoed these conclusions. Captain Thebaud wrote, "All equipment functioned as it should. It is believed that the accuracy of the ship's bombardment fire as directed by the shore fire control party contributed not a little to the discomfiture of the enemy. Communications functioned perfectly." He thought the efforts were simply what was expected of a crew as fine as *Boise*'s, to the point he did not think that the individual actions of any single individual merited "special honors or rewards." Excellence was his standard, and the crew delivered.[95]

Operation Husky's initial landings proved successful. The Allies opened the second front in Europe that Soviet Union leader Joseph Stalin had insisted upon for years. The unleashed forces quickly broke out and conquered the entire island. Some key German generals realized that Husky represented the beginning of the end for the Nazi empire. German Lieutenant General Fridolin von Senger toured the Gela battlefield and wrote "unforgettable it was" about the scene of American military might. He now believed after those first few days that not only was Sicily lost, but Germany was going to lose the war.[96]

The cruisers and their tin cans returned to Algiers, where they had a short period to rearm, refuel, and conduct routine maintenance. Training also continued, particularly AA training where the ship remained at anchor and the SOCs flew past towing targets.[97] On July 16 the crew was reminded that danger was a constant bedfellow to shipboard life. An explosion at a nearby fuel dock sank a Liberty ship and damaged two others. *Boise* had its own scare later in the day, but it turned out to be a false alarm.[98]

Boise, *Savannah*, and *Brooklyn* continued to support the Sicily operation through the later weeks of July and into August, which became a monotonous grind for the crews. The ship returned to Gela and took turns with the rest of the fleet moving from anchorage to anti-submarine patrol sectors and back. They also stood to for numerous air threats that never materialized and made frequent return trips to North Africa to escort friendly vessels. Sailors frequently launched small boats while the ship was anchored to patrol the surrounding waters for threats.[99]

Boise's celebrity status continued. While anchored in Algiers on July 29, the battleship HMS *King George V* signaled, "We are honored to have a United States Ship with such a fighting record as you alongside." The *King George V* was the flagship of the British Home Fleet and a veteran of the hunt for the infamous German battleship *Bismarck*. Praise from the likes of that crew constituted significant bragging rights for the men and was recalled repeatedly at reunions years later.[100]

On August 8, *Boise* left Algeria once more for Sicily.[101] This time they were bound for Palermo on the northern coast. Patton's army had taken the city two weeks earlier nearly without a fight. The Italian army in Sicily was used up. They lacked food, ammunition, and supplies. Few would have wanted to fight a last-ditch battle for Palermo with Patton at their front and the U.S. Navy at their backs.[102]

Patton was now in frenzied competition with Field Marshal Montgomery to capture Messina. Both wanted to cut off and destroy the enemy before they could withdraw, and both equally wanted the accolades that came along with such a conquest. As the British pushed up the heavily populated and defended east coast, the Americans acted as a left hook, pummeling the retreating forces. Patton drove his men hard, and even attempted to outflank his enemy with small amphibious operations that landed limited numbers of American troops behind enemy lines. *Boise* proved critical to these operations, even if they failed to trap the Germans.

Boise joined the fray on August 12 after several days of patrolling Palermo's immediate waters. Two days before, an amphibious force had sailed from Palermo, and *Boise* was coming to aid them and the soldiers of the 3rd Infantry Division pushing east towards Messina. *Boise*'s 6-inchers barked forty-five times before 0800 to take out enemy positions in the village of Gioiosa Marea and a bridge.[103]

The enemy answered with their own heavy artillery. *Boise* had multiple near misses from a mobile gun hiding in a railroad tunnel, showering the topside with shrapnel, damaging one of the SOCs, and injuring six crewmembers. Thebaud avenged his injured men with ninety-one shells fired in the vicinity of the mobile battery's hiding place, ending the cat-and-mouse game with either the gun destroyed or choosing to hide until *Boise* withdrew in the late morning.[104]

The next day *Boise* escorted a group of LCTs carrying artillery to the village of Patti. Before returning to Palermo, they were urgently re-tasked further east to stop a reported attempt by the Germans to evacuate from Milazzo. *Boise* arrived with the destroyers *Benson* and *Rowan* and conducted a search of the area. They did not find any escapees, but they were fired on by several shore batteries. *Boise* answered with gusto. For nearly three hours they shelled the town, surrounding gun batteries, fortifications, and even a radio tower while the destroyers engaged several positions of German 88mm anti-aircraft guns.[105]

None of the ships were hit during the duel. *Boise* alone fired 614 6-inch shells during the match, leading Thebaud to include an interesting note in his report. It revealed the violence that the big guns dealt to their caretakers. He recorded, "All personnel and material functioned perfectly with the exception of minor damage caused by shock of ship's fire, such as jack-box covers blown off, fire control circuits slightly damaged, cease firing gongs broken and minor damage to clocks and clock cases."[106]

The ship spent the following few days in Palermo's harbor. At dusk on the 17th, they set sail to attack mainland Italy under orders directly from the "Commander in Chief, Mediterranean."[107] *Boise* left port with *Philadelphia* and four destroyers. They moved fast with no transports to slow them down. The little task force split up at 0015 with each cruiser leading two tin cans to a different objective. Like a wraith, *Boise* slid into attack position about 15,000 yards from the target. Their mission was to destroy a railway electric power substation while *Philadelphia* attacked a major bridge ten miles to the north, hopefully slowing the retreat of German forces away from Sicily.[108]

Judging by the lack of any fire from the coast, the ships achieved surprise. Unfortunately, *Boise* did not have accurate coordinates for their target, only an intelligence report that the target was "on the outskirts of town." *Boise* applied their professionalism the best they could to destroy the substation. The log reported:

> A power house had been reported at Palmi. However, this could not be picked out on the chart. Since all firing was to be done in darkness with no point of aim it was decided to lay a "checker-board" of salvos over the entire area of the town, using pre-determined spots…. Ships' position was determined accurately by search radars and checked by fire control radar. Correction for height of town (250 meters) was applied to gun elevation. It is believed that all salvos landed in target area.

In only nine minutes, they fired an astounding 292 shells. All five turrets fired non-stop, with some turrets shooting 15 shells a minute! While hardly reassuring to any civilians in the town, the raid is a testament to *Boise*'s ability to deal death as accurately as 1943 technology would allow. Even so, the after-action report recommended future raids avoid firing during the night "except under unusual circumstances."[109]

The raiders arrived back in Palermo by 0700, but there was no rest for the weary. By noon, *Boise* was leaving port with destroyers *Ludlow* and *Bristol* bound for Algiers. *Boise* performed the usual zigzag maneuvers, keeping DB and his fellow quartermasters on their feet by halving the usual time between each course change. An enemy plane found them just before midnight and just missed each of the ships, causing no damage but several casualties aboard *Ludlow*. The threats to a wartime ship continue unabated, so after dodging bombs the ships rigged their paravanes, devices attached to cables designed to snag mines and allow the crew to detonate them before they hit the ship. As they cruised the mine-infested waters north of Tunisia, they witnessed a "heavy raid" by the

Luftwaffe on the port city Bizerte. After a hectic trip, they arrived in the relative safety of Algiers harbor the afternoon of the 19th.[110]

By September 1943, the Allies had failed to trap several enemy divisions in Sicily and the Germans scrambled to new positions on the Italian mainland to thwart the next wave of invasions. Operation Avalanche was launched against the new Axis positions at Salerno early that month. *Boise* was again part of the fleet, ready to take the fight to the European mainland. The crew had spent several weeks training in North Africa. Along with other *Brooklyn*-class cruisers, they conducted live fire training with new shore control parties and practiced amphibious landings with the transports tasked for Salerno.[111]

On September 6 they were sailing a zigzag pattern with *Savannah* and *Philadelphia*, along with escorts and transports. At noon the ship welcomed the SOCs back to the deck and took on last-minute supplies. The crew had these simple sailing maneuvers and reprovisioning operations down cold, and there was no indication of trouble ahead. In the late afternoon the fleet set sail, then shortly after 1800 the *Boise* received an unexpected signal from Rear Admiral Davidson, the task force commander. He ordered the *Boise* to "return at once to Bizerta [*sic*], report to CINCMED."[112]

Captain Thebaud was perturbed, anxiously wondering why his highly experienced ship was being ordered to return to port alone while the rest of the fleet continued into battle. He queried the admiral, stating "please repeat" in hopes of an explanation. The reply was cryptic but encouraging. The original signal was repeated, but this time Davidson added, "Hope this makes you an admiral!"[113] Whatever was in store for *Boise* was bound to be interesting.

A few days before, British Admiral of the Fleet Andrew Cunningham proposed a daring operation to General Eisenhower. The Italian government was on the verge of surrendering to the Allies, including the remains of their fleet anchored at Taranto. The Italians agreed in secret negotiations to open the port and another at Brindisi to the Allies while their remaining fleet sailed to Malta to formally surrender. Cunningham proposed he designate a force of warships to deliver troops directly to Taranto to secure the port and surrounding area, a mission dubbed Operation Slapstick. Eisenhower ordered the British 1st Airborne Division to accomplish the mission, and if the Allies were lucky the action would pull German troops away from Salerno. However, planners quickly realized that a significant portion of their forces would have to remain in North Africa unless additional ships were made available. Unfortunately for the Paras, all the theater's ships and planes were allocated to invasions of the Italian west coast. Enter the *Boise*.[114]

An hour after leaving the column of American cruisers, *Boise* dropped anchor in Bizerte.[115] Captain Thebaud disembarked to learn the details of the plan while the ship began embarking British soldiers. What Thebaud received was more suited for an infantry squad briefing than a conference between senior naval officers. Admiral Cunningham met Thebaud at the pier and took him to his staff car. He proceeded to use his finger to sketch the Italian coastline and Taranto in the dust of the hood, stated *Boise*'s position in the battle line, and sent Thebaud back to the ship. The rest would rely on updates as the fleet progressed and the crew's ability to adapt.[116]

As the soldiers loaded, the SOC airplanes were offloaded so the hangar could be filled with jeeps, motorcycles, field guns, and even bicycles. DB noted they "received aboard 650 troops and about 60 jeeps and equipment. We are to take them to Taranto, Italy, and except [*sic*] the surrender of the Wop fleet." By 1600 the next day, the fleet set sail. *Boise* carried elements of legendary 1st Airborne and an eccentric commando unit known as "Popski's Private Army." They joined four British cruisers and the minesweeper HMS *Abdiel* for the mission, and at 1900 the captain announced to the ship via the loudspeakers that Italy had surrendered to the Allies.[117]

As formidable as five cruisers could be in a stand-up fight, Cunningham thought the force could use a little more firepower. He noted that if the Italian fleet, which

Troops of the British 1st Airborne Division crowded aboard the ship with their equipment before landing at Taranto, Italy, 8 September 1943 (National Archives: 80-G-85577).

included a pair of battleships, opted to get "mixed up" with the Allied force they could create a "jolly nuisance." To overcome such understated concerns, he ordered the British battleships *Howe* and *King George V* to join the party along with six destroyers.[118]

The fleet charged forward, using all the speed available to the most modern of warships. The *Boise* log recorded "flank speed" of 25–30 knots through the night as the fleet zigzagged through the sea with darkened decks and anti-aircraft guns ready. Operations continued similarly the following day, with a section of ships breaking off in the afternoon. As they approached the port, sailors across a dozen ships felt their hearts in their throats as the Italian Navy left port. Sailing towards the *Boise* were two battleships, a heavy cruiser, a light cruiser, and a destroyer.[119] The combined firepower could certainly become a "jolly nuisance" intentionally or by mistake. Morrison noted, "one trigger-happy gun pointer on either side might have set off a minor Jutland," referring to the famously bloody World War I naval battle.[120] Thankfully, cool and calm heads prevailed on both sides as the ships slid past each other. DB expressed the thoughts of a fighting man and disparaged the no-longer-enemy ships by noting "such nice ships to not even put up a fight."[121]

With a costly encounter avoided and the autumn sun setting behind them, the fleet entered the Taranto harbor under the direction of Italian harbor pilots. *Boise*'s assigned pilot suggested a particular mooring in the harbor, but Thebaud declined the position, instead tying up alongside a merchant pier. This decision, which was likely made to expedite the offloading of troops, proved fortuitous for the ship. As veterans noted years later, "The Gods of War were with *Boise*, for during the night, the minelayer *Abdiel*, which had accepted the anchorage previously declined, swung over while at anchor and struck a magnetic mine. The minelayer broke in two and sank within a few minutes."[122] Slapstick's bloodless streak ended as 48 sailors and 101 soldiers went with *Abdiel* to the bottom.[123]

The fleet unloaded quickly and set sail the following morning. There was no need for them to remain in an unsafe anchorage with no room to maneuver if the Luftwaffe came calling. They returned to Bizerte the morning of the 11th to refuel and begin loading additional British paratroopers. That process was abruptly canceled at 1450 and the troops were ordered to disembark.[124] By 1600 they set sail, along with a single destroyer escort, rushing to Salerno where the battle was not going well.

Avalanche failed to achieve surprise. Upon landing on September 9, American troops at the southern end of the beaches were greeted by a loudspeaker proclaiming, "Come on in and give up. We have you covered!" The enemy was ready, willing to fight, held the mountains all around the beaches, and were doing their absolute best to push the Allies back into the sea. Naval gunfire proved critical, hitting enemy guns and tanks and allowing the Allies to desperately cling to their positions. Brigadier General Otto Lange, the assistant commander of the 36th Infantry Division, lauded the *Savannah*, *Philadelphia*, and attached destroyers on the 10th. "Thank God for the fire of the Blue Belly Navy Ships. Probably could not have stuck out 'Blue' and 'Yellow' Beaches. Brave fellows please tell them so. Well done."[125]

The support came at a much greater cost than Gela. Landing craft of all types were shot up badly as they approached the beaches. The HMS *Abercrombie*, a slow "monitor" type of ship built specifically with a giant 15-inch gun to support bombardment operations, struck a mine on the first afternoon and had to withdraw to Palermo. The bigger ships contended with artillery fire from the beaches and with the Luftwaffe above. The destroyer *Rowan* was lost to a torpedo from a German E-boat on the 10th. The torpedo set off a terrifying explosion and the ship sank in forty seconds, taking 202 of 273 men to their deaths.[126]

The butcher's bill grew the following morning, greatly impacting the fire support available to the men ashore. At 0944 on September 11 the lookouts on *Savannah* spotted a German Do 217E-5 approaching out of the sun to their port quarter. The plane was one of many that threatened the beaches that morning, and the Allied air cover failed to intercept this one in time. The German dropped a Fritz-X radio-controlled bomb and controlled its dive towards the ship. A P-38 Lightning and the ship's gunners tried without success to shoot down the glide bomb. Survivors of the attack described a "whooshing" sound as the bomb cut through the top of Turret 3 at over 550 mph and continued belowdecks to explode its 660-pound explosive in the lower ammunition handling room. The resulting blast killed the sailors of Turret 3 and a damage control party nearby. It also ripped a hole in the hull below the waterline. The crew was now in a fight for their lives against their beloved ship, just as the *Boise* had been nearly a year before.[127]

The crew responded quickly and professionally. The ship lost all electric power, and individual damage control parties had to rely on their training to tackle the problems immediately in front of them. Smoke and fumes from the bomb caused additional casualties in the forward turrets, and the ship took on so much water the forecastle nearly dipped below the waterline. Fifteen minutes later a secondary explosion from the destroyed turret rocked the ship, probably from a few 6-inch shells that were ready to launch. Despite this, the damage control parties had the overall fire under control within minutes, and the entire blaze extinguished in two hours. Several of the nation's highest medals were awarded posthumously to crewmembers who sacrificed themselves to save their ship, including a Navy Cross given to Lieutenant John J. Kirwin, a turret officer who "despite the imminent danger of a magazine explosion, stood by his station in the turret booth. With full knowledge of the serious hazards involved and with complete disregard for his own personal safety, he calmly supervised evacuation and deliberately remained behind to aid in saving the lives of as many of his command as possible when he might easily have escaped."[128]

By late morning *Savannah* was moving out of the battle area with the assistance of two tugs. The damage report stated "the bomb detonated in the midst of main and secondary battery magazines—a location usually regarded as certain to cause the immediate and violent destruction of the vessel."[129] But not for the first or last time, the *Brooklyn*-class cruisers and their crews proved that these were not ordinary ships, and they did not succumb to the enemy easily.

Still, the *Savannah* was out of action, leaving a hole in the naval gunfire support that *Boise* was rushing to fill. By noon on the 12th, they threaded a clear channel through the minefields into a support position with *Philadelphia* and awaited calls from the shore parties. The Luftwaffe greeted the men at 1803 with an attack of four "Fock Wolfs [sic]" according to DB. The log noted three dive-bombers, and everyone agreed that the ship was straddled by three near misses. The AA guns chattered and the ship dodged, but this time there was a higher level of angst for the crew as word spread of what had happened to *Savannah* the day prior.[130]

Monday the 13th saw more air attacks, and the spotters watched another radio-controlled glide bomb barely miss the *Philadelphia*. One *Boise* sailor recorded: "Had worst day of air attacks."[131] DB recalled firing at targets on the beach all day along with four air attacks. The log concurs with the air attacks which kept the ship busy all day, but only logged a single target destroyed in the afternoon. The difference in reports was manifested in more than just *Boise*, however. Morison noted that the chaos of repelling German counterattacks was of an "intensity and volume ... in direct support of troop operations [at Salerno] set a new high in that aspect of naval warfare; one that would not be exceeded in the Pacific until Iwo Jima and Okinawa." He continued, "Unfortunately no accurate or complete log was kept of these shoots, or even of the calls."[132] It would seem that everyone involved was more concerned with winning than with proper record keeping.

Boise certainly added literal and figurative weight to the fight on the 14th. They fired 1,046 shells at the Germans that day. Then, shortly after midnight while trolling the beach in hopes of "unmasking" an enemy battery, they received a rare overnight call for fire. An observer embedded with the Army signaled, "We need support. When able, give four minutes' rapid fire." Happy to oblige, *Boise* fired 288 rounds from the big guns. This was much more satisfying to the crew than their late-night raid on Palmi a few weeks prior because this time they knew where to shoot. Three hours after the initial contact, the observer relayed, "Your firing has won our praise. It has Jerry puzzled. Well done. Will be back in 20 minutes." The duo teamed up to drop another 147 rounds on the Germans before sunup.[133]

A new problem arose early on the 15th. *Boise* and *Philadelphia* were running out of ammunition. *Boise* responded to several more fire requests but let the 5-inch guns provide more support than normal. The larger rounds were held for tougher targets and longer ranges. Help was on the way, though, as the U.S. naval commander at Palermo anticipated an ammo shortage and sent his entire supply of 6-inch shells to Salerno on a destroyer early that morning. Admiral Hewitt, the overall naval commander for the operation, also sent the destroyer *Gleaves* on a lightning errand to Malta to scavenge *Savannah*'s remaining stock of shells.[134]

As the ammunition relief ships were approaching the area, *Boise* received orders to withdraw. By 1900 they had passed through the minefield again for open sea, en route to Bizerte. The fight continued without them for about forty-eight hours as they rearmed and refueled at Bizerte. *Boise* returned to Salerno on the 18th. The fight had moved past the point of naval support, however, and by the 19th *Boise* again departed Salerno, this time for Palermo.[135]

On September 25, the crew said goodbye to Captain Thebaud. He was bound for the command of Cruiser Division 10 in the Pacific, and Captain John S. Roberts took over as *Boise*'s latest skipper. He had big shoes to fill. It should be noted that Admiral Davidson's prediction before Slapstick proved correct; Thebaud eventually made Admiral.[136]

Roberts had to wait until October 5 before taking his ship to sea. The crew continued the duties required of a warship but settled into a boring routine of maintenance and watches, particularly spotting for enemy aircraft with radar and the naked eye. When they finally sailed, the crewmembers topside got one last look at Italy when they passed through the Strait of Messina. The ship stopped briefly in Malta, and then continued to Algiers where they remained for several weeks.[137]

The crew did not know it yet, but they were finished with the Mediterranean Theater, and would depart the ancient seas later that month. They had made an indelible mark on Army-Navy cooperation, the war in Europe, and in the lives of countless

Captain Hewlett Thebaud shakes hands with the ship's officers after passing command to Captain John S. Roberts, at Palermo, Italy, 25 September 1943 (National Archives: 80-G-57183).

Allied and enemy soldiers. Their impact was recorded succinctly by a German general at Salerno: "But the greatest distress suffered by the troops was caused by the fire of ships' guns of heavy caliber, from which they could find no protection in the rocky soil."[138] The Germans even went so far as to christen *Boise* and *Philadelphia* with the colorful and accurate nicknames "The Murderous Queens."[139] *Boise* and the men had proven once again they represented the best of the U.S. Navy.

The ship's Mediterranean adventures are best wrapped up with a moment of levity. Thanks to *Boise*'s support of the British Commandos during their bold capture of Taranto, the Royal Navy extended a rare courtesy to the ship's men. On October 18, the Brits opened the Royal Navy Canteen in Algiers for the sole use of the *Boise* crew. To the assured jealousy of the club's usual patrons, the evening's festivities promised the attendance of local French ladies.

With typical wit, a group of sailors identified only as "The Committee" published the rules for the evening and addressed the desires of young men cooped up on a ship during wartime. The instructions included the areas of the club permitted to the crew, the timeline, and a warning for everyone to be on their best behavior. The building's balcony was declared out of bounds, which was probably a wise decision considering the amount of alcohol many of the sailors planned on imbibing. The rules also proclaimed the bad news that only the crewmembers of the standby section could attend, resulting in an almost surely lucrative business of trading watch billets!

Finally, rule number four set the most important commandment of the evening. It stated, "The girls are French and must come in a body and leave in a body. This regulation is laid down by the port authorities. Hence, it will be impossible to take a girl home." Still, the Committee allowed a glimmer of hope with the caveat "there is no rule which will prevent you from getting an address."

While the men almost certainly enjoyed the company of the French ladies as a badly needed distraction from the war, there are no records of whether or not any sailors returned to the ship with an address in hand.[140]

6

The March Up

New Guinea

The crew was allowed a few merciful days of light duty at anchor to nurse their hangovers. On October 23 they weighed anchor in the early afternoon and departed Algiers. They arrived at Mers-el-Kebir near Oran the following morning. It was time to upgrade their armory for an Atlantic Ocean trip where the primary threat was submarines. They transferred their bombardment ammunition in exchange for armor-piercing shells and depth charges.[1]

They waited in port for a few days before authorization to proceed home arrived. On the 29th they started their journey home along with destroyers *Rhind* (DD-404) and *Nicholson* (DD-442). They chased the setting sun and passed through the Strait of Gibraltar just before midnight, finally arriving in Casablanca around 1000 the next morning for refueling.[2]

The ship remained in port for a few days, providing the men a chance to explore a little. The city had been made famous a few months prior thanks to the Humphrey Bogart movie that many of the men probably saw while in Philadelphia. DB noted the city was "a much more modern place than expected."[3] It was not until November 7 that the ship finally set sail for America.[4]

The same destroyers accompanied *Boise* on their Atlantic journey. It was a quiet voyage, only interrupted by a fire "caused by rain entering switch box in whip hoist power supply circuit." Fires at sea are always a threat to ships, so luckily this one was put out in under ten minutes before it grew into mortal threat. They arrived in New York Harbor on the 15th. The first stop was far from the city to unload their ammunition, but the Statue of Liberty welcomed them by 1825 for their own private pass-and-review that ended in Berth 15 of Pier J at the Brooklyn Navy Yard.[5] There was no more iconic American arrival.

On Thursday the 18th the ship moved into dry-dock and remained there for ten days. Since there was little for a helmsman to do while their ship is placed on blocks, DB was granted eight days of leave. He used the time to travel to the home of his friend Estill Drake, one of the ship's boatswains. The two spent a few days relaxing in the hills of Kentucky's western coal country. DB returned to New York in time to celebrate Thanksgiving with his shipmates.[6]

Their period of "repair and maximum improvement" ended on December 6. There would be no stateside Christmas for the men. Captain Roberts was in command and tasked with getting the *Langley* (CVL-27), *Remey* (DD-688), and *Lewis Hancock* (DD-675) to the Pacific. *Boise* was destined for the 7th Fleet supporting General MacArthur's drive across the Southwest Pacific. On the 3rd they began preparations for any possible fight by filling the magazines with a mix of ammunition suited for all sorts of targets. On the 5th they loaded powder for the main guns. They also topped off their fuel and aviation gasoline bunkers before departing New York on the 6th. By 1900 they had collected all ships of their task group and set a course for Panama.[7]

December 7 marked two years that the United States had been at war. The day was suitably stormy for those whose thoughts strayed to all that had been lost. The log noted "sky solid overcast, low ceiling, strong southerly shifting winds, frequent rains; sea rough."[8] Many may have found it fitting, because *Boise* was sailing back into the storm clouds of war. While the Allies had pushed back hard against Germany and Japan since Pearl Harbor, there was still hard fighting ahead as neither country was anywhere near surrendering.

The next day did not brighten anyone's mood. *Langley* lost an aircraft that crashed while attempting to land. It sank in thirty seconds, taking two men to their deaths. One man was rescued. But the task group had no time to mourn and sailed onward. *Boise* conducted routine tasks, launching and recovering SOCs for anti-submarine patrols and transferring fuel to the destroyers.[9] The war continued, and proved once again that lives could be lost far from battle.

On the 10th the task group was alerted to an enemy submarine. *Boise*'s expert radar operators identified the contact at 19,400 yards and tracked it while it slowed and then disappeared. An enemy submarine was known to be operating in the area and had sunk a merchant ship earlier in the week. *Boise*'s log noted, "Conclusion drawn was that submarine on surface was spotted by patrolling aircraft and forced to dive." The ships altered course to the south and kept their speed up. Twenty-five minutes after the radar contact they assumed the danger had passed. They passed word of the contact to U.S. forces in Panama so Allied airplanes could continue the hunt.[10]

They passed through the Panama Canal that afternoon without incident. This was DB's second time seeing the engineering marvel, and he was less impressed than before. He was much more concerned with liberty in Balboa. He and everyone else knew that it could be a long time before they enjoyed the vices of a proper port, and the men reveled.[11]

They left Panama for Milne Bay in New Guinea on the 12th, alone. The gunners conducted firing exercises to shake off any rust and train new crewmembers. It was a good thing they did. Guns from four of the five turrets jammed during the exercise. "These jams were very severe, requiring over thirty minutes to clear." The culprit seemed to be an area of "raised" metal inside the breeches that was causing the shell casings to get stuck after firing. The log did not note the fix, but the crews quickly got to work to ensure that every gun would be available if called upon.[12]

The rest of the trip was uneventful. DB dutifully noted crossing the equator but did not note any shellback ceremony. *Boise* launched SOCs every day the weather allowed, nearly always to support AA exercises. The crew was putting a lot of emphasis on repelling air attacks. The finally arrived at Bora Bora on the 22nd.[13] DB noted, "Hasn't changed much. Took on fuel, underway 2000 tonight for Suva, Fiji."[14]

At 1925 on the 23rd the radarmen again earned their pay. This time they picked up an unidentified ship to the west at 34,700 yards. Roberts ordered an intercept course to silhouette the ship against the setting sun at 12,000 yards, providing an excellent firing solution if needed. Thirty-five minutes later they could see the vessel through binoculars and the crew went to General Quarters. Everyone was on edge for twenty minutes until they identified the ship as the Dutch freighter *Klipfontein*.[15]

The crew was cheated out of a proper Christmas shortly after. At 1006 on the holiday the ship crossed the International Date Line from west to east, essentially jumping forward to the 26th. They arrived at Suva Harbor a few hours later. The ship's sole present was 294,714 gallons of fuel oil, which they received before settling in for the night.[16] The men celebrated with food from the mess and the company of their friends. Many quietly reread letters from home and imagined what families and sweethearts were doing without them. Some sort of religious ceremony was certainly held, as faith was something that helped many men endure the horrors and simple loneliness of war.

Religion has long been a pillar of strength for many of America's fighting men. To help men attend to their spiritual needs, the Navy provided chaplains who served alongside sailors aboard ships and in the field with Marines. DB noted that the *Boise* carried a Catholic chaplain. Services were held on the fantail on Sunday mornings whenever combat operations did not get in the way. DB did not hold any particularly strong religious views at the time, and usually avoided the services that he felt catered too much to the Catholic faith and not enough for the crew's Protestants. Still, the services provided comfort and strength to many of the men that Christmas and throughout the year.[17]

Those who did not partake in religious services probably spent their off time in the same activities they did every day to entertain themselves. Sailors throughout history have been subjected to days of drudgery repeating the same tasks to keep the ship running, and finding new ways to break up the routine can be difficult.[18] A newspaper article after the war mentioned "at night, the crew watched movies on the hangar deck under the stars," and that "cards were forbidden, but some sailors played chess, checkers, and acey ducey," a game similar to backgammon.[19] Men aboard sister ship *Helena* played "pitch or blackjack," but it appears that someone in the *Boise* leadership had something against card games, probably due to the gambling and potential fights that can come along with them.[20]

Others found escape in books, and reading was a pastime for many of the men. In classic military logic, books were assigned to cruisers based on tonnage, not personnel. Navy regulations allowed *Boise* nine hundred volumes in its library, almost enough for one book per man. They were supposed to receive new books each month, but this was a low priority for Navy logistics.[21]

Some preferred to stay busy with their hands. Incredible artistic talent was on display, with men sometimes using unique mediums. Turning brass shell casings into vases, ashtrays, mugs, and display pieces was a common way for fighting men to pass the time. One historian describes such art as "an opportunity to create something at a time when there was so much destruction."[22] Aboard *Boise*, GM2c James Clarence Ledford used the ship's machine shop to convert 40mm shells into something beautiful. He spent hours polishing the casings to a high sheen and then using a small punch to outline intricate letters, the ship, and other objects to commemorate his time at war.[23]

Another way to distract men from the doldrums was exercise. Sailors were required to maintain their physical fitness, even while at sea. Video from the *Boise* demonstrated that every available inch of the aft deck was used for men to accomplish group calisthenics. Many men stripped to the waist under the open sky to accomplish exercises that moved the entire body, starting with each person reaching across their body with the left hand to the right foot, then pulling the arm backward and behind them in a quick motion like they were trying to start a lawn mower. The workout was certain to raise everyone's heart rate while increasing their general strength and range of motion.[24]

The exercise was crucial for the men whose duties could be sedentary. Navy cooks tried hard to provide the men with nutritious food and a balanced diet. The Navy introduced a revised cookbook in 1944 that urged cooks to balance the nutrition of each meal, offer variety, and even consider the "'likes and dislikes' of the men." Most sailors would probably agree that desserts "[give] a feeling of satisfaction."[25] This could be difficult, though, when ships were at sea for long periods of time. Fresh food did not last long and everyone was forced to subsist on canned and frozen food for days and weeks on end. *Boise* veterans would continue to bemoan the ship's "chow" for years after the war, despite the cooks' best efforts.

Sometimes the crew needed to seek medical attention. Light cruisers carried a small medical staff and fully equipped sick bay. Those men were critical to saving lives after the Battle of Cape Esperance, and again treated wounded soldiers at Gela. Besides treating combat casualties, the doctors and corpsmen treated to the day-to-day medical concerns of the crew. For DB, that meant at some point in the war he was circumcised while at sea. Such a procedure is painful, and the recovery may be embarrassing for the patient, yet duty still called. In what may have grown into a "tall tale" over the years, DB claimed that after the procedure he was scheduled to stand watch on the bridge. He reported to duty with a soup can attached to a string around his neck with a hole cut into the side so he could soak "it" in cold water while on duty. When the captain observed his helmsman and his accessory, he quickly relieved him of duty and ordered him off the bridge until he could work without his soup can. Even if the story is nothing more than a myth, it certainly provides insight into the humor of the crew.[26]

The pace of duties could be exhausting. Joseph Fenton recalled they worked "four hours on, four hours off," while at sea.[27] At the end of a shift, many men just wanted to get enough sleep to function for the next go-around. Men had a bunk or used a hammock after stowing their meager possessions into small personal lockers.[28] Often it was too hot to sleep below decks in the South Pacific, so one sailor noted, "I only slept below in my bunk a few times, because it is too hot. You sleep on the steel deck with your clothes on and use your shoes as a pillow."[29]

If sleep failed them, or they were trying to stay awake on watch, many turned to nicotine. Smoking was fairly common for Americans in the 1940s, and many military men used cigarettes to relax when tensions were high, or just to unwind after a shift. Cigarettes were even included in daily rations for soldiers, including 4 per meal in the ubiquitous "K-Rations."[30] The Rho Lamda Phi sorority at Temple University even conducted a "Smokes for Yanks" drive at the beginning of the war to make sure soldiers and sailors could get their fix.[31]

For those needing something harder to relax, there may have been "raisin jack" to be found if you knew where to look. Although alcohol had been banned on U.S. Navy ships since 1914, crafty sailors still found ways to distill their own booze in the darker corners of their vessels.[32] World War II stories abound of this strong drink made from fermented raisins, usually because the proprietors got caught.[33] There is no evidence of any *Boise* sailors producing their own hooch, but DB and his friends probably longed to produce their own. They may even have had a supply squirreled away somewhere.

The ultimate pick-me-up for sailors, besides opportunities to leave the ship, was mail from home. The tenuous links to families and friends back home, or even deployed to other theaters, helped sailors stay grounded in their previous lives and plan for after the war. DB kept postcards from friends deployed to Europe and held on to a photo of his mother that he received sometime in 1944.³⁴ A sailor aboard the *Helena* described the excitement of a potential mail call. "Men lined the rail, waiting. To hell with the war. They were individuals now, not cogs in a machine…. They shuffle their feet, tug at their clothes, try to think of something smart to say to conceal their eagerness."³⁵ If the ship was underway, a cable was run between the resupply ship and the cruiser and the mailbags were slid along the line with any other supplies while the ships held a parallel course about 30–40 feet apart. Sailors had to keep enough tension on the line to make sure the precious cargo did not dip into the sea.³⁶ When the bags containing the mail finally made it to the deck the men would cheer like kids at a baseball game.

Boise left the harbor before 1000 the next morning. The war was calling, and the crew resolutely answered. They ran through firing exercises again that afternoon. The main guns jamming issue still existed. This time they experienced fourteen jammed plugs, some taking an hour to clear. Some were removed thanks to vigorous use of a leather maul to knock the cases loose, but one particularly bad jam could only be removed by ramming down from the muzzle, hardly a viable fix during combat. The gunners again investigated and this time uncovered "the shoulder just inside the powder chamber was unusually sharp" and catching the cases. The men set to work filing down the sharp edges "by stoning."³⁷

They navigated the tricky waters around Milne Bay and arrived in port on the 30th. The 7th Fleet commander wasted no time ordering them to refuel and join the fleet near Buna.³⁸ The men rang in the New Year by transferring the depth charges they had carried since North Africa and bringing aboard the deadliest of firecrackers—more 6-inch shells. They were designated part of Cruiser Division 15 along with sister ships *Phoenix* and *Nashville*.³⁹ They were officially part of MacArthur's navy.

Buna was the site of the Allies first big win in New Guinea roughly one year before. Australian troops, affectionately known as "Diggers," had pushed Japanese forces back

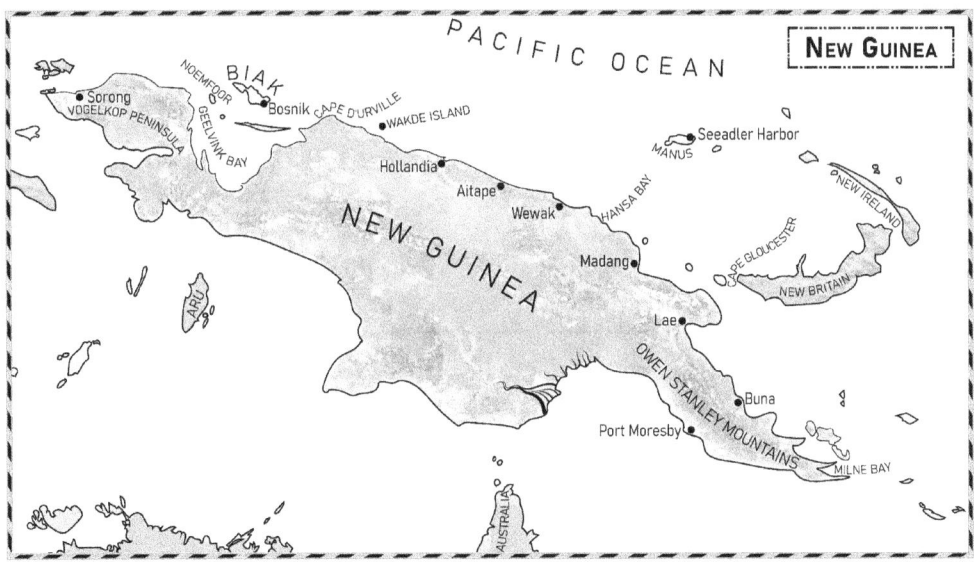

Boise supported General MacArthur's 1944 campaign across the northern coast of New Guinea. It took part in most of the major battles and provided critical support during invasions that often lacked naval air support.

from a thrust to the outskirts of Port Moresby.[40] What followed was a monthslong battle that introduced American reinforcements to hellish jungle-fighting conditions. The campaign was particularly difficult because the Allies lacked artillery and naval support and had only limited air support, which meant the infantry had to fight nose-to-nose in an environment that rarely allowed them to see more than a few feet in front of them.[41]

Since then, the Americans had conducted a two-pronged offensive to wrestle control of the South Pacific from the Japanese known as Operation Cartwheel. Admiral Nimitz commanded forces fighting their way up the Solomon and Admiralty island chains towards the massive Japanese base at Rabaul while MacArthur's forces hacked their way along the northeastern New Guinea coast.[42] Most recently the "Alamo Force" under MacArthur's control landed soldiers and Marines to take and hold Cape Gloucester on the western end of New Britian.[43] The plan called for the Allies to control the surrounding straits and seize an air base for future operations. On December 26, ships provided ninety minutes of supporting fire as the Marines went ashore. The landing went smoothly and is better remembered for the truly miserable conditions of swamp, rain, and general jungle malaise that the men had to survive.[44] Japanese air attacks were able to sink the destroyer *Brownson* (DD-518) and severely damaged the *Shaw* (DD-373).[45]

Boise joined the fellow cruisers on New Year's Day and instantly got to play hero, but not with their guns. They delivered mail to their comrades like a slightly late Santa Claus. They fell into the routine of spending days patrolling near Buna and then anchoring away from shore to make it harder for the Japanese to pull off a surprise night attack.[46]

January was mostly quiet. This was fortunate for *Boise* because they were still troubleshooting the main guns. Test firing on the 1st resulted in more jams, even on the guns that had been rigorously "stoned," so the gunners tried comparing powder received in the U.S. and some picked up in Milne Bay. They found the jams were only occurring when the older powder was used, but that cause was not considered conclusive. The commander of the Cruiser Division brought in expertise from the other ships. Someone came up with the idea to test the pressure used in each gun. They found the pressure differential from the outside air to the inside of the breach was 600 psi, while the other cruisers were using 650 psi. It was possible that the lower pressure was insufficient for the underperforming powder. The pressure was adjusted and on the 10th they conducted another round of testing, firing thirty rounds from the three worst guns. The results were good enough that the commander authorized additional tests on the 21st that performed flawlessly. *Boise* was one hundred percent ready to fight again.[47]

On the 25th they headed back into battle, following *Phoenix* through the darkness along with "3 cans" to bombard Japanese troops at Alexishafen and Madang.[48] A pair of radar-equipped Black Cat spotter planes kept them company overhead, sandwiched between the overcast sky and the choppy seas. At 0151 the guns thundered and did not let up for seventeen minutes. Spotters noted a few splashes around the ships, but the enemy failed to hurt the Americans before they retired back to Buna.[49] It was a simple and low-risk introduction to combat for the new sailors, but the men were "bitterly disappointed at failure to carry out its assigned bombardment mission." They believed that the secondary batteries missed their targets entirely.[50] February proved frustrating for the newer crewmembers, but many of the ship's veterans were happy for a quiet existence mostly spent at Milne Bay, with brief excursions for exercises and the daily drudgery of shipboard life.[51] They did not know that MacArthur was preparing the next phase of the war for the Southwest Pacific, chasing his heart's desire: the liberation of the Philippines. It would take time to gain approval from Washington, so *Boise* waited.

During the wait they hosted Admiral Russell Berkey for a few days.[52] The commander of Cruiser Division 15 had just taken the position at the beginning of the year. Previously he commanded the light cruiser *Santa Fe* (CL-60).[53] He saw combat in the Aleutian campaign and his crew repelled significant air attacks a few months earlier at Bougainville.[54] The *Boise* men respected him and quickly formed a comfortable and effective working arrangement.

Early in the morning of the 26th, *Boise* left New Guinea for Sydney, Australia. They pulled into the harbor on the 29th.[55] The men were chomping at the bit to get into the city and have a good time. For nine days the official log noted only a few instances of ammunition resupply while they rested in the delightfully named Woolloomooloo Bay.[56] While the ship sat at anchor, one third of the crew at a time partied in what some American service members considered the premier liberty location in the Pacific Theater. Sydney was a modern city where everyone spoke English. There was an abundance of women for the sailors to chase, especially with so many Australian men serving abroad. The crew came with an abundance of pay they were looking to burn through.

Shelling the coast of New Guinea in early 1944. This view looks forward on the starboard side from the midships 20mm gun gallery. Note tracers, which appear several feet in front of gun muzzles. Those from the four starboard side 5/25 guns have a higher trajectory than the tracers fired from the forward 6-inch gun turrets. Tracers from the 6-inch guns appear to wobble slightly (National Archives: 80-G-213844).

There were prohibition rules in place that made getting alcohol complicated but still relatively easy.[57]

DB and some friends managed to rent rooms from a middle-aged woman in town that they referred to as "the Old Broad." This way they dodged the early closing times of local bars. They spent their hard-earned paychecks on several types of alcohol and filled the house's bathtubs with ice to keep their drinks cold. By their own admission, the parties got a little too rowdy and the owner threatened to kick them out. Rather than limit their partying, the men took a different approach to appease her. They brought in an older chief from their boat and introduced him to the woman. The two stuck up a congenial relationship that was acceptable enough to allow the parties to continue.[58]

The crew stumbled back to the ship in time to resume operations on the 11th. *Boise* had orders to return to Milne Bay. DB noted laconically that "some hated to leave."[59] On the return journey they resumed their part in a series of wargames that began before their Sydney sojourn. The exercises focused on every type of warfare the ship might see. They tracked other ships by radar and with the SOCs. The pilots and their gunners also practiced finding submerged submarines, while men aboard the ship learned to spot periscopes. The ship maneuvered to avoid incoming shellfire, and dodged dummy torpedoes. The men practiced during the day and in the dark of night, ensuring they were ready for another battle like Cape Esperance. Then there was the gunnery. They fired at simulated bombers. The main batteries engaged surface targets while the SOCs practiced spotting and adjusting the fire. The secondary batteries also fired, with the starboard crews showing exemplary ability. The ship was ready for whatever the Japanese could throw at them.[60]

As the *Boise* approached the rest of Cruiser Division 15 they got the chance to play the bad guy. They were under orders to simulate a Japanese battleship and attack the fleet from the south of Milne Bay. They charged towards their sister ships just before midnight, reminiscent of real Japanese attacks. They commenced fire using their radar to guide the shells at 19,300 yards and continued their mock firing for an hour and a half. *Boise* had a heyday sailing directly at the American fleet, using their radar and targets spotted by star shells to identify and shift between targets. The crew received unique training because they were allowed to throw caution to the wind and attack like a fox in a henhouse.[61]

The last two weeks of March were spent in and around Milne Bay. *Boise* participated in more advanced training that saw cruisers and destroyers synchronizing their efforts. The 7th Fleet divided into two Task Forces, 74 and 75. Task Force 74 consisted of the Australian cruisers *Australia* and *Shropshire* along with two Australian and two American destroyers. Task Force 75 under Admiral Berkey included *Phoenix*, *Boise*, and *Nashville* along with six American destroyers.[62]

Continuous training honed the men's skills but was also incredibly frustrating. There was a war on, and many wanted to either get into the fight or go home. Others, often veterans, were happy to serve in capacities that did not put them in harm's way. They had "been there and done that" and had nothing left to prove. They were not anxious to fight if it was not necessary.

The increased training would prove to be a decisive difference between the Allies and the Imperial Japanese Navy. In many battles the Allies enjoyed a level of tactical superiority that was unknown in 1942. The steady growth of the U.S. military allowed the Allies to outproduce their enemies, so not only were they able to put more ships and planes into battle, they also were increasingly able to rest their forces and provide advanced training. Meanwhile, the Japanese forces were run ragged. According to Japanese records, between April 1943 and February 1944 "the Japanese Navy lost thirty-three ships—twenty-five destroyers, five light cruisers, one escort carrier, one seaplane carrier, and one battleship." This did not include the dozens of damaged ships that filled Japanese ports and dry docks. Replacement ships were also limited, and the totals in all categories lagged far behind the Americans. Those ships still at sea were filled with experienced but tired crews, with little time to train or learn new tactics.[63]

Berkey understood this advantage and continued to train his crews hard in April. The ships practiced shore bombardment operations along with more anti-aircraft drills. The task force attacked en masse, practicing synchronized turns for the cruisers while their destroyers screened the larger ships and conducted their own maneuvers. Thousands of men worked in concert to rain death on simulated targets from dozens of points at once. The air sizzled with steel rounds, the drone of scout planes, and the imperceivable hum of radio and radar waves that allowed the disparate parts to act as one.[64]

The *Boise* gunners had set the bar high in Sicily, but the jungle terrain was proving more difficult. On the 7th Captain Roberts was notably unhappy with the gunnery results, especially the main batteries. He thought delays in shore parties spotting the hits compounded with ship movement caused improper corrections for each salvo. The crew identified the errors and put their final rounds on target, but the captain knew Americans ashore relied on accurate gunnery. Proper corrections would literally mean the difference between life and death. The entire ship performed considerably better during night exercises. They took advantage of a smoke screen set by their destroyers to attack simulated enemy forces with radar. Advanced technology was proving another key advantage held by the Allies.[65]

More bombardment training may have been in order, but circumstances would not allow it. The ship settled into an uneasy wait for MacArthur's next move. On the 15th they sailed north for Buna. That night and through the next day they topped off the fuel bunkers and maximized their ammunition.[66] Operations were brewing.

The Allies had decided in a series of meetings through mid- to late 1944 that the war against Japan would continue along two lines in the Pacific. Admiral Nimitz led efforts through the Central Pacific towards the Marianas Islands. Those islands could support bombing missions by the Air Force's new B-29 bombers on the Japanese home islands while Nimitz continued a drive towards Formosa (modern Taiwan) or the home islands. Meanwhile, MacArthur was granted permission to drive through New Guinea towards the Philippines where the Allies could cut supply lines from the Dutch East Indies to Japan.[67]

The next logical step along the northern New Guinea coast was to invade Hansa Bay. However, a Japanese intelligence blunder provided the outline of a new plan. An unknown Japanese officer reported his code books as destroyed during a tactical retreat, but instead dumped the materials in a muddy pool. The Allies recovered the books and used them to decipher thousands of Japanese messages, including those that indicated a massive trap set for any landing at Hansa Bay. Considering the new information, they decided to bypass the area entirely and jump operations hundreds of miles up the coast to the lightly defended Hollandia area. The plan assumed that the Japanese Eighteenth Army lying in wait around Hansa Bay would be unable to easily move through the swamps and mountains to threaten the Allies. To some the plan was an incredible gamble, and it was dubbed Operation Reckless, but the ability to peer into Japanese plans certainly provided comfort to MacArthur and he greenlit the mission.[68]

The plan was the largest amphibious operation in the Southwest Pacific to date and called for the 41st Infantry Division to land the bulk of its forces in Humboldt Bay with Hollandia at its northern edge. At the same time, elements of the 24th Infantry Division would land roughly thirty miles further west at Tanahmerah Bay. The coast between the two bays was dominated by the Cyclops Mountains that shielded a swampy plain along Sentani Lake ten miles inland which hosted three Japanese airfields. The two divisions were to strike inland and meet in the middle where the airfields could be claimed by MacArthur's air force.[69] At the same time, a separate force would land 100 miles east at Aitape to seize an airfield that could quickly support the broader operation with friendly fighters as well as provide a blocking position against any response from Hansa Bay.[70]

Boise sailed toward battle along with *Phoenix* and three destroyers on April 18.[71] They joined a larger contingent the next day off the recently liberated Manus Island. The bulk of 7th Fleet was present, including escort carriers, tins cans, dozens of transports, and Australian cruisers organized as TF-77. Admiral Nimitz also lent TF-58 and its twelve aircraft carriers to the operation. Although they operated independently and were openly trying to provoke the Japanese Imperial Navy into a fight, their fighters pounded airfields throughout the region along with the Air Force to cripple any Japanese air response to the landings. The fleet's fast battleships, cruisers, and destroyers were also available to support the landings if needed.[72]

The TF-58 strikes began on the 21st while TF-77 approached Hollandia. They bombed and strafed every airfield they could find, with little resistance beyond scattered anti-aircraft fire. The attacks would have been devastating had the Air Force not gotten there first. An after-action report complained that "due to the very large number of aircraft previously destroyed by the [Fifth] Air Force strikes, it is impossible without photographs showing previous destruction, to determine accurately the number of planes destroyed by TF-58."[73] The attacks may have been overkill, but not a single sailor or soldier bound for Hollandia was about to complain.

Late in the afternoon on the 21st TF-77 divided itself. Some headed to the east for the Aitape invasion at 1740 and twenty minutes later more peeled off for the western beaches at Tanahmerah Bay. *Boise* stuck with the Center Attack Group along with *Nashville,* who proudly carried General MacArthur into the fight, and *Phoenix*. While they plodded along at 8 knots, the three spread out in a protective semicircle. Three columns of landing ships followed behind them while the destroyers fanned out in all directions to screen for enemy submarines.[74]

During the night, they were struck by a heavy rain squall. The storm let up as the fleet entered Humboldt Bay, but the rain was still enough to soak exposed men to the bone. *Boise* went to General Quarters at 0502 and crept along at 5 knots toward the north shoulder of the landing beaches. The sea calmed and a slight northeast breeze tried to clear the air. It was enough to launch a SOC at 0552, but not enough to identify the ship's assigned targets through the mist at 0600, so Roberts decided to hold fire for a few minutes in hopes of better conditions. The mist hid another danger that nearly caused a disaster. The calm seas masked a westerly current that was pushing the ship "uncomfortably close to a nearby reef." DB and others remembered well what a reef could do the bottom of a light cruiser, and the ship was forced to take immediate action to turn the ship and back away from the shore to a safer position.[75]

At 0606 they could not wait any longer to fire lest they upset the landing timeline or leave suspected Japanese units completely intact. They based firing solutions on the nearby Cape Soeadja and unleashed the main batteries on targets in the hills south of Hollandia. The resulting impacts filled the air with smoke and debris, but the crew did their best to wreak havoc on the enemy. The secondary batteries got into the fight two minutes later engaging targets north of town. They were heartened by the lack of Japanese fire on the invasion force.[76]

Boise spotted the landing craft at 0631 and watched the first wave hit the beaches right on time at 0700. The landing was unopposed, but American fighter-bombers still swooped in and bombed suspected enemy positions and potential mines on the beach. Landing Craft Infantry (LCI) let loose a fusillade of rockets right as the men stepped ashore. Next, the 5-inch guns took on targets north of Hollandia. The SOCs also participated in the fun by dropping 100-pound bombs on a few targets that managed to avoid the guns.[77]

Two regiments of the 41st achieved surprise across four beaches. Soldiers quickly took Pancake Hill and were shocked to find at least one anti-aircraft gun untouched by the pre-assault bombardment, yet the enemy failed to bring it to bear on advancing troops. Others moved into the heights outside Hollandia. Two companies were tasked with hitting the beach in LVTs (Amphibious Vehicle, Tracked) and charging directly through the mangrove swamps until they reached the bay on the other side so they could continue across the smaller body of water to secure the main Japanese trailhead to the interior at Pim. However, not for the first or last time, the New Guinea swamps proved impenetrable, and the vehicles were forced to withdraw the way they had come and instead move through the exposed channel. The Japanese failed to resist this landing just like the others.[78]

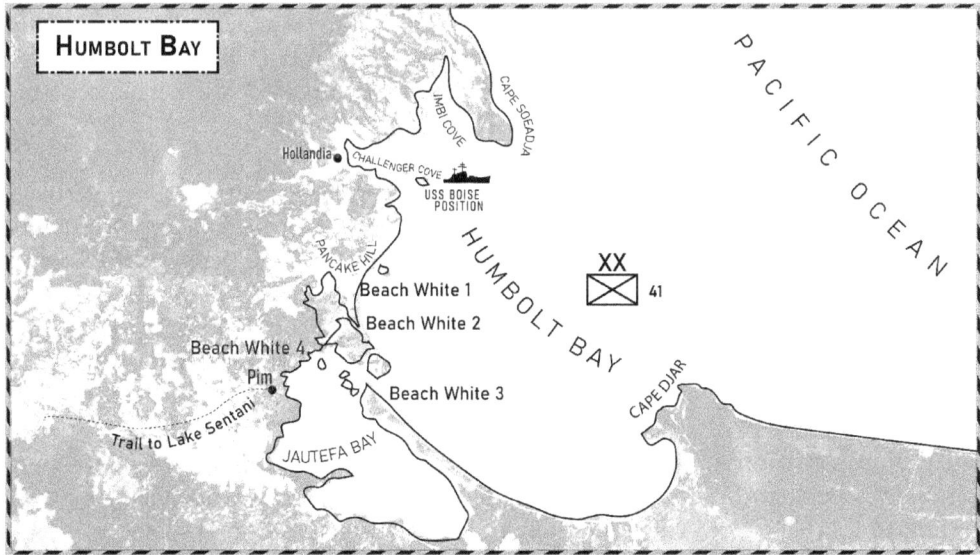

Boise covered the northern shores of Humboldt Bay during Operation Reckless. The operation involved simultaneous landings in three locations and was meant to provide General MacArthur with airfields for the ongoing drive across the Southwest Pacific.

Boise fired a few more times that morning, but by 0945 transitioned to standby, awaiting calls for fire from shore parties. At 1040 the ship was ordered south to cover *Nashville*'s beaches. MacArthur wanted to check on progress at the other two beaches. It took twenty minutes to tiptoe through the landing traffic, but there was little to do when they arrived on station. Heavy rain provided the Japanese some respite from air attacks just before lunch, but the advancing infantry were proceeding just fine without the support. *Boise* recalled the SOCs and put them on standby. The pilots joined the rest of the crew, waiting. At 1745 the commander of the landing forces radioed Berkey and the cruisers, "Please consider your job well done at 1800. Thank you very much." The cruisers withdrew shortly after lest they become easy targets for Japanese night attacks.[79]

The biggest problem ashore was that Japanese supplies filled the same places the Americans were trying to land their own. Naval gunfire had set some of it afire. The result was mountains of ammunition, rations, spare parts, and gasoline on the beaches on the 23rd. That night, a lone Japanese bomber dodged the American fighters and was drawn to the still smoldering fires of Japanese equipment like a moth to flame. It dropped a stick of bombs that found a Japanese ammunition cache. The ammo blew sky-high, and the raining debris started additional fires, one of which found an American gasoline dump which then went up in a spectacular explosion. The resulting fire killed twenty-four men and wounded another hundred. It took days to extinguish, and in the process destroyed 60 percent of the rations and ammunition on the beaches. This was equivalent to eleven fully loaded LSTs and compounded the ongoing campaign's supply issues.[80]

The *Boise* crew was proud of their contribution to Reckless. Morison described the operation as gaining "complete and overwhelming" surprise that caused a near collapse of enemy resistance in the area.[81] Commander Wolverton concluded the crew performed in a "uniformly exemplary manner."[82] DB wrote that they helped land 50,000 troops during the operation, which was certainly an exaggeration. He added correctly that they "shelled beach. No opposition."[83] The problem was that their contributions were limited by poor visibility that radar could not remedy. They also recorded a few main battery malfunctions. These issues were not present at Guadalcanal or in the Mediterranean and were cause for worry among the ship's leadership.[84]

On the 23rd they pulled into Seeadler Harbor on Manus Island. Navy engineers had been working day and night to turn the harbor into a logistics hub for MacArthur's drive. DB counted "6 carriers ... plus *Nashville* and about 20 destroyers," but the log only acknowledged four escort carriers. They sailed again on April 26, returning to the Hollandia area to support the ongoing operation. The cruisers were assigned to cover four escort carriers, a mission they were designed for but had rarely had an opportunity to execute. Throughout the day any man with an outside view was treated to the unique sight of waves of aircraft taking off and recovering to the flattops. By the 27th the force was fifty miles northeast of Humboldt Bay. The next three days were an endless cycle of aircraft operations interrupted repeatedly by the threat of enemy air attack. Several times the radars picked up unidentified aircraft referred to as "bogies." Crews across the fleet had to rush to battle stations to fend off air attacks that never came. The usual culprits were Allied aircraft failing to broadcast proper IFF codes. The mistakes were frustrating to the sailors as the encounters interrupted routines, meals, and worst of all—sleep.[85]

On the 29th the three cruisers went on a mission to deny Japanese soldiers of sleep. Along with five tin cans, they charged up the New Guinea coast like galloping horses. The formation ran at 26 knots through the evening while enjoying remarkably good weather. The targets were the enemy airfields at Wakde and Sawar, about 120 miles from Hollandia. The airfields had been pummeled during previous weeks, but this was the Navy's chance to make sure the Japanese received no respite during the hours of darkness. The ships approached like phantoms and at 0029 unleashed hell on Sawar. *Boise* was the final cruiser in line, fired for fourteen minutes on all assigned targets, and was rewarded with a large explosion that was probably an ammunition or fuel dump. Berkey demanded precision and ordered the ships tighten their formation before the next target. They arrived off Wakde at 0127. *Boise* contributed twenty-two minutes of punishment, focusing on the barracks, personnel, and dump areas on the southeastern side of the airstrip. Spotters noted a large fire sprouted in the target area as the entire force withdrew into the night. *Boise* had performed remarkably and, even better, there was only a single main battery misfire which was attributed to poor powder, not the gun itself. Their pride was affirmed a few days later when they learned that "photos taken by carrier plane yesterday show target areas well pockmarked with both strips unserviceable X It looks like a good job was done by all hands."[86]

The cruisers rejoined the carriers and remained in the Humboldt Bay area until the evening of May 4. They arrived back at Seeadler Harbor, replenished their fuel and ammunition, and then settled in for a few days of maintenance and rest. On the 8th they conducted anti-aircraft gunnery exercises. The training was incredibly useful thanks to the help of a B-26 target plane towing banners at 240 knots and 12,000 feet, providing "the most valuable AA practice that this ship has had," and all types of AA scored multiple hits on the difficult targets.[87]

Everyone in the Navy realized the danger Japanese planes still posed to the fleet. *Boise* returned to the AA range on the 12th for more drills. The crew again proved the seamless fusion of radars, fire direction equipment, guns, and men by performing so well they repeatedly shot down the banners before the scheduled end of the exercise.[88]

MacArthur was ready to make his next jump up the coast. TF-75 left Seeadler on the 15th along with the Australian cruisers in TF-74. It was time to revisit Wakde and Sawar, but this time the Allies were coming to stay. They needed Wakde because the South West Pacific Area (SWPA) lacked fleet carriers and required an airfield for smaller planes that could cover the upcoming Biak operation. MacArthur badly needed Biak because it was the only island that could host heavy bombers after the Hollandia area proved unsuitable.[89]

They met the transports off Tanahmerah Bay at 1900. The amphibious operation was again under TF-77. All ships proceeded slowly through the darkness, reaching their destination around 0430.[90] *Boise* fired on the assigned areas at 0605. There was little to target, but the SOCs reported "good coverage of target areas" in and around Maffin Bay and the associated airfield. For forty-three minutes they punished the jungle and any living creature within it. Destroyers, LCI rockets, and aircraft continued to pound the beach for another hour until members of the 163rd Regimental Combat Team (RCT) of the 41st Division hit Yellow Beach, but *Boise* fell silent while awaiting calls for support. The soldiers, encountering no resistance, quickly secured their objectives on the mainland. The second phase of the day's operation could begin. Another battalion of the 163rd landed on the tiny island of Insoemanai to set up artillery positions. They were likewise unopposed.[91]

By noon, a call went out: "You are relieved from present assignment. Thank you for splendid job." *Boise* had fired 776 total rounds without any major incidents or malfunctions.[92] Wakde was invaded the next day. Although the Japanese put up a fierce fight where they could, the island was secure by the 20th and the first planes landed at the newly repaired airstrip on the 21st.[93]

On the 21st they returned to the Wakde area. During the following night the cruisers pushed further west in a probing operation. At 0058 the vanguard destroyer *Hutchins* (DD-476) detected a contact at 1,000 yards, practically spitting distance. The intrepid ship began probing the contact while the rest conducted a rapid reversal of course. *Hutchins* searched for over an hour without any results. The contact may very well have been a submarine, but the aggressive American response sent it into hiding.[94]

May 22 and 23rd continued the aggressive patrolling. *Boise* also fine-tuned their radar systems with the help of a few civilian contractors. On the 24th they returned to Humboldt Bay on orders to replenish. It was time for MacArthur's next jump.[95]

MacArthur's eyes were set on Biak. Until recently the island was within the latest Japanese defensive line, and they intended to robustly defend it. A convoy of reinforcements bound for the island was sunk on May 9, but the island still held around 10,000 enemy troops.[96] Several thousand of them were China combat veterans, but MacArthur's staff severely underestimated that strength. This was a growing problem, but one the general seemed content to accept as the rosy assessments allowed him to push hard for his desired objectives with minimal resources.

Troops were set to hit the beach on the 27th. Early morning on May 26 *Boise* and the rest of the cruisers met several fast transports carrying members of the 41st Division. DB wrote, "met *Shropshire*, *Australia*, LCI's and LST's. Proceeding to the Biak, Schouhton [sic], Islands to land troops and take possession."[97]

Passage was slow to accommodate the troopships. The fleet navigated the islands

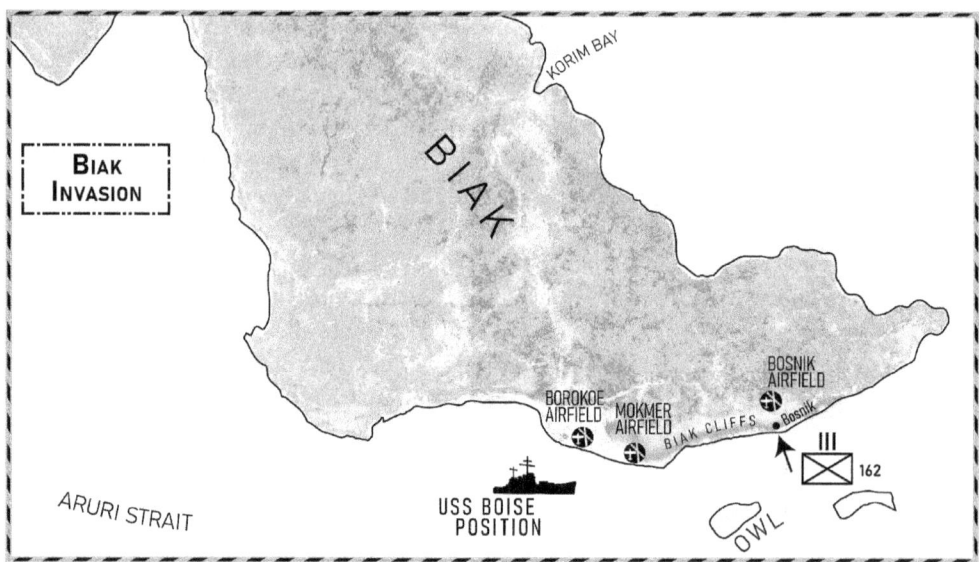

Boise supported the Biak operation by bombarding targets in and around the western airfields. The landings went well, but after *Boise* departed the U.S. Army faced significant resistance in capturing the island.

and shoals southeast of the landing beaches under the cover of darkness. *Boise* stood to General Quarters at 0435 and readied for battle. The cruisers launched their SOCs a little after 0600.[98] They settled into a comfortable position six miles south of the island abeam the center airfield at Borokoe. In what was becoming a tradition, rain fell just before the landings.[99]

At precisely 0630, forty-five minutes before the first landings, the naval contingent opened fire. *Boise* focused the main guns on targets from Borokoe airfield down to the shore and east to Mokmer Airfield. The 5-inch guns attacked targets of opportunity, starting with a pair of barges near the shore. The guns thundered for twenty minutes until everyone caught their breath while the first B-24 airstrike of the day arrived. There was barely time to grab a sip of coffee, because three minutes later the planes departed and *Boise* got back into action. At 0715 they ceased firing as the preinvasion bombardment came to its scheduled completion. There was scant response from the Japanese, and Army leadership believed they had achieved a tactical surprise. This was largely true, as the local Japanese commander believed the invasion would come at a later date and the Americans would land at Mokmer, and thus concentrated his forces directly in the path of *Boise*'s shells.[100]

The first assault troops hit the shore around 0730, but not where they intended. Many of the landing craft had difficulty identifying landmarks on the beach due to smoke. Combined with a stronger than anticipated current, this pushed troops 3,000 yards west, into a nasty mangrove swamp. Subsequent waves landed at Bosnik as intended. The entire operation became confounded when units in the wrong locations had to cross over the paths of other advancing units, all while the reserve elements began landing and tried to claim space on the crowded shore. Thankfully, the Japanese were in no condition to offer significant resistance.[101]

Other enemy units along the coast were less benign. A hidden gun near Mokmer took the *Hutchins* under "well controlled" fire. One shell found the ship and caused slight damage and casualties, but it was frustrating that something survived *Boise*'s assault. That would be dealt with, but first *Boise* had to recover their SOC and launch another. A few minutes into the recovery, the fresh plane proudly reported they had bombed and destroyed a Ki-57 "Topsy" transport plane.[102] The aircrew now had bragging rights to hold over their comrades.

At 0759 the SOC spotted "a powerful group of 40mm guns" similar to the *Boise*'s own anti-aircraft batteries. Roberts wasted no time requesting permission to "investigate" the threat by dropping steel on top of them. It was quickly granted. *Boise* pounded the target area for fifteen minutes. Fire missions trickled in for the next few hours, making this the busiest invasion *Boise* had contributed to since Italy. The enemy conducted a half-hearted air raid around 1100, but none managed to inflict serious damage.[103]

Boise called All Clear from the air threat at 1130 and the ship had thirty minutes of relative calm for men to grab a bite delivered by the mess-men or smoke a cigarette. At 1205 they reengaged several of the targets they had attacked earlier. They ceased firing at 1313, but the secondary batteries pounced on some troops and a truck foolish enough to come into the open at 1326.[104]

At 1621 the cruisers were reaching the end of their day and preparing to depart, lest they get caught close to shore by Japanese bombers after friendly air cover was forced to fly home. Just then bogies were detected by radar fifty-four miles west. The enemy arrived overhead at 1640. At least two bombers swept in across a cliff north of Bosnik and attacked

LSTs. They were so low that although the bombs flew true and struck their targets, they could not arm and thus did not explode. Two of the bombs were recovered nonchalantly by sailors and thrown over the side so they could continue their business.[105] A few minutes later four more bombers accompanied by fighters tried the same trick of hiding from radar in the terrain, but the Americans were ready. The enemy got off a few bombs and strafing runs; these also failed to explode and the damage was minimal. An explosion of AA fire greeted them.[106] All enemy bombers were shot down or damaged. One strafed *Sampson* (DD-394), and after being damaged tried to crash into the ship before losing its wing and slamming into the ocean 400 yards off the starboard side.[107]

After the air attack it was time for the cruisers to depart. Several destroyers would remain in the area to assist the Army. By 1747 the cruisers were clear. The crew was pleased with the day's events and noted "the results of the shooting were gratifying."[108] DB recorded "landed 20,000 troops on Biak. Shelled positions all day."[109] His troops numbers were a little closer than his Hollandia recording. The Army had about 12,000 troops ashore by the time *Boise* departed, along with 12 tanks, 3,000 tons of cargo, 500 vehicles, and about 30 various artillery pieces.[110] Within a few days they would wish DB had been correct.

The Army was in for a tough time on Biak, but they would do it without *Boise*. TF-75 pulled back to within 150 miles of Wakde so the planes there could provide daytime air cover. At night the task force conducted sweeps west of Biak in search of the Japanese fleet. Early on the 31st they swapped out with TF-74, who delivered mail before *Boise* departed for Humboldt Bay.[111]

The Japanese were busy during the same period. They quickly developed Operation KON to reinforce the island and hopefully deal a serious blow to the American 7th Fleet. They sent 166 planes to New Guinea, ready to strike by June 2. A considerable contingent of surface vessels began assembling to ferry 2,500 troops to the island. A light cruiser and three destroyers were conscripted as transport vessels, protected by a pair of heavy cruisers, five destroyers, and the battleship *Fuso*. The command ship for the entire operation was *Boise*'s old nemesis *Aoba*.[112]

On June 2, the Japanese struck hard with a fifty-four-airplane raid over the Biak beaches. Bad weather near Wakde grounded friendly air cover and forces at Biak had to rely on ship and shore-based AA fire. Fortunately for the Americans, despite over an hour of attacks no bombing or strafing runs resulted in meaningful casualties or damage. The AA gunners acquitted themselves well, shooting down twelve of the marauding aircraft.[113]

On the 3rd, the KON task force set sail. They were quickly spotted by a submarine. By noon the force was being shadowed by American bombers. The jig was up. Japanese reconnaissance pilots reported seeing aircraft carriers and battleships in the waters around Biak. MacArthur dreamed of such a naval force, but the 7th Fleet was desperately outgunned by the KON force and had nothing larger than a destroyer immediately around Biak.[114] The stage was set for an epic naval showdown until the Japanese blinked and scrubbed the reinforcement mission.

Instead, they sent another wave of bombers on the 3rd. Over forty planes attacked, forcing the destroyers to rapidly maneuver in the narrow channels. The AA gunners dueled with their foes until friendly air support broke through the clouds and drove off the enemy. The Japanese again failed to inflict any serious damage and lost a quarter of their force.[115]

All available ships in TF-74 and -75 were combined and ordered to proceed to Biak on the 4th under the command of the British Vice Admiral Victor Crutchley. Their orders were to patrol and attack any inferior force they met but withdraw in the face of superior strength. If they did not encounter the Japanese fleet, they were to withdraw during daylight and try again the following evening.[116]

They weighed anchor just before midnight and spent the following day sailing towards Biak. DB wrote "underway with *Phoenix, Australia, Nashville* for area north of Biak. Jap ships in that area."[117] The men were clearly expecting a fight. Japanese planes spotted Crutchley's force around noon. The resulting air raid was timed to arrive after American air cover returned to Wakde for the night. At 1740 three Zeke bombers dove out of the sun making a beeline for the four cruisers at the center of the formation. *Boise*'s gunners fired furiously, disrupting the bomb-run of one plane vying for the ship. Starboard gunners meanwhile engaged a bomber focused on *Phoenix* and helped disrupt that attack as well. Overall the mission was undeterred.[118]

The night's sweep failed to uncover any enemy ships. Crutchley maneuvered the force back towards Biak. A little after midnight the ships were passing between the narrow straits when *Boise* picked up intermittent bogies, who closed to within 10,000 yards while the ships sped up to 25 knots. The Japanese had caught the formation in tight confines where they would have difficulty evading torpedoes. At 0106 the ship was rocked with "moderate violence" by an underwater explosion. Reports from around the ship poured into the bridge, but apparently there was no damage to the ship. The formation crackled with AA fire and *Australia* reported they were under attack by three or four torpedo planes. *Boise* conducted rapid rudder maneuvers, fishtailing the ship from side to side. They fired on one of the planes. A minute later the ship was again rocked by an explosion, although less violent than the first. Everything was over in twelve minutes, and once again the enemy missed *Boise* and everyone else, but *Boise*'s gunners found the range of one of the attackers and sent it to a watery grave.[119]

An hour later *Mullany* picked up a sonar contact a mere 1,000 yards away. The fleet took evasive actions while the intrepid destroyer pounced on the contact with depth charges. They hounded the area for over an hour while the rest of the ships escaped, and after an hour of no further contact *Mullany* rejoined the formation. DB noted how the action kept the ship at "I Easy all night," suggesting most of the men spent the night at their battle stations.[120]

A far more devastating air raid hit Wakde that night. Japanese bombers pummeled the island, causing significant damage. One report suggested two-thirds of Air Force planes were damaged or destroyed. This would severely restrict air support to Biak in the coming days.[121]

June 5 passed quietly. They tried another eastern sweep the next night but saw nothing. The 6th was also a quiet day for *Boise*. They were ordered back to Humboldt Bay.[122] In fact, most of the naval support at Biak was called away due to the threat of air attacks.[123] DB noted the more important world events of the day. "Left Biak for Humboldt Bay. Received word of Europe invasion 0500 GCT—1500 this time."[124] The long-awaited invasion of Northwest Europe remembered as D-Day was underway.

After determining there were no Allied carriers supporting Biak, the Japanese embarked on a smaller effort to reinforce the island. Two cruisers and three destroyers escorted three additional destroyers loaded with troops under command of Rear Admiral Naomasa Sakonju. The escort destroyers also towed barges carrying additional troops.[125] That force was underway by midnight on the 7th and on a collision course with TF-74, now operating without the *Nashville*. They set sail for Biak just before midnight.[126]

While *Boise* trucked towards Biak on the 8th, the Air Force visited the approaching Japanese fleet with a few B-25s and P-38s. They sunk one of the destroyers and damaged several others, but the Japanese persisted. The cruisers escaped the attack because they had been ordered to withdraw from the formation and await further orders that morning.[127] The IJN reciprocated with a single G4M Betty picked up by *Boise*'s SK radar at fifteen miles. It did not approach any closer and instead reported Allied strength. Both sides now knew what they were up against.[128]

The Allies held a clear advantage with their three cruisers and fourteen destroyers, but the Japanese had proven themselves highly adaptable. KON forces could also conceivably use night bombers to sow confusion. TF-74 was fifty miles northeast of the island by sundown. Crutchley had diverted forty miles north to evade any bombers sent in response to the reconnaissance. The plan was to move to the western side of the island and stay close to the coast to intercept any troops trying to land near Korim Bay on the Japanese-occupied eastern coast.[129]

The task force arrived in the area a little before 2200. *Boise*'s radar operators had been busy all night tracking bogies that never approached close enough to engage. The crew had been at their battle stations since 1900 and tensions were running high. Veterans like DB knew what a night battle could turn into and did their best to mask any fear and perform their jobs. At 2152 *Mullany* was sent into Korim Bay to snoop around. A 20-minute search uncovered nothing, so the ship was ordered to rejoin the task force. A Black Cat reported five unidentified ships seventy-seven miles to the northwest at 2200.[130]

At 2220 a plane dropped flares over the destroyer. *Boise* was close enough to pick up the plane by radar and their AA gunners joined with *Mullany* to strike back. The aircraft managed to drop bombs but missed. The first action of the night was a draw.[131]

The Allies pushed west into the black. A full moon lit portions of the sea not obscured by rain showers, providing a melancholy semidarkness suitable for enemy ghosts to appear at any minute. Thankfully, *Boise* and others were peering through the night beyond the sharpest-eyed lookouts, and at 2321 *Boise* picked up a surface contact to the northwest at 26,000 yards. Crutchley ordered his cruisers into a column behind the *Australia* and its 8-inch guns. He swung the column due north to intercept, with *Boise* in the second spot and *Phoenix* in the rear while destroyers formed a protective perimeter.

Boise hummed in anticipation. The Combat Information Center (CIC) took in updated radar contacts while the gunners, loaders, and fire directors itched for a chance to fire. The initial plot of the enemy showed them on a course of 015° at 12 knots. By 2330 Crutchley's cruisers charged forward at 25 knots. While they closed on their quarry the Japanese had picked up the Allies on their own radars. At 2328, radar reports showed the enemy destroyers splitting into two columns that both altered course to the northwest and "retired at high speed."[132]

Sakonju had no stomach for a lopsided fight and decided to run. He ordered the troop barges cut free and fled away from the Allies after launching a torpedo volley to cover his tracks.[133] With the entire formation in a stern chase, Crutchley ordered his vanguard destroyers to attack at 2332. *Boise* spotted a torpedo off the port quarter at 2336 but no evasive actions were needed. The cruisers continued to increase speed to 29 knots. At 2345 the leading destroyers passed the discarded troop barges and peppered them with fire. The cruisers passed the same barges at 2359 and *Phoenix* also engaged the abandoned troops. The soldiers still posed a threat, but there was no need to stop and deal with them so far from shore.[134]

TF-74 continued the chase past midnight, but the frustrated radar operators watched the range slowly increase. Around 0030 the enemy ships began dropping off radar scopes as they sailed out of range. The cruisers slowed and turned back to Biak.[135]

This did not mean Crutchley was letting the Japanese off the hook. He ordered a pair of Australian destroyers to mop up the barges and unleashed eight destroyers to hound the fleeing enemy. The pursuing destroyers sped up to their top speed of 35 knots and slowly gained ground. They tried to force the Japanese to zigzag by firing on them. The enemy replied with shells of their own and clouds of smoke.[136]

The Americans had a time limit. The chase had taken the destroyers so far from Biak that they risked being fired on by friendly submarines or aircraft, so Crutchley ordered them to break off pursuit and return to Biak no later than 0230. Around 0130 the southern American column tried to drive a portion of the fleeing Japanese closer to their northern colleagues. The four ships turned hard to port to unmask all their guns and fired a tremendous volume of fire on the Japanese. The maneuver worked, and two of the enemy turned and unwittingly closed the distance with the other American ships. At 0205 the northern American destroyers fired on the Japanese and were rewarded with a large explosion aboard the *Shiratsuyu*. The ship was significantly damaged but still managed to retire when the Americans hit their deadline.[137] The final engagement of the night was a resounding American success but was deeply dissatisfying to the Allies who had hoped to deal a crushing defeat to the IJN.

The night of June 9 teased a rematch. Shortly after sunset a Black Cat reported "3 to 5 enemy ships … course southeast, speed 20." The position meant the contacts could be heading to Noemfoor or Biak, but the distance was too great to intercept. The TF sailed to the north of Korim Bay at 25 knots. When they arrived shortly after midnight, they witnessed AA fire from Biak and tracer fire inside the bay. *Boise* readied for action, but a radio call quickly confirmed that the surface action was Allied PT boats firing on beached barges, suggesting that a few survivors from the previous night may have made it ashore. Although the U.S. Army later assessed that fewer than 100 troops survived the trip to Biak, the second KON operation spurred American commanders to send another regiment of their own.[138]

The contacts from earlier in the evening were apparently not bound for Biak, so at 0137 Crutchley withdrew for Humboldt Bay. The task force arrived in the relatively safe harbor in the early afternoon, but they did not stay long. The following day they sailed east for Seeadler along with *Phoenix* and eight destroyers.[139]

Boise arrived at Seeadler on June 12. The crew received a little downtime while the ship took on supplies. Two notable events took place before the ship set sail again for training exercises on the 19th. The first was the invasion of Saipan in the Marianas Islands on the 15th.[140] Allied control of the islands would provide a base for bombers capable of hitting the Japanese home islands. The fighting was brutal, but Nimitz needed the islands to continue his Central Pacific thrust.

The second event was one of DB's greatest sea stories of the war. One evening the *Boise* officers were invited ashore for a party. DB and a few friends managed to get selected as the soiree's bartenders. On the night of the festivities, DB and friends arrived on shore wearing their dress whites adorned with their combat medals. Their first order of business was cleaning out a few empty buckets and placing them behind the bar. As they made the rounds delivering drinks to the officers, they quietly picked up the drinks left behind by the men busy dancing with the attending nurses. The collected half-drinks were poured into the buckets, forming an unholy but potent grog. Each time the sailors returned to the bar, they took a swig. By the middle of the evening the admiral hosting the party stepped up to the bar and observed the sailors in their deteriorating state. He declared, "It's a bad thing when the enlisted guys are having more fun than my officers!" and made a deal with DB and his coconspirators. If they knocked off their drink collecting and grog consumption, he would make sure they had plenty of their own booze for a private after-party. This deal was too good to pass up, so the sailors exhibited their best behavior for the remainder of the party, and then drank themselves unconscious on the beach under the stars.

The next morning arrived with the men seriously hungover or, in some cases, still drunk. To their astonishment, their company had gained a man—one of the officers from the party! When he came to, he asked DB what they were doing. He told the officer they were waiting on a lift back to *Boise*. The man said not to worry, he would give them a ride, while he called for a boat. It turns out the man was the captain of the USS *Trathen*, one of the destroyers from Biak. The boat picked up the partiers and as it approached *Boise* the watchmen of the ship saw that the small craft carried the captain of another vessel. They scrambled to assemble the appropriate greeting party, including a senior chief petty officer. The chief nearly blew a gasket when four of his drunken sailors stumbled aboard and waved goodbye to the *Trathen*'s captain, who declined to come aboard. DB and his friends were saved by the chief's propriety, as he merely growled threateningly, "Get below...."[141]

From the 19th through the 27th the ship conducted a series of training exercises reminiscent of March. The last few months of operations helped, but the men needed to keep their skills sharp because the Battle of the Philippine Sea happening west of the Marianas on June 19 and 20th changed the war. Morison described it as the "greatest carrier battle of the war" where hundreds of American planes launched from carriers intercepted multiple Japanese air raids.[142] Using radar to vector aircraft and guide AA fire, the Americans decimated Japanese forces. The Japanese lost 476 aircraft, including an astounding 92 percent of their participating carrier aircraft. The Americans dubbed it the Great Marianas Turkey Shoot and lost only 130 of their own aircraft. The Japanese lost two aircraft carriers. Still, six Japanese carriers survived the encounter to haunt the Americans, even if they lacked planes and pilots.[143]

On June 29 *Boise* sailed for combat along with *Australia*, *Phoenix*, and their bevy of destroyers. MacArthur's next target was the eleven-mile-diameter Noemfoor Island, which held three airfields in various stages of development ten miles west of Biak. The Cyclone Task Force consisted of 8,000 men. They were to land at Kamiri and take the airfield there. Follow-on landings across the Vogelkop Peninsula were planned in rapid succession over the next few weeks. D-Day was scheduled for July 2. The Japanese commander had a paltry force of 2,000 demoralized and underfed troops, but thanks to the discovery of an American scout team, he oriented his forces at Kamiri. Japanese air support in the area was practically nonexistent.[144]

The task force approached Noemfoor under the cover of darkness. At 0640 the *Boise*'s main and secondary batteries fired on the airstrip. The first volley fell short by fifty yards but SOC #19 easily provided corrections and the second volley struck home, resulting in a satisfyingly large explosion. All guns continued firing until they expended their allotments. *Boise* ceased firing at 0710 and stood by. The bridge crew watched B-24s strike suspected supply dumps and bivouac areas and a radio call at 0812 informed them that troops landed unopposed. Support calls never came and by noon the cruisers departed.[145]

Roberts was pleased with the ship and crew's performance. These landings had become routine, and the biggest danger seemed to be crew complacency that could lead to accidents. The bombardments had achieved some of the best preinvasion results of the war. Japanese survivors at Kamiri put up little resistance, and many were so disoriented from the attack they could not resist.[146]

July 3 found *Boise* back at Humboldt Bay for resupply. Two days later they sailed for Seeadler. The crew was tired and in need of a serious break, but there was still work to be done. They languished at Seeadler until the 27th when MacArthur was ready to establish air bases on the Vogelkop Peninsula. Because the Allies anticipated so little opposition, they decided to conduct the mission using stealth. The naval forces approached the coast before sunrise on the 30th using strict radio silence. Landing craft filled with 6th Infantry Division troops hit various beaches beginning at 0700 without preparatory naval bombardment or airstrikes and achieved complete surprise.[147] There was nothing for *Boise* or any other warships to accomplish. The landings were the simplest of *Boise*'s career and they departed by 0900.[148]

Finally, *Boise* was bound for Sydney and some well-deserved R&R. They arrived on August 10.[149] The crew spent a glorious fifteen days repeating their March reveries. For DB and his friends, it meant several nights at the "Old Broad's" residence.[150] They and millions of Allied troops across the Pacific deserved some celebrating in August. They now controlled most of the South Pacific and were ready to push on to the Philippines. The Marianas Islands were beginning their conversion to massive aircraft carriers from which B-29 bombers could strike Japan. Eisenhower's forces were galloping across northern and southern France. In the east, the Soviets wrapped up Operation Bagration, a massive summer offensive that pushed the Nazis back across the front. Despite these gains, neither the Germans nor Japanese planned on surrender. Many miles and months stood between the Allies and victory, and far too many people would die along the way. DB and his friends knew this, and that their odds of surviving were less than ideal. So, in Sydney, they partied like each day could be their last.

7

Ship of the Line

Leyte Gulf

DB and the rest of the men were required back in time to host Admiral Thomas Kinkaid for an inspection and tour at 0925 on August 24. Hangovers were probably forgiven provided the men could mask them and not embarrass the ship in front of the commander of 7th Fleet. There also may have been passes available the following day to enjoy Australia one last time before shipping out. *Boise* left Woolloomooloo at 0837 on the 26th for another round of exercises.[1]

Their departure was ignominious thanks to an overeager tug operator who rammed into the ship and rankled the superstitious sailors. The collision caused "minor damage to shell plating and bulkheads," and much of the day was spent assessing damage and making repairs before finally departing that afternoon.[2]

They made radar contact with TF-74 and -75 at 0230. *Boise* took the center cruiser position between *Phoenix* and *Australia* by 0800 and the fleet sailed north while conducting radar exercises with the destroyers. The crew placed a disappointing fourth among their comrades, but their gunnery performance against a towed surface target that afternoon was significantly better. The following day *Boise* ranked second in tracking exercises. The ships continued north and on the 29th the AA gunners practiced. They were ragged and inconsistent in the first passes, but by the end were noted "satisfactory."[3]

The month ended with a quick stop in Milne Bay on the 30th for fuel before continuing to Seeadler with night exercises along the way.[4] They would soon enter a new phase of the war that was bound to take 7th Fleet into contact with the enemy on a scale not seen in years. The tensions felt at Biak could easily manifest into real encounters with Japanese battleships and swarms of aircraft at any time. They needed to be ready for it all as they pushed towards and into the Philippines.

September 1944 is a bit of a mystery in *Boise*'s story. The month's War Diary is missing from the National Archives, so there is no day-to-day record of events. DB provided a few notes, which help, but two of *Boise*'s most reliable chroniclers were not aboard the ship. Langelo was away attending a radio school while Moneymaker had been promoted to ensign and left the ship in February after becoming seriously disgruntled with *Boise* leadership.[5]

DB recorded the ship arriving at Seeadler on the 2nd. On the 4th he noted "*New Jersey* came in today. Also thirteen carriers in here."[6] The *Phoenix* log added an admonishment to DB's report. When the battleship pulled into the harbor it "immediately ordered all vessels present to get 'on their toes' when they were slow in answering a flag-hoist." This was the type of pomp and circumstance that most sailors hated.[7]

On the 10th they "left Seeadler with a hole [sic] task force. Another deal coming up."[8] DB was correct, even if he did not know what the "deal" was. The operation underway was MacArthur's final one of the New Guinea campaign. Japanese garrisons around Halmahera needed to be isolated and eliminated, and the Allies wanted one last group of airfields that could support operations in the Philippines. Morotai was a small island north of Halmahera with a Japanese airstrip and potential for a larger aerodrome. The effort also tied into Nimitz's plans for the Central Pacific and the invasion of Palau roughly 500 miles to the northeast of Morotai, as between the two operations MacArthur could be reasonably sure his flanks were secure for the drive on the Philippines.[9]

The journey to Morotai was uneventful, but apparently tense. They stopped at Humboldt Bay on the 11th for fuel, and on the 12th DB simply recorded "Underway—." The following day they met the amphibious forces. Later that day they were joined by escort carriers, hopefully ensuring that Japanese airpower could not pose a threat even when timing and weather kept Air Force planes away. By 0500 on the 15th everyone was in position for members of the 31st Infantry Division to attack.[10]

The overall story from there is familiar. The cruisers took their positions, searched for navigational marks, launched planes, and at the appropriate time fired their main guns on targets on the main island of Halmahera, across Galela Bay from the landing beaches on the smaller target island. *Boise* fired alongside *Phoenix* and *Nashville*, which carried General MacArthur, while Australian cruisers bombarded the landing beaches. Leadership hoped to achieve a tactical surprise so the area was not attacked by air before the invasion fleet arrived. The Navy made up for the previous peace and quiet with relish. *Boise* fired over 1,000 rounds at various targets labeled as "stores and personnel." Destroyers found multiple barges to engage. The overall naval bombardment helped ensure the surprised defenders were unable to fight at the beach, and no reinforcements could be sent from Halmahera.[11]

The interesting part of the Morotai landings is not how successful the landings were, but rather how successful the operation was despite the terrible terrain and navigation information available to the Allies. Because tactical surprise was considered paramount, no scouting or reconnaissance of the area was permitted. *Boise*'s official report complained of poor charts making navigation hazardous and precise firing almost impossible. Correcting for these shortcomings through annotations and keen watchmen took concentration, professionalism, and more than the usual manpower.[12] The Army also suffered. Their expectations for sandy beaches were instead met with clay and mud covered by a thin layer of sand. The northernmost Red Beach was described as "undoubtedly the worst encountered in the Southwest Pacific Area throughout the entire war." Had the enemy put up a fight, they could have massacred the Army on the beach.[13] All services would have to collect much better intelligence before attempting operations in the Philippines.

Boise departed Galela Bay a little after 2000 along with *Phoenix* and attached destroyers. They intended to join with the escort carriers but their services were not required. They spent a boring night and the following day cruising in zigzag patterns until released at 1800 to return to anchorages near Biak.[14]

DB noted that they spent nine days at the tiny harbor at Mios Woendi off the southeast Biak coast.[15] The *Phoenix* deck log noted that the stay was uncomfortable at best. Although there was a small Officer's Club for the higher-ranking members, there were few boats available to take men ashore and that the "swimming facilities are poor." This

Bombarding the Galela sector of Halmahera Island during the Morotai invasion, 15 September 1944. Guns in the foreground are port-side 5/25s, but the firing is being done by the forward 6-inch guns. Note the ammunition passing party at work in the lower right (National Archives: 80-G-301528).

made it almost impossible for men to escape the unrelenting heat and humidity, which could reach 130° below decks.[16]

September was nearly over when the force left for Seeadler. They arrived on the 29th to a "bustling" port, far busier than previous visits. Much of the 3rd Fleet was at anchor, suggesting the next operation could be the biggest *Boise* had seen since Italy.[17] DB recorded the astounding sight. "Ships present: *Boise, Phoenix, Nashville, Australia, Shropshire, Denver, Cleveland, Boston, Canberra, Witcha* [sic]*, Minneapolis–Indiana, Tennessee, Mississippi, California, Idaho, Pensylvania* [sic]*, Maryland–Hornet, Wasp* and 8 converted carriers plus destroyers and D.E.'s."[18]

The next few weeks were "hurry up and wait." There were a handful of drills and exercises, but mostly they waited. The ship received operational plans on the 6th but did not depart until the 11th.[19] During the wait DB caught an old friend aboard the destroyer escort *Suesens* (DE-342). William Henry Shand was also from Salt Lake City, and it is possible the men knew each other from boot camp or even before.[20] Running into a familiar face in a war zone is always a notable event, even if there is nothing to do but share stories of hardship, danger, and deprivation. Preferably over a few drinks. Commiserating can be great for morale.

The fleet stopped at Humboldt Bay on the 12th to refuel. When they left the next day, DB noted, "Left Humboldt for operation in the Philippines. A large force with us." General MacArthur had argued vehemently for this campaign. Through 1943 and even into 1944 some of America's top military leadership thought that bypassing the Philippines entirely was the correct strategic path, and the next invasion should be Formosa. In contrast, with the exception of Nimitz, most military commanders in the Pacific were opposed to the Formosa plan, agreeing with MacArthur that liberation of Luzon would allow for the Allies to bypass Formosa and jump next to Okinawa at the southern end of the Japanese islands.[21]

In February the Joint Chiefs of Staff ordered the Pacific commanders to draw up plans for both options.[22] On the line were vast, but not infinite military resources. In the eyes of the Pacific commanders they were also competing for the glory of leading America's main effort against Japan, the quickest way to end the war, and according to MacArthur the very honor of the United States.

The decision was pushed all the way to the top. In July, President Roosevelt traveled to Hawaii to personally meet with MacArthur and Nimitz.[23] The three posed for photographs and newsreels and adjourned until the next day, when they toured Oahu together while inspecting troops of all services. It was not until the second evening that the president gave his commanders a chance to make their case. MacArthur urged there was a "moral obligation" for the U.S. to liberate the Philippines, and failing to do so would negatively impact the president's reelection chances. He also noted geopolitical concerns of British desires to liberate the Dutch East Indies, setting up potential future conflicts with their Dutch allies. If U.S. forces took the Philippines, they could send their own forces to the East Indies. Discussions continued into the night, but when they met the following morning MacArthur seemed to have won the day. In public the president praised both commanders, but on the strategic issue said, "We are going to get the Philippines back, and without question General MacArthur will take a part in it. Whether he goes direct or not, I can't say."[24]

Boise was now bound for Leyte Gulf. They were joined by an armada that consisted of not only 7th Fleet but the fast carriers of Halsey's 3rd Fleet. Several battleships were included that dwarfed *Boise*'s firepower. At the heart of it all were enough transports to carry two full Army Corps. The Allies were not only going to knock down the door to the Philippines, they were coming to stay. Most American planners believed the Japanese navy would not try to intervene. Still, the possibility existed, so 3rd Fleet was given a caveat. If the IJN made a concentrated effort to thwart the Leyte operation, destruction of that enemy fleet would become their primary mission.[25]

The events at Leyte have filled many books over the years. The official U.S. Army and Navy histories each devote an entire volume to the campaign, and many prominent historians have analyzed the battle. This story will stick closely to the events and stories that impacted the ship, DB, and his shipmates.

Leyte is a large island in the central Philippines. To its south is the large island Mindanao and north is Luzon, the largest island and MacArthur's eventual goal. Leyte was at the maximum range for land-based air cover from Morotai. The Air Force planned to construct airfields immediately after the invasion to cover the rest of the island chain and free up the 3rd Fleet carriers.[26] The island itself is covered in lush jungles and a mountain range runs across its center like a spine, but its eastern side is a relatively flat plain with the city of Tacloban and an airstrip at the northern end of the bay. It was along this eastern coast the Army chose to land.[27]

The Army expected over 21,000 defenders across Leyte, and another 160,000 in the Philippines, so they needed a significant invasion force and plenty of reinforcements. MacArthur redesignated Lieutenant General Walter Krueger's Alamo Force as 6th Army for the invasion. They were ordered to seize Leyte Valley for construction of airfields and logistics bases for the follow-on drive into the Philippines, and eventually to clear the rest of the island. Major General Franklin Sibert's X Corps would land the 1st Cavalry Division and 24th Infantry Division near Tacloban, while XXIV Corps under Major General John Hodge led the 7th and 96th Infantry Divisions ashore at four beaches further south. The 32nd and 77th Infantry Divisions were held in reserve. Tens of thousands of service troops and additional fighting men were also involved, resulting in a force of 174,000 for the invasion. A-Day was set for October 20.[28]

Boise approached Leyte as part of TF-78, the Northern Attack Force commanded by Vice Admiral Daniel Barbey. Admiral Berkey led his cruisers as the Close Covering Group, which consisted of the usual suspects *Boise*, *Phoenix*, *Australia*, *Shropshire*, and seven destroyers. *Nashville* was busy ferrying MacArthur.[29] Berkey's group was protecting the Northern Attack Force and tasked with helping destroy Japanese army, naval, and air forces that could threaten the landing.[30]

Leyte Gulf received plenty of attention from the Allies before *Boise* and the transports arrived. Minesweepers began the dangerous task of clearing the sea-lanes under the nose of the enemy on the 17th. Army Rangers captured small islands that could be used to fire on the transports as they entered the gulf. On the 18th cruisers and battleships entered the gulf and began shelling the beaches while planes from escort carriers worked over the region's airfields. Underwater demolition teams cleared the final approaches to the landing beaches while trading fire with Japanese defenders. There were a few casualties to men and ships, but the enemy was either unable or unwilling to counter the preinvasion operations.[31]

Boise entered the gulf at 0130 on October 20 with their paravanes out in defense of any threats the minesweepers may have missed. The log noted several unidentified aircraft in the area starting around dawn along with sporadic AA fire from other ships, but *Boise* did not fire. Shortly after the first rays of light the skies filled with friendly planes.[32]

Normally the cruiser would begin shelling assigned targets as the sun came up, but for several hours *Boise* was at anchor roughly three miles from the beach. They had to wait their turn while the battleships had their fun with the opening bombardment. The big guns went silent at 0900 and the large ships withdrew while swarms of friendlies pounced on select targets. *Boise* moved in and took up a position. They were south of Tacloban, but north of the Southern Attack Force's areas. The SOCs were already airborne when the main guns swung to port and thundered.[33] They put significant effort into Highway 1 parallel to the coast to help isolate the landing beaches. The crew was extremely satisfied with their performance, noting that the charts provided were exceptional. The SOC pilot gloated "it was the most effective firing he had ever witnessed."[34]

While the Allies were pleased with the amount of steel they sent ashore, most of the Japanese troops had withdrawn to positions outside the range of naval guns and hid in locations unlikely to draw the attention of aerial bombs. They planned to quickly return to their prepared defenses after the bombardment to fight for control of the Leyte beaches.[35] It was here that *Boise* really aided the operation.

The first X Corps troops swarmed ashore after a final deluge of rocket fire from landing craft. The men were greeted by minor rifle and machine-gun fire, but their worst experience came from the swamps with armpit-deep mud just beyond the beaches. Further south, troops encountered mortar and artillery fire targeting the landing craft. A few Higgins boats were struck and the enemy homed in on three LSTs, setting one afire and forcing others away from the beaches.[36]

Boise was called upon to help silence some of the guns. At 1136 the SOC identified one. *Boise* let loose, and "completely knocked out" the threat. The gunners had a quick twenty-minute break before they were back in action. Four separate targets were passed to the ship, but the men attacked them all in the next hour without issue. They were called upon one last time at 1630.[37]

The real drama of the day came just after noon on Red Beach. The beach was crowded with boats, men, and equipment. The front was less than half a mile inland, but this is where General MacArthur chose to visit because he wanted to understand the battle at its most contentious point. At 1247 he splashed ashore, accompanied by his entourage and the President of the Philippines. His boat's draft was too deep to allow it to reach shore, so the group was forced to wade ashore, despite MacArthur's crisp, clean uniform. Photos and videos of him striding through the surf quickly became iconic. He soon took to the airwaves to address the people of the Philippines. He urged them to "rally to me" to eject the Japanese from their country, but most importantly for the general's ego he was able to truthfully announce to the world, "I have returned." After two and a half years, he was finally fulfilling his promise.[38]

MacArthur departed for *Nashville* at 1600. The first day of the invasion was a resounding success. The 6th Army reached all its objectives in the face of light resistance thanks to a well-devised and -executed plan and the fact that the Japanese were husbanding their forces for an inland fight away from the Navy's big guns. The situation was calm enough by nightfall for *Boise* to anchor a few miles offshore and for the men to get some rest.[39] DB described "things going pretty easy" after the day's actions and that they simply "shelled beach" along with the help of "6 wagons here."[40]

At 0525 *Boise*'s men ran to their battle stations to repel an air attack. Thirty minutes later a pair of Japanese bombers flew in low from the south. Intense AA fire from the Southern Attack Force gave them away. One of the planes made a beeline towards *West Virginia* within sight of *Boise*, who lashed out with 5-inch and 20mm fire at 4,000 yards. The shells found their mark and the plane was smoking when it broke off its attack and passed between *Boise* and *Australia*. The pilot bid towards shore and *Boise*'s gunners lost sight of the aircraft among clouds of exploding AA shells and the dark hills.[41]

This pilot was determined to hurt the Allies at all costs. He swung his plane in a wide arc and set his sights on *Australia*. The ship's gunnery officer called to the captain, "Just look at this. She's aiming for us." No one knows what the pilot's intentions were, but after firing his cannon at the ship he dove directly at the bridge. His wing struck the foremast and the plane tumbled into the sea, but not before its fuel tank ruptured. The bridge was instantly engulfed in a gasoline inferno that killed twenty men including the captain and wounded fifty-four others. Historians debate whether the pilot intended to strike the ship or not, but survivors insisted this was the first kamikaze attack of the war.[42] *Boise* saw the entire incident and DB wrote, "*Australia* hit this morning with bomber." His choice of words suggests that he at least thought the attack was intentional.[43]

Boise spent the remainder of the day on standby. Repeated radio calls to the shore fire control parties did not produce any fire missions, so their guns sat quiet even as others were called upon. They watched *Australia* finally depart the area around noon as many of the crew remembered the feelings of grief over fallen comrades they felt at Guadalcanal.[44]

By the afternoon the fleet was on the verge of a crisis. The battleships and cruisers were nearly out of ammunition. One report estimated that ships equipped with 6-inch or larger guns were down to 10 percent of their ammo, and the destroyers assigned to bombardment missions had fired all their allotted shells and now had only their "service ammunition." The only solution was to bring ammunition resupply ships into the crowded gulf, despite the added risks. Plans were set for the next morning so warships could begin taking turns replenishing.[45]

At 2100 *Boise* and their compatriots repositioned to cover the southeastern flank of the transport group.[46] DB's notes on the second day reveal growing stress and fatigue for the crew. He recorded, "Still here firing at targets ashore. 4 air raids today. *Honolulu* took a torpedo. Did not sink."[47] His misattribution of events from the day prior suggest he may have written his remarks later, but one cannot miss the anxiety and exasperation that comes with the words "still here." *Boise* had not stuck around after an invasion like this since Italy, and it was an uncomfortable feeling to remain at a location waiting for an enemy response. The men were not used to playing defense.

At 0500 on the 22nd they moved back towards shore. The men stood to General Quarters at 0528. Shortly before seven they were greeted by another Japanese bomber. This one came in at a medium altitude and tried to use Leyte's hills to hide its approach. Ship radar picked up the approach and the Mk-35 Fire Director slewed the guns on target. The Val dove on the *Boise* but a hail of fire from the 5-inch, 40mm, and 20mm guns caused the plane to veer down the ship's port side at 1,000 yards before disappearing back into the island's interior. Thankfully, this time the plane did not return for a suicide attack.[48]

Boise passed another quiet day at anchor without any further action. They again retired to the southeast at dark and spent the night making a slow patrol to protect the transports.[49] DB wrote, "Still here. Firing at targets when called. 7 air raids. *Australia* hit this morning with bomber."[50] Again, his details seem to reflect the broader Leyte battle, not just *Boise*'s specific events, and his timing is a little scrambled. What is clear is that on the 22nd the dangers posed by the enemy were still present, and that the massive operation was continuing.

The 23rd started like previous mornings with an enemy air raid, but it failed to cause any problems to the Close Covering Group or their transports. *Boise* was soon anchored in Area Dog and waiting for calls. Around 1000 the Army decided they could use some help and called for them to reposition for afternoon support. They arrived as requested by noon, but the troops were not quite ready. Finally at 1345 SOC #20 catapulted into the air to help guide *Boise*'s shells. It was finally time to show off their precision gunnery. The first call was to destroy enemy personnel and their pill boxes just in front of advancing troops at San Joaquin. The forward observer (FO) requested "6 gun salvos main battery. Try to settle [straddle?] road. Suggest 10 salvos on 2 special points previously designated." *Boise* responded with zeal, firing on the target for almost an hour.[51]

An hour later the FO called again. This time the Army spotted enemy personnel in the open. *Boise* punished them with the main batteries as they fled the battle. The secondary batteries took over and continued to punish the enemy holding a small river crossing. American troops followed close on the enemy's heels and *Boise* ceased fire at 1622 to let the situation develop. They were called again at 1707 for twenty minutes of firing on enemy forces in San Joaquin. The FO described the target as "pill boxes and machine guns. Fire according to ammunition available not to exceed 200 rounds." When the smoke cleared the FO called "Army observers report excellent firing. Two Japs blown to bits as they ran. Other enemy casualties not known yet." Shortly after *Boise* recovered their SOCs and departed for their nightly patrol stations.[52]

Boise's performance was exemplary. The Army passed on such praise that Berkey wrote a letter to Admiral King himself, stating, "The effectiveness of the called fire of the USS Boise served to destroy large numbers of enemy personnel and thereby materially contributed to the rapid advance of our forces during the early stages of the exploitation of the occupation of LEYTE." He singled out the performance of the SOC pilots who accurately spotted fire when ground controllers could not get a vantage point.[53] Gunnery officer Commander William Cassidy, navigator George Beardslee, and eight other officers were recommended by Commander Wolverton to Captain Roberts for commendations. None of the enlisted men were identified for individual medals.

Successful gunnery has elements of art, science, and a little luck, but *Boise*'s gunners had added something to the science aspect that may have added to their impressive results at Leyte. They developed a gadget that they dubbed a "gyamo." It provided "instantaneous and continuous means of determining from reference point the correct range and deflection spot to place opening salvos on target areas." It was a simple plexiglass overlay for charts with known range and deflection data etched into its surface that allowed the gunners to calculate their opening shots quickly and accurately. The simple but ingenious idea was quickly adopted by the other cruisers in 7th Fleet.[54]

There remained room for improvement in other areas. The biggest shortfall of the operation so far was intercom discipline. The official battle report surprisingly calls out officers as the main culprits. They are accused of taking over as radio operators but not bothering to learn the standards. They also talked too fast, tying up individual circuits longer than necessary because everything had to be repeated. This was a serious problem when communication was essential for passing target information, damage reports, and equipment updates around the ship. Many of the enlisted men probably felt vindicated that an official report called out their leadership in such a bold manner. It may even have been an enlisted man that added "some individuals simply cannot make themselves understood and should not be allowed to use voice radio."[55]

DB's most accurate statement for the day was "Still here." After that he wrote, "10 raids today. Our planes shot down 46 jap planes today. Not bad."[56] The crew was clearly tiring of continuous duty in the narrow confines of Leyte Gulf, even if they were providing meaningful impacts on the battlefield. Official reports do not seem to support DB's assertion of major air raids that day, and again suggest he muddled his dates after the events. Instead, his entry now reads as foreshadowing for the near future.

The 24th was a day of anticipation for *Boise*. It was their turn to refuel, so *Phoenix* and the destroyers were sent in early to support the troops. But they were interrupted early on when the Japanese kicked off their response to the invasion. Around 0830 a massive air raid approached. Allied pilots tore into the enemy and *Boise*'s log recorded "about 40 enemy planes of various types shot down," while an LCI was sunk and another cargo ship damaged. Three aircraft dove on *Nashville* and MacArthur but failed to score any hits. Ultimately the raid achieved little. *Boise* did not get a shot but spent the raid conducting evasive maneuvers in a continuous right-hand circle with *Phoenix* and *Louisville*. *Boise* started refueling operations at 1100 but was interrupted twelve minutes later with another air raid. They again formed their cruiser-circle, and *Shropshire* joined the group. The Combat Air Patrol (CAP) fought off the raiders without any damage, and the cruisers finally topped off their fuel bunkers by late afternoon.[57]

The enemy also tried to strike at Halsey's carriers. Multiple raids were fended off, but one enemy bomber crept through the high clouds to plant a 550-pound bomb on the flight deck of the light carrier *Princeton* (CVL-23). Sadly, the fires reached the ship's torpedo storage room, resulting in 237 sailors killed, 4 missing, and 211 seriously wounded. The carrier was abandoned and sunk by an American torpedo.[58]

These were the initial jabs of the Japanese Operation SHO-1. The plan called for the majority of Japan's remaining naval power conducting a three-pronged attack. Admiral Takeo Kurita was leading the Center Force towards the San Bernardino Strait on the north side of Leyte and neighboring Samar Island. Admiral Nishimura was taking his Southern Force and a force of transports through the Surigao Strait to the south of Leyte. They intended to wreak havoc on Kinkaid's fleet in a pincer attack that trapped U.S. forces in Leyte Gulf. The genius of the plan came in the third prong. Admiral Ozawa was ordered to use the remaining Japanese carriers of the Northern Force, now largely bereft of aircraft since the Great Marianas Turkey Shoot, to lure Halsey's fleet carriers away from the fight. They were betting that after the Japanese carriers escaped destruction in June, Halsey's aggressive spirit would compel him to give chase, hopefully leaving Leyte Gulf with seriously depleted air cover.[59]

The Allies were largely aware of the plan thanks to incredible submarine surveillance and broken codes. On the 23rd a pair of American submarines caught the Center Force and sunk two heavy cruisers and damaged a third enough that it needed to withdraw.[60] On the 24th Halsey sent hundreds of planes to the Sibuyan Sea against the Center Force, who had no air cover of their own. They pummeled the monstrous battleship *Musashi*. The loss of one of the largest battleships in the world was a huge blow to the IJN. Three other battleships were also damaged, but Kurita was still following the plan with four battleships, six heavy cruisers, two light cruisers, and at least ten destroyers.[61]

The Southern Force continued towards Leyte unabated, but not undetected. Admiral Jesse Oldendorf was developing a plan including the bulk of 7th Fleet's surface power. It was in the north that decisions were made that could sway the battle. Some of Halsey's pilots spotted Ozawa's Northern Force. Halsey decided to follow Nimitz's instructions to destroy the enemy fleet, and he assumed that the Northern Force with its carriers was the superior threat. He had the entirety of 3rd Fleet chasing Ozawa. Historians have since argued that he had more than enough carriers and surface ships to handle both the

Central and Northern Forces, but still decided to take everything with him in his pursuit. This left only a thin screen of escort carriers and destroyers between Kurita's battleships and the transports of Leyte.[62]

Boise readied for surface combat in the south. Berkey received news of the impending attack around 1500. The Close Covering Group would join Oldendorf's battleships. DB included a pre-engagement entry in his log: "Still here. Large Jap force reported steaming this way through Mindinao [*sic*] Straits. 1800—underway with other ships to engage them."[63]

Oldendorf pulled out all the stops and ordered overwhelming force to greet the IJN. He believed in an old aphorism "never give a sucker a chance," and the approaching IJN force was a bunch of suckers in his mind.[64] The anchor of his plan was six battleships and their 14- and 16-inch guns. Six destroyers provided them security. Five of the battleships had been sunk or damaged at Pearl Harbor, and now sat ready to personally deliver their vengeance.[65] Forward of the largest ships were two lines of cruisers. *Boise* was a part of the Right Flank Force in between *Phoenix* and *Shropshire*. One sailor thought they were bait to bring the enemy under the battleship guns.[66] They also had six destroyers with them to protect the western side of the Surigao Strait. On the eastern side the Left Flank Force waited with five more cruisers and nine destroyers. Further south skulked thirty-nine PT boats sent to monitor Japanese actions and harass them with torpedo attacks.[67]

The Allies knew where and when the enemy would come, and their overwhelming number of ships should have no problem with Nishimura's Southern Force. He had two old battleships, *Fuso* and *Yamashiro*, along with the heavy cruiser *Mogami* and four destroyers under his command, and with a little patience would be reinforced by a follow-on force consisting of heavy cruisers *Nachi* and *Ashigara*, light cruiser *Abukuma*, and nine destroyers under the command of Vice Admiral Kiyohide Shima. A small five-ship transport unit guided by two cruisers and a destroyer was also designated to land troops in western Leyte.[68] However, even if the enemy consolidated, they were still outgunned.

The thing that worried Oldendorf was a serious shortage of ammunition for all those guns. The entire fleet was hurting for shells, and the number of armor-piercing shells needed to take on battleships were in particularly short supply. The battleships had originally sortied to the region intending to bombard Yap, and thus had magazines filled with high-capacity ammunition. Less than a quarter of their stock was armor-piercing. Therefore, the Battle Line was prepared to hold their fire until the enemy closed to 17,000–20,000 yards, almost assuring the enemy would also come within range of the cruiser guns before the battleships opened fire. As another hedge against limited ammunition, the destroyer squadrons prepared to hug the coasts and fire swarms of torpedoes at the oncoming enemy.[69]

Late in the afternoon, all SOCs that could not be stowed in ship hangars were flown to shore. Their wooden frames were a serious fire hazard, and since the concussion from main battery volleys could damage the aircraft, it made sense to send them away. They could still be called upon to take off and drop flares if needed, but everyone expected the surface radars to do most of the work.[70]

By sunset *Boise* was cruising back and forth in a tight pattern that kept them on the western half of the twelve-mile-wide channel. There was nothing to do but wait. The nervous tension that all fighting men know prevailed across the ship. They tried to distract themselves with routine tasks, but most besides DB at the helm had little they could do. Small talk, jokes, and cigarettes were the only refuge. But there was excitement as well. This time was not like Guadalcanal. They were professionals, and they were ready to unleash hell.

The moon set on a glassy sea just after midnight, plunging everyone into a Stygian darkness only the radars could penetrate.[71] The Japanese Navy loved a good night fight and had trained relentlessly for such a battle for years. But the Americans were not the novices they had been in 1942. Many sailors' attitudes could now be boiled down to "bring it on," and one historian of the battle described the officers as waiting "rigid with excitement" thanks to their tactical advantages.[72]

The first indication of the enemy came to Roberts at 2310 when *PT-127* provided a contact report. It was followed at 0040 by a second report from the same boat. Two more reports helped everyone plot the enemy's advance and by 0202 it was clear to *Boise* that the IJN was approaching Surigao Strait. They were expecting "at least two very large targets, and several smaller ones."[73] The PT boats served their purpose well by relaying their reports back to the fleet. Thirty of the boats got into action that night and fired torpedoes before the enemy identified and repelled them under hails of gunfire. Nishiura's force fought through the harassment undeterred.[74]

At 0252 *Boise* picked up their first enemy contact by SG radar at 47,900 yards. A few minutes later they picked up a second contact, and then the entire enemy force began to coalesce on the scope. They saw "two columns of three or four ships each, with a large ship in the lead of each column." At the same time, American destroyers from the forwardmost Picket Line snuck towards the Japanese along the sides of the channel. They fired volleys of torpedoes and quickly retired back up the channel even as Japanese destroyers reached out with their 5-inch guns and the *Yamashiro* tried to find the range. The destroyer crews were rewarded with several large explosions among the enemy ships.[75]

Despite clear damage to his force, Nishimura continued to advance, possibly not comprehending what was waiting for him. From 0300–0400 the destroyers of both Flank Forces made their own torpedo attacks with additional satisfying explosions. Berkey experienced a moment of terror when the Battle Line reported "have group of small ones followed by heavy group; when large group reaches 26,000 yards I will open fire." Berkey understood the current score, and that the "small ones" were friendly destroyers returning from their attacks. He quickly ordered them to flee the center of the channel to clear up the larger ships' radar screens to avoid friendly fire incidents.[76]

Boise watched all this from a distance. Radio reports kept them abreast of the destroyer attacks while everyone looking south could see scattered gunfire, large explosions, and the eerie glow of Japanese star shells. The fight was getting closer, but still they waited.[77] At 0351 Oldendorf allowed the Flank Forces to break their tension with three simple words: "Cruisers, open fire."[78]

Thirty seconds later, *Boise* was the first of the big ships to fire. Range to the lead ship, the *Yamashiro*, was 18,100 yards. *Phoenix* bit into the battleship thirty seconds after.[79] *Boise*'s superb gunnery was instantly on display. Their initial salvo was "up 300" and rapid adjustments dropped the next salvos directly on target. Satisfied with the initial rounds they quickly switched to rapid-fire, pumping out rounds as fast as they could load. Berkey had to temper his force's exuberance at 0355 when he ordered them to "fire slow and deliberately," lest they burn through their limited ammunition too quickly.[80] Roberts complied and the gunners settled into a smooth rhythm of firing.

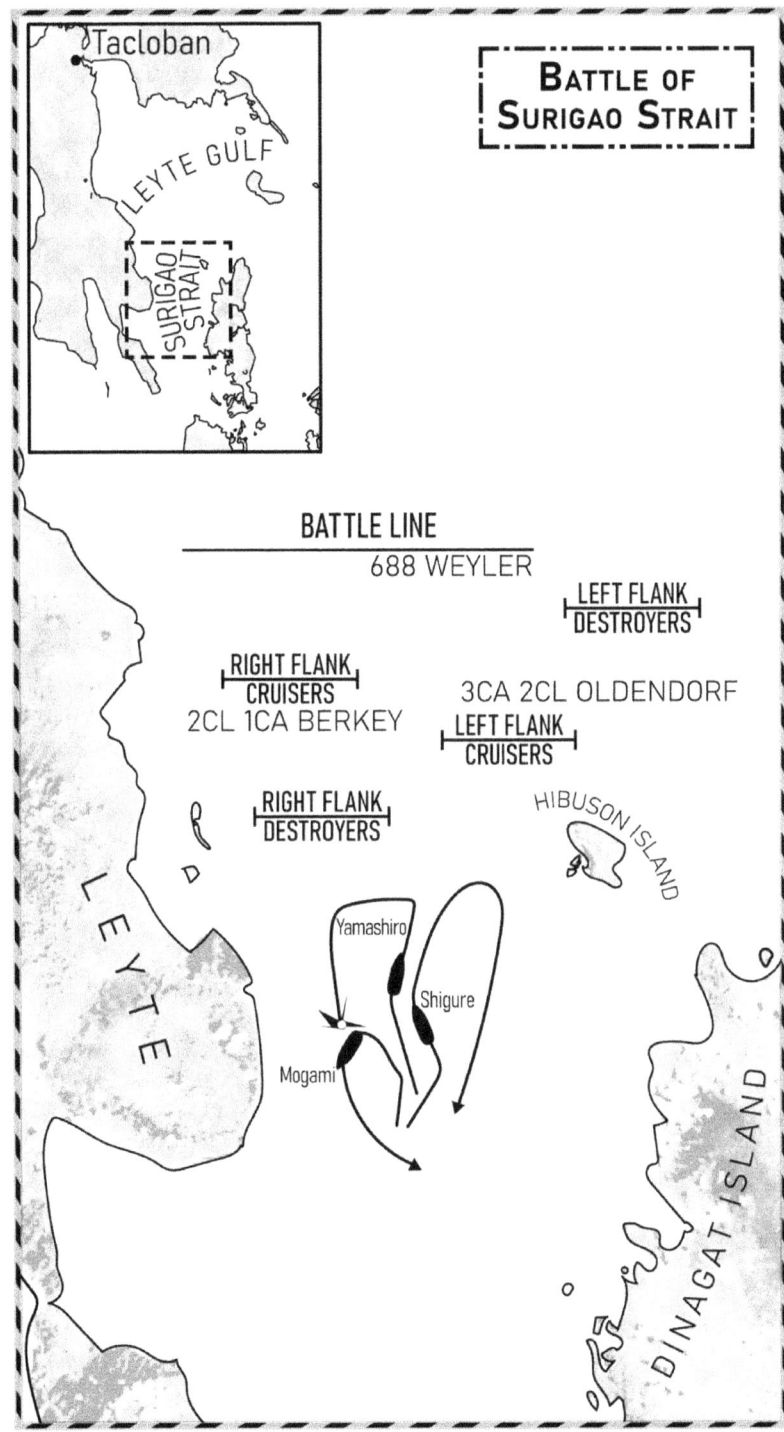

Boise supported landing beaches around Tacloban during the invasion of Leyte in October 1944. In the early morning of October 25, *Boise* was a part of Rear Admiral Oldendorf's force that "crossed the T" of a Japanese fleet at Surigao Strait.

Shropshire finally joined the match at 0356. All three continued engaging multiple targets. At 0357 the Right Flank Force was approaching the center of the channel. They risked interfering with the heavy cruisers of the left flank and leaving an open channel along the shore that enemy ships could exploit to get behind the Battle Line and into Leyte Gulf. *Boise* and *Phoenix* checked fire while each ship executed their turns. DB cranked the wheel to the right and the bow churned through the sea until they faced westward a few minutes later. *Shropshire* was in a safe enough position to continue firing through the turn, and they never let up their murderous fire on the enemy, even as shells splashed around them.[81] *Boise* and *Phoenix* both resumed fire at 0400. Shells were now heard by *Boise*'s crew and splashes observed, but they were spared any hits or damage.[82]

The battleship was now aflame and continued to draw fire from across the Allied fleet. They continued to hammer the remaining Japanese ships until 0410 when the left flank destroyers reported receiving friendly fire. Oldendorf called for all ships to cease fire while the destroyers withdrew.[83] By then the leading enemy target had closed to 12,800 yards but was "burning fiercely," and a second target was also aflame nearby.[84]

At 0416 Berkey's ships had again run out of room and conducted a hard left turn to reverse course. They were in position by 0420 when they were ordered to resume fire. *Boise* searched for targets but found none within range. The crew settled back into waiting and watching. Over the next hour the two largest enemy targets disappeared from the radar scopes. Status reports were passed, revealing that many of the destroyers were low on fuel, ammunition, and few had torpedoes left. By any measure the Allies had dominated the fight against Nishimura, but they needed to ensure that surviving enemy ships did not escape. Oldendorf also had to prepare for additional waves of Japanese attacks.[85]

Boise had fired 439 shells, the most rounds of any of Berkey's ships, but that was a third of their ammunition.[86] Another fight like this could leave them empty and exposed. *Phoenix* and *Shropshire* were similarly depleted. The entire force desperately needed resupply.

Berkey's force had hardly fought the battle alone. The five cruisers of the Left Flank Force added 3,100 rounds to the hellish demise of Nishimura's force. The Battle Line added 274 man-sized projectiles that could weigh more than a ton each. *West Virginia*, *Tennessee*, and *California* provided the most to the battle thanks to their advanced Mark-8 FCR.[87]

Boise relaxed their readiness at 0450, but ten minutes later an air attack was reported "imminent," so everyone scrambled back to their battle stations. The planes never materialized, but Shima's force was still advancing up the channel. A PT struck the light cruiser *Abukuma* and forced it to retire. Shima ordered a torpedo attack by his remaining ships and turned south to reassess the situation. He tried to flee the area before American airpower could find them.[88]

Oldendorf led his Left Flank Cruisers in pursuit and ordered the Right Flank to do the same. Thirty minutes later the admiral's cruisers sunk a fleeing vessel. A few minutes after, *Boise* was ordered to steam north towards their original position, only to be turned around again to investigate "three large columns of heavy black smoke" visible in the predawn light. One of the damaged destroyers tried to make a last stand but was quickly cut down when Left Flank cruiser fire found the magazine, causing a "large tongue of flame shoot high into the air" observed by *Boise*. Several destroyers encountered survivors in the water. They were ordered to rescue them but "do not overload your ships—about 50 to 75 per ship—search each man—kill every man who shows resistance. Be careful of enemy attempt to damage your ship." Many refused rescue at first, but the desire to live was strong in at least some Japanese sailors who began accepting help by taking lines at 0625.[89]

At 0732 they received orders to proceed back up the channel because trouble was brewing to the north. Further pursuit was handed off to Allied planes who would claim more kills on Shima's force and severely damage the small transport unit sent to western Leyte. Due to the cold calculus of war the Americans could not continue recovery efforts. One destroyer reported more than 300 "Nip survivors" nearby. They were told, "Regarding Nips in the water—let them sink."[90]

Everybody wanted to know the score from the night's action. DB wrote, "0400—caught Jap force completely by surprise in Surigao Strait, south of Leyte gulf. We sunk them all.... Some show. It was all over when the sun came up." After listing the participants he recorded, "Japs sunk—2 BB 2 CA 1 CL 6 DD's; Damaged—1 CA 1 CL 5 DD."[91] One can only imagine the fireworks present for the laconic sailor to write "some show." His score was inflated, but this was common for all battles during the war. *Boise* sailors claimed years later that during the battle the IJN lost two battleships, two heavy cruisers, and six destroyers.[92] This is more accurate if one considers all the ships sunk by torpedoes, gunfire, and air attacks before and after the climactic battle at the northern end of the Strait. In reality, the Japanese lost two battleships, two heavy cruisers, two light cruisers, and several destroyers. Of all the ships involved, only five destroyers and heavy cruiser *Ashigara* remained afloat.[93] It was a resounding victory for the Allies that demonstrated the value of combining all elements of naval warfare to relentlessly strike the enemy from multiple directions. It was also the culminating moment of centuries of naval warfare theory. Oldendorf had "crossed the T" of his enemy, raining fire from all his fleet's guns on the vulnerable enemy. Airpower was rapidly making such tactics antiquated and irrelevant, but for eighteen glorious minutes the Americans applied the leading naval theory with resounding success, perhaps for the last time.

Wolverton again singled out several officers for commendation. This time he noted an enlisted man, S1c Clayton Boone. The seaman was a "projectileman" in Turret 2 with the job of loading shells into the right gun breech. During the fight he fractured a bone in his hand but continued to "load his gun without regard to his own injury."[94] Professionalism and bravery abounded on the ship, and it was certainly nice to see one of the regular sailors noted for his performance.

Meanwhile, a dangerous situation was developing off Samar Island. American forces in the area consisted of destroyers and escort carriers since Halsey had taken everything larger to hunt Ozawa. At 0645 a pilot reported enemy battleships, cruisers, and destroyers a mere twenty miles from the closest American carrier. The ships had escaped radar detection and practically stumbled upon the Americans. Kurita's force had rallied from the prior day's air attacks and stolen the march on their opponents.[95] What followed should have been a melee of gunfire that culminated in sunken American carriers before they waded into the transport ships like a scythe through wheat.

At 0657 the commander of the carriers, Rear Admiral Clifton Sprague, ordered his ships to run east while launching planes. He called for help from anyone in the area. What followed was a battle full of confusion that the Americans only survived thanks to Kurita's poor ship handling and understanding of the situation, Allied air prowess, covering rain squalls, and valiant attacks by woefully outgunned destroyers. Although he sunk one carrier and several destroyers, Kurita was convinced he was up against a much stronger force and decided to withdraw rather than press home his attack.[96]

Boise and the rest of Oldendorf's forces moved into Leyte Gulf to secure the transports and the beaches. They were greeted by an air raid that targeted the escort carriers. It turned into the first recognized kamikaze attack.[97] Japan started forming these "special attack units"—that Americans eventually called kamikazes—in response to Allied air dominance during 1944. The Battle of the Philippine Sea proved that Japanese pilots were no longer good enough to penetrate Allied air patrols, evade AA fire, and drop their bombs with any accuracy. Instead, beginning in October 1944, some pilots were trained to deliberately target enemy ships with their aircraft, dropping their bombs at the last second to maximize damage.[98] As the carrier *St. Lo* and others learned off Samar, this was a devastating new tactic that all Allies had to adapt to quickly, because their very survival depended on it.

Boise was spared the chaos off Samar. Their day was spent patrolling and waiting. They tried to get an ammunition resupply but were denied as other ships were more desperate.[99] Many wondered how their brilliant victory could be soured by Kurita's force. Those thoughts were inflamed as news of a message from Pearl Harbor that seemed to chastise Halsey made its way around the ship. At least that is how many veterans recalled it. Nimitz had been monitoring the Samar battle from Hawaii and reached out with a radio message asking "WHERE IS TASK FORCE THIRTY-FOUR." However, due to security protocol, the message included extraneous phrases before and after the message to confuse Japanese codebreakers. Typically those extra words were not included when messages were passed to commanders, but apparently the technician thought the phrase at the end was intended to be part of the message, so Halsey was given "WHERE IS TASK FORCE THIRTY-FOUR THE WORLD WONDERS." The last three words should never have been passed, but Halsey took it as a sarcastic rebuke to his Ozawa chase and swung his ships around to help at Samar.[100] It is highly unlikely the same mistake was made aboard *Boise*, but DB swore for years that the crew got word of the message with its mistake and similarly wondered with anger, where was Halsey?[101]

By evening the situation around Leyte Gulf had quieted. There was no attack that night, and the 26th started slowly. The air raids did not come until 0830 when a pair of Helens came out of the clouds at 14,000 feet. The 5-inch gunners got off a few rounds that helped alert the rest of the fleet to the enemy's presence. The enemy ducked into another cloud bank before the gunners could get their number, but the bombers failed to cause any problems.[102]

Boise finally got their turn to resupply when they pulled alongside the Merchant Marine ship SS *Durham Victory*. According to DB, the encounter went poorly. The civilian sailors were striking for higher wages, so when *Boise* threw lines to secure the ships the men just dropped them into the water. The crew had to call for their Marines to board the ship, round up the crew, and threaten to shoot anyone who interfered with the resupply. It took a long time for the *Boise* men to figure out how to operate the crane, but eventually they were able to get their allotted 750 6-inch rounds and smokeless powder.[103] There may have been a bit of truth to DB's sea-story, but the sailors probably took the situation out of context. A history of the Pacific War's sustainment operations reported that the *Durham Victory* "had a very small civilian crew, no winchmen, and no previous experience with ammunition handling." The same report also noted that at Leyte Gulf "the taking of ammunition was, as usual, slow, difficult, and unsatisfactory."[104] It is unlikely that the Marines were needed, but there was ample room for frustration over the four-hour process.

The evening was filled with air attacks, but the pilots were focused on the Battle Line's big ships and transport areas.[105] DB summed up the day succinctly: "Returned to Leyte Gulf for ammunition. A few air raids. Patrolled in entrance of gulf all night."[106]

They moved out of the gulf to provide protection to the escort carriers. *Boise* and *Nashville*, now free from flagship duties, watched over six carriers while *Phoenix* and *Shropshire* had six more. The *Suesens*, with DB's friend Shand, joined their formation the following day with three additional destroyer escorts.[107] They all continued carrier support through the 29th.[108]

They were back in Leyte Gulf the following morning when the bulk of the fleet departed for Ulithi to refit and resupply. *Boise* remained in the area with the rest of Berkey's force, three battleships, and thirteen destroyers. That night they rode out a "severe local cyclonic disturbance." Winds blew up to 75 knots and the rain came in heavy sheets. Despite the rough seas and accompanying excitement, the entire system blew through by morning.[109] The rest of the month passed quietly with routine patrols to protect the gulf.

November dawned with renewed air attacks. The Japanese had pushed fresh planes and pilots into the region while American carrier-based airpower was worn down from weeks of combat. The Air Force had not yet been able to base significant forces on Leyte due to limited space on the airfields and difficult construction conditions.[110] The enemy took advantage of the relative equity in airpower and attacked with vigor, including kamikaze attacks.

Boise recorded attacks early on the 1st. AA fire rose from ships around them, but nothing approached *Boise* and at 0334 they relaxed from General Quarters. The attacks resumed in earnest at 0928 with a string of dive-bomber and torpedo attacks. The starboard gunners fired on a Val and forced it to turn away. A few minutes later a plane crossed in front of their formation and several guns set it ablaze just before it crashed into the destroyer *Ammen*. Another plane streaked in and crashed off *Boise*'s port bow. The attacks drew blood on two more destroyers. Another wave arrived. The cruisers fired on a bomber to port and forced it away. Attacks continued across the area, but the planes seemed to focus on the destroyers.[111] Although several enemy planes were destroyed, three destroyers had been hit, two of them taking serious damage.

Even as the fleet licked their wounds from the air attacks, they were forced to form a new battle line across Surigao Strait. Contact reports said that two battleships, three heavy cruisers, and eight destroyers were heading towards Leyte. To make matters worse, three other large ships were reported in a position to rendezvous before they entered the Strait. *Boise* took a position on the right flank while the other ships tried to recreate the same formations from October 25, but with significantly fewer ships. Everyone was in position by 2030 and tensions ran high. Later in the evening it was determined that the enemy contact reports were part of a Japanese deception plan designed to force Allied ships into narrow confines where the kamikazes could target them.[112]

November 2 was a tense day full of patrolling and air raid alerts. None of them came close enough to *Boise* to merit evasive maneuvers, but the constant stress was wearing on everyone's nerves.[113] DB summed up the past two days as "5 of our D.D.'s damaged. *Abner Read* sunk. 3 or 4 crash dives." He also claimed six enemy aircraft downed.[114] The next day they were greeted by another air attack. At 0503 radar picked up a threat at 16,000 yards. The crew never saw the threat, but radar showed that their AA fire was enough to force the aircraft away.[115]

With the passing of that threat the crew finally got some peace. They had several days of quiet patrolling interrupted by air alerts and the foul weather that came from a typhoon passing two hundred miles from Leyte. Not until November 11 did an air raid approach close enough to draw defensive fire from *Boise*'s defensive screen.[116]

On the 16th *Boise*'s duty at Leyte was complete. A new task group arrived allowing a changing of the guard. The men were exhausted after weeks of fighting, patrolling, and air attacks. With great relief DB wrote, "Left Leyte Gulf for Seeadler Harbor […] *Boise*, *Phoenix*, *Nashville*, *Shrop[shire]*, *Mississippi*, 5 destroyers."[117]

It took several days to reach Seeadler. While en route the Navy insisted on continued training, even for exhausted men who just fought one of the greatest battles in U.S. history. On the 18th a destroyer stood out from the column while the *Mississippi* fired offset rounds at it. The cruisers maneuvered into columns to defend against multiple targets on both sides of the task group if needed.[118] On November 20 they launched SOCs for AA gunnery practice. With the growing threat of kamikaze attacks, everyone understood the proficiency of those gunners could mean the difference between life and death. The next day they conducted an even larger AA exercise, firing at targets towed by B-26s. They fired thousands of rounds, ensuring that everyone qualified to pull a trigger received plenty of practice.[119] Later that morning they pulled into Seeadler and refueled. By dinner they were safely at anchor and able to breath a collective sigh of relief.

The crew now had a chance to rest and reflect. They were integral to MacArthur's return to the Philippines. Their shore bombardment and on-call gunnery were superb and reasons for pride. They had taken part in one of the Navy's greatest battles, but also witnessed the terror and confusion the enemy could wreak. Many wondered what was coming next.

The Navy had the same questions at strategic and institutional levels. The IJN had limited surface forces available and another major battle was unlikely. But friendly ships were constantly threatened by submarines, mines, bombs, and kamikazes. Even land-based artillery could take a toll when they had to operate near shore.

While the crew recovered from weeks of taxing operations, the stress took a heavy toll on at least one of them. On the 28th a call went out for medical aid. Captain Roberts was having a heart attack. The Senior Medical Officer examined him and diagnosed him with coronary heart disease and arteriosclerosis. He was transferred to the hospital on Manus Island. Commander Wolverton was given command of the *Boise*.[120] The man who led *Boise* through the New Guinea campaign and Leyte Gulf eventually recovered and retired as a Rear Admiral. He was awarded a Navy Cross for his leadership at Surigao Strait.[121]

There was no time to lament the loss of their skipper. *Boise* set sail that same evening with *Nashville* and some tin cans. The constant flow of Leyte-bound transport ships filled with supplies, replacement troops, and construction material needed protection. They crossed the equator on the 29th, and the following day slowed their speed to refuel the accompanying destroyers. Once everyone's fuel was topped off, the ships practiced evasive maneuvers to evade air attacks.[122] The exercise required precision and coordination for each ship to move unpredictably while also avoiding collisions.

They made contact with the rest of the fleet on December 2 and joined their ranks. The battleships and heavy cruisers departed that afternoon along with a flock of destroyers. Leyte's defense was in the hands of Berkey, his four cruisers, and fifteen destroyers. The Japanese reminded everyone they were in a war zone when a lone bomber approached undetected. He missed his target and paid for the attack with his life. On the 3rd another lone-wolf plane flew a torpedo attack against the transport *Hope* but missed.[123]

December 4 was the quiet before the storm. They spent hours in the morning sailing in a circle around *Portland*, who was having propeller problems and sent divers to make repairs.[124] The next day the air raid alerts started well before dawn. From 0353 to 0621 there were five separate alerts. Then everything was calm for a few hours while half the force sailed to San Pedro Bay to replenish their stores. *Boise* and *Phoenix* remained on patrol at the gulf's southern entrances when an air raid alert was received at 1115.[125] The CAP swooped in on the threat and downed several bandits, but not quickly enough to stop three aircraft from diving on a convoy at the western side of the gulf. The pilots dove through a maelstrom of AA fire. The first sunk *LSM-20*, the second missed but still damaged *LSM-23*, and the final one landed a glancing blow on the *Drayton* before crashing into the water.[126]

The enemy returned at 1700. A Val snuck through the CAP and made a run on *Boise*. It was time to put the AA training to the test. The gunners started firing at 5,500 yards with the 5-inch batteries, followed shortly after by the 40mm and 20mm guns. The plane played chicken with the incoming bullets and barreled towards *Boise*'s bridge. Bullets streamed towards the plane for thirty seconds when a 5-inch shell exploded "almost directly on the plane," killing the pilot as the plane veered sharply and crashed about 1,000 yards from the ship.[127]

Before the men could exhale and let the adrenaline dissipate another Val came out of the clouds on the port side. They spotted it at 10,000 yards and began firing at 8,000. The guns hammered for almost a minute. The 5-inch guns scored early hits and the 40mm's started the plane burning at 3,000 yards. The plane set up a glide profile directly towards *Phoenix*. Both ships kept firing until the plane crashed into the sea a mere twenty-five yards shy of *Phoenix*.[128]

Meanwhile, the CAP continued to chase their counterparts around the sky, claiming at least two kills. A Val dropped a bomb 200 yards short of destroyer *Mugford*, but swung around and crashed into the ship, killing two and setting the ship aflame. The attacks were costly for the Japanese, but it was clear that the suicide attacks could overwhelm Allied defenses to kill men and sink ships.[129]

There were more alerts during the late afternoon, but no more attacks on the cruisers. *Boise* fired almost 1,200 rounds from the AA guns to ward off the attackers. It was a small dent in their stores, but the fight demonstrated the fury needed to defend from the kamikazes.[130] DB wrote with pride but also with a little anxiety, "Shot down two Vals. One tryed [sic] to crash the *Phoenix*, we got it, another off our stbd."[131] Wolverton must have ended the day with similar pride for bringing his men through battle without any losses. Although he was a veteran of every one of *Boise*'s fights, this was the first time he had been in command and responsible for the ship and everyone onboard.

The following day *Boise* welcomed Captain Willard M. Downes aboard as their new skipper. Wolverton had acquitted himself well, but the Navy was not going to leave a cruiser in the hands of a mere commander. Downes was an interesting choice, as he had spent the war thus far commanding submarine operations.[132] Regardless, he was entering directly into the fray. The Japanese gave him enough time to drop his seabag in his quarters before sending their own greeting at 1812 by way of another air raid. The formation accelerated to 25 knots with evasive maneuvers. The gulf erupted with pockets of AA fire. A plane at wavetop level came out of the darkness towards the ship. The port 5-inch guns fired across the water until the plane crossed the bow and the starboard gunners picked up the fight. The plane approached to 1,500 yards and appeared to drop something before turning its tail towards *Boise*'s bullets. Nobody wanted to stay on their current course to find out what was dropped, so the ship turned hard to starboard. None of the formation's ships were struck, but they did get the satisfaction of seeing another flaming plane crash into the water before the night went quiet.[133] Hopefully Downes felt satisfaction knowing he was inheriting an experienced ship and crew.

Boise was sent to San Pedro Bay for replenishment on the 7th during a lull, when DB pulled off a caper that became ship legend. *Boise* took aboard a veritable feast of foods that men far from home craved during the holiday season. The supplies were meant to be split between *Boise* and *Phoenix*, which was serving as Berkey's flagship. Everything was stacked neatly in the hangar bay until it could be distributed. During the night, "about half of the canned turkey and chicken and innumerable cases of fruits and juices were taken from the hangar by members of the crew" to the deepest recesses of the ship, hidden in the labyrinth of spaces, compartments, and holds that the enlisted men knew intimately. Downes tried to recover the missing items and save face with his new boss, but the crew kept their secret like Mafia dons. No one broke. Instead, *Boise* was forced to transfer their half to *Phoenix*, as they had been entrusted with the precious cargo. In a ship-wide "Orders for the Day" the officers chastised the men: "In effect a comparatively few men have beaten the whole crew out of a turkey and chicken dinner." In truth it was mostly the officers who lost out. Years later DB wrote for their reunion, "Perhaps the entire crew still enjoyed their turkey dinners, if not, at least a turkey sandwich while on the mid-watch." From that day forward the phrase "Who stole Admiral Berkey's turkey?" became a rally cry for the men. DB was clearly a ringleader of the event later dubbed the "Turkey Snatcher," and in his files was a list of memories sent to him by an unnamed crewmate where DB had circled and wrote in December "that's when I stole Berkey's turkey!"[134] The list of his coconspirators is now lost to history.

On the 9th *Boise* rejoined *Phoenix*. The day was quiet, and the log made no mention of turkeys. The following day brought more patrolling and another air raid just before sunset. This bomber came in from the west with the setting sun covering its approach. *Boise* fired on it with the starboard batteries until it crossed the bow and portside took up the fire. They think they hit the plane because after the initial pass it turned back towards the formation "with apparent intention of making a suicide dive." The port gunners gave it everything they had as it again crossed the bow screeching towards *Phoenix*. The starboard 40mm found the mark and chewed the plane to pieces, forcing it into a crash 200 yards from *Phoenix* and 800 yards from *Boise*.[135] Another close call.

The rest of the fleet did not have nearly the AA firepower of the cruisers. The *Boise* log noted that *Hughes* (DD-410) was struck by a bomb and a suicide attack near Surigao Strait. The cruisers were quickly dispatched to help secure the struggling vessel. The same air raid also sunk the Liberty ship *William S. Ladd*, *PT-323*, and *LCT-1075*. This is on top of the loss of multiple destroyers a few days earlier during an invasion of Ormoc on western Leyte.[136] The attacks were taking a serious toll on the Navy's smaller vessels that were crucial for amphibious operations.

On the 12th it was time once more for major action.[137] Mindoro sits south of Luzon and was lightly defended. Unfortunately, to reach it the fleet would have to pass several areas still teeming with Japanese troops and would be closer to enemy airfields than friendly. It was a gamble, but MacArthur wanted the island as a base for his upcoming Luzon campaign, and his gambles had paid off in the past. Still, to hedge his bet, the invasion force would have six escort carriers for direct air support and three battleships with three additional cruisers for fire and AA support.[138] The plan called for units from the 24th Division and the 503rd Parachute Regiment to land at 1500 on the southwest coast. The initial target would hopefully bag three airfields and set up advances. "U-Day" was set for December 15.[139]

The 13th was an unlucky day for the invasion force. It started easy with the fleet pushing through the Surigao Strait and the Mindanao Sea. CAP aircraft buzzed overhead, and the fleet's radars hummed looking for threats. Despite the precautions, a Val snuck up just as they were leaving confined waters for the Sulu Sea.[140] The aircraft made a suicide run on the flagship *Nashville*, pushing through AA fire to release two 63-kg bombs just before impact. The pilot struck amidships and exploded in a massive fireball, sparking intense fires "from the foremast to the mainmast topside." The damage was extensive, 133 men were killed, and 190 were injured, including several of the mission's commanding officers. MacArthur was not aboard. The crew valiantly fought fires to save the ship, even as stored AA ammunition cooked off around them. Within ten minutes the fires were under control, and in twenty everything was extinguished. The ship was saved, but out of action. Fleet command shifted to *Dashiell* (DD-659).[141]

The enemy was not finished yet, returning around sunset with multiple bombers. *Boise* had barely begun firing at one when a P-38 swooped in and shot it down. Another plane dropped bombs on the destroyer screen. Two planes were seen crashing into the sea, and ten minutes later an American Corsair shot down a Nick. Still the enemy persisted. Four Sally's passed over the formation and *Boise* watchmen reported splashes in the wake and off the starboard.[142] DB summarized the chaos in his entry the next day. "*Nashville* hit by crash dive. Our fighters shot down a bunch of planes. Couldn't count for sure how many."[143]

The 14th was "remarkably quiet" according to the ship log. This was because a massive air raid ran into Halsey's planes. Two-thirds of the sixty-nine enemy aircraft launched never made it back home. By 1900 the Close Covering Group was in position five miles off the landing beaches.[144]

The rest of the force trickled into position overnight. *Boise* was the only cruiser designated to directly support the landings, so they moved towards the beaches at 0700 with a pair of destroyers. The tin cans fired a brief bombardment for about ten minutes, but *Boise* was only on call. The first troops splashed ashore right on time at 0730 to no opposition. It did not take them long to secure all their objectives.[145]

A dozen enemy aircraft arrived at 0856 and tried to crash dive the transport ships. They were quickly intercepted by the CAP, but two survived long enough to crash into *LST-472* and *LST-738*. Both ships were set ablaze and eventually sank. The kamikaze hit a few other ships including escort carrier *Marcus Island*.[146]

The troops' advance was going so well that at 1254 *Boise* rejoined the Close Covering Group's patrol.[147] DB wrapped up the day succinctly. "Landed 16,000 troops on Mindoro. One air raid. Ships shot down 6 planes. 2 LST's hit, one by bomb, the other crash

Boise steams past a burning LST hit by a kamikaze during the invasion of Mindoro, Philippines, on 15 December 1944 (National Archives: 80-G-294541).

dive. *Boise, Portland, Phoenix,* covering operations. 3 wagons, 6 carriers 4 cruisers covering us."[148]

Boise departed the area with the bulk of the convoy on the 16th.[149] The Pacific Theater in its entirety was fairly quiet that day. *Boise* pulled into San Pedro Bay for resupply as Hitler's legions were unleashing a surprise campaign in the Ardennes region of Belgium. The hammer blow pushed the Allies nearly 70 miles and created a giant salient on the Western Front that took weeks for the Allies to reduce. It was the beginning of the Battle of the Bulge.

Boise remained at anchor for several days. They were still moored on the evening of the 20th when the next air raid arrived. The attack was spotted seventy miles out. CAP was sent to intercept but missed them in the dark. The planes commenced their attack at 1830. AA guns ashore lashed out first, but a bogie locked its sites on *Boise* and started its attack. Every ship in the area fired on the attacker, forcing it to crash without causing any damage. There was intense AA fire in the area for a few more minutes until the air was clear at 1856.[150]

The *Boise* men tried to rest, but their slumber was interrupted every night by enemy "snoopers" and nuisance raids. None of them caused any material damage, but constant alertness and stress took its own toll. *Boise* finally left anchor on the 26th. A contact report suggested a battleship, heavy cruiser, and six destroyers were 100 miles from Mindoro and approaching at a high speed. *Louisville* took the lead and *Boise* fell in with

Phoenix and *Minneapolis*. Eight destroyers formed a protective circle around the cruisers, and they made their way at 20 knots.

Boise's group had no chance to win this race. The Japanese, led by Admiral Masanori Kimura, had too much of a head start thanks to poor weather masking their movement for days. The enemy force cruised down the western Mindoro coast. All that stood between them and the airfields were American PT boats ... and all the aircraft that had begun operating on the island. Kimura began shelling the area at 2240 but was attacked constantly by every aircraft available. Over 100 planes swarmed his ships. They caused distraction and destruction on such a scale the shelling was completely ineffective. There were no casualties or significant damage during the 20–40 minutes of firing, but Kimura's force suffered heavy damage. As he withdrew around midnight, a PT boat put several torpedoes into destroyer *Kiyoshimo*, sinking it on the spot.[151]

Boise arrived around 0700 primed for a fight. Everyone was on alert for "stragglers or cripples" that might put up a fight. They patrolled all day finding only fires and a single Japanese survivor.[152] DB's notes from the chaotic night were hasty. Sometime on the 26th he wrote, "Left Leyte for Mindoro to intercept Jap force. *Louisville, Phoenix, Minneapolis*," but the script for the next day was nearly incomprehensible: "Force went [undecipherable] couldn't find. Bombers bombed them." It was rare for him to record anything so sloppily, even after Cape Esperance, so it is interesting to consider his state of mind that night. The *Boise* reunion papers referred to the event as a "high-speed covering operation" occurring during the "'relative quiet period.'"[153]

They hung around Mindoro until sunset on the 28th and then retired back to Leyte. They refueled and settled into anchor at San Pedro for a few days. The Japanese threatened to ring in the New Year with an air raid at 2030, but the planes never approached the gulf. The men were left to wonder what 1945 would bring them.

8

Liberation

Luzon, Philippines

Once again *Boise*'s proud bow carved a path through the waters west of Luzon. The last time they had been in these waters they had been alone, fleeing the Japanese forces attacking Manila. Now *Boise* sailed at the heart of an armada. On all sides sailed cruisers, destroyers, light carriers, and most importantly: troopships. Aboard *Boise* sailed the arguably most important American in the Eastern Hemisphere in January 1945. General Douglas MacArthur stood at the rail of the *Boise*'s battle bridge, gazing out at the island that he called home for years. Every fiber of his being longed to win the island back. It was the site of his biggest disgrace, and the avenue towards his final redemption.

MacArthur's collar now carried the weight of five stars. He was one of only seven American officers in history chosen to advance to the rank of General of the Army.[1] This was his moment, and he had chosen *Boise* as his chariot towards this ultimate battle. MacArthur seemingly had an affinity for the *Brooklyn*-class ships. In February 1944, he undertook Operation Brewer, a daring invasion of the Admiralty Islands by a small Army force. The operation was a "gamble" according to Morison, but if successful it could help isolate the Japanese stronghold on Rabaul. Against the recommendations of his staff, MacArthur chose to personally oversea the operation, and selected the *Phoenix* as his flagship.[2] It was the general's first time aboard a Navy vessel larger than a PT boat, and he thoroughly enjoyed it. During the invasion *Phoenix* used its 6-inch guns to destroy Japanese gun positions, and the incident turned MacArthur into something of a naval gunfire acolyte.[3] *Nashville* served as his flagship for several operations after that.

In early January 1945, MacArthur was ready for his grandest amphibious assault of the war. Operation Mike I would put more American divisions ashore in its opening effort than Eisenhower landed in Normandy on D-Day.[4] It also had multiple naval fleets assigned and legions of airplanes dedicated.

Mike I planned to invade Luzon at Lingayen Gulf, the wide stretch of flat sandy beaches flanked by mountains that opened up to vast plains leading to Manila. The plains contained road and railroad networks that would be crucial to reaching the capital city and ensuring supplies could flow quickly from the beach to the combat units as they advanced.[5] The route would also secure Clark Air Base, which could support U.S. heavy bombers attacking Japan.

The initial day of the operations was branded "S-Day" as opposed to the conventional military term of D-Day.[6] Overall, the Mike I plan included 191,000 men, 131,000 of them combat troops. Additionally, Lieutenant General Robert Eichelberger's 8th Army would conduct landings elsewhere on Luzon shortly after S-Day. Luzon would become the largest battle in terms of U.S. forces in the Pacific War.[7]

Allied planners expected heavy resistance to the invasion. Submarine attacks were a key concern, and concentrated air attacks focused first on transports and then on the carriers would come at dawn and dusk. Night attacks from motor torpedo boats were also likely. They thought the landing beaches would be "well defended in many places by barbed wire, beach obstacles, land mines, trenches and pillboxes." The Americans expected a stiff fight to the landing beaches, and for upward of 160,000 Japanese troops to battle the Americans from the beaches to Manila.[8] The potential for high casualties during the initial phase of the invasion was real.

Admiral Oldendorf commanded the armada that preceded the amphibious fleets. Oldendorf's fleet of 164 vessels included the entire gamut of U.S. naval power with the exception of the largest fleet carriers. Their job was to "kick down the door" by clearing the sea-lanes of enemy ships, subs, and mines while softening up the beaches with pre-invasion bombardment.[9]

The Japanese hit hard with their remaining air forces and kamikazes. On Jan 5th they sank the escort carrier *Ommaney Bay* and struck several other vessels including escort carrier *Manila Bay*. On the 6th they countered the mine-clearing operations in Lingayen Gulf by sinking one ship and damaging eleven more vessels. They also killed a U.S. Navy Rear Admiral, a British Army Lieutenant General, and hundreds of sailors. The following two days leading to the invasion included more air attacks and kamikazes, including the incredible fourth hit on the Australian cruiser HMAS *Australia*. The crew of that valiant ship fought off the flames, repaired what they could, and refused an offer from the task force commander to withdraw in order to stay in the fight.[10]

One benefit of the repeated attacks on Oldendorf's vessels was that they saved the amphibious forces from much larger attacks. Yet the amphibious force's passage was not without threats. *Boise* specifically seemed to wear a bullseye for the entire trip.

Boise welcomed General MacArthur aboard on January 4. He was accompanied by a staff of thirteen officers, a chief warrant officer, and nine enlisted troops. Three reporters rounded out the "CinC SWPA Afloat" court.[11] The presence of MacArthur merited a separate line from DB.[12] What was apparently not notable enough for DB's log was his own promotion to Quartermaster Third Class (QM3c) three days prior.[13]

MacArthur was pleased with his flagship, writing to his wife, "The *Boise* is the most comfortable cruiser on which I have traveled. The suite I occupy is much larger, has artificial ventilation and better cooking than the others."[14] He noted that overall the ship was still and tense, and that "only the pulse of her engines and the wash of the waves broke the quiet," as they steamed.[15]

They sailed as part of Admiral Berkey's Close Covering Group that also included cruisers *Phoenix*, *Denver*, and *Montpelier* and eight destroyers. Under their watchful eyes were hundreds of transports stretching forty miles loaded with troops, tanks, jeeps, gasoline, ammunition, and rations. The Close Covering Group spread itself out on a general heading of 270° while readying for battle.[16]

They cruised quietly for almost twenty-four hours. By noon they were approaching the Sulu Sea, but still sailing within the twenty-mile-wide channel between Mindanao to the south and Negros to the north.[17] The task force was still visible to nefarious eyes on both islands, and hiding a large naval force in such an area was nearly impossible.

Word reached the IJN, and at 1509 they took their shot. The destroyer *Nicholas*

General Douglas MacArthur (hand extended to a saluting sailor) and staff coming aboard USS *Boise* for Operation Mike I, the invasion of Lingayen Gulf on Luzon (Naval History and Heritage Command: 80-G-304363).

(DD-449) reported "torpedo off our starboard bow." At the same time sharp lookouts from the *Phoenix* relayed "torpedo on course south—torpedoes are headed towards *Boise*." Everyone knew the havoc a torpedo could wreak on a cruiser, and while Berkey ordered *Boise* into an "Emergency 20 turn," the crew scrambled to General Quarters and the spotters sighted the torpedoes off the port bow at 6,000 yards, bearing down on them with murderous intent.[18] Captain Downes already had his helmsman cranking the wheel while the engines strained to displace the warship. The radical maneuvers and high speed allowed *Boise* to dodge yet another attempt on their lives.

MacArthur was a veteran of many types of combat, and to his credit he set an example of professionalism, courage, and perhaps fatalism during the attack while he "calmly watched the action."[19] The general's personal physician, Colonel Roger Egeberg, had a reaction to the attack more akin to most sailors who just wanted to survive the war. He recalled, "as I watched, I couldn't help thinking of my cabin at the waterline with those water-tight doors locking me in."[20]

The *Nicholas* was soon joined by *Taylor* (DD-468) to hunt for enemy submarines. At 1516 *Taylor* observed what they thought might be a periscope, and shortly after a midget submarine surfaced directly behind the destroyer. *Taylor* came around with full rudder and flank speed. Meanwhile, an Avenger torpedo bomber keeping watch over the task force spotted the sub and dropped its bombs. The bombs missed the Japanese by about

8. Liberation

50 yards. *Taylor* rapidly moved in for the kill. The sub was damaged so the destroyer adjusted course, slowed to 20 knots while firing a spread of six depth charges forward at their target, and thirty seconds later rammed the Japanese sub. According to their report, "several shocks were felt after initial jar. Personnel in magazines and engineering spaces distinctly heard scraping noises along hull."[21] The destroyer suffered minor damage to the hull, but an oil slick made the crew confident they had killed their prey.[22]

The Japanese had another chance to take out MacArthur that night. The general wrote years later that the Japanese were targeting *Boise* deliberately because "careless publicity" had informed them of his whereabouts. If true, his assertion drips with irony considering how MacArthur constantly used publicity to promote his own image. That night a force of fifteen enemy aircraft were observed, but the Japanese pilots must have had other targets in mind.[23]

The next day *Boise* steamed north without incident. DB noted that they "met troop convoy, the biggest one yet. Another one a day behind us."[24] The plan was coming together with ships and personnel from across the Pacific coalescing in time and space for the assault. Despite the cogs of the war machine meshing as intended, it is unlikely the average sailor had any idea how large MacArthur's invasion force truly was.

On the 6th the skies over *Boise* remained clear. That luck lasted a mere twenty-four hours. At 0621 on the 7th, Downes ordered the crew to precautionary General Quarters. Anxious but professional eyes kept watch. Despite the vigilance, danger found them once again at 0645. The crew observed a large explosion 1,000 yards off their starboard bow from a Japanese bomb. A single Ki-45 "Nick" bomber had hidden itself among a flight of American aircraft approaching Mindoro, thus evading radar. Like a ghost, it approached the fleet from the inky western sky, dropping to the deck and making a run at the *Boise*. The crew never saw the aircraft cloaked in the early morning darkness, only hearing the bandit as it crossed the bow and the succeeding explosion.[25] Luck and poor aim saved MacArthur this time, but the rest of the day would require skill to keep everyone alive.

In response to the air threat, Berkey ordered his ships to accelerate to 20 knots and maneuver independently to make themselves more difficult targets. They slowed back to 10 knots at 0700, but five minutes later a second Nick bomber dove on the fleet. This time the spotters and the gunners picked up the target at 5,000 yards and opened fire, driving off the threat before it could effectively target the *Boise* or anyone else. About ninety minutes later, another Nick tried to sneak in for a shot on the fleet. *Boise*'s starboard gunners again went to work, possibly damaging the aircraft before a shore-based P-47 Thunderbolt swept in for the kill.[26] These enemy attacks were definitely uncoordinated, but still represented a clear threat to everyone.

Japanese aircraft appeared again at dusk. At 1814, a bomber braved the guns and crossed the formation a few miles off *Boise*'s bow.[27] A few minutes later the plane reversed its course and began a kamikaze dive on *Phoenix*. The cruiser was already at 20 knots, and they applied left rudder to unmask their starboard guns against the threat. The crew held their collective breath as the streams of fire desperately tried to destroy their foe. The log recalled, "We kept him under fire. At about 1817, when the Val was only about 50 feet from the starboard side of our bridge, the plane's right wing was shot off and fell into the water ... the plane went into a snap roll, cleared the ship, and plunged into the water on our port side just aft of the bridge!"[28]

Boise helped engage another bomber a few minutes later. The pilot decided discretion was the better part of valor and retired without attacking.[29] One Japanese pilot snuck through and managed to dive on the transport *LST-912*. Luckily his aim was off and the ship took only minimal damage, but four men perished.[30]

MacArthur reportedly stood stoically by one of the starboard anti-aircraft batteries and gazed eastward at his beloved Philippines. According to his biographer, in the late afternoon the general gazed upon Corregidor and Bataan and later recalled of the moment, "there they were, gleaming in the sun far off on the horizon…. I could not leave the rail. One by one, the staff drifted away and I was alone with my memories. At the sight of those never-to-be-forgotten scenes of my family's past, I felt an indescribable sense of loss, of sorrow, of loneliness, and of solemn consecration."[31] He may have been leading his men north to invade Luzon, but his heart's desire was to liberate Manila.

The fleet declared All Clear about an hour later. They reduced speed but did not slacken their steady vigilance. The fleet was fifty miles west of Manila Bay when another potential threat emerged. Around 2100, aircraft flying protection for the fleet reported a surface contact emerging from Manila Bay. Four destroyers were dispatched to deal with what turned out to be the destroyer-escort *Hinoki* who was attempting to flee the area for Indochina.[32] The American destroyers made quick work of the Japanese vessel, sinking the ship at 2255. *Boise* could see the fireworks from the bridge, reporting star shells and 5-inch gunfire that resulted in a satisfying explosion.[33] *Hinoki* never stood a chance in a stand-up fight with the Americans but, like the midget sub and the bombers, held the potential to inflict significant pain if they had been able to strike home with their torpedoes.

DB and his comrades were at their battle stations with the dawn. Hundreds peered at the skies, the sea, and their instruments looking for signs of the enemy. They were tired yet determined after several days of harassing attacks. At 0752 the sun was still low in the sky when the first wave of Japanese planes greeted the convoy from the west.[34]

The attacks on the 8th lacked surprise as *Boise*'s radars picked up the first threat thirty miles out. The task force once again increased their speed and their spacing from one another. *Boise*'s port side batteries opened up on a Nick at 0806 at a range of 8,000 yards. Multiple ships let loose with their own guns, and in ninety seconds the encounter was finished as the Nick crashed into the sea.[35]

Colonel Egeberg provided an insightful description of the air attacks. He wrote that while MacArthur was "avidly interested, twisting his head as the action moved from one part of the sky to another…." Egeberg was also fascinated by the sailors as they went about their work. "Each Navy man was intently watching or doing," he wrote. The doctor felt out of place and found himself walking the deck until he found a position towards the stern. He finally settled near a machine gun position manned by "some men from the mess." He marveled that despite the limited range of their weapon compared to 5-inch and 40mm positions, the men still "pulled their triggers and they coupled that with full and oft-repeated and rounded oaths." He envied the sailor's comradery and ability to vent their frustrations directly at the enemy.[36]

The doctor provided a heart-stopping account of the last few seconds from one kamikaze attack: "It came on, growing bigger by the fraction of a second, and many pieces of metal flew off its wings and fuselage. The noise of the shooting was terrific, and certainly the excitement was intense. When the pilot was about 400 yards away (2 seconds) he veered, seemed to change his aim to the ship parallel with us and a couple of hundred yards off our starboard beam. More metal came off his wing and fuselage, he veered again, probably not intentionally, maybe even dead by now, and would appear to be coming up between the two ships. As he was almost even with our stern, the tail of his plane came off and it plunged into the water between the two ships. The tremendous column of water and smoke that went up bespoke the large load of explosives that were aboard so the pilot could use his plane as a directed bomb."[37]

The kamikaze attacks could be terrifying. Joseph Dyar described them as "the scariest time" of the war. Yet the men had to stand and fight. Joseph Fenton said of one close call that he "threw my [head]phones off and went down the ladder" from his gun position. He was later demoted for leaving his station.[38]

Up and down the convoy anti-aircraft guns fired at the Japanese bandits. Many were shot down, but some were surviving their gauntlets of fire to reach American targets.[39] The transport ship *Calloway* (APA-35) engaged in a remarkable battle with a "Tony." The plane reportedly missed with its bombs on the initial run but returned for a strafing attack from the rear. The Tony then banked to starboard and despite the best efforts of the anti-aircraft gunners it crashed into the transport taking the lives of thirty-one sailors. Still, the ship's war diary proudly declared that not a single soldier embarked on the ship was killed, and all men were soon delivered into the ground offensive.[40] *Phoenix* reported one plane nearly hit the destroyer *Fletcher* (DD-445), but the most desirable targets to the kamikaze pilots seemed to be the escort carriers.[41]

That morning the Japanese homed in on the *Kadashan Bay* (CVE-76). The ship's radar picked up between fifteen and twenty enemy aircraft, and they launched sixteen fighters to intercept. The fighters sliced into the enemy, and by 0748 the carrier's lookouts could see the dogfights with their own eyes. The War Diary noted this enemy attack was "of no mean proportions," and the crew spotted one enemy bomber escape the melee and swing towards the carrier. At 5,000 yards the 40mm guns fired away, followed shortly after by the 20mm guns. Twice they observed the aircraft burst into flames while it dove. At the last second, the aircraft plunged further, missed the bridge, but struck the ship at the waterline. Its two underslung 250 kg bombs detonated inside the ship, destroying "the junior officer's country" aft of the gasoline pump room. Fires broke out and the ship listed 20°, but in under two hours the damage was controlled and the ship was even able to recover aircraft in a limited capacity. Remarkably no one was killed and only two men were injured in the attack, but one standby pilot was missing. Lieutenant A.F. Buddington had been in his quarters when the aircraft hit. He was knocked unconscious and miraculously washed through the hole in the hull without snagging on the jagged metal. He awoke later, alone and afloat on the open ocean until an American patrol craft (*PC-1600*) came across the airman and picked him up.[42]

The attacks did nothing to delay the invasion. By early afternoon the various elements of MacArthur's fleet were rendezvousing and readying for the following day's operation, but the enemy was still determined to exact a heavy toll. Around 1800, radar scopes around the fleet again blinked the return of enemy aircraft.[43]

Boise and a pair of escorts detached from Berkey's group to join Attack Group Baker under the larger Lingayen Task Force (TF-79).[44] They soon joined the new formation and were steaming with the escort carrier *Kitkun Bay* (CVE-71) nearby off the port bow. Six enemy bombers approached the two warships and their escorts. Twelve American fighters pounced the enemy formation, quickly shooting down four, but two aircraft slipped past.[45] The two bombers circled the ships and lined up for an attack. *Boise*'s gunner fired on the closest plane at 1850, adding to the cacophony of the fleet's anti-aircraft fire. In under a minute the plane was severely damaged and the pilot nosed over in a final dive. The kamikaze managed to steer into the carrier, striking the ship at the waterline only 1,000 yards from *Boise*. The resulting explosion ripped a 20-by-9-foot hole in the hull, almost entirely below the waterline. The engine room and other spaces quickly flooded, but valiant work by damage control parties and solid engineering kept the ship afloat. Additional damage was caused by falling American 5-inch shells, demonstrating an unintended hazard of so many close ships firing at aerial targets. Seventeen men were killed and another thirty-six wounded, but the ship was saved for another day.[46]

Just a few minutes later *Boise*'s 5-inch guns barked again. This time the fleet brought down the enemy bomber before it could find an American ship.[47] It slipped beneath the waves along with the last rays of dusk. At 1937 Downes gave his ship All Clear, allowing off-duty sailors to breath a small sigh of relief.[48] DB retired to his bunk and caught up on the prior few days. Exhaustion seeped in as he misattributed the dates of events he witnessed from the bridge. He wrote on the 7th, "Air raids today. *Kitkun Bay* crashed dived by Jap fighter plane. Not badly damaged." His short entry for the 8th recorded, "More air raids. Force shot down two."[49] The division of the coinciding events into two days attests to the mental strain the entire fleet was under.

The repeated air attacks certainly took a toll. Multiple escort carriers, cruisers, and even battleships were targeted and hit over several days. Yet the enemy missed the point. The attacks did not focus on the transports. MacArthur himself noted from his cabin on the *Boise*, "Thank God they're after our men-of-war." His reasoning was warships were better able to defend themselves and were ultimately designed to survive damage from enemy bombs and planes. The transports were less resilient, and the loss of too many soldiers before they could land may have jeopardized the invasion.[50] Despite the air attacks and other diversions sent against the fleet, none had succeeded in forcing the Americans to delay or abandon their mission. The following morning, MacArthur would return to Luzon.

January 9 was S-Day. DB and the rest of the *Boise* men had ringside seats for the main event. The weather was remarkably good for the tempestuous Lingayen Gulf, with calm seas and a slight breeze blowing north from the beaches.[51] All night the invasion force had sorted itself into the proper elements at the gulf's mouth. By 0400 the two attack convoys pushed into the twenty-mile-wide body of water, carefully following the lanes cleared over previous days by minesweepers. Destroyers, cruisers, and even battleships led the transports of both the Lingayen Amphibious Force destined for the western landing beaches and the San Fabian Force heading for the eastern zones.[52]

The landing zones were divided into 13 different beaches.[53] All were wide, sandy expanses that sloped gently into the sea. Soldiers would need to cover dozens of yards before they could find any sort of cover. The sand was soft enough that a man's feet could sink into it, so the passage of wheeled vehicles was bound to be a challenge, but tracked vehicles should have an easier time.

Boise joined the ships streaming towards Lingayen and followed their familiar routine of standing to General Quarters well before sunrise to fend off the pervasive air attacks. They maneuvered independently, enjoying the freedom that came with hosting the invasion's leader. They were shadowed by destroyers *Edwards* and *Coghlan* (DD-606) who acted as bodyguards.[54]

Japanese planes were proving unsettlingly adept at sneaking close to the fleet undetected, partly due to the gulf being straddled to the east and west by mountain ranges. That high terrain so close to the ship was playing havoc with *Boise*'s SK radar.[55] The first

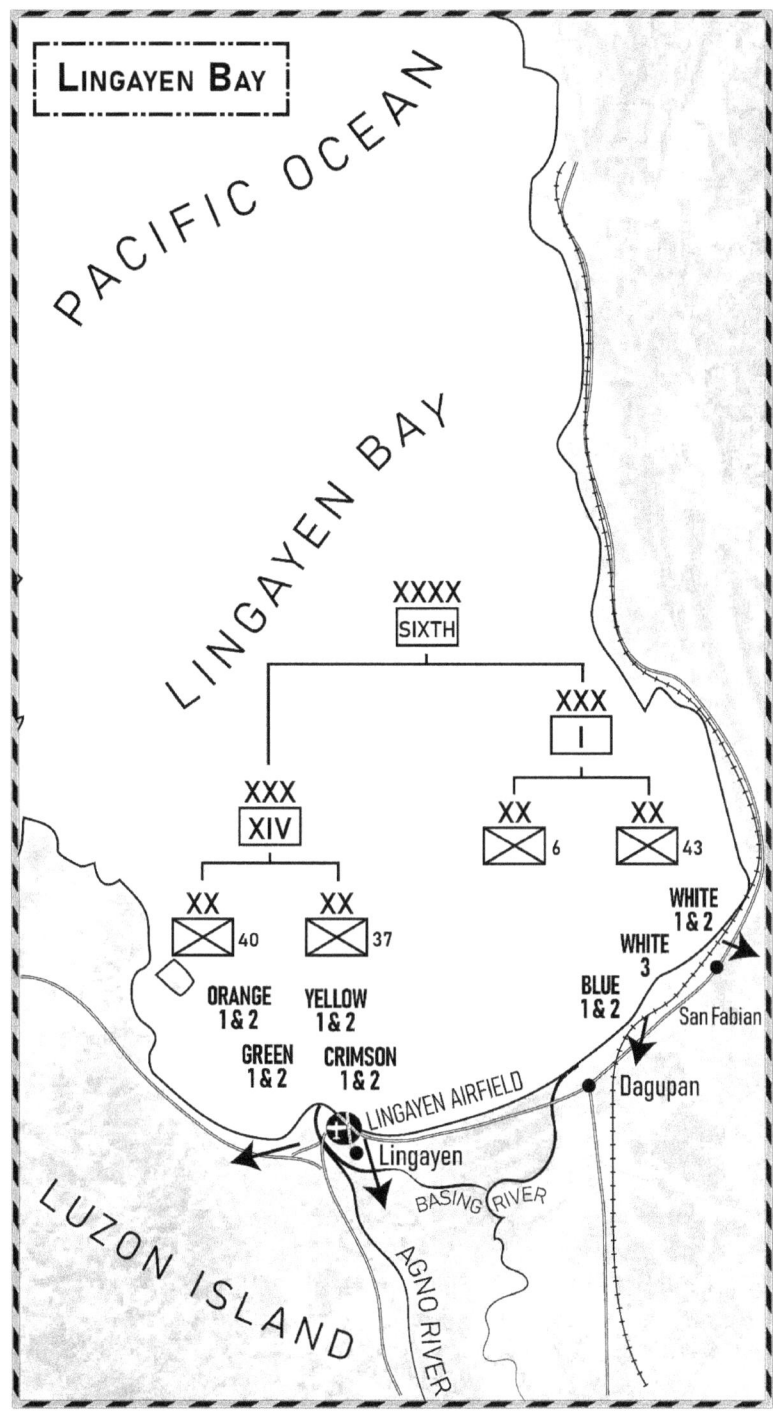

"S-Day" of Operation Mike I on 9 January 1945 was General MacArthur's triumphant return to Luzon, the main island of the Philippines. He selected *Boise* as his flagship for the operation that landed more American troops in one day than during Operation Overlord in Normandy the previous June.

few Japanese planes dove on their targets but largely missed.⁵⁶ Shortly after, another kamikaze made a run at the *Mount Olympus* (AGC-8), the flagship for the Lingayen Amphibious Force, but was driven off by murderous anti-aircraft fire. A third kamikaze found the *Columbia* stuck between waves of landing craft and unable to maneuver. The ship had already been hit twice previously, one causing significant damage. This latest blow struck the forward main battery director, killing and wounding dozens of men. Despite the loss of 191 men in the past few days, *Columbia*'s survivors quickly put out the fires and resumed their bombardment missions.⁵⁷

The men aboard *Boise* had their own Japanese threat to worry about. A Zeke played hide-and-seek with the clouds and made it within four miles of the ship before spotters sighted it. Individual gun captains opened fire on the plane until the fire directors could take control and switch to automatic. The Zeke turned away in hopes of finding an easier target. Still, the crew observed three bombs hit the water 4,000 yards away.⁵⁸ After those attacks the skies quieted.

The warships were undeterred by the air attacks. At 0700 they opened fire on the beaches. DB could see the ships stretched across the bay and made note of the heavy hitters. He recorded that "the Battle ships have been bombarding the beach since the sixth. *Tenn[essee], Miss[issippi], Calif[ornia], New Mex[ico], Penns[ylvania], Mary[land], Columbia, Ast[oria], Shrop[shire], Portland.* The *Louisville* has been crashed dived and

Anti-aircraft fire from ships of the U.S. Navy task force in Lingayen Gulf, Luzon. Taken from USS *Boise* (CL-47) on 10 January 1945 (Naval History and Heritage Command: 80-G-304354).

Anti-aircraft gunners try to shoot down Japanese kamikazes at Lingayen Gulf, Luzon (Naval History and Heritage Command: 80-G-304355).

left."[59] His ship identification was less precise than during other operations, but his count was near complete and accurately portrayed the amount of firepower available. The Bombardment and Fire Support Group included a total of six battleships, seven cruisers, and several destroyers.[60] The big guns of the fleet punished the shore, villages, airfields, and roads leading to the landing beaches. By 0900 the area was thoroughly saturated and the landing craft started their runs. LCIs carrying 20mm, 40mm, 50 caliber guns and rockets added to the carnage while the big guns shifted fire to the flanks to ensure the beaches remained isolated. A veritable alphabet soup of landing craft including LCVPs, LVTs, LCMs, LSMs, and DUKWs began swarming towards the beaches in waves.[61]

By early 1945 the U.S. Navy was the undisputed master of preinvasion bombardments. The flat, sandy beaches were peppered with deep holes from the impact of tens of thousands of shells. The villages, often still filled with local Filipinos, were leveled. In Lingayen, the capital of Pangasinan Province, the big guns targeted the magnificent capitol building. After a few hours, the building was a jagged shell that now stood as a testament to the sad nature of war.[62]

Tragically, the destruction was for naught. The Japanese had elected not to defend the beaches. It was the civilian population that bore the brunt. To make matters worse, the destruction of so much civilian property and the corresponding loss of innocent lives could have been averted. The Filipino guerrilla movement was incredibly active before the invasion, and Allied submarines had helped prepare Luzon for the invasion with the distribution of propaganda materials. Buttons with MacArthur's visage proclaimed "I shall return." One pamphlet showed MacArthur striding ashore at Leyte, and another announced, "The Warriors of Freedom have landed on your island!" next to a drawing of an American soldier running forward with his rifle leveled at the enemy. Others urged Filipinos to "clear the way for the fighting men" and "don't block the roads" in hopes that throngs of cheering locals would not hinder the Army's progress. Despite these warnings, many Filipinos remained in their homes along the Lingayen shore on the 9th. Modern Filipinos celebrate the bravery of a single man who charged into the surf that morning waving an American flag. The man was spotted by an observation plane as he desperately tried to signal to the landing forces that the area was safe and clear. Sadly, his message was either not relayed, was misunderstood, disbelieved, or simply ignored.[63]

At 0930 *Boise*'s log noted "'H' Hour. First assault wave of troops landed on San Fabian beaches." In only twenty-two minutes the amphibious forces landed five waves of troops on the various beaches.[64] Scared but determined troops ran through the soft sand and into the tree lines and villages nearly unopposed. There was nary a Japanese soldier to be found, but the locals greeted the soldiers enthusiastically. They had suffered for three years under the brutal occupation of the Japanese Empire, and many wanted to greet their liberators in person. Others were more practical. In Dagupan, Dr. Pedro Balolong rushed towards the Americans and immediately requested medicine and supplies. He had been treating those injured by the shelling and had exhausted his supplies. Others across the area "brought out long-hidden American flags and greeted the liberators with joyful celebration."[65]

All morning the various types of landing craft and ships brought wave after wave of soldiers ashore. The Americans found little resistance except the sand. The Japanese were only able to muster limited mortar and artillery fire, and they could only reach the San Fabian beaches from their hidden positions in the mountains.[66] One pesky 320-mm gun survived counter-battery fire for days and gained the nickname "Pistol Pete," but despite its perseverance it failed to inflict any serious damage on the Americans.[67]

Around lunch time *Boise*'s world was once again dominated by airplanes. At 1205 a PBY flying boat landed next to the ship and delivered Lieutenant General Richard Sutherland, MacArthur's chief of staff. He arrived just in time to bask in his boss's glory, but also in time to witness the next wave of kamikazes. At 1306 enemy aircraft crashed into the battleship *Mississippi* and the cruiser HMAS *Australia*. Despite the tragic blows to the fleet, the invasion continued without skipping a beat.[68]

At 1407 MacArthur called for a boat to take him ashore to check on operations firsthand.[69] His arrival was well choreographed, with photographers standing by to record the event. Despite a crude pier already constructed by the Seabees, MacArthur insisted his landing craft drop its ramp a few yards from the sand so he could tromp ashore with wet feet like his soldiers. He strode onto Luzon with his entourage in tow, gazing through his signature sunglasses beneath his iconic campaign hat. He was whisked away to tour the battlefield and receive briefs from his commanders.[70] Interestingly enough, the exact location of his triumphant return has been lost to history. Today no less than three separate locations claim to be his exact landing spot. The upkeep of these sites and local rivalries over eighty years after the landings demonstrates the enduring gratitude the Filipino people have for the general.[71]

8. Liberation

MacArthur returned to *Boise* before evening. The final phase of his campaign to liberate the land he loved finally reaching fruition. By nightfall 68,000 troops were ashore and some had advanced nearly 6,000 yards inland.[72] The next step was to consolidate the beachhead and begin pushing into the interior, especially towards Manila.

One factor aiding the success of S-Day was the defensive strategy of General Tomoyuki Yamashita. He had learned that battling the Americans at the beachheads was costly for both sides, but allowed the Americans to utilize their massive sea and airpower advantages to destroy Japanese forces in decisive battles. Yamashita felt this would squander his forces, already isolated and unable to obtain reinforcements. He planned a defensive battle for Luzon where his forces would draw MacArthur's forces into the mountains and exact high costs in American equipment, lives, and time.[73] Most of Yamashita's strength was beyond the range of the fleet's guns.

Just because the Japanese chose not to contend the beachheads does not mean they were not looking for ways to make the Americans bleed.[74] That night they unleashed a new suicide weapon. The Japanese Army had created a regiment of suicide boats, hidden away in various coves and under the cover of overhanging vegetation around Port Sual.[75] At least seventy boats had gone undetected and survived the preinvasion bombardments, and between midnight and 0200 they were launched to seek out and destroy American ships. The 18-foot plywood vessels could make 26 knots with their converted automobile engines, and each carried a pair of 120 kg depth charges. The small crew was tasked to maneuver the boat next to an American ship, drop the depth charges, and then escape before the six-second fuse expired. If everything went well for the Japanese, they could trade an insignificant boat for an American warship.[76]

During the darkest hours of the night, the suicide boats played a perverse game of blind man's bluff with the anchored fleet. The ships were blacked out, and the only sound besides anchor chains would have been the soft rumble of the Japanese boats. Many lookouts and gunners would be loath to fire at noises lest they highlight their own position or, worse, inadvertently shoot a friendly ship. *Boise*'s log dripped with tension as it recorded the confusion like a thriller movie.

> 0348—LST 925, bearing 250°T., distance about 8000 yards reported that she had been attacked by a torpedo boat, and has sustained underwater damage.

This report caused confusion and consternation, but without any other information the *Boise* apparently decided there was no need for additional concern.

> 0420—ROBINSON (DD 592) and LEUTZE (DD 481) reported receiving underwater damage from hand launched depth charges from enemy PT boats which approached them from close aboard. Went to general quarters to repel air attack.

With additional reports of PT boats it was only logical to wake the crew and ready for battle. Whether the men now watched for airplanes, boats, or both, it would now be incredibly difficult to approach the *Boise* unnoticed and without a fight. Still, the men could now appreciate the fear that their Army and Marine comrades felt as they huddled in their foxholes awaiting attacks.

> 0428—WAR HAWK (AP 168) reported receiving underwater damage from unknown source and that ship was being abandoned. At about this time an underwater explosion was both heard and felt. Later learned that LCI-974 had been attacked and sunk, bearing 336°T., distance 1270 yards.

If any *Boise* crewmember had doubts about the deadliness of the new threat, they were quickly cast aside. Feeling the shudder of an explosion is a terrifying experience, but to feel one without seeing its source is cause for fear and doubt that can break a man.

> 0536—Observed destroyer illuminate and fire on enemy PT boat, bearing 320°T., distance about 2000 yards.[77]

Finally, the crew had a little closure. Even if the destroyer failed to destroy the suicide boat, members of the crew could at least report to their leadership and friends that they were fighting something real, not a boogeyman.

Despite the damage noted, the suicide boat attacks were largely a failure. All seventy boats were lost and many failed to even conduct an attack. They were simply lost to the sea. Ten Allied ships were damaged, but only *LCI-974* was lost. This was a far cry from the twenty to thirty ships that Radio Tokyo later claimed were sunk by the suicide boats. At 0558 *Boise* welcomed two officers and twenty-eight men from the sunken LCI.[78]

Dawn greeted the crew with another wave of kamikazes while they sat at anchor. At 0634 a bomber used the combination of sunrise and the smoke screen to disguise its approach on *Boise*. The entire complement of AA guns took shots at the bomber and drove it off with an intense thirty seconds of firing. The smoke swirled and obscured the skies as the bomber maneuvered for another attack. Ten minutes later the plane again targeted the ship and this time approached without the sting of anti-aircraft fire. The plane dropped two bombs, but the smoke that hid its approach also obscured the *Boise*, resulting in the bombs straddling the ship. The men could only wonder what was happening around them as the air filled with the sounds of anti-aircraft fire. One *Boise* man, Coxswain Howard Schofield, was wounded in the foot from a falling 20mm shell casing. Despite the military trope of leaving combat due to a gunshot to the foot, Schofield stayed aboard and continued his duties.[79]

The weather worsened that day, causing difficulties for the landing craft and unloading crews. The Lingayen airfield was ready to receive emergency aircraft by the afternoon, and soldiers pushed inward.[80] *Boise* passed mail and a handful of passengers to *Edwards*, who was preparing to join a convoy of ships departing the area. The LCI survivors were transferred to *Monrovia* to start their long journey home. Evening settled in with another wave of enemy aircraft that failed to cause any damage.[81]

The following day was a day of parting as the bulk of the fleet left Lingayen Gulf. "All warships left today except us and some tin cans. The *Phoenix*, *Denver*, *Montpillier* [sic] is with a carrier force outside the gulf."[82] *Boise* would linger for as long as MacArthur required, allowing for the arrival of a ghost from *Boise*'s past. At 1200 the officer of the deck received word that a long-lost crewmember wanted to come aboard. The man was Officer Steward 2/c Estaneslas Bandong, a Filipino American who had been granted leave from *Boise* on December 4, 1941. He left Manila to see his family on Luzon and was scheduled to return by midnight on the 8th. Unfortunately *Boise* had had to depart early. His hometown was four miles south of Lingayen. He spent three years hiding from the occupying Japanese, but when the American fleet returned to his home he faithfully reported for duty. By extreme luck or providence his ship was the flagship for the liberation of his village, province, and country. To its credit, the Navy accepted Bandong back into service without prejudice, and gave him three years of back pay.[83]

Boise fired on two more aircraft that evening. The second incident involved every gun on the port side sending up an incredible wall of lead. The aircraft was later confirmed as killed by a nearby ship. When the unnamed, exhausted sailor designated to write up the report for the attack reached the required item "Best estimate of size of gun or guns responsibile [sic] for each [plane shot down]," he sarcastically wrote, "Sure."[84]

The 12th started with even more air attacks.[85] With fewer ships in Lingayen Gulf, the hard calculus of war meant *Boise* and its exhausted crew had a greater chance of being hit than before. At 0807 one attacker survived long enough to drop a bomb that missed the stern by a mere 200 yards before it crashed into the beach. Still, the duties of a flagship continued among the danger. MacArthur hosted the top brass of the invasion, providing opportunities for the enlisted men to either witness the war's heavy hitters or, more likely, to avoid public spaces and chance encounters with flag officers. Lieutenant General Krueger reported aboard in the morning and discussed with MacArthur a follow-on operation to land troops at Bataan. In the afternoon Vice Admiral Kinkaid and Vice Admiral Theodore Wilkinson conferred with MacArthur.[86] The campaign was about to enter its next phase and its leaders needed to ensure they were on the same page, especially as naval assets were leaving Lingayen Gulf for their next missions.

While the gunners fired on Japanese planes and the brass held their war councils, DB witnessed an attack that proved closer to home than any since Guadalcanal. From the bridge he learned of an air attack on the *Suesens* with his friend Shand aboard. His atypical note of "The *Suesens* came pretty close I couldn't see where she was hit" betrayed a level of fear that he did not usually record. A Japanese Hamp bomber had closed on the destroyer escort around 0730. The DE began maneuvering erratically and turned hard towards the aircraft while its anti-aircraft gunners fired frantically. The plane dove on the ship in a steep turn at 400 knots while the gunners shot chunks out of the plane. The pilot was likely killed before he could finish his attack and the plane missed the aft 40-mm gun mount by five feet and exploded on impact with the sea. The explosion looked impressive but left only a 10-inch gash in the hull and cut some cables along the mast. Eleven men were injured, but there were no deaths thanks in large part to the judicious use of steel helmets by men on deck.[87] DB had no way of knowing the reality, and it would be several agonizing days before he could learn the fate of the man that connected him to home.

On the 13th *Boise* relinquished the role of General MacArthur's residence and command post. He went ashore at 1415 along with his staff, allowing the ship and crew to resume their duties as warfighters. Enemy aircraft tried to harass the remaining ships but failed to sneak past the growing combat air patrols now operating from Luzon airfields. By evening it was time to leave.[88]

The crew was immensely proud of their contribution to the invasion as MacArthur's flagship. Future *Boise* reunions shared a letter of thanks from the general to Captain Downes from his time aboard. The note was first shared with the crew on January 14, just days after they departed the invasion area. It read:

Dear Captain Downes:
Before disembarking from the *Boise* I wish to offer my high commendation of the outstanding manner in which you and your officers and crew have participated in the restoration of our flag in the Philippines.

Your highly professional seamanship and the magnificent discipline and fighting spirit of your crew in hazardous circumstances have fully upheld the high traditions of the United States Navy. For myself and my staff I thank you for the many courtesies we have enjoyed during the time the *Boise* has served as my headquarters afloat.

With my sincere appreciation of a job well done.

Faithfully yours,
/s/ Douglas MacArthur[89]

Boise sailed away from Lingayen Gulf in triumph. Not only had they hosted General MacArthur, they had done their part to protect themselves and the fleet. They had stood to General Quarters every day from the 9th through the 13th, never relaxing during daylight hours as they waited and responded to air attacks. Ship veterans reminisced years later that "the ship was subjected to extensive attacks from enemy aircraft (including kamikaze pilots attempting to crash dive) and in two cases was bombed resulting in near misses. Throughout these attacks and during the long uncomfortable periods of general quarters, the crew performed their assigned duties with courage and intelligence. The Combat Information Center team functioned in such an efficient manner as to gain the praise and commendation of Commander Support Aircraft. The gunners assisted in shooting down two sure kills and took all attacking aircraft under such an effective fire that they were either destroyed or driven off before any damage could be done to the ship."[90]

The battle that began at the beaches of Lingayen Gulf now pushed beyond the range of naval guns. It was time for *Boise* and other ships to redeploy and ready themselves for new missions. The men needed a break, but MacArthur's plans for Luzon included more landings up and down the western coast, and those troops required support. *Boise* would soon find itself back in the thick of the fighting.

The remainder of January was quiet. The Army was battling its way to Clark Air Base and then Manila, so *Boise* fell into a routine of helping secure Lingayen Gulf. The men were in place to ensure the endless convoys bringing supplies and reinforcements to Lingayen were safe. It was a chance for the crew to catch their breaths, but the work continued and tedium grew. They were at General Quarters from before sunrise to after sunset. Sometimes they provided protection for aircraft carriers covering the area, which DB noted on the 19th involved six of the massive vessels. At other times they scouted for Tokyo Express ships attempting to resupply or evacuate Japanese forces. All surface radar contacts turned out to be nothing, and *Boise*'s guns remained silent. The Japanese simply did not have the resources to attempt operations near Luzon.[91]

Boise was ready for action on January 29 when 8th Army's XI Corps landed near the village of San Antonio in the Zambales Province, completing Operation Mike VII. *Boise* was in the area to provide on-call fire for the 30,000 troops going ashore on B-Day, but this time the Navy acted more cautiously in terms of civilians. Intelligence reports from Filipino guerrillas suggested the beaches were virtually empty of Japanese forces, and the designated bombardment forces held their fire. The landing troops were greeted not by bullets but by mobs of Filipino civilians cheering "Liberty!" The troops quickly moved inland and began sealing off the Bataan Peninsula to prevent the Japanese from using the area in the same manner as General Wainwright three years before. The following day soldiers took possession of the abandoned port at Subic Bay.[92]

Boise wrapped up the month with a surface contact on their radar. The target soon disappeared from their scopes, but the commander dispatched destroyers for a hunter-killer operation to pursue what could be an enemy submarine. At least one was suspected to be in the area since the transport *Cavalier* suffered a crippling explosion thought to be from a torpedo. The American ships searched the area and pounded suspected sonar contacts with depth charges until they were satisfied they had killed their quarry.[93]

In early February the ship was sent to Mangarin Bay on the island of Mindoro. They were joined by other elements of the Task Group including fellow light cruisers *Phoenix*, *Denver*, and *Montpelier*. Their first day was spent replenishing the ship. It is a testament to the miracle of American logistics that supplies were available in a recently occupied bay within 150 miles of the ongoing fight.[94]

Over the next week the men finally received some badly needed rest. There are no reports of air attacks, General Quarters, or threats from surviving bands of Japanese on the island. Some men were even granted passes away from the ship. DB made his way to *Suesens* on the 4th. He tracked down his friend Shand and was able to put his concerns to rest, and the two were able to revel in stories of survival.[95]

Boise left Mindoro on the 8th with a bevy of eight destroyers. By morning their formation joined with their sister destroyers and escorts to enter Subic Bay. The military adage of hurry up and wait kicked in, and the fleet remained mostly at anchor until the morning of the 13th. MacArthur's plans for the Philippines called for the ships to help retake Bataan and Corregidor, but the pieces were not yet in position. So the crew waited, periodically refueling in operations that shuffled the ships around the bay. The men were rested and the ship was ready.

The force sallied forth on the 13th at 0630. It was a short trip down the coast to their assigned positions off Corregidor at the mouth of Manila Harbor, where *Boise* and *Phoenix* pushed to within 8,000 yards of the shore while the other warships protected minesweeping operations and watched the skies for air attack. *Boise* launched a pair of SOCs at 0945 to scout enemy gun positions, mines, and submarines, but one landed on the water fifteen minutes later with engine troubles. The Air Force arrived at 1015 for their latest bombing raid on the island and the Bataan port at Mariveles Harbor.[96] The crew was treated to an impressive display of airpower as B-24 Liberators pounded known and suspected enemy positions while A-20 Havocs and P-47 Thunderbolts bombed and strafed targets with impressive dives and gut-wrenching pullouts.[97]

Corregidor, known as "The Rock," was the impressive monolith seated at the mouth of Manila Bay. The outward facing cliffs rose hundreds of feet straight from the ocean. Nearly three years had passed since the Japanese wrestled control of the bastion from General Wainwright and his beleaguered troops. The jungle had reclaimed much of the island and greenery covered the scars caused by Japanese bombs and shells in 1942.

The western portion of the island towered above the water and was known as Topside. It housed the original living space of the U.S. garrison, including barracks, officer's quarters, command buildings, a parade field, a golf course, and the various American gun batteries. The eastern portion descended to a small dock area, the airfield, and the massive Malinta Hill with its significant tunnel complex that previously housed MacArthur, Wainwright, their staff, and a hospital.[98]

Lush tropical plants had also begun to overgrow the numerous American gun emplacements across the island. Those guns sat forever silent since the soldiers destroyed the firing pins before they surrendered. The Japanese had been busy in the intervening years, honeycombing the island with cave systems that linked their artillery positions hidden beneath the canopy.⁹⁹ Those guns and their supporting troops now stood between the U.S. Navy and the desperately needed shipping capacity of Manila Bay.

The fortified positions containing the U.S. Army's guns' remains was each a possible redoubt for the Japanese defenders. The island was a thorn in MacArthur's side because it threatened any shipping into the bay. Corregidor's capture also held moral significance to the general and much of his staff. The official U.S. Army report of the battle said, "Many officers at GHQ SWPA fervently awaited the recapture of 'The Rock' and if it could be done dramatically—by means of a parachute drop, for instance—so much the better." American planners had a hard time determining the strength of the Japanese garrison on the island and arrived at the laughable number of 850 defenders. In reality the invasion force would face over 5,000 Japanese soldiers backed up by two artillery batteries dispersed across the island.¹⁰⁰

The men of *Boise* did their best to whittle away at the defenders. They moved into position along with tin cans *Nicholas* and *Taylor*.¹⁰¹ The guns thundered at 1107 and fired at targets on Corregidor and nearby islands until 1334. They then sailed west to allow the other cruisers to move in and take a turn pummeling the island. American shells tore into the jungle in search of Japanese troops and heavy guns. Admiral Berkey hoped the Japanese would fight back and reveal their positions. They did not take the bait, and Berkey complained, "Juicy targets were placed under the Nip's nose, but he declined to take a crack at them."¹⁰² For the time being the enemy kept their heads down and hid in their caves, saving their strength for the coming battle.

The Task Group retired back to the relatively safe harbor of Subic Bay late in the afternoon. The men knew they were helping clear a stain from the honor of the United States. The highlight of the day was the news that minesweepers had completely cleared areas west of the island, slowly paving the way for the American return.¹⁰³

On Valentine's Day they left Subic Bay well before sunup. The ship played double-duty as a gun platform as well as the Fighter Director responsible for coordinating actions between the surface ships and Army bombers. At 0710 the first waves of fighters in the CAP checked in to keep the skies clear of Japanese, and by 0800 *Boise* was ready to share "love" with the Japanese along the southern side of the island.¹⁰⁴

At 0845 *Boise* engaged a surface ship with all guns near San Jose Point. Their fire was interrupted by Air Force strafing runs, and the ship slipped away in the resulting smoke. *Boise* shifted its guns elsewhere while trying to keep the friendly aircraft out of the impact areas. At 0937 the SOCs observed AA fire near Geary Point. The gunners were unwise enough to fire on the continuous armada of American planes and *Boise* took issue with that. Several rounds from the main and secondary batteries silenced the position, but just as quickly new targets popped up for *Boise*'s attention.¹⁰⁵

The men in the CIC were as busy as ever. Targets came in from the SOCs and orders were issued to the guns. At the same time, they coordinated air strikes to avoid and assist surface actions. Around 1000, they simultaneously engaged enemy guns who were firing on the minesweepers while also coordinating airplanes to lay smoke screens around the vessels. The next hour was a symphony of violence where A-20s swooped in and pumped clouds of smoke, followed immediately by *Boise* firing at the enemy's guns. As the smoke dissipated *Boise* silenced the guns for a few minutes to allow additional smoke screens, just to be followed by additional gunfire. At 1043 another flight of B-24s entered the fray to strike preplanned targets. This sequence continued until 1100 when the guns were either destroyed or their crews retreated to their caves for respite. *Boise* simply moved on to new targets.¹⁰⁶

Boise's turn on the firing line ended at 1200. The ship sailed away to a holding point about ten miles west of the island and went into reserve. The next few hours of the log read like a sports broadcast. Destroyers were sent to sink "floats and buoys" that were interfering with the minesweepers. One destroyer was hit in the forecastle by a shell from Corregidor, so others were pushed close to the island to punish the Japanese. *Boise*'s 20mm gunners sank an oil drum rather than risk the chance it was some sort of improvised explosive. SOCs were recovered and launched again for anti-submarine patrols. Minesweepers took damage and needed to be evacuated from the fighting, all under the cover of additional smoke screens.¹⁰⁷

Breaktime was over at 1445. Admiral Berkey ordered *Boise* to swap positions with *Phoenix* on the north side of the island and recommence bombardment. The men resumed their battle stations. They let the fleet know that the aerial attacks were shifting to Bataan. The ship darted in close to Mariveles on the mainland, but kept their fire focused on the northern shore of Corregidor. Berkey continued to refine the placement of his forces and soon sent *Boise* south while *Montpelier* moved in to continue the attacks on the north side and the mainland.¹⁰⁸

Rear Admiral Russell S. Berkey (with binoculars around his neck) gives orders aboard *Boise* during a bombardment of Corregidor, February 1945. Note anti-flash clothing on some men and the Mk 33 director in background (National Archives: 80-G-259152).

In the midst of the fighting an A-20 performed a crash-landing 2,000 yards off the port bow. It is a testament to the radar operators, CIC, and the AA gunners that no one fired on the crashing plane, despite the lasting nervousness of kamikaze attacks from the weeks prior. The aircrew survived their crash and *Boise* directed *Nicholas* to pick them up. The men of *Taylor* were quicker and had a boat in the water six minutes after the crash. The crew was safely recovered four minutes after that, which almost certainly had to be a record for the shortest amount of time spent in the water by a downed aircrew in World War II.[109]

At 1533 the crew was rewarded in their bombardment efforts when the men on the bridge witnessed a "large fire and explosion in target area." The target was probably an ammunition dump. Before the excitement had a chance to die down, *Boise* was again shuffled to a reserve position while others continued the pressure. The afternoon proved tough on the Americans as the destroyer *Lavallette* (DD-448) struck a mine while approaching Mariveles. The ship sustained heavy damage and casualties, so *Radford* (DD-446) took it under tow, only to strike another mine. With two destroyers hit Berkey had no choice but keep additional destroyers back until minesweepers could clear the area and pull the damaged vessels to safety. While the rescue was underway *Boise* transferred CAP control to *Montpelier* and withdrew with the rest of the cruisers to Subic Bay.[110]

The day was best described as steady. The threats were ever-present and real, and the American military was raining death on the Japanese. Yet, to the men of *Boise*, the death-dealing was routine. DB's entry after the long day was essentially the same as the prior. On the 13th he simply recorded, "Left Subic Bay with TG 77.3. Bombarded Corregidor and Bataan. Returned to Subic Bay and anchored." The 14th he wrote, "Left Subic as before and bombarded Corregidor and Bataan. Returned to Subic."[111] If DB or any other crewmembers still maintained sympathy for their enemy or pondered the impact of their actions, those sentiments were dimming. These warriors were growing increasingly callous, and their humanity was fading.

The 15th was D-Day for operations in Mariveles Harbor on Bataan. *Boise* was second in the line of five light cruisers that left Subic at 0507 while destroyers took their screening positions. Shortly before 0700 the cruisers were ordered to act independently. *Boise* took up position on the northwestern side of Corregidor. Their primary mission was to provide fire support for amphibious landings in Mariveles. The ship stopped and the SOCs were put in the air.[112]

The Japanese took offense and began lobbing shells in their direction. The closest barely got within a mile. Downes had his men hold their fire until the SOCs or another asset could fix the guns' locations. The first American shots of the morning came at 0800 when P-47s arrived and began strafing the harbor. *Phoenix* and some of the destroyers added their shells to the assault when the planes departed, but *Boise* was ordered to limit their fire to counterbattery operations. P-38s attacked at 0900 as the assault craft entered the harbor. *Boise* observed geysers of water from Japanese shells fired from Corregidor. The SOCs were able to locate the guns and Downes let loose with the main and secondary batteries on different targets. The well-placed salvos silenced the Japanese.[113]

At 0925 the ships checked their fire. It was time for other Americans to showcase their destructive power. First came the B-24 heavy bombers who dropped massive amounts of bombs on the town. P-38s hit the northwest tip of Corregidor just after the bombing raid, and before the fighter-bombers were finished the LCIs approaching Mariveles fired swarms of rockets. At 1012 the men of the 151st Regimental Combat Team hit the beach. They encountered little resistance.[114]

8. Liberation

The rest of the morning *Boise* took turns with the B-24s in making sure anything above ground on Corregidor had a limited lifespan. Shortly after, American planes dropped leaflets to the Japanese survivors.[115] The papers extolled Japanese soldiers to surrender. The message was blunt, stating that the Americans "are strong. We are determined," and that "help will not reach you." It is unlikely the appeal worked on many enemy soldiers, and the follow-on attacks by A-20s a mere 20 minutes later may have raised doubts of American sincerity.[116]

By early afternoon, the American commanders were growing frustrated. Despite a near-continuous rain of bombs and shells, the enemy was persisting. At 1225 spotters noted the Heavy Cruiser Unit moving into position to add their 8-inch guns to the fight. The deluge of American firepower grew so intense that *Boise* stopped logging individual attacks from their own weapons or anyone else. They simply wrote, "Note:—From 1400 to 1800 Corregidor was bombed almost continuously by A-20's, P-47's, strafing [sic] and bombing, using fire bombs, para-frags, and skip bombs."[117] The effect was devastating to the landscape and shredded vegetation. The remaining concrete buildings were also punished, along with any position that seemed remotely offensive. Unfortunately, no one could know how many of the enemy had been killed, or how many still huddled in their tunnels and caves. Only the following day could reveal the score.

The naval force withdrew around sunset with high hopes. Tired sailors cleaned weapons, maintained vigilance for enemy subs and aircraft, and readied their stations for the next day's combat. Whenever possible they grabbed hot meals and dropped bone-tired into their racks.

February 16 was D-Day for Corregidor. The small fleet of landing craft waiting in Mariveles Harbor was visited in the night by Japanese suicide boats. The enemy found more success than at Lingayen. They sunk three American landing craft in the assault but sacrificed their entire flotilla of about thirty boats.[118]

At dawn, 200 miles to the south on Mindoro the men of the 503rd PIR stuffed themselves into C-47s. The unit was the only independent airborne regiment in the theater, and despite two combat jumps during the war they were itching for a prominent role in the Luzon campaign. They were dubbed Rock Force and they would try to catch the Japanese defenders by surprise with an audacious and risky drop onto Topside. The available drop zones were on the golf course and parade field, both incredibly small and pockmarked with bomb craters, shell holes, and debris. Rock Force planners believed they would lose 29 percent of the force to jump-related casualties even before the bullets started flying.[119] While the paratroopers dropped, amphibious forces were scheduled to land on the east side of Corregidor.

Boise and the rest of the naval ships were on station west of Corregidor by 0630. They put the SOCs up thirty minutes later and stood by while the heavy cruisers once again pounded the island from their positions to the south. The sun came up at 0725, and a few minutes later *Boise* was asked to help a fellow ship out of a quandary. The destroyer *Claxton* (DD-571) was operating five miles west of La Monja Island. The island was barely a speck of rock and was in the middle of an area previously considered clear of sea-mines. Unfortunately for *Claxton*, regardless of their origin, mines now surrounded them.[120]

Shortly after 0800 the A-20s arrived for one last attack mission before the paratrooper's drop. They worked the island over for nearly twenty minutes. Meanwhile, *Boise* sent one of their SOCs away from the battle to help *Claxton* tiptoe through the new minefield. That crew was much more concerned with the floating explosives than the ongoing invasion. *Boise*'s men were enjoying their front-row seats to history. Their log recorded at 0838 "observed paratroopers landing on Corregidor from C-47's." DB remembered it from the bridge as "0840 Paratroops landed on Corregidor. Really some show."[121]

The drop looked like an airshow to those not involved. Due to the extremely small drop zone, the paratroopers dropped from 400 feet or lower. The small space also meant only six to eight soldiers could jump on any pass, so individual planes had to circle the drop zone multiple times. Two columns of C-47s passed over the island nearly wingtip to wingtip. After they cleared the drop zone, they banked hard away from the island in opposite directions to rejoin the end of their respective column. Above and around the transports zipped fighter and attack planes like sheep dogs ready to pounce on any wolf that threatened their flock. A-20s also pummeled the island's eastern tail in preparation for the amphibious landing. It was "some show" indeed. *Boise* soon recalled their second SOC to hold northwest of the battle lest they attract the ire of an overeager American fighter jock.[122]

An hour after the C-47s arrived they had disgorged their troops and headed back to Mindoro for a second wave. *Boise* recovered their SOCs before moving onto a new mission. They were to take *Taylor* and *O'Bannon* to the north side of the island to cover minesweeping operations. Theirs would be the biggest guns in the area and they were ready to silence any enemy gunners more interested in the minesweepers than the American infantry breathing down their necks. The cruiser was in position by the time the amphibious landings began on Bottomside on the opposite side of the island's tail at 1028.[123] The first four waves landed unopposed, but eventually the enemy woke up and began to resist. Several vehicles were destroyed by mines, but the men of the 34th Infantry Regiment were undeterred and within thirty minutes were standing atop Malinta Hill.[124]

The paratroopers caught the defenders completely by surprise. The first wave secured the drop zone and managed to place a pair of .50 caliber machine guns overlooking the landing beaches on Bottomside.[125] Some paratroopers were pushed off course by strong winds. Several splashed into the warm waters of the harbor and were rescued by PT boats. Others found themselves in unexpected parts of the island. One lucky group missed the drop zone and sailed over the cliffs near Breakwater Point only to drop around the position of Captain Akira Itagaki, the Japanese garrison commander. He had been observing the movement of American landing craft and was apparently oblivious to the danger of paratroopers in the middle of his forces. A brief firefight ensued, and the paratroopers killed Itagaki, depriving the enemy of leadership and their best hopes at a coordinated defense.[126]

The fighting for Topside quickly devolved into small but vicious actions between small groups of soldiers. The second wave of paratroopers began descending under full canopies at 1240. They jumped from lower altitudes and most landed within the secure drop zone before quickly assembling and moving out to find the enemy. Of 2,050 men who made the jump, only 280 men were killed or wounded, far less than planners anticipated.[127] The rest were eager for a fight and began the difficult and deadly task of rooting the Japanese out of their caves.

Boise kept a watchful eye on the northern minesweeping operations. Some brave but foolish Japanese survivors on La Monja Island fired their mortars at the nearby minesweepers. *Taylor* made short work of the threat. At 1440 the battle-hardened sailors dealt with waves of complex emotions when they observed the stars and stripes being raised on the island.[128]

The naval battle for Corregidor was essentially over by that afternoon. Destroyers were called close to shore at times to help seal Japanese soldiers in their caves.[129] *Boise* launched the SOCs once again to help spot for mines, but with paratroopers quickly spreading across the island it was difficult to employ naval gunfire without risking collateral damage unless shore parties were attached to the infantry. The log noted minesweepers calling out machine-gun fire from Japanese caves near the waterline, but there is no record of who silenced them.[130]

Boise remained in the area overnight. The following day they again acted as the fleet's Fighter Director. At 0816 one of the SOCs reported "a man on log in water" 2,500 yards from the ship. Further investigation by the *Abbot* (DD-629) revealed three Japanese men who were inexplicably floating among some debris. PT boats assisted in capturing the men, who were whisked away for interrogation.[131]

Cargo planes began arriving around 0900. They dropped food, water, and ammunition to the Rock Force, but no reinforcements. The commander, Colonel George Jones, had opted to bring his last battalion to the island via landing craft instead of airdrop. Much to the disappointment of those soldiers, they did not get to complete a combat jump, but they still managed to get shot at while approaching the island.[132]

Boise spent the late morning snooping around La Monja at only 1,000 yards. None of the spotters could detect surviving Japanese, so they moved on. In the early afternoon they began receiving calls for fire from shore fire control parties. The targets were small, but the *Boise* gunners were experts at dropping shells exactly where requested. At 1400 they engaged an enemy force of machine guns and mortars. They fired off and on for over thirty minutes, pausing only for C-47s dropping supplies. The eyes on the ground made a world of difference as *Boise* needed only 20 rounds to kill these targets.[133]

At 1725 *Boise* was ordered to depart the area.[134] The men ashore would continue to fight pockets of Japanese soldiers for several days. On the 19th several hundred Japanese soldiers attempted a major counterattack. The fury of their effort drove the Americans from their initial positions on Topside until after dawn when the paratroopers countered and slaughtered the Japanese. When the butcher's bill was tallied there were over 500 enemy dead to thirty Americans killed and seventy-five wounded.[135] Those holed up in the Malinta Tunnel system refused to surrender and the Americans were still deciding how to eliminate them when a massive explosion rocked the hill during the darkest hours of February 21–22. The Japanese had planned to conduct a controlled explosion to start a major counterattack from the tunnels, but something went wrong. Hundreds of the approximately 2,000 soldiers were killed in the blast, but a few hundred survived long enough to be cut down by American infantrymen or escape into the jungle. The blast filled the historic tunnels with rubble that took months to sift through for answers.[136]

On the 23rd the last meaningful fighting on Topside occurred near Wheeler Point, when enemy forces conducted a final banzai charge at the American lines. The next two days saw Rock Force attack across the remainder of the island's tail, killing over half the Japanese with artillery fire and airstrikes until the final troops were literally pushed into the sea to either surrender to the PT boats or suffer the wrath of their machine guns. Finally, on the 26th, the last bastion of enemy forces set off a massive explosion near

Monkey Point that sent debris flying for thousands of yards. The blast killed over 200 Japanese holdouts, but also took 50 American lives and injured another 150.[137]

General MacArthur returned to Corregidor on March 2. He remarked to Colonel Jones, "I see the old flagpole still stands. Have your troops hoist the colors to its peak and let no enemy ever haul them down." Shortly after, Jones saluted sharply and reported, "Sir, I present to you Fortress Corregidor." The general later grandiosely stated, "No soil on Earth is more deeply consecrated to the cause of human liberty than that of the island of Corregidor."[138]

The men of the USS *Boise* were immensely proud of their participation in the battle. They fired almost 1,800 shells and noted with pride that "the results of the shooting were very gratifying." They were particularly proud of a strike on the 14th where they fired on the remains of a building that burned for about ten minutes before exploding into a conflagration lasting two hours. They also noted a "very satisfactory explosion" from a presumed ammunition dump they hit on the 15th near Morrison Point. The final report for the mission remarked almost amusingly at the inconsistency of enemy gunnery. "On several occasions, the splashes were so far from the ships that it was hard to decide at which ship the gun had fired. On other occasions there were no splashes at all."[139]

The crew's reward for their part in the fighting was several days of relaxing duties at Subic Bay. They replenished their stores, especially ammunition. The SOCs occasionally flew in support of mine-clearing operations in Manila Harbor, but the ship remained at rest. On the 25th they joined a group of warships bound for Lingayen Gulf, but after a few days at anchor they returned to Subic.[140]

While *Boise* rested, the war raged. Signs of defeat were everywhere for the remaining Axis powers, but neither the Japanese nor the Germans were willing to admit it. The Marines were waging a battle of pure annihilation against the obstinate Japanese defenders of Iwo Jima. They had stormed ashore just three days after the paratroopers dropped on Corregidor. By the end of the month they were still fighting a fanatic enemy that was determined to fight for every yard until they all died at their posts.[141]

Meanwhile, the Russians were steamrolling the Germans on the Eastern Front. Stalin's armies advanced on a front three hundred miles long. By the end of the month they were threatening Berlin. On the Western Front the Americans had reduced the salient created by the Battle of the Bulge and were pushing on the Rhine. Further north the British and Canadians were sweeping into Denmark.[142] The cracks were definitely showing in parts of the German war machine, but many Nazis and patriotic Germans were still willing to defend their homeland, even while others thought it was simply delaying the inevitable.

March brought more invasions for *Boise*. MacArthur devoted significant resources to clearing the entirety of the Philippines of Japanese troops. Some argued that these efforts were a waste of resources when many of those troops were isolated and posed little to no threat to the Allied war effort, but MacArthur was on a crusade.[143]

DB certainly represented the tired attitudes of much of the crew. His log consisted of only nine entries for March. Each were simple variations of when they left or arrived in Subic Bay and the islands they helped invade.[144] The boredom with such routine was palpable. There was no glory in these operations, and while a few artillery shells were fired at the ship, the enemy's naval and air resistance "was nil."[145] The historical record seems to agree with the sentiment, as there is no ship's log available for that month or the following in the National Archives, only individual mission reports.

8. Liberation

On March 10 *Boise* supported Operation Victor IV, the invasion of Zamboanga.[146] The city lies on a peninsula of the same name in the westernmost part of Mindanao. The operation was preceded by two days of minesweeping and bombardment by *Boise*, the rest of the escorting surface ships, and of course Air Force bombers. Military intelligence had already identified several enemy positions, and the *Boise* log noted several instances of large explosions from main battery fire. On the 9th the ship employed a new weapon of war when ordered to jam enemy radars in the frequency of "600 mcs." The effort helped hide the approach of a fleet of B-24s. Ten minutes into the attack the men on the bridge watched with horror as one of the bombers flew into the stream of bombs from a preceding aircraft. One detonated on contact with the B-24 and nearly obliterated it in a cascading explosion. The crew captured the moment forever in a grainy photograph that displayed a cloud of debris and a smoke trail of the wreckage. Only one of the 10-man crew escaped.[147]

Soldiers from the 41st Infantry Division set out in their landing craft at 0747 and the first men dashed ashore against light resistance at 0915. Intelligence initially estimated around 4,500 defenders in and around the city, but later adjusted that figure to 8,300. Regardless of the actual number, they put up minimal resistance until the next day. Whenever the enemy congregated or offered an enticing target like an artillery piece, *Boise* and *Phoenix* got involved.[148]

By midafternoon on the 12th *Boise* was released from fire support duties at Zamboanga. They departed the area to the north to cover yet another invasion. The operation report praised the performance of the Mark-8 FCR, noting that "it is difficult to imagine conducting a bombardment without its use," and that "the effectiveness of the firing was very satisfactory."[149] While the sailors could leave the area with pride, it took another three weeks of tough fighting before the 41st and Filipino guerrillas managed to defeat major Japanese resistance on the peninsula.[150]

The rest of the month passed quietly for the ship, and official records are sparse. DB simply noted time spent in Subic Bay, and then on the 21st repositioning to Mindoro.[151] Morison noted that *Boise* was part of the bombardment group for the invasion of Cebu on the 26th. The enemy made a unique decision for this point of the war and contested the landings on the beaches with a dense field of landmines and obstacles that the naval shells failed to detonate.[152] For ninety minutes soldiers held their position at the waterline while more troops arrived and crammed into the small safe spaces until safe paths were cleared. Fortunately for those men, the Japanese did not occupy positions close enough to pour fire into the Americans, or Cebu could have been remembered as a major disaster for the U.S. Army. For the rest of the day *Boise* provided unspecified counterbattery fire for the Americal Division's drive into the devastated Cebu City. By the afternoon the task group commander decided further support could be provided by destroyers and released *Boise* back to Subic Bay.[153]

Boise's return to Luzon soon provided a unique opportunity for the men. With Corregidor back in American hands, the way was cleared for American sea power to return to Manila Bay. This meant that Manila itself could again serve as a major supply base for the Allies as they readied for the invasion of the Japanese home islands. Many American fighting men remembered the city fondly from before the war and hoped to visit the "Pearl of the Orient."

DB and his friends got their chance to make memories in early April, although they would prove to be vastly different from the ones they had from 1941. The battle to free Manila from the Japanese had been a monthlong grind that saw American soldiers fighting block by block in a manner rarely seen in the Pacific War. Yamashita had originally ordered his troops to withdraw from the city because he knew it was impossible to hold and the troops assigned there could serve his purposes better helping defend the northern mountains. His deputies ignored that order and instead prepared the city for a defense that would bleed the Americans at every step. They also committed the unforgivable sin of refusing to allow civilians to evacuate the city.

MacArthur had hoped to liberate the city and its people with minimal suffering. He refused to allow aerial bombardment in hopes of sparing civilian lives. The soft-touch approach proved impossible, and after heavy casualties in early fighting MacArthur relented and allowed artillery to be used in the city. The carnage was palpable and many blocks of the city simply ceased to exist. The battle culminated in an apocalyptic fight for the ancient walled city of Intramuros. It was preceded by intense artillery fire and concluded only after the Japanese were ferreted out of buildings, basements, tunnels, and ultimately the remains of Fort Santiago. A few Filipino survivors were rescued from the ruins, all of them traumatized by unspeakable brutality.[154]

Worse than the fighting were the deliberate atrocities conducted by the Japanese defenders. Many of the soldiers chose to inflict unspeakable cruelties on the population in a last orgy of violence that included arson, mass rapes, and mass murders. Over 100,000 Manila civilians died during the battle, and the survivors faced mountains of rubble, no electricity, shortages of food, lack of water, destroyed shelter, and a cityscape that was utterly ruined. Those lucky enough to live through the battle faced the grief and trauma of searching for loved ones, burying mountains of the dead, and processing unspeakable horrors. The overwhelming stench of death and decay permeated the city for weeks.[155]

The Allies quickly jumped into the endless list of actions needed to recover Manila's port, rebuild the city, and provide aid to civilians. In the process, MacArthur insisted that the city remain open for his troops. He wanted them to see the carnage and carry the stories back home. He also wanted them spending money and helping the locals in ways big and small. His insistence led to the proliferation of prostitution and an accompanying rise in venereal disease among Americans and Filipinos alike, but MacArthur felt the benefits outweighed the damage. When asked to close Manila to visiting troops, he replied, "These men have fought their way through the jungles to get to Manila, and now you're asking me to tell them they can't go into Manila. Besides, do you realize the money they bring into town to buy things with, whether it be a bottle of liquor, or a meal, or a souvenir they send home, that is becoming the new economic life blood of Manila? Manila needs it, and these people have been through this war need that kind of help, particularly when it comes willingly. No, I'm not going to put Manila out of bounds to our troops." He even quipped that modern medicine was pretty effective at treating the diseases in question.[156]

The city that DB and his friends knew from the eve of the war was gone. The crew had only a few hours from the time their boats scraped the pier until they needed to return to the ship. DB called it a "sightseeing tour." There was not much left to see. The structures of the Army-Navy club and nearby Intramuros were in ruins. It is likely that even the Whoopee Cabaret was now smoldering rubble. The Manila Hotel that MacArthur called home with his family before the war was a skeleton with pockmarked bullet holes and shrapnel. DB simply wrote, "there isn't much left of the city."[157] The men saw what they could and many certainly imbibed in the pleasures they could find. DB collected a handful of the now-worthless occupation currency that the Japanese issued for his souvenir stash. Yet it was obvious to all of one's senses that the Filipino people had suffered severely under the thumb of their occupiers, and few ever saw the benefits of the Greater East Asia Prosperity Sphere. The people of Manila suffered more than most. The quick trip inflamed the crew's hatred of the Japanese, and the results of the wanton violence hardened many hearts on that April day. They may have been tired from the continuous stream of invasions and bombardments, but deep down they were more resolved than ever to help usher in the final defeat of the Japanese Empire.

9

The Long Way Home

Borneo and Operation Magic Carpet

War weariness was palpable aboard *Boise* in April 1945. The crew had been fighting for months and had not seen America since December 1943. The kamikaze attacks had dried up, but every day at sea held the risk of death by submarine attack, submerged mines, foul weather, hidden reefs, or even a lucky enemy shot. Many dreaded the climactic battle they were certain to support in the coming months.

April allowed the men a little respite. Official records are sparse, but DB recorded their movements after Manila. The ship stopped briefly in Subic and then again at Leyte before sailing alone to Seeadler.[1] April 12–15 the ship was loaded into the USS *Advance Base Sectional Dock-4* (ABSD-4). The ABSD-4 was a marvel of modern engineering. It was a seven-section floating dry dock that could lift fifty-six thousand tons from the water for hull repairs. A small army of mechanics, welders, painters, and others worked three shifts to continue repair operations twenty-four hours a day, seven days a week. *Boise* was a simple job and received "routine underwater inspection and painting." Some of the cruiser's older hands certainly wondered how their war may have changed if such a facility was available in 1942 when they were forced to do their own repairs in Bombay.[2]

DB crossed paths with another old friend, Stan Beau. The pleasant distraction was soured when the crew received news of Franklin Roosevelt's death.[3] The president had led the United States for so long many of the sailors had no practical recollection of any other American leader. He had led the country through the darkest days of the Great Depression and World War II, only to die with victory on the horizon.

Boise left Seeadler on the 16th bound for Leyte. The ship's lucky star guided them as before. Less than two weeks after they left dry-dock, a rare Japanese raid managed to hit the ABSD-4 with a torpedo. The vessel's remarkable engineering and fast-acting sailors limited the damage and even protected the three ships within from any damage. The vessel only needed nine days to repair their own damage before they were back at full capacity.[4]

On the 24th, the *Boise* rejoined Berkey's unit and readied themselves for the invasion of Borneo.[5] The entire operation was of dubious strategic value, but MacArthur pushed for it. The Australians wanted to liberate thousands of their POWs held in ever-worsening conditions in labor camps on the island. They also wanted a larger role in the war. The British and Dutch governments wanted to assist to start reclaiming their colonies, but the British Navy had little desire to take part in the operation. They were more concerned with supporting operations in Okinawa and the upcoming invasion of Kyushu in the home islands and believed Borneo was too distant from those theaters.[6]

What the *Boise* crew knew was they had the opportunity to kill more Japanese, and right then that was what mattered to them. The crew manned their watches and conducted drills. The log noted one instance of General Quarters for a possible air attack, but the near constant combat air patrols kept stray enemy aircraft at bay.[7]

Late on the 26th the TG came across more macabre signs that they were approaching the enemy. At 1609 the *Nicholas* came across a small craft with two Japanese men. As the destroyer moved to intercept the vessel the two inhabitants "committed suicide by blowing themselves up." Sixteen minutes later *Taylor* came across "4 small boats filled with Japanese" and managed to take five prisoners who were transferred to *Boise*. There were apparently additional Japanese in the area who were killed when the CAP strafed them.[8]

The next several days were spent supporting painstaking mine-clearing operations. *Boise* snagged a few with their paravanes, but mostly they were on standby. On the 30th they provided overwatch for Australian troops landing on the small island of Sadau, but the big show came the next day.[9] Unbeknownst to the fighting men, Adolf Hitler committed suicide around the same time the men ate their dinner.[10] The war in Europe was ending, but the fight for the Pacific continued.

Tuesday, May 1, was P-Day for Operation Oboe 1, the invasion of Tarakan Island on the northeast coast of Borneo. The 26th Brigade Group from the Australian 9th Infantry Division rode predominantly American landing craft to the beaches, and shortly before sunrise were greeted by a handful of enemy torpedoes. Shortly after a Japanese submarine was spotted. The deadly fish failed to hit anything, and the landings continued while the small sub managed to sneak away. At 0729 *Boise* opened up on preplanned targets. Their impressive rate of fire averaged 12.5 shells every minute, despite a tricky current that DB fought at the helm to keep the ship steady.[11]

Beyond the beaches the oil fields burned brightly, filling patches of sky with thick, black smoke.[12] The first troops ashore remarked that "the beach appeared to be an inferno and was continually aflame from the crimson flashes of bursting bombs and shells." The worst foe the Australians met on the first day was mud, up to three feet deep on some landing areas. The Diggers quickly advanced through their objectives and by nightfall commanded a landing zone 2,800 yards wide by 2,000 deep with fewer than a dozen casualties.[13]

Oboe I continued without any significant participation from the *Boise*. The SOCs helped scout for enemy positions and mines. The only significant enemy resistance directed towards the Navy came on the 2nd when a handful of hidden artillery pieces fired on the minesweepers. Their fire was deadly accurate and sunk one minesweeper and left two more burning. The survivors called for immediate assistance, and Allied fighter-bombers pounced on the guns before *Boise* could get into range. Nearby LCS ships also added their firepower to the response along with the tin can *Cofer* (DE-208). The response was enough to silence the guns for the day, but the position remained a threat for nearly a month.[14]

The following day the ship set sail to return to the Philippines. *Boise* welcomed seventy-five sailors from the *Jenkins* who were hitching a ride back to Subic after their ship was damaged by a mine during the operation. The ship linked up with *Phoenix* and bid adieu to the Australians at 1300.[15]

The rest of May was as quiet as April. The war in Europe officially ended on the 8th, but if *Boise* celebrated there is no record. Many of the men were veterans of that theater thanks to their work in Sicily and Italy, but the end of the fighting there did not change their prospects in the Pacific. DB did not bother to record anything that day, but since the ship was anchored in Subic Bay it is possible he and his comrades went ashore in search of a drink to celebrate.

On the 12th Admiral Berkey came aboard to conduct the ship's annual Military Evaluation. The men certainly grumbled about the need for an inspection while serving in a war zone, but by this point in the war military procedures were again being adhered to. The crew called what they perceived as unnecessary and senseless duties "chickenshit."[16] Berkey arrived at 0828 and spent half an hour inspecting the personnel. The ship then got underway and was tasked to defend against a simulated air attack. The highly proficient gunners proved "very accurate" and knocked down every target offered. After that came the "battle problem" where the ship tracked the *Taylor* and simulated engaging the enemy with the main guns. Finally, the ship tackled the "damage control problem" and simulated handling the ship after receiving two hits by 6-inch shells. While managing the problem, the evaluators added in a simulated kamikaze attack that forced ship operations to move from the bridge to an alternate location. The exercise was a breeze for the veteran crew, and the evaluation team declared *Boise* "handled all problems very well." They returned to port and the admiral departed by 1330.[17] It is unknown if he had forgiven the men for his missing turkeys, but he at least did not apply any grudge to the evaluation.

On the 29th, Admiral Berkey returned to the ship. This occasion was much more positive. The crew assembled on the aft deck under the hot sun in their best uniforms. Berkey proceeded to award medals to the officers and crew for their actions at Surigao Strait and Lingayen Gulf.[18] While certainly appreciated, what the men really wanted was a trip home.

Their desire to see home again would be granted soon, but MacArthur called on the *Boise* first. The general had been informed he would be commanding all ground forces during Operation Olympic. It was the first phase of the broader Operation Downfall, the conquest of Japan that would also be led by MacArthur.[19] He would have to depart the Philippines to take charge of the planning, but before leaving he wanted to tour his beloved islands once more and visit the troops across the theater.

He came aboard on June 3 at Manila along with an impressive entourage. Lieutenant General Eichelberger, 8th Army Commander, was the highest-ranking until General George Kenney, Commander of the Far East Air Forces, joined a few days later. Two other brigadier generals, two colonels, three additional officers, and eight enlisted troops crammed into *Boise*'s extra spaces. MacArthur also traveled with five journalists to ensure his exploits were properly distributed to the folks back home. MacArthur himself gave the order to depart Manila Harbor at 1811.[20]

DB kept the itinerary in his journal. His description of MacArthur's journey could easily be mistaken for a modern band tour listed on a T-shirt:

June 3

General MacArthur and staff came aboard. Underway at 1800 to take the General on a tour of the Philippines. At following places are date indicated:

June 4 San Jose, Mindoro Is.
5 Cagayan Bay, Mindanao
6 Cebu, Cebu Is.
7 Iloilo, Panay Is
8 Puerto Princesa, Palawan

9 Joined invasion force.
10 Landed troops at Brunei Bay, Borneo. After bombarding beach.
12 Left Brunei Bay
12 Arrived at Jolo Island.
13 Arrived at Davao, Mindanao
14 Arrived at Zamboanga.
15 Arrived at Manila MacArthur left ship.[21]

At each stop the general and his staff would depart the ship in the morning to tour the battlefields. At the first stop in Mindanao the general drove 120 miles by jeep to observe fighting on the front lines. On Cebu he toured the recently cleared Japanese caves where the enemy held out to the end. On Palawan he visited the block houses where 139 U.S. Marines were tortured and killed before U.S. forces could rescue them. Each stop connected the general to his troops, and the stories made their way back to *Boise* before departing each afternoon.[22]

The tour and the accompanying invasion were almost like a pleasure cruise for MacArthur. He wrote years later, "I can still taste those chocolate ice cream sodas the Navy stewards served me and remember the movie shows each night." He marveled at the peacefulness of operating in waters that were essentially an American-owned lake. The enemy no longer had any means to resist, a marked contrast to his last journey to Lingayen.[23]

On the morning of the 10th *Boise* was in position to cover the second phase of the Borneo landings. The target was the oil-rich Brunei Bay, a Sultanate formerly under British protection. Two landings were scheduled for that morning and *Boise* was covering those going ashore on Labuan Island.[24] The crew manned their battle stations before sunrise. At 0655 a single enemy bomber dropped a stick of bombs near the transports about 8,000 yards from *Boise*. The pilot was clearly braver than skilled and the bombs failed to hit anything.[25]

This time the men had the opportunity to show off their offensive capabilities to MacArthur. At 0727 the SOCs were hoisted out and took to the air. At 0805 the main batteries and starboard secondaries fired on their assigned targets in Victoria Town and Ramsey Point. The rapid fire of the guns showcased the crew's prowess for an hour until an untimely glitch took the rear half of the ship out of action. The No. 4 main generator tripped offline causing the aft sections to go dark. Turrets 4 and 5 along with 5-inch batteries 5 and 7 lost power. The FH radar went offline as well as all the gyro compass equipment. The veteran crew did not miss a beat and electricians had power restored in less than a minute.[26] The incident was a chance to show off their ability to solve problems and stay in the fight. Joseph Fenton remarked, "we were so darned good because we trained, trained, trained! They could do their job standing on their heads!"[27]

With power restored, they shifted to targets further inland. *Boise* fired 1,803 rounds and outpaced their incredible rate of fire from the previous month. In one twenty-one-minute period they averaged nearly twenty-four shells per minute![28] This was just an example of what a professional crew of warfighters could accomplish after three and a half years of war.

Two PT boats came alongside thirty minutes later. Much to his glee, MacArthur was going ashore amid the assault landings by the remaining two brigades of the Australian 9th Infantry Division. By the time MacArthur made it ashore, the first tanks were arriving and driving into the interior. The most excitement of the morning came when two Japanese soldiers hiding in a culvert along the general's route of travel were discovered shortly before his arrival.[29]

While the boss was away the ship continued the mundane tasks required of a warship. They recovered, refueled, and launched the SOCs. Additional dignitaries were piped aboard, only to depart shortly after to chase down MacArthur on the beaches. They sidled up to the *Winooski* (AO-38) and took on fuel oil. MacArthur was back aboard by 1430 to help welcome survivors of the USS *Salute* (AM-294). Their minesweeper had been sunk two days before and they would begin their journey home or to new assignments via *Boise*.[30]

The next day MacArthur made another trip ashore with the top brass. He returned in time to witness Admiral Berkey award Captain Downes a Gold Star for his Legion of Merit. Pictures show Downes smiling while MacArthur pumps his hand and grips his shoulder with a proud, fatherly expression on his face. By early afternoon they weighed anchor and departed the area for the Philippines.[31]

The remainder of the tour was of little consequence to the *Boise*. MacArthur came and went from the ship each day until the crew bid him farewell in Manila Harbor on June 15, 1945. There was no fanfare, but MacArthur passed his "heartiest congratulations for the flawless performance of the difficult and dangerous mission assigned…."[32] When considered against some of *Boise*'s earlier exploits this mission had been a cakewalk, but everyone still appreciated his praise. What they appreciated even more was that they were finally cleared to start the long voyage home.

They left Manila on the 16th. Two days later they stopped briefly at Leyte to refuel.[33] Even after so many years of war, DB could not stop marveling at the sight of America's sea power. At Leyte he recorded "Task Force 58" in port consisting of "4 S.D. class BB's, 3 Iowa class BB's, 1 Alaska class C.B., 8 Essex class CV's, 6 small CV's, 18 CL's and CA's plus DD's," and "3 old BB's."[34] He was right to be impressed. The forces gathering around the world for the final hammer blow against Japan were nearly incomprehensible compared to those available in 1941.

Boise wasted no time and by early afternoon was pointed towards Pearl Harbor. They were alone and unafraid. They ran up the engines in a fashion not typically seen during their months of escort duty, hitting 20 knots before slowing to 16 before sunset. During the evening of the 20th they passed near Ulithi. Their simple duties and contemplations of home were rudely interrupted when they were informed enemy subs were still active and sunk two ships that night. The following day their progress was slowed by employing zigzag patterns along their course. Two days later Downes authorized 20 knots again to "expedite clearing submarine infested waters."[35]

On the 26th the crew watched a partial lunar eclipse. It must have been a relief to look to the skies with interest rather than dread. Twenty-four hours later the ship crossed the International Date Line and experienced "two Tuesdays" according to DB. *Boise* approached Hawaii on the 28th while witnessing the steady flow of combat ships bound for the Pacific War. The following morning they arrived at Pearl Harbor for a quick fuel stop.[36]

It took another week for *Boise* to reach Los Angeles and several hard hours of work unloading the last of the ship's ammunition. On the 8th the ship moved into dry-dock for forty-seven days of long overdue repairs and upgrades.[37] The entire gamut of American equipment and expertise was on hand to prepare the ship for the final phase of the war.

9. The Long Way Home

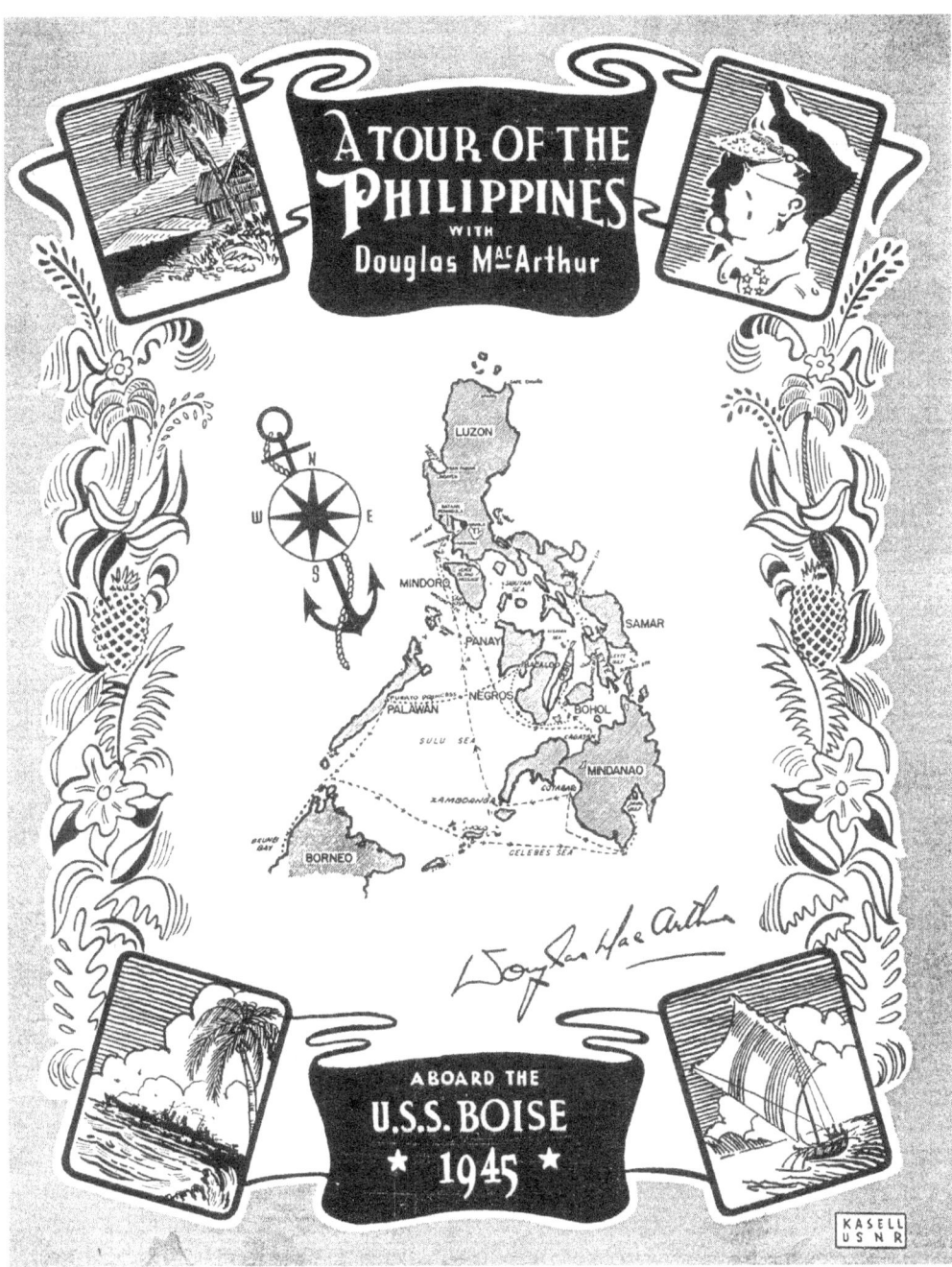

This map was drawn by a crewmember named Kasell for a *Boise* reunion. It shows the route traveled while the *Boise* served as MacArthur's flagship late in the war (Fitch Family Private Collection).

The men also received a well-earned break. DB departed before the ammunition was even offloaded. He traveled back to Salt Lake City and did his best to enjoy twenty days of leave.[38] He left no record from the trip, but it is likely he tried to forget the war by spending time fishing and drinking. The year and a half spent in the Southwest Pacific exposed him to different traumas than previous *Boise* deployments. The ship amazingly avoided nearly all threats, but they were exposed to long periods of exhausting readiness and combat. They dodged submarines, bombs, kamikazes, and enemy gunfire. They sailed through storms and DB had the added stress of driving a 10,000-ton warship through poorly charted waters. On top of processing or trying to forget the past, contemplations of the upcoming invasion invaded his quieter moments.

In August 1945, the war was winding down in scale but was still as bloody as ever. The U.S. Army units that *Boise* supported in the Philippines had chased the surviving Japanese forces into the mountains of eastern Luzon. On Okinawa, Marine and Army divisions were licking their wounds and readying for the largest amphibious operation in history. Other divisions trained in Hawaii and around the Pacific, and combat units from Europe prepared to swap the Nazi enemy for the Japanese.[39]

Preparations were also underway for Operation Downfall. MacArthur planned to land 436,486 troops under Krueger's expanded 6th Army on Kyushu in November.[40] Eichelberger would follow-up in March 1946 with the invasion of the Kanto Plane along with General Courtney Hodges' 1st Army coming from Europe. Admiral Nimitz would support the operations with the largest fleet the world had ever seen. The armada would consist of three thousand ships. Among those would be twenty-two battleships, sixty-three aircraft carriers, and fifty cruisers.[41] *Boise* was readying to join that fleet.

Before the invasion, Japanese cities were scheduled for near-continuous bombing by Air Force B-29s. In August they used a new weapon of unimaginable power. On the 6th, the *Enola Gay* dropped a single atomic bomb on Hiroshima. Despite the destruction of the city from a single weapon, the Japanese government persisted, with a significant segment of military and civilian leaders willing to continue the war.[42]

Just two days later the Soviet Union fulfilled their promise to declare war on Japan. They poured across the border into northern China with 1.6 million troops.[43] The troops were veterans of the brutal fighting on the European Eastern Front and mechanized in a manner inconceivable to the Japanese soldiers in their path. Many were killed and hundreds of thousands were taken prisoner to linger in Siberian labor camps for years. At the same time the Soviet troops unleashed atrocities of murder, theft, and rape that rivaled their horrific exploits in Germany a few months prior.[44]

While the Soviets invaded, the Americans readied another terrible blow to the Japanese homeland. On the 9th, *Bockscar* dropped a second atomic bomb on Nagasaki. The two nuclear attacks killed over 100,000 people instantly or shortly after the blasts; some were simply incinerated. At least another 100,000 people died slowly from the effects of the bombs, including from horrible radiation poisoning.[45]

Historians continue to debate the exact reason the Japanese government surrendered, but the nuclear weapons were certainly a factor. The home islands were also being starved of resources thanks to years of Allied submarine attacks that devastated Japanese shipping and Air Force bombings that decimated manufacturing. The Soviet invasion along with the pending American-led invasion of the home islands also contributed. Regardless of the specific reason, Emperor Hirohito surrendered with the only qualification that he be allowed to remain in his position as the symbolic head of the Japanese people. The Allies accepted the surrender on August 12.[46] The war was over.

While the world celebrated the end of the war, the crew of the *Boise* continued their efforts to refit their ship. DB's log was quiet throughout August and his immediate thoughts on victory and peace are lost to history. The ship's log is similarly quiet.

However, photos from around Los Angeles that joyous day are considerably more insightful. Soldiers and sailors danced, drank, and cavorted with local women in the streets. Military vehicles paraded through the streets loaded down with amorous couples kissing and laughing on hoods or grasping onto tailgates and each other. Confetti rained and flags waved. Bands and amateur musicians created a triumphant and chaotic atmosphere for the revelers that shut down traffic. *Boise* men who were allowed passes certainly joined in the festivities wherever they could, dropping their guards in a raging river of conflicting emotions ranging from grief to pure elation.[47]

At the end of the month *Boise* said goodbye to Captain Downes and welcomed Captain C.C. Hartman as their new skipper.[48] On the other side of the world efforts were underway to liberate Allied POW camps throughout Asia and inform far-flung Japanese troops that the war was over.[49] On September 2 General MacArthur accepted the formal Japanese surrender in Tokyo Harbor aboard the battleship *Missouri*. The officer who received the Japanese delegation was none other than *Boise*'s former assistant navigator, James Starnes. He played a role in awing the defeated enemy, and for the official party he "had my side boys, four on each side, and I picked out ones at least six feet tall, to give some dominance feeling."[50]

MacArthur was surrounded by some of the most notable leaders of the war, including Admirals Nimitz and Halsey. Generals Krueger and Eichelberger also attended, along with the newly liberated General Wainwright. The event was also attended by hundreds of Allied ships that filled the harbor, and at the conclusion of the ceremony hundreds of B-29s and Navy fighters conducted a thirty-minute flyover.[51]

Boise spent the first few weeks of the month in dry-dock. On the 12th, the ship slipped back into the water where it belonged and began loading ammunition. The war may have been over, but the ship must still be ready when called. The crew spent the rest of the month training new and old crewmen alike to operate the ship's systems at the high level of expertise they had known just a few months prior. By the end of the month the ship was finished with their training, exercises, and final inspection and awaiting assignment in San Pedro, California. DB only noted that they completed a "10 day shake down" cruise, as such training was likely dull, repetitive, and hardly of note to a veteran such as himself.[52]

They did not wait long for orders. On October 3 they sailed again on another grand adventure. They were not being asked to brave submarine-infested waters or face enemy guns. This time they were bound for New York City to take part in a grand victory celebration. They would then report to the Atlantic Fleet. Five destroyers joined them as they set sail for the Panama Canal.[53]

The trip south was filled with daily drills. The captain conducted several inspections of the ship's living spaces. With the men's proven ability to hide contraband as large as turkeys, it is unlikely the new skipper found anything inappropriate or out of order. On the 11th they arrived at Balboa and tied up in the harbor. The next morning *Boise* greeted the most notable ship from the recent Japanese surrender when the *Missouri* tied up next to them. The battleship stayed only a night, but it is likely that some of the men from both ships mingled and shared drinks in the balmy Panamanian evening.[54]

The next day *Boise* got a taste of their future missions. They welcomed aboard 6 officers and 436 enlisted soldiers who were eager to hitch a ride home.[55] Their transport was a small part of Operation Magic Carpet, what the National World War II Museum described as "the largest combined air and sealift ever organized."⁵⁶ While occupation forces would remain for years in many places around the world, there was a rush to demobilize the United States military and quickly bring service members home.

They passed through the Panama Canal on the 14th, rejoined their destroyer escort, and continued to New York. It took six days to sail across the Caribbean and up the East Coast before docking in New York City. En route, they received orders to report to the Navy Yard "for the purpose of installing standee bunks and other facilities." The ship was officially transitioning from a warship to a transport.⁵⁷

Boise received celebrity status when they arrived in New York Harbor. One source claimed "reporters rented two tugboats to guide the ship in." Not to be outdone, the *New York Daily News* rented a plane to take aerial photos of the ship.⁵⁸

Navy celebration events kicked off on the 21st. The ship opened for public visits from 1000 to 1130 and 1300–1630 for four days. Each day civilians scrambled aboard and got to see the "Noisy Boise" firsthand while talking with the veterans.⁵⁹ Undoubtedly many of the crew tried to arrange future meetings with some of the female guests. The ship repositioned on the 25th in preparation for the upcoming Presidential Review. The crew cleaned, scrubbed, and shined an already sparkling ship to prepare for their Commander in Chief.

The crew lined the decks as USS *Boise* pulled into New York Harbor for Navy Day in October 1945. In another copy of this photograph, DB had circled the individual on the top deck just left of the "scoreboard," claiming, "That's me!" (Fitch Family Private Collection).

9. The Long Way Home

The 27th was Navy Day. President Harry S. Truman gave a speech in Central Park praising the assembled ships and all veterans. He declared that they had "won the greatest naval victories in history," and urged people to visit the ships and speak with the sailors. He also told the assembled New Yorkers "battleships and cruisers ... swept the enemy ships from the seas and bombarded their shore defense almost at will," something that DB and his friends were proudly aware of.[60] The president then moved to the destroyer *Renshaw* (DD-499) where he reviewed the parade of American sea power. *Boise* joined forty-seven warships including heavyweights *Missouri* and the carrier *Enterprise* for the procession up the Hudson River attended by up to five million people lining the riverbanks, all while 1,200 Navy aircraft flew circles over the fleet.[61] One attendee remembered it as "the most spectacular home front display of American military might the nation had ever seen."[62] For decades the *Boise* men proudly recounted a quote attributed to *Time* magazine: "The ship they were waiting for came in and you could almost hear the sighs of thousands as she nosed past the Battery in New York Harbor toward her pier in the North River. Some said that the fleet had arrived when *Boise* rode by, the sun playing on her metal and the welcome of thousands in her ears."[63] *Boise* was finally being recognized as one of the finest warships of the war.

After Navy Day *Boise* docked for a few more days of tours with the public. On the 30th they moved into the Navy Yard and moored at Pier George, Berth 14. They underwent fifteen days of modifications to ready the ship for Magic Carpet. The following day, they left their last official entry. "This is the last War Diary to be submitted by this command as provided for in Cominch Restricted Letter FF1/A12–1, Serial 7425, dated 18 September 1945." The war was over. The requirement to log ship actions was over. But the missions continued.[64]

Without official records the rest of *Boise*'s story is remembered through DB and his comrades. He finished up the training course required for promotion to the next rate on the 11th, proving he did more than just drink while the ship was in port.[65] DB wrote that the ship left the Brooklyn Navy Yard on November 15 "for Plymouth England with 500 soldiers." Fresh American troops were still needed around the world for occupation duty even as combat veterans returned home. They arrived in England on the 22nd and stayed a single night before continuing to Le Havre, France. On the 25th they set sail for the United States with twelve hundred passengers.[66]

American commitment to "bringing the boys home" was massive. The commander of naval forces in Europe noted sixteen ships dedicated to the mission. Eight of those were aircraft carriers of various sizes, and *Boise* was joined by *Savannah* and *Philadelphia* to show the world the versatility of the *Brooklyn*-class cruisers at least one more time. All the ships except for a few carriers were expected to make four round trips by the end of January.[67] On top of this effort, over seven hundred additional ships of various types and nationalities participated in transporting millions of fighting men and women, civilians, and even "war brides" who had married Americans back to the United States. Some ships carried passengers both ways, returning repatriated POWs held in America.[68]

Boise issued a booklet to each of the passengers. It told the history of the ship while also setting expectations and giving instructions. Captain Hartman emphasized that the men needed to conserve fresh water, many ship spaces were off limits, and the soldiers must keep their spaces clean. In exchange for a lack of comfort amenities he highlighted that *Boise* was considerably faster than other Magic Carpet participants. Mess times were clearly stated, and soldiers were reminded not to take food or items from the mess hall. In other words, souvenir hunting was off limits. The soldiers were also forbidden from drinking liquor, interfering with crewmembers, possessing firearms, or gambling. These were imposed to maintain harmony among the soldiers and sailors, but it

U.S. Army Private First Class Felix A. Uva (left) and Corporal Donald A. Purdy examine a memorial plaque on the cruiser's main deck, while they were being transported to the United States from Europe as part of Operation Magic Carpet in November 1945. This plaque was presented to the ship by the citizens of Boise, Idaho, in memory of the 107 crewmembers who lost their lives in the Battle of Cape Esperance (National Archives: 80-G-701627).

is likely that at least the final rule was disregarded. Finally, male and female passengers were not permitted in each other's berthing areas, lest someone get a head start on the baby boom.[69]

The soldiers disembarked upon arrival in New York Harbor on December 1, excited to process out of the Army and make it to their homes before the holidays. Indeed, one of the themes for Magic Carpet was "Home Alive By '45," where the public was clamoring for troops to return by Christmas.[70]

DB also made it home for Christmas during his thirty-six days of leave. He did not record his activities, but he may have taken the time to visit friends around the country before landing in Utah. While away he missed *Boise*'s last trips to Europe. He was probably happy to let someone else drive the ship for a while. He returned to the ship on January 6, eager to end his own service but still owed six months on his 1944 contract extension. The pain from continued service was salved, though, as he was promoted to Quartermaster Second Class on New Year's Day.[71]

Boise left New York on January 15 for the short trip to Philadelphia. They arrived the next day and DB left no record of his or the ship's activities for the next several months until he wrapped up both of their stories. He wrote on May 1, "Put Boise in reserve." He left out what was certainly dull duty for the quartermaster of a ship continuously in port and his trips to local jazz clubs for dancing, drinking, and general carousing. DB left *Boise* for the last time on June 20. He was discharged from the Navy at Lido Beach in New York on the 23rd and somehow made it home to Salt Lake City the following day. He had $1,000 in his pocket and big dreams of making his way in peacetime America. His last entry was simple but held significant patriotic overtones when he wrote on the Fourth of July "Boise in decommission."[72] It was a very fitting way to mark the end of DB's war.

Epilogue

With the war over the crew of the *Boise* quickly went their separate ways. Many found their way back to hometowns and tried to make their way in a civilian world that was rapidly adjusting. Millions of veterans were looking for jobs, even as the wartime industries drew down. Some of the men certainly got caught up in the nationwide housing crisis and were forced to move back in with family members or find space in barns, sheds, or even tents.[1] A few continued careers in the Navy. Others leaned on the generosity of family, friends, and veteran connections to build their lives. The camaraderie that they had built on the ship took a back seat to life, but the fire of connection still burned for many of them, and some managed to stay in touch through letters and occasional phone calls.

Peace brought about elucidation of many of the war's battles. Allied officers conducted hundreds of interviews with their recent enemies. They also dug through surviving official records and reports. For *Boise* that meant increased clarification of their battle off Guadalcanal. Japanese reports adjusted what Americans thought they knew about that night, leading to a slight revision to *Boise*'s record. Captain Hartman's guide to the Magic Carpet passengers in late 1945 reflected this. He explained the ship's history and noted during the battle they were "credited with sinking or assisting in sinking one cruiser and two destroyers of the Japanese Navy."[2] The correction in no way took away from the crew's heroic actions that night.

The proud *Boise* spent several years languishing at anchor as part of the 16th Reserve Fleet.[3] The salt water, weather, time, and lack of upkeep slowly deteriorated the ship. In 1951 the Argentinian navy purchased the cruiser along with sister ship *Phoenix*. *Boise* was renamed the *Nueve de Julio* in honor of Argentina's independence day, and *Phoenix* became the *General Belgrano*.[4]

The *Nueve de Julio* took part in the Revolución Libertadora, the Argentine coup d'état where a military junta overthrew the government. On September 19, 1955, the ship was dispatched to attack the oil tanks at Mar del Plata. The guns roared in anger for the first time in a decade and proved just as destructive as they had been in Sicily, New Guinea, and the Philippines. The crew destroyed nine out of eleven oil tanks. The attacks were accompanied by a rebel message to President Peron demanding his surrender lest follow-on attacks focus on the capital. The nation's leader soon acquiesced, as the ship's attack foreshadowed the horrors a civil war would unleash on the country.[5]

Sadly, by the 1970s the ship was again sitting tied up to a pier, slowly succumbing to the elements.[6] The ship's honor was besmirched in the worst possible way when it was used in 1976 as a location for the Argentinian government to commit atrocities against its citizens as part of their "Dirty War." The conflict saw thousands of people "disappeared" because of real or imagined ties to anti-government terrorist forces.[7]

The ship was decommissioned and sold to an American company for scrap. The ship sailed one last time into U.S. waters before settling in Brownsville, Texas. The Manchester Sling Company cut it apart for scrap metal. Thankfully, they preserved sections of the main deck planks. Those pieces were "suitably engraved" and were given to men who served onboard *Boise* when it was commissioned. The men who attended the 1981 reunion took the final loss of their ship with grace and humor, suggesting "who knows, maybe your next shave will be with Boise steel or your next automobile may contain some of her armor!"[8] A local Brownsville paper ran a center-spread story about the *Boise* when it arrived. Pictures showcased the still-proud guns pointed slightly to the sky, as if they only needed an order from a long-gone captain to again engage America's enemies.[9]

That is not the final chapter of *Boise*'s story. A few pieces of the ship remain and are on display with the Idaho Military History Museum in Boise. Visitors can see the original ship's bell, a range indicator from the 1942 FCR, and a U.S. Navy Mark I Deck Clock that still has pieces of embedded shrapnel from a Japanese shell. They can also see a piece of armor from the ship's bridge that proudly displays the six Japanese ships that *Boise* claimed as sunk at the Battle of Cape Esperance.[10]

The U.S. Navy bestowed the proud *Boise* name on a new ship in 1990. On October 20, the nation christened the USS *Boise* (SSN-764), the latest *Los Angeles*-class of attack submarine. DB learned about the new ship in 1989 and told fellow veterans that they "should start *MAINLINING* that Geritol and Vitamin C so we will still be around and healthy...."[11] Along with some World War II crewmembers, Alice Salone Clark Springer was invited to attend the ceremony, just like she had in 1936 when she christened the cruiser.[12] The submarine was designed to echo its namesake with the ability to seek out America's enemies and destroy them if necessary. The new *Boise* had the munitions and training to both protect the fleet, attack the enemy ashore with cruise missiles, or even hunt enemy ships with its torpedoes.[13] DB was present for the christening and said simply "it was great, very moving," and "I'm just proud to be here."[14]

The last note from the ship's story is one of redemption, a constant theme of the mighty ship. In 2015, the Argentinian government tried hundreds of Dirty War perpetrators for their atrocities. Survivors and families had waited decades for justice. Finally, twenty-two officials, including naval officers, were convicted of various charges including "unlawful deprivation of liberty," "torments," "torture," and "homicide." All the men were imprisoned, most of them for life.[15] In this manner, the best of humanity helped remove the only truly black mark from the record, the decks, and the very soul of the USS *Boise*.

The *Brooklyn*-class cruisers served honorably throughout the war. They served in every naval theater and proved that light cruisers possessed incredible versatility. The rapid-fire guns were a solid investment, and the ships fought America's enemies in every conceivable type of mission. They guided convoys, engaged enemy fleets, bombarded shores, and battled fleets of enemy aircraft. They repeatedly proved that they could take a hard blow from the enemy, survive, and return to the fight. It is hard to find any major engagement during the war that did not involve a *Brooklyn*.

Many *Boise* sailors continued to find success in their Navy careers. Captain Moran was promoted to Commodore, commanding Motor Torpedo Boat Squadrons in the ongoing battles for the Solomon Islands. After the fighting died down, he was assigned as the Commander Naval Forces, Northern Solomons, for the remainder of the war. He was promoted to Rear Admiral in 1947 shortly before he retired. He was an active

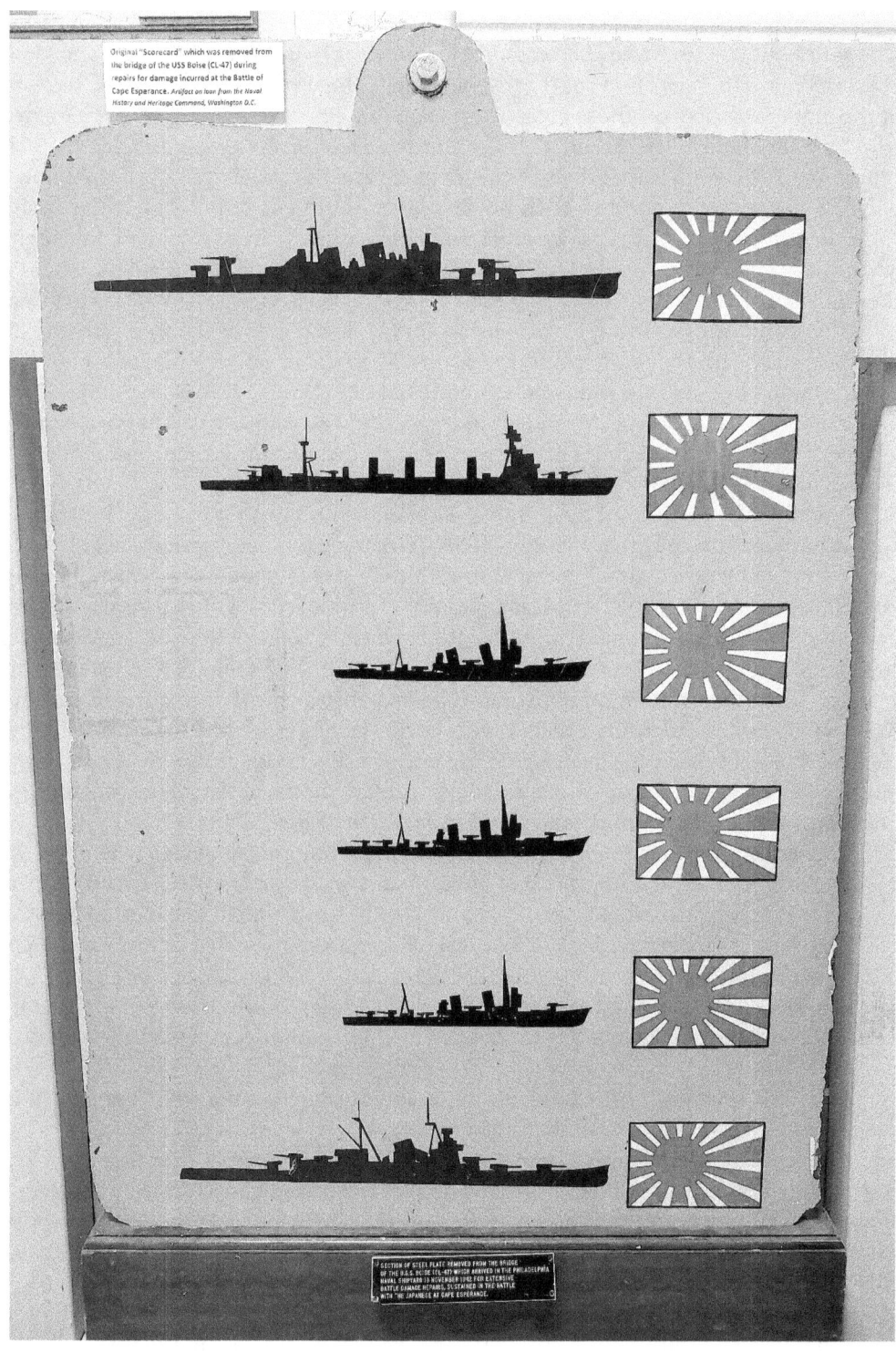

The "scoreboard" is one of the few remaining pieces of the *Boise*. This section of the bulkhead was removed before the ship was sold, and is now at the Idaho Military History Museum in Boise (author photograph).

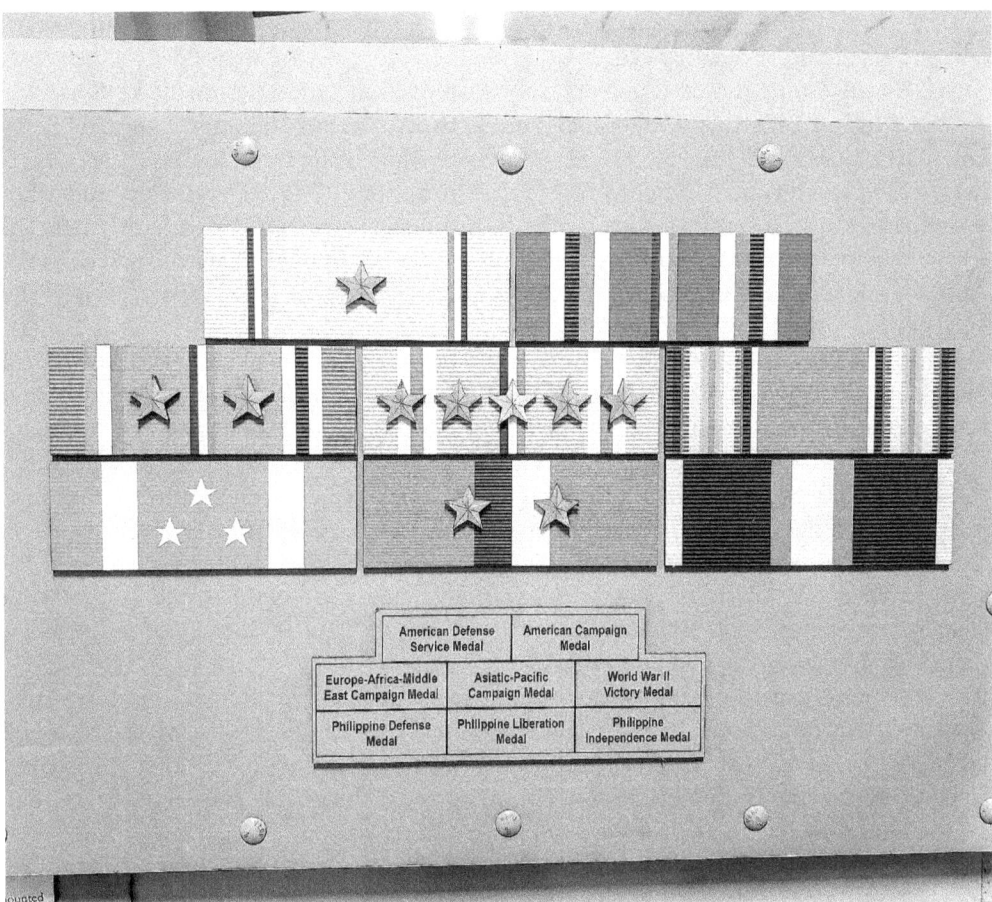

***Boise*'s campaign ribbons showing its service in nearly every theater of World War II (author photograph).**

member of the Bohemian Club, an influential San Francisco group that promoted the arts. Moran passed away on April 20, 1957.[16]

Thebaud eventually made admiral, just like Admiral Davidson said he would before the Taranto invasion. He commanded a cruiser division in the Pacific and was then made the Director of Naval Intelligence. He continued to serve after the war as Inspector General and eventually U.S. First Naval District Commandant where he rubbed elbows with the Secretary of the Navy and even President Truman. He earned medals from the French and British governments in addition to accolades from the U.S. Navy. After completing an astonishing fifty-two years of service, he retired to Washington, D.C., and spent his summers quietly in Quebec. He died on April 18, 1980, and was buried at the U.S. Naval Academy.[17]

Robinson, after he was removed from command of the *Boise*, was eventually put in command of the naval base at Tacloban. He retired from the Navy in 1947 and practiced law for many years in California. He reconnected with the crew later in life and fostered a grandfather-like relationship with the men, taking a keen interest in their lives and well-being. He lived to be a centurion, passing away in 1990 at 101.[18]

The ship's gunnery officer for much of the war, Lieutenant Commander William C.

Butler, retired as an admiral.[19] Others found success in all walks of life including sales, law, and medicine.

DB's life after the war was a juxtaposition of highs and lows, just like *Boise*. He returned to Salt Lake City and took his shot at the American Dream. He married Betty Lou Eileen Owsley on June 5, 1947. He and fellow Navy veteran Dale Larsen were partners in the United Fence Company that helped him and his family prosper. He and other veterans in the area supported each other's businesses, creating strong family ties. DB was also active in his community through a laundry list of organizations including the American Legion, Elks Club, and the Navy League where he eventually served as the local chapter president.[20]

He and Betty Lou had four children, all boys. He insisted they name the oldest Mark after a friend that died right next to DB at Cape Esperance, but never revealed anything further about the shipmate.[21] The boys inherited their father's penchant for mischief and neighborhood pranks that nearly drove their mother insane. At the same time, the partying lifestyle that DB developed during the war to blow off steam followed him into his marriage. When drinking he could become mean-spirited and relationships with some of his siblings soured, including with a brother who had served in the war as a Navy officer. DB had no respect for the man, who never saw combat, and accused him of spending the war "teaching navy wives to play tennis." The resentment hung between them and was unresolved when he died.[22]

DB always played down his wartime experiences in public. An article from Veterans Day, 1962, interviewed the "personable, quick-talking 'fence salesman,'" where he joked, "we spent half the war in the navy yard." But when asked if the war changed him, he deflected, saying, "I don't think so. You forget those things. We buried 107 in one day at Guadalcanal—but you forget those things."[23]

But he did not forget those moments, and it was most evident with his drinking. What had been a crutch to help quiet the demons during the war metastasized into a miserable coping mechanism to hide from the past. He told his family he did not understand how anyone could experience what he had and not drink, and that since he could drink all night and not suffer from a hangover the following day it meant he was not an alcoholic.[24]

Despite his shortcomings, he tried in his own way to raise his sons to become men like himself. He shared his passion for baseball, hunting, and fishing. Weekends were almost always spent in the mountains chasing deer, snagging trout, or on the banks of the Great Salt Lake tagging ducks. During the summers they spent the days on the water, hosting friends from around the country for hours of sun-drenched fun water-skiing or simply cruising and drinking. The booze-soaked expeditions were less loved by his family, sometimes even requiring the boys to drive everyone home, despite sometimes being too young to hold a driver's license.

The parties did more than release DB's tension—they also displayed a much more positive aspect of his character, that of a gracious host. He also used his well-honed charisma to make friends with prominent figures around the country. He was half-obsessed with maintaining and strengthening the bonds of brotherhood established on the *Boise*. He corresponded with fellow enlisted sailors and officers alike, demonstrating that military stratifications could not keep veterans apart. The communication salved his pain and allowed him to reminisce the good and bad times with old friends.

He befriended the Utah National Guard adjutant general while some of his sons served. Major General Maurice L. Watts started his career as an enlisted man and was in the first wave of troops to land at Luzon. He later led the state's forces from 1964 to 1980.[25] He once remarked to DB that "if I'd known then that you were in the *Boise* I would have felt more secure as I waded ashore that morning."[26] The comment was more than a platitude and demonstrates the bonds that World War II veterans felt.

His desire to connect with people from the war did not end with American veterans. At one point he tried to find the German POWs who were taken aboard at Gela.[27] His willingness to reach out to former enemies did not extend to the Japanese, however, and he never missed a chance to curse the entire country and its people.[28]

His connections extended even to the ship's leadership. He kept up correspondence with at least one of *Boise*'s skippers. In a 1979 letter, Captain Robinson, then eighty-four years old, expressed his appreciation to DB for keeping the crew connected through reunions. He thanked him for his "very well expressed description of the present activities of our crew of the Boise and of the cross section of America that they represent." He beamed with pride at the memory that "they were such a wonderful crew."[29]

DB's oldest son was amazed by the vast quantity and quality of his connections around the country. He seemed to know someone everywhere, from simple businessmen to politicians and flag officers. He recalled meeting Robinson, who asked him if he had ever seen his father afraid. When he responded no, the captain simply said, "That's because after you've been in a naval battle like Leyte Gulf, you'll never be afraid again."[30]

DB's efforts were instrumental in coordinating *Boise*'s reunions, which began in 1970 in Long Beach, California. The events were filled with tours, speeches, dinners, dancing, and of course alcohol. DB reveled in the events, always bringing his wife and sometimes enlisting the assistance of his oldest son. DB chaired the following year's event in Boise, which proved raucous and included a musical fashion show that bordered on burlesque thanks to the lead performer Diamond Tooth Lil.[31] He recounted in a newsletter afterward that "those who came to Boise for fun, had fun. Those who came to fight the war all over again couldn't find a sober fighter." He claimed they provided one bar its best business since the Gold Rush, and as a result two of the men ended up falling drunkenly into a local creek. He jokingly praised their navigator, Commander George Beardslee, for finding his way to the meeting as effectively as he had navigated the ship around the world. Then DB wrote, "I do remember having a little problem finding our position in the review line in the Hudson River on Navy Day, 1945. Seems none of the instruments would work."[32] One wonders if DB's mischief had been at play.

Two years later 400 crewmembers gathered in Philadelphia. The local paper recorded that DB "came in Wednesday night and by yesterday morning they were younger than anybody, partly because of a magic potion they had been drinking from bottles." They even quoted DB: "To tell you the truth, I'm drunk."[33] The desire to live like they were young again was ever-present, and while meeting old comrades could be cathartic these reunions seemed to drown the past more than provide healing.

In 1975 his continued work with Navy veterans earned him the opportunity to sail aboard an active-duty warship once again. DB and nineteen other veterans of the Navy League stepped aboard the USS *Denver* (LPD-09) for a cruise from San Diego to Hawaii before the ship departed for Southeast Asia to take part in evacuations after the Vietnam War. He bragged about being "last out of the sack and first in the chow line" in postcards to Betty Lou and his friends at work.[34] The time at sea sounds peaceful and he noted in a letter a few weeks later to a *Denver* crewman that the trip reminded him "of my days from 1940 to 1946 as a USO dancer on the Boise."

Apparently, the time in a Pearl Harbor hotel was reminiscent of DB's wild days during the war. The *Denver*'s captain commented how great it was having DB and everyone else aboard, and specifically mentioned that many sailors mentioned "the fine time" they had and it was a "port call ... to be remembered."[35] Upon returning to Salt Lake City, DB wrote, "we arrived back ... all hung over and still drunk ... damn hard to do." Their party got out of hand and required "the assistant manager and his 'goons' coming up to the room to quiet us down," all thanks to several rounds of drinks he called "loudmouth." DB clearly reveled in memories and comradery, but his letter displays a longing for days past. He wrote:

> Hope Jim finally made chief and gets his pay. Hello to Hauser, Dick, with the Flag group.... The High Lord Sheriff, Master at Arms, McCoy, and all the rest of that great bunch. ... A guy has to travel a long time to find a better bunch than I met on your ship. Thanks for a great time.[36]

Despite the use of alcohol to dull the pain from the war, DB showed real concern and love for his shipmates, their families, and other veterans. His surviving correspondence held touching letters. In one from 1987, the sister of John F. Watson, who had died at Guadalcanal, wrote to him after hearing of a *Boise* reunion. She wanted to find anyone who might have known John. DB wrote back and said he sadly did not remember him, but enthusiastically promised to share her contact information with other survivors and encourage them to reach out. He tried to reassure her even after forty-five years: "The Boise was a wonderful ship and her crew was a bunch of good American and fighters to the end. I am sorry we had to lose your brother in that tough battle." In another instance he saved a heartfelt letter from James D. Johnston, a sailor aboard the USS *Salute*. He and fellow survivors from the minesweeper had hitched a ride on *Boise* after they had been sunk at Brunei Bay. Johnston remarked many of them "had never sailed on a large 'Ship of the Line' and especially one with the Boise's reputation." The spirit of comradery touched DB deeply, even among veterans he did not know.[37]

Tragedy struck DB in 1980 when Betty Lou passed away on January 21. Although certainly filled with grief, he pushed his feelings down deep and carried on with his life. Eight months later he wedded Jenna Vee Lundahl Soeffker.[38] She seemed to offer him peace through an outgoing attitude and zest for life that matched his own.

The crew met officially for the 10th time in 1987 in Boise, Idaho. DB chaired the event and planned the usual local excursions, cocktail hours, and jazz bands. There were also more solemn moments. The city dedicated a memorial to the men containing the original ship's bell that notified the crew of watch changes and a bronze "Honor Roll" plaque that displayed the names of the crewmembers lost at Guadalcanal. Shipmate Al Hunnicutt was "overcome with great emotion" at the event, and Marine Colonel Harold L. Hiner, who had been a First Lieutenant aboard the ship at Guadalcanal, gave the memorial address.[39] The Mayor attended and read a proclamation that declared September 6 to be "USS *Boise* Crew Member Day."[40] Pictures from that weekend show the men and their wives with drinks in hand, laughing while sharing stories of their exploits. They ate, danced, and helped each other forget the hard times in favor of the happy memories from their time aboard the ship and their lives since the war.[41] Letters of appreciation to DB poured in from around the country for months after.

By 1991 his health was beginning to turn. Photos show him leaning heavily on a cane, but his charismatic smile was ever-present.[42] He and Jenna Vee continued to live

DB and second wife Jenna Vee at a *Boise* reunion (Fitch Family Private Collection).

life to the fullest until 1997, when she passed away on June 10. She had been a light in his darkness, and now he was an old man still battling the demons of his youth. In August he traveled to Natick, Massachusetts, for the ship's 15th reunion. Only eighty-three crewmembers were able to attend, and while they certainly reminisced, the event

U.S.S. BOISE   10th REUNION

RED LION INN - RIVERSIDE   BOISE, IDAHO

SEPTEMBER 23 - 26, 1987

Boise veterans met at reunions several times after the war, and each time they made a pamphlet filled with pictures, history, and their best stories from the war (Fitch Family Private Collection).

seemed more subdued than previous gatherings. Just after the reunion DB was honored in Washington, D.C., as an Honorary Admiral of the Asiatic Fleet. In a five-day event America finally celebrated its Forgotten Fleet from 1942 and unveiled a monument to their lost cause. The ship and crew had officially buried the "Reluctant Dragon" moniker from the beginning of the war and were accepted as peers within another sacred brotherhood. These would be the last *Boise* events DB would attend.

DB passed away on July 8, 1998. Over 250 people attended his funeral where family and friends recalled good times and DB's zest for life.[43] In quieter spaces, many shared some measure of relief that he would suffer no more pain or anguish over those lost before.[44] In the end, they simply hoped that the old sailor had finally found peace.

Chapter Notes

Abbreviations for Chapter Notes

The following citations will be listed the first time, and then abbreviated for succeeding entries:

Fitch Diary (FD)
Fitch Family Private Collection (FFPC)
Idaho Military History Museum (IMHM)
Naval History and Heritage Command (NHHC)
Office of Naval Intelligence (ONI)
USS Boise Hull Repairs to USS *Boise*: Jan to Apr 1942 (HR)
USS *Boise* 1987 Reunion Papers (RP)
USS *Boise*—War Diary / *Boise*—War Diary (UBWD)

Prologue

1. Ian W. Toll, *Pacific Crucible: War at Sea in the Pacific, 1941–1942* (Norton, 2012), 36.
2. Morison, Samuel Eliot. *The Rising Sun in the Pacific, 1931–1942*, vol 3: *History of United States Naval Operations in World War II*. 1948. Reprint (Little, Brown, 1988), 81.
3. Morison, *Rising Sun in the Pacific*, 159.

Chapter 1

1. *USS Boise 1987 Reunion Papers (RP)*, prepared for Chairman Don B. Fitch, Fitch Family Private Collection (FFPC), 1.
2. Richard B. Frank, *Tower of Skulls: A History of the Asia–Pacific War: July 1937–May 1942* (Norton, 2020), 229.
3. Norman Friedman, *U.S. Cruisers: An Illustrated Design History*, 163.
4. U.S. Department of State, *The London Naval Conference, 1930*, Milestones 1921–1936, Office of the Historian, [https://history.state.gov/milestones/1921-1936/london-naval-conf].
5. Naval Treaty between the United States, France, the British Empire, Italy, and Japan for the Limitation and Reduction of Naval Armament, April 22, 1930, Article XVI.
6. *RP*, Fitch, FFPC, 1.
7. U.S. Navy, *Gun Mount and Turret Catalog*, Ordnance Pamphlet 1112, 1945, available through the San Francisco Maritime National Park Association, https://maritime.org/doc/guncat/index.php#toc.
8. Friedman, *U.S. Cruisers*, 183, 210.
9. "6"/47 (15.2 cm) Mark 16," NavWeaps: *Naval Weapons, Naval Technology and Naval Reunions*, 10 Sept 2023, www.navweaps.com/Weapons/-WNUS_6-47_mk16.php.
10. Friedman, *U.S. Cruisers*, 474.
11. Vincent A. Langelo, *With All Our Might* (Eakin Press, 2000), 73–37; "Radar Equipment of World War II," *NavWeaps*, http://navweaps.com/Weapons/WNUS_Radar_WWII.php#Mark_3; Richard B. Frank, *Guadalcanal: The Definitive Account of the Landmark Battle* (Penguin, 1990), 294; Friedman, *U.S. Cruisers*, 193.
12. Robert L. Lawson, *The History of U.S. Naval Air Power* (Temple, 1985), 25.
13. William T. Larkins, *Battleship and Cruiser Aircraft of the United States Navy: 1910–1949* (Schiffer Publishing, 1996), 145.
14. Steve Ginter, *Curtiss SOC Seagull*, Naval Fighters Number 89 (Ginter Publishing, 2011), 16–22.
15. Friedman, *U.S. Cruisers*, 187, 474.
16. Friedman, *U.S. Cruisers*, 187, 210 474.
17. Mark Stille, *U.S. Navy Light Cruisers 1941–45* (Osprey, 2016), 22; Friedman, *U.S. Cruisers*, 187, 474.
18. Friedman, *U.S. Cruisers*, 474; *RP*, Fitch, FFPC, 12.
19. Friedman, *U.S. Cruisers*, 210.
20. CL 47 Hull Corrected Working Drawings, 25 July 1957, Reel 32560 1–6, National Archives, College Park, Maryland.
21. CL 47 Hull Drawings.
22. Frank D. Morris, *"Pick Out the Biggest": Mike Moran and the Men of the* Boise (Houghton Mifflin, 1943), center diagram; Friedman, *U.S. Cruisers*, 474.
23. Friedman, *U.S. Cruisers*, 474; *RP*, Fitch, FFPC, "Roster page 6."
24. *RP*, Fitch, FFPC, 1; "Benjamin Vaughan McCandlish," *Hall of Valor*, Military Times, https://valor.militarytimes.com/recipient/recipient-9787/.
25. Larkins, *Battleship and Cruiser Aircraft*, 150.
26. *RP*, Fitch, FFPC, 1.

27. The quote was made by Secretary of War Henry Stimson on Dec 16 claiming solidarity with Secretary Knox in firing the top Army and Navy leadership at Pearl Harbor. Gordon W. Prange, Donald M. Goldstein, and Katherine V. Dillon, *At Dawn We Slept: The Untold Story of Pearl Harbor*, 60th Anniversary Edition (New York: Penguin, 1991) 589–590; *RP*, Fitch, FFPC, 1.

28. U.S. Department of the Interior Heritage Conservation and Recreation Service, *William and Martha House* National Register of Historic Places Inventory, approved January 15, 1982, [https://npgallery.nps.gov/NRHP/GetAsset/NRHP/82004164_text].

29. Mark Fitch, interview by author, Salt Lake City, January 26–29, 2021.

30. Mark Fitch, interview.

31. Mark Fitch, interview.

32. Mark Fitch, interview.

33. Douglas F. Bennett and James W. Woolley, "Mass Transit in the Salt Lake Valley: 1872 to 1960," *Utah Economic and Business Review*, vol 37, num 9, Sept 1977, College of Business, Bureau of Economic and Business Research, University of Utah, accessed through Utah Rails.net [https://utahrails.net/articles/uebr_37-9.php].

34. I.C.B. Dear, ed, *The Oxford Companion to World War II*, Paperback ed. (New York: Oxford, 2001), 1021–1022.

35. Toll, *Pacific Crucible*, 91.

36. Frank, *Tower of Skulls*, 124–129.

37. Frank, *Tower of Skulls*, 100, 138,

38. Delta High School Class of 1941: 1991 Reunion papers, FFPC.

39. Fitch Diary (FD); Selective Training and Service Act of 1940, 76th Cong., 3d sess. (September 16, 1940), 895.

40. Jennifer A. Garey, *San Diego's Naval Training Center*, Images of America Series (Arcadia Publishing, 2008); 7–12.

41. Garey, *San Diego's Naval Training Center*, 32–33.

42. Gilbert Hotchkiss to "Folks," Letter, 7 Jan 1940, National Museum of the American Sailor.

43. Hotchkiss to "Folks," 7 Jan 1940.

44. FD.

45. Naval History and Heritage Command (NHHC), *Wharton (AP-7): 1940–1947* [https://www.history.navy.mil/research/histories/ship-histories/danfs/w/wharton.html].

46. FD.

47. "N. Nav 351," Enlistment paperwork, FFPC.

48. Fitch Papers, Idaho Military History Museum (IMHM), 2008.60.3/1–3/8.

49. NHHC, "U.S. Navy Interviewer's Classification Guide," NAVPERS 16701 December 1943 [https://www.history.navy.mil/research/library/online-reading-room/title-list-alphabetically/u/us-navy-interviewers-classification-guide.html#qm].

50. NHHC, "Classification Guide."

51. Brian Morris, interview, January 26–29, 2021, by author.

52. NHHC, "Classification Guide"; FD.

53. FD; Hawai'i Tourism Authority, "Moloka'I Historic Places," 2022 [https://www.gohawaii.com/islands/molokai/things-to-do/land-activities/historic-places].

54. Stetson Conn, Rose C. Engelman, and Byron Fairchild, *Guarding the United States and Its Outposts* (U.S. Government Printing Office, 1964), 210.

55. Mark Fitch, interview.

56. Dear, ed, *Oxford Companion to World War II*, 1024; Frank, *Tower of Skulls*, 185.

57. FD.

58. *Boise (CL-47), 1/28/39–7/1/46* https://catalog.archives.gov/id/125563586?objectPage=120, 120.

59. FD.

60. Frank, *Tower of Skulls*, 217.

61. *RP*, Fitch, FFPC, 1.

62. FD.

63. William Mulvey, "Mulvey, William (Interview outline and video), 2009," *Digital Collections*, https://digitalcollections.library.gvsu.edu/document/29314.

64. Fitch's dates sometimes conflict with other reports by a day or two. Whenever possible I have included the date from his memory as well as event dates from official sources such as the *Boise* War Diary. Fitch Papers, IMHM, 2008.60/1/2, 31.

65. Fitch Papers, IMHM, 2008.60.1/19.

Chapter 2

1. FD.

2. Morison, *Rising Sun*, 150.

3. Morison, *Rising Sun*, 150.

4. Morison, *Rising Sun*, 158–159.

5. Clayton James, *The Years of MacArthur*, Vol. 1, *1880–1941* (Houghton Mifflin, 1970).

6. Phillips Payson O'Brien, *How the War Was Won: Air-Sea Power and Allied Victory in World War II* (Cambridge University, 2015), 88.

7. John C. McManus, *Island Infernos: The U.S. Army's Pacific War Odyssey, 1944* (Caliber, 2021), 24.

8. Morison, *Rising Sun*, 154.

9. Morison, *Rising Sun*, 154.

10. Morison, *Rising Sun*, 154–155.

11. Morison, *Rising Sun*, 187, 230.

12. Morison, *Rising Sun*, 169.

13. Campbell, Roy Allen, *Roy Allen Campbell Collection*, https://www.loc.gov/item/afc2001001.75599/.

14. Klemm, Frederick Robert, *Frederick Robert Klemm Collection*, interviewed by Leslie Harrold, January 27, 2004, Library of Congress, Veterans History Project, https://www.loc.gov/item/afc2001001.10835/.

15. Fenton, Joseph Franklin, *Joseph Franklin Fenton Collection*, interviewed by Constance Jones, Dec 2007, https://www.loc.gov/item/afc2001001.82111/.

16. Since keeping a personal log was against regulations, Moneymaker managed to hide his inside the searchlights he maintained on the mast. Garnett Bailey Moneymaker and Henry Shapiro.

Garnett Bailey Moneymaker Collection, 1937, Personal Narrative. https://www.loc.gov/item/afc2001001.83353/.

17. James Starnes, interviewed June 10, 2010, Digital Collections of the National WWII Museum, Oral Histories. https://www.ww2online.org/view/james-starnes#segment-1.

18. Morris, *Pick Out the Biggest*, 3–6; Klemm interview.

19. Morison, *Rising Sun*, 193; FD.

20. FD.

21. I.C.B. Dear, ed, *The Oxford Companion to World War II*, Paperback ed. (New York: Oxford, 2001), 32.

22. Joseph Franklin Fenton, *Joseph Franklin Fenton Collection*, interviewed by Constance Jones, Dec 2007, https://www.loc.gov/item/afc2001001.82111/; Marlin A. Levin, "Only Our Job," *Temple University News*, January 25, 1943, from Temple University Libraries Digital Collections, https://digital.library.temple.edu/digital/collection/p16002coll11/id/5411/rec/22.

23. FD.

24. NHHC, *Crossing the Line: Pollywogs to Shellbacks*, July 9, 2019, https://www.history.navy.mil/browse-by-topic/heritage/customs-and-traditions0/crossing-line.html.

25. "Imperium Netuni Regis" certificate, FFPC.

26. NHHC, USS Indianapolis Scrapbook: 1936, in "President Franklin D. Roosevelt's 1936 Cruise to Latin America on USS *Indianapolis* (CA—35): A Scrapbook," 28 January 2019, https://www.history.navy.mil/research/library/exhibits/roosevelt-1936-cruise-to-latin-america.html.

27. *Enlisted Man's Jacket–Fitch*, FFPC.

28. USS *Boise*–War History https://catalog.archives.gov/id/77622643?objectPage=2, 2.

29. FD.

30. Frank, *Tower of Skulls*, 336, 348–354.

31. Morison, *Rising Sun*, 187–190.

32. Morison, *Rising Sun*, 179–183.

33. Morison, *Rising Sun*, 255–256.

34. Office of Naval Intelligence (ONI), Navy Department–Java Sea Campaign, https://catalog.archives.gov/id/134249895?objectPage=22, 22.

35. Toll, *Pacific Crucible*, 182, 185

36. Morison, *Rising Sun*, 313.

37. Morison, *Rising Sun*, 50.

38. FD.

39. John W. Masland, "American Attitudes toward Japan," *The Annals of the American Academy of Political and Social Science*, May 1941, Vol. 215, America and Japan, 163.

40. Films for the Humanities & Sciences (Firm), Films Media Group, and Prelinger Archives, dirs. 20101943. *Prelinger Archives. Our Enemy–The Japanese (1943)*. Films Media Group, https://archive.org/details/OurEnemy1943.

41. "When Spoiler bumped into the monkeys he was a trifle short on 1. body balance 2. timing 3. teamwork 4. stamina 5. tricks 6. the old fight." United States Navy Department Bureau of Aeronautics Training Division; Richard W. Cheek WWII Graphic Arts Collection (Boston Athenaeum) (Contributor), Osborn, Robert Chesley, 1904–1994, artist (Creator) U.S. Government Printing Office https://cdm16057.contentdm.oclc.org/digital/collection/p16057coll48/id/706.

42. Morison, *Rising Sun*, 284.

43. Langelo, *With All Our Might*, 44.

44. Mulvey interview.

45. Morris, *Pick Out the Biggest*, 11.

46. Spencer Duckworth, *Destroyers on the Rocks: Seven Ships Lost* (Cyprus, 2005),75–81, 83, 222–231.

47. Morison, *Rising Sun*, 284.

48. NHHC, *S-36 (SS-141)*, Jan 31, 2017, https://www.history.navy.mil/research/library/online-reading-room/title-list-alphabetically/u/united-states-submarine-losses/s-36-ss-141.html; ONI, Java Sea , 60.

49. Morison, *Rising Sun*, 284.

50. FD.

51. Langelo, *With All Our Might*, 44.

52. USS *Boise*–Hull Repairs to USS *Boise*: Jan to Apr 1942 (HR), https://catalog.archives.gov/id/133895997, 1; FD.

53. ONI, Java Sea, 27.

54. Morison, *Rising Sun*, 285.

55. Morison, *Rising Sun*, 286–287.

56. Morison, *Rising Sun*, 287–288.

57. Welford C. Blinn, interviewed October 22, 1945, by U.S. Navy. https://catalog.archives.gov/id/278475679, 3.

58. Morison, *Rising Sun*, 289.

59. ONI, Java Sea, 39.

60. Blinn interview, 3.

61. ONI, Java Sea, 40.

62. Morison, *Rising Sun*, 289–290.

63. Morison, *Rising Sun*, 290; James D. Hornfischer, *Neptune's Inferno: The U.S. Navy at Guadalcanal* (Bantam, 2012), 41.

64. CINCAF–Report of naval engagement off Balikpapen, Borneo. 1/24/42, https://catalog.archives.gov/id/133898701?objectPage=11, 11.

65. FD.

66. Hornfischer, *Ship of Ghosts,* 7.

67. Fitch Papers, IMHM, 2008.60.1/30.

68. HR, 1.

69. HR, 23.

70. HR, 2.

71. FD.

72. FD.

73. HR, 2–3.

74. *Colombo–Information for Visiting Troops*, Fitch Papers, IMHM, 2008.60/1/33.

75. *Colombo*, Fitch Papers, 2008.60/1/5, 28, 33.

76. HR, 11.

77. Hornfischer, *Ship of Ghosts*, 69–70.

78. ONI, Java Sea, 86, 99, 108–109, 118–120; Hornfischer, *Ship of Ghosts*, 85–89, 92–93.

79. ONI, Java Sea, 123.

80. Hornfischer, *Ship of Ghosts*, 107–145.

81. Hornfischer, *Ship of Ghosts*, 2.

82. Morris, *Pick Out the Biggest*, 13–14.

83. Mark Fitch interview.

Chapter 3

1. FD.
2. NHHC, *USS Mississippi (BB-23)*, https://www.history.navy.mil/content/history/nhhc/-our-collections/photography/us-navy-ships/battleships/mississippi-bb-23.html.
3. HR, 4.
4. HR, 12. According to the *Boise* muster rolls, CM1c W.H. Martens was catching a ride back to the U.S. for a medical survey aboard the *President Polk* and would have witnessed the SOCs in their search. *Boise (CL-47), 1/28/39–7/1/46*, 262.
5. HR, 6.
6. Mulvey interview.
7. HR, 6. The Indian workers did not participate in 24-hour work, and instead assisted 16 hours each day.
8. HR, 25–31.
9. HR, 12, 14.
10. HR, 14.
11. HR, 15.
12. Langelo, *With All Our Might*, 49–50.
13. Mulvey interview.
14. Fitch Papers, IMHM, 2008.60/1/1–14.
15. Mark Fitch interview.
16. HR, 17.
17. HR, 6, 23.
18. HR, 4–6.
19. HR, 35.
20. USS *Boise*–War Diary (UBWD), 4/1–30/42, [https://catalog.archives.gov/id/134012386?objectPage=5], 5–6.
21. Frank, *Tower of Skulls*, 505–507.
22. UBWD, 4/1–30/42, [https://catalog.archives.gov/id/134012386?objectPage=5], 5–6.
23. UBWD, 4/1–30/42, [https://catalog.archives.gov/id/134012386?objectPage=10], 8–10.
24. FD.
25. Enlisted passengers were not listed on the surviving Muster Roll, which only includes forms titled "List of Non-enlisted Passengers," *Boise (CL-47), 1/28/39–7/1/46*, 273.
26. FD.
27. Frank, *Tower of Skulls*, 517–521; James M. Scott, *Rampage: MacArthur, Yamashita, and the Battle of Manilla* (Norton, 2018), 6.
28. John C. McManus, *Fire and Fortitude: The U.S. Army in the Pacific War, 1941–1943* (Caliber, 2019), 109–117.
29. McManus, *Fire and Fortitude*, 157. McManus wrote that MacArthur actively resisted Wainwright being awarded the Medal of Honor, believing that it would dishonor the men who fought on Bataan and Corregidor. However, Wainwright was deservedly awarded the Medal of Honor by President Truman after the war. Congressional Medal of Honor Society, *Jonathan Mayhew Wainwright IV*, https://www.cmohs.org/recipients/jonathan-m-wainwright-iv.
30. McManus, *Fire and Fortitude*, 134–143, 157.
31. Carroll V. Glines, *The Doolittle Raid: America's Daring First Strike Against Japan* (Schiffer, 1991), 12–15.
32. Glines, *The Doolittle Raid*, 16–17.
33. Glines, *The Doolittle Raid*, 28–29, 36–37.
34. Glines, *The Doolittle Raid*, 43; Morison, *Rising Sun*, 392–394.
35. Toll, *Pacific Crucible* 287–88.
36. Toll, *Pacific Crucible*, 290–291; Morison, *Rising Sun*, 394.
37. USS *Nashville*–*War Diary 4/1–30/42 (Enc A)*, https://catalog.archives.gov/id/133968929?objectPage=21, 20–21.
38. USS *Nashville*–*War Diary 4/1–30/42*, 22; Morison, *Rising Sun*, 397.
39. USS *Nashville*–*War Diary 4/1–30/42*, 25–26.
40. JAPAN REPORTS TOKYO, YOKOHAMA BOMBED BY 'ENEMY PLANES' IN DAYLIGHT; New York Times (1923–); Apr 18, 1942; ProQuest Historical Newspapers: *The New York Times* with Index pg. 1; TOKYO BOMBED!: Allied Craft Hit Capital Broadcast by Japs Says Nine. *Los Angeles Times* (1923–1995); Apr 18, 1942; ProQuest Historical Newspapers: *Los Angeles Times* pg. 1; PLANES BOMB TOKIO OM TOKI: JAPANESE RADIO REVEALS FIRST ATTACK; CLAIM. *Chicago Daily Tribune* (1923–1963); Apr 18, 1942; ProQuest Historical Newspapers: *Chicago Tribune* pg. 1; Toll, *Pacific Crucible*, 298.
41. Toll, *Pacific Crucible*, 295.
42. *Command Summary of Fleet Admiral Chester W. Nimitz, USN: Nimitz "Graybook," Vol 1*, Internet Archive, 368.
43. USS *Nashville*–*Ship's Record*, https://catalog.archives.gov/id/77539226?objectPage=3, 3.
44. Langelo, *With All Our Might*, 26.
45. FD.
46. FD.
47. [USS] *Honolulu (CL-48)–December 1941*, https://catalog.archives.gov/id/78104503?objectPage=28, 28.
48. UBWD, 5/1–31/42 https://catalog.archives.gov/id/134012400?objectPage=5, 3–5.
49. Bureau of Naval Personnel, *Navpers 16118: Seamanship*, June 1944, 132.
50. Naval Personnel, *Seamanship*, 132.
51. Morris, *Pick Out the Biggest*, 19–20.
52. Langelo, *With All Our Might*, 66; UBWD, 5/1–31/42, 5; FD.
53. NHHC, "Battle of Midway," Infographic [https://www.history.navy.mil/content/history/nhhc/news-and-events/multimedia-gallery/infographics/history/battle-of-midway.html].
54. UBWD, 6/1–30/42, https://catalog.archives.gov/id/133942770?objectPage=1, 1; Roy Campbell recalled that 40mm cannons were added at this time, but the author was unable to confirm. Roy Allen Campbell, Roy Allen Campbell Collection, interviewed by Carl Cox, July 14, 2010., https://www.loc.gov/item/afc2001001.75599/; Langelo, *With All Our Might*, 71.
55. Langelo, *With All Our Might*, 73–74.
56. UBWD, 6/1–30/42, 1.
57. *Boise (CL-47), 1/28/39–7/1/46*, 333–337,

357; Langelo wrote that a few months later "all one hundred men (his estimate from scuttlebutt) appeared at captain's mast for punishment," *With All Our Might*, 69; *United States Navy Regulations: 1920*. Internet Archive, https://archive.org/details/unitedstatesnavy00unit/page/2/mode/2up, 2.

58. UBWD, 6/1–30/42, 4–5.

59. Morris's book should be considered a 'hagiography' that overly promotes the *Boise* and Captain Moran. It was published during the war and was a useful piece of American pro-war propaganda. Still, the work is useful for its descriptions of the ship, its crew, and events if the reader 'takes it with a grain of salt.' I strove to use it only for those descriptions and not its conclusions. All events have been cross referenced with other sources whenever possible. Morris, *Pick Out the Biggest*, 25–29.

60. LT John W. Alexander, *Origin of Navy Terminology*, U.S. Navy Pamphlet, NHHC [https://www.history.navy.mil/content/history/nhhc/research/library/online-reading-room/title-list-alphabetically/o/origin-navy-terminology.html#cap].

61. AO3/(AW/IW) Julian Olivar interview, 13 March 2022.

62. These punishments were listed in a manual for Navy officer recruits published in 1944 but are similar to those found in the *United States Navy Regulations: 1920* that were still in effect in 1942. Naval Personnel, *Seamanship*), 322.

63. FD; *Enlisted Man's Jacket–Fitch*, FFPC.

64. FD.

65. Moneymaker, *Diary*.

66. FD.

67. The Naval and Merchant Navy Patriotic Sub-Committee, of the Auckland Metropolitan Patriotic Committee, "Information for Men of Visiting Warships," Auckland 1942, Fitch Papers, IMHM, 2008.60.1/16.

68. FD.

69. Kaplan, *World War Two at Sea*, 64–67.

70. *Graybook*, Vol 1, 710.

71. Samuel Elliot Morison, *The Struggle for Guadalcanal: August 1942–February 1943* (Little, Brown and Co, 1989), 14–15.

72. *Graybook*, Vol 1, 737, 777.

73. FD.

74. UBWD, 7/1–31/42, 9.

75. Hornfischer, *Neptune's Inferno*, 27; FD.

76. FD. DB's accounting of the battleships at Pearl Harbor was not entirely accurate. There were eight active battleships in port on December 7, and the Japanese succeeded in sinking the *California*, *Oklahoma*, *West Virginia*, and *Arizona*. They also severely damaged the *Nevada*, and dealt minor damage to the *Maryland*, *Tennessee*, and *Pennsylvania*. The USS *Utah* was also sunk but had been reconfigured to a radio-controlled gunnery practice ship in 1932. Frank, *Tower of Skulls*, 280, 288.

77. Langelo, *With All our Might*, 87.

78. UBWD, 7/1–31/42,10; *Graybook*, Vol 1, 782.

79. FD; Langelo, *With All Our Might*, 83.

80. FD; John Macomber quoted in Larry Gardner, "USS Boise: Navy Crew, Historians Puzzle Over Artifacts" *The Idaho Statesman*, D 1–2, September 26, 1987; Starnes interview.

81. UBWD, 8/1–30/42 [https://catalog.archives.gov/id/133979957?objectPage=3], 3.

82. UBWD, 8/1–30/42, 3.

83. W.C. Butler, interviewed October 18, 1943, by U.S. Navy. https://catalog.archives.gov/id/2784776192.

84. FD.

85. UBWD, 8/1–30/42, 4.

86. Butler interview, 3.

87. UBWD, 8/1–30/42, 4.

88. Lawson, *U.S. Naval Airpower*, 25.

89. UBWD, 8/1–30/42, 4. Moneymaker, *Diary*.

90. Langelo, *With All Our Might*, 85.

91. UBWD, 8/1–30/42, 23.

92. Mike Stankovich, "The Hardest Choice," *Naval History*, U.S. Naval Institute, Winter 1988, Volume 2/1/2, 31.

93. FD, Langelo, *With All Our Might*, 86.

94. UBWD, 8/1–30/42, https://catalog.archives.gov/id/133979957?objectPage=25, 17, 25.

95. UBWD, 8/1–30/42, 17.

96. UBWD, 8/1–30/42, 19.

97. UBWD, 8/1–30/42, 19.

98. UBWD, 8/1–30/42, 5, 20.

99. UBWD, 8/1–30/42, 21.

100. UBWD, 8/1–30/42, 13.

101. FD.

102. *Graybook*, Vol 1, 857.

103. UBWD, 8/1–30/42, 13; Stankovich, "The Hardest Choice," 33.

104. UBWD, 8/1–30/42, 6.

105. *Graybook*, Vol 1, 698.

106. Frank, *Guadalcanal*, 35.

107. *Graybook*, Vol 1, 782.

108. *Graybook*, Vol 1, 792; ONI, *The Aleutians Campaign*, 1945, NHHC, https://www.history.navy.mil/research/library/online-reading-room/-title-list-alphabetically/a/the-aleutians-campaign.html#chap3.

109. ONI, *Miscellaneous Actions in the South Pacific: 8 August 1942–22 January 1943*, NHHC, https://www.history.navy.mil/content/dam/nhhc/research/library/online-reading-room/war-and-conflict/wwii/MiscellaneousActions/misc-actions-south-pacific-reduced.pdf, 1–13.

110. Frank, *Guadalcanal*, 655.

111. Matome Ugaki, *Fading Victory: The Diary of Admiral Matome Ugaki, 1941-1945* (University of Pittsburgh Press, 1991), 182–183.

112. *Graybook*, Vol 1, 857.

113. Macomber, "Historians Puzzle Over Artifacts."

Chapter 4

1. USS *Jarvis* attempted to leave the area for repairs the following morning when it was tracked by the Japanese who mistook the ship for a New

Zealand cruiser. The Japanese mounted an air-raid with over 30 aircraft that overwhelmed the intrepid ship, sending it to the bottom along with all hands. NHHC, *Jarvis II (DD-393): 1937-1942*, https://www.history.navy.mil/research/histories/ship-histories/danfs/j/jarvis-ii.html; Morison, *Guadalcanal*, 14-16; Frank, *Guadalcanal*, 72-79.

2. Tameichi Hara, Fred Saito, and Roger Pineau, *Japanese Destroyer Captain: Pearl Harbor, Guadalcanal, Midway-The Great Naval Battles as Seen Through Japanese Eyes* (Naval Institute Press, 1967), 95.

3. Jonathan Parshall, "How Can they Be That Good? Japan 1922-1942," in *Fighting in the Dark: Naval Combat at Night: 1904-1944*, Vincent P. O'Hara and Trent Hone, eds. (Naval Institute Press, 2023), 142-144.

4. Morison, *Guadalcanal*,18-20.

5. Morison, *Guadalcanal*, 26; 29-32.

6. Paul S. Dull, *A History of the Imperial Japanese Navy: 1941-1945* (Naval Institute Press, 1978), 187.

7. Morison, *Guadalcanal*, 15-20.

8. Morison, *Guadalcanal*, 37-39; Dull, *Imperial Japanese Navy*, 188.

9. Morison, *Guadalcanal*, 41-44; Dull, *Imperial Japanese Navy*, 190.

10. Morison, *Guadalcanal*, 44-46.

11. Morison, *Guadalcanal*, 47-49.

12. Hara, *Japanese Destroyer Captain*, 95.

13. Morison, *Guadalcanal*, 66.

14. "America's First Offensive Proves a Miserable Failure," Japan Center for Asian Historical Records (JACAR) Ref.C14020686300, Official Journal of the Military Administration. No.6. October 15, 1942 (National Institute for Defense Studies), 115-118.

15. Parshall, "How Can they Be That Good?" in *Fighting in the Dark*, O'Hara and Hone eds., 168.

16. Dull, *Imperial Japanese Navy*, 193.

17. Hornfischer, *Neptune's Inferno*, 89.

18. Morison, *Guadalcanal*, 61 notes.

19. Morison, *Guadalcanal* 66.

20. FD.

21. UBWD, 8/1-31/4211; FD.

22. Ian W. Toll. *The Conquering Tide: War in the Pacific Islands, 1942-1944* (Norton, 2015), 132-133; Lowry interview.

23. Toll, *The Conquering Tide*, 132-133; Lowry Interview; Morison, *Guadalcanal*, 106, 113.

24. UBWD, 9/1-30/42 https://catalog.archives.gov/id/134000568?objectPage=3, 3.

25. Langelo, *With All Our Might*, 91.

26. New Zealand History, *HMNZS Leander* https://nzhistory.govt.nz/war/hmnzs-leander; Frank, *Guadalcanal*, 252; Vice Admiral George Carroll Dyer, USN (ret), *Amphibians Came to Conquer: The Story of Admiral Richmond Kelly Turner*, Vol 1 (Government Printing Office, 1972), xix.

27. UBWD, 9/1-30/42, 4; FD.

28. UBWD, 9/1-30/42, 5.

29. UBWD, 9/1-30/42, 5; FD.

30. *Graybook*, Vol 2, 1036.

31. Dyer, *Amphibians Came to Conquer*, 442.

32. Dyer, *Amphibians Came to Conquer*, 442; Morison, *Guadalcanal*, 130-131.

33. Morison, *Guadalcanal*, 132-135.

34. Morison, *Guadalcanal*, 133-134.

35. Morison, *Guadalcanal*, 136.

36. *Amphibians Came to Conquer*, 442.

37. FD; USS Crescent City-War Diary, 9/1-30/42 (Enc A), https://catalog.archives.gov/id/133994257?objectPage=51, 51.

38. FD; Morris, *Pick Out the Biggest*, 30

39. UBWD, 9/1-30/42, 6; FD.

40. Dyer, *Amphibians Came to Conquer*, 442.

41. UBWD, 9/1-30/42, 6-7; Morison, *Guadalcanal*, 138.

42. Morison, *Guadalcanal*, 138.

43. UBWD, 9/1-30/42, 7; Frank, *Guadalcanal*, 252.

44. FD; *Graybook*, Vol 2, 1040.

45. FD.

46. FD.

47. *Graybook*, Vol 2, 1036.

48. UBWD, 9/1-30/42, 8-10; USS San Francisco-War Diary 9/1/42 to 10/31/42 https://catalog.archives.gov/id/134005142?objectPage=28 28.

49. UBWD, 10/1-31/42 (Enc A-B) https://catalog.archives.gov/id/134000579?objectPage=3, 3; Naval Personnel, *Seamanship*, 89, 98; FD.

50. Dull, *Imperial Japanese Navy*, 216.

51. *Helena* would actually join the Task Force near Guadalcanal. FD; UBWD, 10/1-31/42, 4-5.

52. UBWD, 10/1-31/42, 5; FD; Moneymaker, *Diary*; Captain Edward J. Moran (Commander USS *Boise*), interviewed February 15, 1943, by U.S. Navy. https://catalog.archives.gov/id/278490145.

53. USS Salt Late City-War Diary, 10/1-31/42 https://catalog.archives.gov/id/134001322?objectPage=12, 12; UBWD, 10/1-31/42, 17. Wave height was taken from the Beaufort Scale. Naval Personnel, *Seamanship*, 270.

54. Butler interview.

55. Salt Late City-War Diary, 10/1-31/42, 12; UBWD, 10/1-31/42, 6.

56. FD.

57. Salt Late City-War Diary, 10/1-31/42, 11; UBWD, 10/1-31/42, 6.

58. UBWD, 10/1-31/42, 18; San Francisco-War Diary 9/1/42 to 10/31/42, 51; Morison, *Guadalcanal*, 152; Salt Late City-War Diary, 10/1-31/42, 12; FD.

59. Dull, *Imperial Japanese Navy*, 216.

60. Bob Hackett and Sander Kingsepp, "IJN Submarine I-26: Tabular Record of Movement," *Combined Fleet* webpage, Revision 4, http://www.combinedfleet.com/I-26.htm; Hornfischer, *Neptune's Inferno*, 166.

61. Butler interview.

62. The exact times of events for the following battle sometimes differ between the logs of the various participants and secondary sources. Where possible, I have used the times in the *Boise* log. Morison, *Guadalcanal*, 153.

63. Hornfischer, *Neptune's Inferno*, 169-170.

64. UBWD, 10/1–31/42, 18.
65. Morison, *Guadalcanal*, 154; UBWD, 10/1–31/42, 18.
66. *RP*, Fitch, FFPC, 3.
67. Scott was like many senior officers in 1942 and did not fully understand the new SG radar or its capabilities. It is possible that even if he had received the information from the SG radars, he would not have acted more quickly than he did. Morison, *Guadalcanal*, 154.
68. Morison, *Guadalcanal*, 156–157; Hornfischer, *Neptune's Inferno*, 170.
69. Langelo, *With All Our Might*, 97.
70. "They, Too, Were Expendable," *Time*, Vol XL, no. 22, November 30, 1942. Variations of this line have been repeated in numerous articles and books since the battle.
71. Butler interview.
72. UBWD, 10/1–31/42, 20.
73. FD.
74. UBWD, 10/1–31/42, 20.
75. Hornfischer, *Neptune's Inferno*, 173.
76. Captain Edward J. Moran (Commander, USS *Boise*), interviewed February 15, 1943, by U.S. Navy. https://catalog.archives.gov/id/278490145.
77. Morris, *Pick Out the Biggest*, 40; Butler interview.
78. Hornfischer, *Neptune's Inferno*, 173; Butler interview.
79. Moneymaker, *Diary*.
80. UBWD, 10/1–31/42, 21; Hornfischer, *Neptune's Inferno*, 174.
81. Langelo, *With All Our Might*, 98.
82. Morris, *Pick Out the Biggest*, 45.
83. Moran Interview.
84. Morison, *Guadalcanal*, 160.
85. UBWD, 10/1–31/42, 21.
86. Dull, *Imperial Japanese Navy*, 219.
87. UBWD, 10/1–31/42, 21; Moneymaker, *Diary*.
88. Although this is an amusing line, it could not be verified outside of Morris's book. Morris, *Pick Out the Biggest*, 42.
89. UBWD, 10/1–31/42, 21–22; Butler interview.
90. Moran interview.
91. Morison, *Guadalcanal*, 163; UBWD, 10/1–31/42, 22.
92. FD.
93. Morris, *Pick Out the Biggest*, 54; Langelo, *With All Our Might*, 99.
94. UBWD, 10/1–31/42, 22.
95. The ship's after-action report tried to downplay the danger of using searchlights, stating that the muzzle flashes from the main batteries was more than enough light for enemy ships to track *Boise*. Hornfischer, *Neptune's Inferno*, 180; Langelo, *With All Our Might*, 100; FD; UBWD, 10/1–31/42, 22; Morison, *Guadalcanal*, 161–162.
96. UBWD, 10/1–31/42, 23; Morison, *Guadalcanal*, 163–164.
97. UBWD, 10/1–31/42, 23.
98. Morris, *Pick Out the Biggest*, 60; Boise–War Diary, 10/1–31/42 https://catalog.archives.gov/id/134000579?objectPage=24; 24.
99. UBWD, 10/1–31/42; 24.
100. UBWD, 10/1–31/42, 23.
101. Hornfischer, *Neptune's Inferno*, 180; Frank, *Guadalcanal*, 306.
102. UBWD, 10/1–31/42; 25.
103. UBWD, 10/1–31/42; 25.
104. Moneymaker, *Diary*.
105. UBWD, 10/1–31/42, 23.
106. Morris, *Pick Out the Biggest*, 59.
107. UBWD, 10/1–31/42; 24.
108. UBWD, 10/1–31/42; 24; Moneymaker, *Diary*.
109. UBWD, 10/1–31/42; 25.
110. Fenton interview; Klemm interview.
111. Mulvey interview.
112. Salt Late City–War Diary, 10/1–31/42, 35.
113. Salt Late City–War Diary, 10/1–31/42, 35.
114. FD.
115. *RP*, Fitch, FFPC, 6.
116. UBWD, 10/1–31/42; 26.
117. UBWD, 10/1–31/42; 25.
118. UBWD, 10/1–31/42; 26.
119. UBWD, 10/1–31/42; 26.
120. Moran interview.
121. *RP*, Fitch, FFPC, 5.
122. UBWD, 10/1–31/42; 26.
123. Morris, *Pick Out the Biggest*, 68.
124. Morris, *Pick Out the Biggest*, 66; UBWD, 10/1–31/42, 40.
125. Morris, *Pick Out the Biggest*, 67; Anthony S. D'Angelo Papers, D'Angelo Family Private Collection.
126. Morris, *Pick Out the Biggest*, 57; Moneymaker, *Diary*.
127. The "First Aid treatment for Survivors of Disasters at Sea" that provided guidance to wounded and shipwrecked sailors was published in 1943 but was compiled from the "experiences and needs of 9,114 survivors of 167 ship disasters" including those at Ironbottom Sound. It is logical that many of *Boise*'s crewmembers provided similar care to their wounded after the Battle of Cape Esperance. The Bureau of Medicine and Surgery, Navy Department, *First Aid Treatment for Survivors of Disasters at Sea*, 1943, https://www.history.navy.mil/research/library/online-reading-room/-title-list-alphabetically/h/handbook-first-aid-treatment-survivors-disasters-sea.html#s9.
128. UBWD, 10/1–31/42, 36.
129. Moneymaker, *Diary*.
130. UBWD, 10/1–31/42, 40.
131. Larry McMullen, "The Time Machine," *Philadelphia Daily News*, October 5, 1973, FFPC.
132. Moneymaker, *Diary*.
133. Langelo, *With All Our Might*, 102.
134. Morison, *Guadalcanal*, 165.
135. Hornfischer, *Neptune's Inferno*, 184.
136. UBWD, 10/1–31/42, 27.
137. Butler interview.
138. UBWD, 10/1–31/42, 28.
139. *RP*, Fitch, FFPC, 5; UBWD, 10/1–31/42, 30.
140. FD.
141. UBWD, 10/1–31/42, 32.

142. Moran interview.
143. *Graybook*, Vol 2, 1089.
144. UBWD, 10/1–31/42, 29.
145. UBWD, 10/1–31/42, 28.
146. Morison, *Guadalcanal*, 151; Frank, *Guadalcanal*, 297; Dull, *Imperial Japanese Navy*, 220; Hornfischer, *Neptune's Inferno*, 170.
147. Dull, *Imperial Japanese Navy*, 216–221. Frank, *Guadalcanal*, 307, 309.
148. Morison, *Guadalcanal*, 168.
149. Morison, *Guadalcanal*, 168.
150. Morison, *Guadalcanal*, 162.
151. Hornfischer, *Neptune's Inferno*, 187.
152. NHHC, *The Battles of Cape Esperance: 11 October 1942 and Santa Cruz Islands: 26 October 1942*, Combat Narrative Series, WWII 75th Anniversary Series (NHHC, 2017), 15.
153. Morison, *Guadalcanal*, 147.
154. UBWD, 10/1–31/42, 40–41.
155. Congressional Medal of Honor Society, *Norman Scott*, https://www.cmohs.org/recipients/norman-scott.
156. Although the column technique Scott used was utilized again elsewhere, further analysis revealed that many of his contemporaries took the wrong lessons from Cape Esperance and employed the tactic in the wrong situations, leading to inefficiencies and losses. Morison, *Guadalcanal*, 170.
157. The following *Boise* men were awarded the Navy Cross from the Battle of Cape Esperance: Capt. Edward Moran, Lt Cmdr John James Laffan, Lt Cmdr Edward Kenney, Lt Cmdr William Butler Jr., Lt John Lee, Lt John Howell, Lt (jg) William Thomas (posthumously), Lt (jg) Milo Evarts (posthumously), Ens Theron Duncan, Chief Harold Thomas, B.M.1c Philip Donahue, G.M.1c Mino Poole (posthumously), Sea.1c Vint Eden. UBWD, 10/1–31/42, 36–37; Department of Defense, *Navy Cross Recipients, World War II, 1941–1945*, https://valor.defense.gov/Portals/24/Navy%20-%20Navy%20Cross%20List%20-%202021%2002%2002.pdf?ver=d2g_29o48C-uP_kGnci3kg%3d%3d; Hall of Valor Project, *Thomas Wolverton*, https://valor.militarytimes.com/hero/56689.
158. Hara, *Japanese Destroyer Captain*, 113.
159. Kikunori Kijima, Interrogated by Captain C. Shands, USN, 27 November 1945, Interrogation Nav No. 106, USSBS No. 464, in "Interrogations of Japanese Officials: Volume II," *United States Strategic Bombing Survey (Pacific), OPNAV-P-03-100* (GPO, 1946), 456–460.
160. FD, Mark Fitch interview.
161. *Boise (CL-47), 1/28/39–7/1/46*, 330.
162. Tripp Family Papers. American Legion Post 357 in the author's hometown of Ashby, Minnesota, added Robert Tripp to their post name to remember him and the other young men lost during the war.

Interlude

1. *Graybook*, Vol 2, 1088.
2. The log and DB disagree on the number buried that day. UBWD, 10/1–31/42, 7; FD.
3. Fitch noted 16 crewmembers buried that day, while the log stated 19. FD; Moneymaker, *Diary*; UBWD, 10/1–31/42, 8.
4. FD.
5. UBWD, 10/1–31/42, 8.
6. FD.
7. FD; UBWD, 10/1–31/42, 10.
8. UBWD, 10/1–31/42, 10; FD.
9. FD; UBWD, 10/1–31/42, 11.
10. FD; UBWD, 10/1–31/42, 12; FD.
11. FD.
12. Moneymaker, *Diary*; "Hold That Ghost," *Turner Classic Movies*, https://www.tcm.com/tcmdb/title/78178/hold-that-ghost#overview.
13. Phillip W. Stewart, "A Reel Story of World War II: The United News Collection of Newsreels Documents the Battlefield and the Home Front," *Prologue Magazine*, Fall 2015, Vol 47, No. 3, https://www.archives.gov/publications/prologue/2015/fall/united-newsreels.html.
14. UBWD, 11/1–30/42 https://catalog.archives.gov/id/134037340?objectPage=5, 5; FD.
15. Captain Harry S. Knapp, "The Navy and the Panama Canal," *Proceedings* Vol 3–1913, included in Thomas J. Cutler's *The U.S. Naval Institute on the Panama Canal* (Naval Institute Press, 2016), 52–53.
16. R. E. Bakenhus, "The Panama Canal," *Proceedings* Vol 1–1913, included in Thomas J. Cutler's *The U.S. Naval Institute on the Panama Canal* (Naval Institute Press, 2016) 24–26.
17. Conn, Engelman and Fairchild, *Guarding the United States*, 424–431.
18. Friedman, *U.S. Cruisers*, 255.
19. UBWD, 11/1–30/42, 5;
20. UNESCO is the United Nations Educational, Scientific, and Cultural Organization; "Fortifications on the Caribbean Side of Panama: Portobelo-San Lorenzo," *UNESCO World Heritage Convention*, https://whc.unesco.org/en/list/135/.
21. UBWD, 11/1–30/42, 6.
22. Rick Atkinson, *An Army at Dawn: The War in North Africa, 1942–1943* (Henry Holt, 2002), 31.
23. Stetson, *Guarding the United States and Its Outposts*, 434.
24. UBWD, 11/1–30/42, 7; *RP*, Fitch, FFPC, 6.
25. *RP*, Fitch, FFPC, 6.
26. UBWD, 11/1–30/42, 7.
27. Morison, *Guadalcanal*, 170.
28. FD.
29. Moneymaker, *Diary*.
30. Several headlines were used without specific reference in a collage. *RP*, Fitch, FFPC.
31. *RP*, Fitch, FFPC.
32. FD.
33. Mark Fitch Interview.
34. Mark Fitch Interview.
35. FD.
36. Jack McCarthy, *Philadelphia Jazz: A Brief History*, May 24, 2017, https://www.allaboutjazz.com/philadelphia-jazz-a-brief-history-by-jack-mccarthy.
37. Delmar Postcard, FFPC.
38. Invitation Card, FFPC.

39. Invitation Card, FFPC.
40. Marlin A. Levin, "Only Our Job," *The Temple News, 1942-1943*, Jan 25, 1943, https://digital.library.temple.edu/digital/collection/p16002coll11/id/5411/rec/22; Mulvey Interview.
41. FD.
42. UBWD, 2/1-28/43 https://catalog.archives.gov/id/134103680?objectPage=1, 1, 28.
43. UBWD, 2/1-28/43, 1, 4, 5, 8, 20.
44. UBWD, 2/1-28/43, 54.
45. Friedman, *U.S. Cruisers*, 319, 474.
46. Friedman, *U.S. Cruisers*, 320.
47. Friedman, *U.S. Cruisers*, 339.
48. Stille, *U.S. Navy Light Cruisers 1941-1945*, 27; Friedman, *U.S. Cruisers*, 339-341.
49. Friedman, *U.S. Cruisers*, 343.
50. Ginter, *SOC Seagull*, 250; Larkins, *Battleship and Cruiser Aircraft*, 153.
51. UBWD, 2/1-28/43 https://catalog.archives.gov/id/134103680?objectPage=24, 24; *Rear Admiral Edward J. ("Mike") Moran, USN (Retired) (1893-1957)*, The Public's Library and Digital Archive, https://ibiblio.org/hyperwar/OnlineLibrary/photos/pers-us/uspers-m/ej-moran.htm.
52. UBWD, 2/1-28/43, 57.
53. Naval History Division, "Vice Admiral Leo Hewlett Thebaud: United States Navy, Retired," NHHC.
54. UBWD, 2/1-28/43, 55.
55. FD.
56. UBWD, 4/1-30/43 https://catalog.archives.gov/id/134162986?objectPage=13, 13.
57. UBWD, 4/1-30/43, 17.
58. UBWD, 4/1-30/43, 18.
59. UBWD, 4/1-30/43, 18-19.
60. FD.
61. FD.
62. NHHC, *U.S. Navy PT Boats*, https://www.history.navy.mil/content/history/nhhc/research/histories/ship-histories/u-s-navy-pt-boats.html.
63. UBWD, 5/1-31/43 https://catalog.archives.gov/id/134281872?objectPage=31, 31.
64. Moneymaker, *Diary*.

Chapter 5

1. James Holland, *Sicily '43: The First Assault on Fortress Europe* (Griffon Merlin, 2020),158.
2. FD.
3. Samuel Eliot Morison, *Sicily, Salerno, Anzio, June 1943-June 1944*, Vol. 9 of the *History of United States Naval Operations in World War II*, 1954, Reprint (Little, Brown, 1990), 57.
4. Holland, *Sicily*, 149.
5. Gela observations, author.
6. Holland, *Sicily*, 105.
7. Albert N. Garland, Howard McGaw Smyth and Martin Blumenson, *Sicily and the Surrender of Italy*, United States Army in World War II: The Mediterranean Theater of Operations (Office of the Chief of Military History, 1965), 81, 136.
8. Thomas L. Jentz, ed., *Panzertruppen: The Complete Guide to the Creation & Combat Employment of Germany's Tank Force-1943-1945* (Schiffer, 1996), 102-103.
9. Mitcham and Stauffenberg, *The Battle of Sicily*, 41.
10. FD.
11. *RP*, Fitch, FFPC, 6.
12. FD.
13. UBWD, 7/1-31/43, https://catalog.archives.gov/id/78143885?objectPage=17, 17.
14. Morison, *Sicily, Salerno, Anzio*, 28-29.
15. Garland, *Sicily*, 4-5.
16. Holland, *Sicily*, 51-52.
17. Morison, *Sicily, Salerno, Anzio*, 28.
18. Garland, *Sicily*, 99-100.
19. Morison, *Sicily, Salerno, Anzio*, 61-64.
20. Morison, *Sicily, Salerno, Anzio*, 96.
21. Morison, *Sicily, Salerno, Anzio*, X.
22. Author Unknown, *Sicilian Invasion*, Fitch personal papers, FFPC.
23. Holland, *Sicily*, 110.
24. FD
25. Holland, *Sicily*, 197.
26. UBWD, 7/1-31/43, 23.
27. USS BOISE—Shore Bombardment, Gela Area, Sicily (Boise-Gela), 7/10-12/43, https://catalog.archives.gov/id/134315526?objectPage=7, 7.
28. Morison, *Sicily, Salerno, Anzio*, 100; Boise-Gela, 7.
29. Boise-Gela, 7/10-12/43, 2, 9.
30. Garland, *Sicily* 139.
31. Holland, *Sicily*, 197.
32. Boise-Gela, 7/10-12/43, 3.
33. Boise-Gela, 7/10-12/43, 3.
34. Boise-Gela, 7/10-12/43, 3.
35. Holland, *Sicily*, 198, 245.
36. Pyle, *Brave Men*, 31-32.
37. Bertram, personal photos of Sicily battlefields.
38. Holland, *Sicily*, 217.
39. Holland, *Sicily*, 203-204.
40. Holland, *Sicily*, 204-205.
41. Morison, *Sicily, Salerno, Anzio*, 103.
42. Holland, *Sicily*, 228.
43. Holland, *Sicily*, 159, 217.
44. Harold Grant, Gen, USAF. Oral History. U.S. Air Force Oral History Interview, 12-13 Sep 1984. #K239.0512-1609. United States Air Force Academy, 51.
45. Holland, *Sicily*, 247.
46. Holland, *Sicily*, 205.
47. USS Shubrick, War Diary, 7/1-31/43, [https://catalog.archives.gov/id/135907857], 10.
48. Boise-Gela, 7/10-12/43, 3-4.
49. Boise-Gela, 7/10-12/43, 5.
50. Boise-Gela, 7/10-12/43, 6.
51. FD
52. UBWD, 7/1-31/43, 24; Boise-Gela, 7/10-12/43, 11.
53. USS MADDOX—Report of Battle and Loss of, https://catalog.archives.gov/id/134275989; Morison, *Sicily, Salerno, Anzio*, 108.
54. UBWD, 7/1-31/43, 23-24
55. UBWD, 7/1-31/43, 25-26.

56. Holland, *Sicily*, 243.
57. Holland, *Sicily*, 243, 245.
58. FD
59. FD; Morison, *Sicily, Salerno, Anzio*, 110.
60. Holland, *Sicily*, 243, 247–248.
61. Holland, *Sicily*, 247.
62. Holland, *Sicily*, 248–251.
63. Holland, *Sicily*, 248–251.
64. Morison, *Sicily, Salerno, Anzio*, 110.
65. UBWD, 7/1–30/43, 26; Morison, *Sicily, Salerno, Anzio*, 110.
66. Morison, *Sicily, Salerno, Anzio*, 111.
67. Morison, *Sicily, Salerno, Anzio*, 112; Holland, *Sicily*, 253–254.
68. Holland, *Sicily*, 253; Morison, *Sicily, Salerno, Anzio*, 115–116.
69. UBWD, 7/1–30/43, 26.
70. UBWD, 7/1–30/43, 27.
71. Holland, *Sicily*, 254–257; Garland, *Sicily*, 170.
72. Garland, *Sicily*, 170.
73. UBWD, 7/1–30/43, 26.
74. UBWD, 7/1–30/43, 27.
75. *S.S. Robert Rowen ("Liberty" Ship)*, 1943, photograph (https://www.history.navy.mil/our-collections/photography/numerical-list-of-images/nhhc-series/nh-series/80-G-180000/80-G-180986.html)
76. FD; Holland, *Sicily*, 273–274.
77. Morison, *Sicily, Salerno, Anzio*, 117.
78. Boise–Gela, 7/10–12/43, 8.
79. UBWD, 7/1–30/43, 28–30.
80. Garland, *Sicily*, 175–182.
81. Garland, *Sicily*, 180.
82. Garland, *Sicily*, 181–182.
83. UBWD, 7/1–30/43, 30.
84. Holland, *Sicily*, 287.
85. Holland, *Sicily*, 278–279.
86. Morison, *Sicily, Salerno, Anzio*, 122.
87. UBWD, 7/1–31/43, 31.
88. UBWD, 7/1–31/43, 31; FD.
89. UBWD, 7/1–31/43, 34, 36.
90. Morison, *Sicily, Salerno, Anzio*, 122.
91. Morison, *Sicily, Salerno, Anzio*, 118.
92. Morison, *Sicily, Salerno, Anzio*, 117.
93. Morison, *Sicily, Salerno, Anzio*, 118.
94. Morison, *Sicily, Salerno, Anzio*, xii.
95. Boise–Gela, 7/10–12/43, 1.
96. Holland, *Sicily*, 287. Some scholars now believe that Husky caused Hitler to withdraw forces from the offensive at Kursk, possibly impacting the outcome of the war on the Eastern Front. If true, *Boise* would have indirectly contributed to success in another major theater of the war. Sean McKeekin, *Stalin's War: A New History of World War II* (Basic, 2021), 470–471.
97. UBWD, 7/1–31/43, 40.
98. UBWD, 7/1–31/43, 41.
99. UBWD, 7/1–31/43, 43–73; FD.
100. RP, Fitch, FFPC, 7.
101. UBWD, 8/1–31/43 https://catalog.archives.gov/id/78165450, 15.
102. Holland, *Sicily*, 400–403.
103. UBWD, 8/1–31/43, 24.
104. UBWD, 8/1–31/43, 25.
105. USS Boise–Shore Bombardment, Cape Milazzo Area, Sicily (Boise–Cape Milazzo), 8/14/43 https://catalog.archives.gov/id/135969461, 3–6.
106. Boise–Cape Milazzo, 8/14/43, 2.
107. UBWD, 8/1–31/43, 36–38.
108. UBWD, 8/1–31/43, 39; USS Boise–Shore Bombardment, Palmi, Italy (Boise–Palmi), 8/17/1943 [https://catalog.archives.gov/id/135930935], 1.
109. (Boise–Palmi), 8/17/1943, 2–4.
110. UBWD, 8/1–31/43, 40–43.
111. UBWD, 8/1–31/43, 46–67.
112. UBWD, 9/1–30/43 [https://catalog.archives.gov/id/78210567], 14; Morison, *Sicily, Salerno, Anzio*, 235.
113. Morison, *Sicily, Salerno, Anzio*, 235.
114. Morison, *Sicily, Salerno, Anzio*, 235.
115. UBWD, 9/1–30/43, 14.
116. Morison, *Sicily, Salerno, Anzio*, 235.
117. RP, Fitch, FFPC, 8.
118. Martin Blumenson, *Salerno to Cassino*, United States Army in World War II: The Mediterranean Theater of Operations (Center of Military History, 1969), 41–42; Morison, *Sicily, Salerno, Anzio*, 236.
119. UBWD, 9/1–30/43, 17–19.
120. Morison, *Sicily, Salerno, Anzio*, 236.
121. FD
122. RP, Fitch, FFPC, 8.
123. Morison, *Sicily, Salerno, Anzio*, 236.
124. UBWD, 9/1–30/43, 23–23.
125. Morison, *Sicily, Salerno, Anzio*, 259–265; NHHC, *Savannah IV (CL-42)* https://www.history.navy.mil/research/histories/ship-histories/danfs/s/savannah-iv.html.
126. Morison, *Sicily, Salerno, Anzio*, 265–266, 298–299.
127. Morison, *Sicily, Salerno, Anzio*, 283–284; NHHC, *Savannah IV*.
128. NHHC, *Savannah IV*.
129. NHHC, *Savannah IV*.
130. FD; UBWD, 9/1–30/43, 27.
131. Author Unknown, *Special Events of 1943*, Fitch personal papers, FFPC.
132. FD; UBWD, 9/1–30/43, 29; Morison, *Sicily, Salerno, Anzio*, 280.
133. UBWD, 9/1–30/43, 31–32; Morison, *Sicily, Salerno, Anzio*, 295.
134. UBWD, 9/1–30/43, 32–33; Morison, *Sicily, Salerno, Anzio*, 295.
135. UBWD, 9/1–30/43, 35, 38–43.
136. NHHC, *Leo Hewlett Thebaud* https://www.history.navy.mil/research/library/research-guides/lists-of-senior-officers-and-civilian-officials-of-the-us-navy/district-commanders/-first-naval-district/thebaud-leo-hewlett.html.
137. UBWD, 9/1–30/43, 49–58; UBWD, 10/1–31/43 [[https://catalog.archives.gov/id/135967581], 1–32.
138. Morison, *Sicily, Salerno, Anzio*, 314.
139. Rick Atkinson, *Day of Battle: The War in Sicily and Italy, 1943–1944* (Henry Holt, 2007), 230.
140. Fitch Papers, IMHM, 2008.06.1/59.

Chapter 6

1. UBWD, 10/1–31/43, 40–45.
2. UBWD, 10/1–31/43, 47–51.
3. FD.
4. UBWD, 11/1–30/43, https://catalog.archives.gov/id/136027132?objectPage=12, 12.
5. UBWD, 11/1–30/43, 22, 28–29.
6. UBWD, 11/1–30/43, 32–43; FD; Obituary, "Estill Cleo Drake," Unknown newspaper, *Find a Grave*, https://www.findagrave.com/memorial/144534393/estill-cleo-drake.
7. UBWD, 12/1–31/43, https://catalog.archives.gov/id/78271017?objectPage=2, 1–2.
8. UBWD, 12/1–31/43, 3.
9. UBWD, 12/1–31/43, 3–4.
10. UBWD, 12/1–31/43, 5.
11. UBWD, 12/1–31/43, 5; FD.
12. UBWD, 12/1–31/43, 6. Full entry: "Casualties occurring during this firing were four jammed plugs, one each in turrets I, II, IV, V. These jams were very severe, requiring over thirty minutes to clear. On one gun, it required twenty minutes to clear the case from the powder chamber after the plug was opened. On each jammed case a definite shoulder had been built up about ¼ inch above the base of the case and a raised area was noted on the base where it was in contact with the cut-away portion of the breech plug. This raised area was wiped by the plug in opening. Cases which did not jam were not so marked."
13. UBWD, 12/1–31/43, 7–11.
14. FD.
15. UBWD, 12/1–31/43, 12.
16. UBWD, 12/1–31/43, 13.
17. Mark Fitch interview.
18. Interview with AO3/(AW/IW) Julian Olivar, November 2023, Interview by author.
19. Bonnie Docherty, "USS Boise Crew Members Gather in Natick: Navy Veterans Drop Anchor to Reminisce about World War II." Unknown newspaper clipping, 1997, FFPC.
20. C. G. Morris and H. Cave, *The Fightin'est Ship: The Story of the Cruiser Helena in World War II*, Reprint (Zenger, 1979), 129.
21. "U.S. Navy Libraries, World War II," NHHC, Jul 20, 2020, https://www.history.navy.mil/research/library/online-reading-room/title-list-alphabetically/u/us-navy-libraries.html.
22. Tom Czekanski, Curator, "Trench Art Exhibition Virtual Opening," The National World War II Museum, Online, March 4, 2021, https://vimeo.com/517202828.
23. "Shell," James Clarence Ledford, *Soldier | Artist: Trench Art in World War II*, Temporary exhibit at National World War II Museum, New Orleans, LA, 2009.605.001.
24. "Convoy Crosses the Atlantic, Headed for Invasion Points," Video, National Archives, June 1943, https://catalog.archives.gov/id/77835.
25. Bureau of Supplies and Accounts, *The Cook Book of the United States Navy*, NAVSANDA Publication No. 7, 1944, https://archive.org/details/TheCookBookOfTheUnitedStatesNavy1944/page/n3/mode/2up, 4, 5, 7.
26. Mark Fitch interview.
27. Fenton interview.
28. Langelo, *With all our Might*, 16; Edward Roth Oshier, *Edward Roth Oshier Collection*, interviewed by Jolene Pierson, August 8, 2007, Library of Congress, Veterans History Project. https://www.loc.gov/item/afc2001001.54941/.
29. "Seaman First Class James Fahy and the Eternal Aspects of War," Robert J. Schneller, Jr., Naval Historical Center, June 2008. Accessed through *Navy History and Heritage Command*, https://www.history.navy.mil/browse-by-topic/wars-conflicts-and-operations/world-war-ii/world-war-ii-profiles/s1-c-james-fahy.html.
30. "K Ration," https://kration.info/.
31. "Rho Lambda Phi Sponsors 'Smokes For Yanks' Drive," *Temple University News*, Dec 2, 1942 Vol XXII-No 29, https://digital.library.temple.edu/digital/collection/p16002coll11/id/5356/rec/22.
32. "General Order 99, [Prohibition in the Navy]," 1 June 1914, NHHC, https://www.history.navy.mil/research/library/online-reading-room/title-list-alphabetically/g/general-orders/general-order-no-99-prohibition-in-the-navy.html.
33. James Younkin wrote in his diary how the gunners aboard the USS *La Salle* made raisin jack under one of their 20mm gun platforms, while a story from the Second Battle of Guadalcanal mentioned a sailor named Johnny Brown breaking out a jug belowdecks of the battleship *Washington* to release the tension of the battle. James Melvin Younkin, *World War II: Through a Porthole–A Memoir of Wartime*, edited by Diana (Younkin) Egan, Part 3 of 4, https://www.minerd.com/memoir-younkinjamesmelvin3.htm; David H. Lippman, "Second Naval Battle of Guadalcanal: Turning Point in the Pacific War," *HistoryNet*, June 12, 2006, https://www.historynet.com/second-naval-battle-of-guadalcanal-turning-point-in-the-pacific-war/.
34. FFPC.
35. Morris, "*The Fightin'est Ship*," 132.
36. "Convoy Crosses the Atlantic, Headed for Invasion Points," Video, National Archives, June 1943, https://catalog.archives.gov/id/77835.
37. UBWD, 12/1–31/43, 13–14.
38. UBWD, 12/1–31/43, 15–16.
39. UBWD, 1/1–31/44, https://catalog.archives.gov/id/78293780?objectPage=2, 1.
40. Gordon L. Rottman, *FUBAR: Soldier Slang of World War II* (Osprey, 2011),144.
41. Harry A. Gailey, *MacArthur's Victory: The War in New Guinea, 1943–1944* (Presidio Press, 2004), 1–2.
42. John Miller Jr., *Cartwheel: The Reduction of Rabaul*, The United States Army in World War II: War in the Pacific (Office of the Chief of Military History, 1959), 272.
43. Miller, *Cartwheel*, 275–276.
44. Miller, *Cartwheel*, 290–294.
45. Samuel Eliot Morison, *Breaking the*

Bismarcks Barrier, 22 July 1942–1 May 1944, Vol 6 of the *History of United States Naval Operations in World War II*, Reprint (Little, Brown, 1988), 386.

46. UBWD, 1/1–31/44, 1.
47. UBWD, 1/1–31/44, 15–16.
48. FD.
49. UBWD, 1/1–31/44, 11–12.
50. RP, Fitch, FFPC, 8–9.
51. UBWD, 2/1–29/44, https://catalog.archives.gov/id/78341968?objectPage=1.
52. UBWD, 2/1–29/44, 2–3.
53. "Admiral Russell Stanley Berkey: United States Navy, Retired," Official Navy Biography, 13 Sept. 1950, https://www.history.navy.mil/content/dam/nhhc/research/library/research-guides/modernbios/b/berkey-russell-stanley_Redacted.pdf.
54. *Santa Fe (CL-60)*, NHHC, https://www.history.navy.mil/research/histories/ship-histories/danfs/s/santa-fe.html.
55. UBWD, 2/1–29/44, 9, 11.
56. UBWD, 3/1–31/44, https://catalog.archives.gov/id/78363536?objectPage=2, 1.
57. E. Daniel Potts and Annette Potts, *Yanks Down Under 1941–45: The American Impact on Australia* (Oxford University Press, 1985), 104, 145; Nick Hordern, "Kings Cross in World War II," *Naval Historical Society of Australia*, June 2020, https://navyhistory.au/kings-cross-in-world-war-ii/; Joseph Eugene Dyer, Joseph Eugene Dyar Collection, interviewed by Daniel Lacasse, January 15, 2003. https://www.loc.gov/item/afc2001001.07912/.
58. Mark Fitch interview.
59. FD.
60. UBWD, 3/1–31/44, 1–5.
61. UBWD, 3/1–31/44, 6–7.
62. UBWD, 3/1–31/44, 8–16.
63. Dull, *Imperial Japanese Navy*, 299.
64. UBWD, 4/1–30/44, https://catalog.archives.gov/id/78425813?objectPage=2, 1–2.
65. UBWD, 4/1–30/44, 3–4; O'Hara and Hone, eds, *Fighting in the Dark*, 254–255.
66. UBWD, 4/1–30/44, 7–8.
67. Robert Ross Smith, *The Approach to the Philippines*, United States Army in World War II: The War in the Pacific (Office of the Chief of Military History, 1953), 12.
68. McManus, *Island Infernos*, 129–131, 136.
69. Samuel Eliot Morison, *New Guinea and the Marianas, March 1944–August 1944*, Vol. 8 of the *History of United States Naval Operations in World War II*, 1953, Reprint (Little, Brown, 1990),68; "The Hollandia Operation: 22–26 April 1944," Map III, in Smith's *The Approach to the Philippines*.
70. Smith, *Approach to the Philippines*, 22.
71. UBWD, 4/1–30/44, 8–9.
72. Morison, *New Guinea and the Marianas*, 34–37; Smith, *Approach to the Philippines*, 28.
73. Morison, *New Guinea and the Marianas*, 37.
74. USS BOISE–Rep of Bombardment of Humbolt Bay, New Guinea, in Support of Landing Ops 4/22/44, https://catalog.archives.gov/id/78440196?objectPage=2; UBWD, 4/1–30/44, 9.
75. USS BOISE–Rep of Bombardment of Humbolt Bay, New Guinea, in Support of Landing Ops 4/22/44 (Boise–Humbolt Bay), https://catalog.archives.gov/id/78440196?objectPage=3, 3, 5, 14.
76. Boise–Humbolt Bay, 3, 6, 10.
77. Boise–Humbolt Bay, 4, 7–8.
78. Smith, *Approach to the Philippines*, 68–72.
79. Boise–Humbolt Bay, 9.
80. Smith, *Approach to the Philippines*, 78–79.
81. Morison, *New Guinea and the Marianas*, 88.
82. Boise–Humbolt Bay, 15.
83. FD.
84. Boise–Humbolt Bay, 10.
85. FD; UBWD, 4/1–30/44, 12–15.
86. UBWD, 4/1–30/44, 15–17; Morison, *New Guinea and the Marianas*, 96; USS BOISE–Rep of Sawar-Wakde (New Guinea) Bombardment, Night 4/29–30/44 https://catalog.archives.gov/id/78421295.
87. UBWD, 5/1–31/44, https://catalog.archives.gov/id/78469116?objectPage=5, 1–3, 6.
88. UBWD, 5/1–31/44, 8.
89. UBWD, 5/1–31/44, 10; Morison, *New Guinea and the Marianas*, 94–95.
90. UBWD, 5/1–31/44, 12–13.
91. USS BOISE–Act Rep of Bombardment of Wakde-Toem Area, New Guinea, In Support of landing Ops, 5/17/44 (Boise-Wakde-Toem) https://catalog.archives.gov/id/78449570?objectPage=3, 3, 5–6; Smith, *Approach to the Philippines*, 219–221.
92. Boise-Wakde-Toem, 8.
93. Smith, *Approach to the Philippines*, 231.
94. UBWD, 5/1–31/44, 16–17.
95. UBWD, 5/1–31/44, 17–18.
96. Morison, *New Guinea and the Marianas*, 107, 117.
97. FD; Smith, *Approach to the Philippines*, 286.
98. UBWD, 5/1–31/44, 21.
99. USS BOISE–Act Rep of Biak I[n] Bombardment in Borokoe-Mokmer Area in A9-8 Support of Landing Ops at Bosnik, New Guinea, 5/27/44 (Boise-Biak) https://catalog.archives.gov/id/78468842?objectPage=2, 2.
100. Boise-Biak, 4; Smith, *Approach to the Philippines*, 290; Morison, *New Guinea and the Marianas*, 107.
101. U.S. Army documents use the spelling "Bosnek." Smith, *Approach to the Philippines*, 293–294.
102. Boise-Biak, 5.
103. Boise-Biak, 5, 6; Smith, *Approach to the Philippines*, 296; Morison, *New Guinea and the Marianas*, 113.
104. Boise-Biak, 6.
105. Morison, *New Guinea and the Marianas*, 113.
106. Morison, *New Guinea and the Marianas*, 113; Smith, *Approach to the Philippines*, 297; Boise-Biak, 7.
107. USS SAMPSON–AA Act Rep, 5/27/44, Off Biak Is, New Guinea, https://catalog.archives.gov/id/78467387?objectPage=2, 2.
108. Boise-Biak, 9.

109. FD.
110. Smith, *Approach to the Philippines*, 298.
111. UBWD, 5/1–31/44, https://catalog.archives.gov/id/78469116?objectPage=25, 23.
112. Morison, *New Guinea and the Marianas*, 117–118.
113. Morison, *New Guinea and the Marianas*, 119; Smith, *Approach to the Philippines*, 352.
114. Morison, *New Guinea and the Marianas*, 120; Smith, *Approach to the Philippines*, 353.
115. Morison, *New Guinea and the Marianas*, 121.
116. UBWD, 6/1–30/44, https://catalog.archives.gov/id/78516127?objectPage=4, 2; Morison, *New Guinea and the Marianas*, 123.
117. UBWD, 6/1–30/44, 2; FD.
118. UBWD, 6/1–30/44, 3.
119. UBWD, 6/1–30/44, 4; USS BOISE–AA Act Reps, 6/4, 5, & 8, 1944, off Biak Is, New Guinea https://catalog.archives.gov/id/78476856?objectPage=7, 7–9.
120. UBWD, 6/1–30/44, 5; FD.
121. Morison, *New Guinea and the Marianas*, 125.
122. FD; UBWD, 6/1–30/44, 5.
123. Morison, *New Guinea and the Marianas*, 125.
124. FD.
125. Morison, *New Guinea and the Marianas*, 125.
126. UBWD, 6/1–30/44, 6.
127. Morison, *New Guinea and the Marianas*, 125–126.
128. The report incorrectly listed Allied ships as 1 battleship, 4 cruisers, and 8 destroyers, but the Japanese commander likely concluded the report was incorrect and decided to continue. Smith, *The Approach to the Philippines*, 356; UBWD, 6/1–30/44, 7.
129. Morison, *New Guinea and the Marianas* 126–127; UBWD, 6/1–30/44, 6.
130. UBWD, 6/1–30/44, 7.
131. UBWD, 6/1–30/44, 7.
132. UBWD, 6/1–30/44, 8.
133. Morison, *New Guinea and the Marianas*, 127.
134. UBWD, 6/1–30/44, 8–9.
135. UBWD, 6/1–30/44, 9.
136. COMDESRON 24–War Diary, 6/1–30/44, https://catalog.archives.gov/id/78533682?objectPage=5, 5–6.
137. Morison, *New Guinea and the Marianas*, 129–130.
138. UBWD, 6/1–30/44, 11; Smith, *Approach to the Philippines*, 357.
139. UBWD, 6/1–30/44, 11–12.
140. Morison, *New Guinea and the Marianas*, 186.
141. Mark Fitch interview.
142. Morison, *New Guinea and the Marianas*, 277.
143. Morison, *New Guinea and the Marianas*, 318–321.
144. UBWD, 6/1–30/44, 20–22; Smith, *Approach to the Philippines*, 397–404; Morison, *New Guinea and the Marianas*, 136–137.
145. USS BOISE-Report of Bombardment of Noemfoor Island, New Guinea, in Support of landing OPS On Kamiri Airstrip, Noemfoor Is, https://catalog.archives.gov/id/78541497?objectPage=2, 2–6.
146. Morison, *New Guinea and the Marianas*, 138; Smith, *Approach to the Philippines*, 411–416.
147. UBWD, 7/1–31/44, 4–11; Smith, *Approach to the Philippines*, 440; COMTASK-UNIT 77.2.4-Report of Landing Operations at Warsai, Cape Sansapor Area, New Guinea on 7/30/44, https://catalog.archives.gov/id/78620643.
148. UBWD, 7/1–31/44, 14.
149. UBWD, 8/1–31/44, https://catalog.archives.gov/id/78622557?objectPage=5, 4.
150. FD.

Chapter 7

1. UBWD, 8/1–31/44, 6–7.
2. UBWD, 8/1–31/44, 7.
3. UBWD, 8/1–31/44, 8–9.
4. UBWD, 8/1–31/44, 12–13.
5. Langelo, *With All Our Might*, 220–221; Moneymaker, *Diary*.
6. FD.
7. USS Phoenix–War Diary, 9/1–30/44, https://catalog.archives.gov/id/134374839?objectPage=4, 3.
8. FD.
9. Smith, *Triumph in the Philippines*, 450–453.
10. FD; USS BOISE–Rep of Bombardment of Galela Bay Area, Halmahera Is in Support of Morotai Occupation on 9/15/44 (Boise–Galela Bay), https://catalog.archives.gov/id/134357217?objectPage=2, 2.
11. Boise–Galela Bay, 2–5, 18; Morison, *Leyte*, 22–23; Smith, *Triumph in the Philippines*, 482–483.
12. Boise–Galela Bay, 6.
13. Smith, *Triumph in the Philippines*, 483.
14. Boise–Galela Bay, 6; Phoenix–War Diary, 9/1–30/44, 9.
15. FD.
16. Phoenix–War Diary, 9/1–30/44, 10; Fenton interview.
17. Phoenix–War Diary, 9/1–30/44, 13.
18. DB was mistaken, *Canberra* sank in 1942.
19. UBWD, 10/1–31/44, https://catalog.archives.gov/id/139767203?objectPage=6, 3.
20. "William Shand Obituary," The *Salt Lake Tribune*, 24 January 2006, https://www.legacy.com/us/obituaries/saltlaketribune/name/william-shand-obituary?id=16254210.
21. Smith, *Triumph in the Philippines*, 4–6, 10.
22. Smith, *Triumph in the Philippines*, 4–6.
23. D. Clayton James, *The Years of MacArthur*, Vol. 2, *1941-1945* (Houghton Mifflin, 1975), 527; Nigel Hamilton, *War and Peace: FDR's Final Odyssey; D-Day to Yalta, 1943-1945* (Mariner Books, 2020), 476.
24. James, *The Years of MacArthur*, Vol. 2, 531, 534.

25. Richard W. Bates, *The Battle for Leyte Gulf, October 1944. Strategical and Tactical Analysis*, vol 1, "Preliminary Operations Until 0719 October 17th, 1944 Including Battle off Formosa," (Bureau of Naval Personnel, 1953), 22–23; Cannon, *Leyte*, 30; Morison, *Leyte*, 58, 415–429.
26. Bates, *The Battle for Leyte Gulf*, vol 1, 34–36.
27. M. Hamlin Cannon, *Leyte: The Return to the Philippines*, United States Army in World War II: The War in the Pacific (Office of the Chief of Military History, 1954), 11–12.
28. Cannon, *Leyte*, 22, 24–26.
29. Bates, *The Battle for Leyte Gulf*, vol 1, 187; Morison, *Leyte*, 415, 421.
30. UBWD, 10/1–31/44, 10.
31. Morison, *Leyte*, 119–126.
32. UBWD, 10/1–31/44,, 10–11; USS BOISE–Rep of Ops in Support of the Invasion of Leyte Is, Philippines, 10/13-24/44 (Boise–Leyte), https://catalog.archives.gov/id/78684668?objectPage=3, 3.
33. Bates, *The Battle for Leyte Gulf*, vol 3, 32a; Boise-Leyte, 2–3; Cannon, *Leyte*, 60.
34. Boise-Leyte, 9–10.
35. Bates, *The Battle for Leyte Gulf*, vol 3, 12–13.
36. Cannon, *Leyte*, 62–68; Morison, *Leyte*, 134.
37. Boise-Leyte, 4–5.
38. James, *MacArthur*, vol 2, 554–555, 557; Bates, *The Battle for Leyte Gulf*, vol 3, 3–4.
39. Cannon, *Leyte*, 79–80; Bates, *The Battle for Leyte Gulf*, vol 3, 4; Morison, *Leyte*, 145; UBWD, 10/1-31/44, 12.
40. FD.
41. USS BOISE–Form Reps of AA Acts in San Pedro Bay & Leyte Gulf, Philippines, 10/21/44–11/3/44 (Boise–AA Leyte), https://catalog.archives.gov/id/78686596?objectPage=3, 1–3.
42. Robert Nichols, *The First Kamikaze Attack?* Australian War Memorial, https://www.awm.gov.au/wartime/28/kamikaze-attack.
43. FD.
44. UBWD, 10/1–31/44, 13; Boise–AA Leyte, 10/21/44–11/3/44, 5; Bates, *The Battle for Leyte Gulf*, vol 3, 282.
45. Bates, *The Battle for Leyte Gulf*, vol 3, 267, 269.
46. Boise-AA Leyte, 10/21/44–11/3/44, 5.
47. FD.
48. UBWD, 10/1–31/44, 13; Boise–AA Leyte, 10/21/44–11/3/44, 4–6.
49. UBWD, 10/1–31/44, 13.
50. FD.
51. UBWD, 10/1–31/44, 14; Boise–Leyte, 6.
52. Boise–Leyte, 7–8, 11.
53. Letter, Commander Task Group 77.3 to Commander in Chief, United States Fleet, 14 November 1944, quoted in Boise-Leyte, 22.
54. Boise-Leyte, 13.
55. Boise-Leyte, 12–13.
56. FD.
57. UBWD, 10/1–31/44, 15–17; Bates, *The Battle for Leyte Gulf*, vol 5, 89.
58. Morison, *Leyte*, 178–182; USS BIRMINGHAM–War History, https://catalog.archives.gov/id/77526273?objectPage=8, 8.
59. This text uses the IJN designations given by Morison to simplify understanding of the several IJN units used for SHO-1. See Morison's *Leyte*, 161 for IJN nomenclature; Dull, *Imperial Japanese Navy*, 315.
60. Morison, *Leyte*, 174.
61. Morison, *Leyte*, 184–187.
62. Morison, *Leyte*, 193–195.
63. Bates, *The Battle for Leyte Gulf*, vol 5, 112; FD.
64. Ralph Teatsorth, "Admiral Hints Foe Lost 3 Battleships," *New York Times*, October 28, 1944.
65. UBWD, 10/1–31/44, 18; Morison, *Leyte*, 200, 224.
66. Raymond Hirsch, Raymond Hirsch Collection, interviewed by Joanna Roussis, May 28, 2004, Library of Congress, Veterans History Project https://www.loc.gov/item/afc2001001.13485/.
67. Morison, *Leyte*, 204.
68. Shima's force was reduced to four destroyers by the time they attacked at Surigao. Morison, *Leyte*, 164; Dull, *Imperial Japanese Navy*, 315, 319.
69. Morison, *Leyte*, 201; Bates, *The Battle for Leyte Gulf*, vol 5, 122.
70. Bates, *The Battle for Leyte Gulf*, vol 5, 123.
71. Morison, *Leyte*, 206.
72. This account of the battle was gifted to DB by a friend, and he kept it with his official papers. Adrian Stewart, *The Battle of Leyte Gulf* (Charles Scribner's Sons, 1980), 111.
73. USS BOISE–Rep of Engagement with Jap Surface Forces in Surigao Strait, Philippines, Morning 10/25/44 (Boise–Surigao), https://catalog.archives.gov/id/78684528?objectPage=2, 2.
74. Morison, *Leyte*, 211.
75. Morison, *Leyte*, 215–216.
76. Bates, *The Battle for Leyte Gulf*, vol 5, 517.
77. Boise-Surigao, 5–8.
78. Bates, *The Battle for Leyte Gulf*, vol 5, 517.
79. Bates, *The Battle for Leyte Gulf*, vol 5, 518.
80. Boise-Surigao, 8–9, 14.
81. Bates, *The Battle for Leyte Gulf*, vol 5, 519–520.
82. Boise-Surigao, 10.
83. Bates, *The Battle for Leyte Gulf*, vol 5, 522.
84. Boise-Surigao, 9.
85. Boise-Surigao, 10.
86. Bates, *The Battle for Leyte Gulf*, vol 5, 523.
87. Morison, *Leyte*, 221–224, 227.
88. Morison, *Leyte*, 232–233.
89. Boise-Surigao, 12.
90. UBWD, 10/1–31/44, 19–20; Dull, *Imperial Japanese Navy*, 322; Boise-Surigao, 14.
91. FD.
92. *RP*, Fitch, FFPC, 10.
93. Morison, *Leyte*, 221–222, 239–240.
94. Boise-Surigao, 21.
95. Morison, *Leyte*, 246.
96. Morison, *Leyte*, Chapter 12 "The Battle of Samar–The Main Action."
97. Morison, *Leyte*, 300–303.

98. Robin L. Rielly, *Kamikaze Attacks of World War II: A Complete History of Japanese Suicide Strikes on American Ships, by Aircraft and Other Means* (MacFarland, 2010), 45–46.
99. UBWD, 10/1-31/44, 21.
100. Captain Andrew Hamilton, USNR, "Where is Task Force Thirty-Four?" *Proceedings*, October 1960, vol. 86/10/692.
101. Mark Fitch interview.
102. UBWD, 10/1-31/44, 23; Boise-AA Leyte, 10/21/44-11/3/44, 7–9.
103. UBWD, 10/1-31/44, 23.
104. Worrall Reed Carter, *Beans, Bullets, and Black Oil: The Story of Fleet Logistics Afloat in the Pacific During World War II* (Department of the Navy, 1953), 238–239.
105. UBWD, 10/1-31/44, 24.
106. FD.
107. FD.
108. UBWD, 10/1-31/44, 25–27.
109. UBWD, 10/1-31/44, 28–30; Morison, *Leyte*, 343.
110. Morison, *Leyte*, 344.
111. UBWD, 11/1-30/44, https://catalog.archives.gov/id/139777270?objectPage=3, 1–2.
112. UBWD, 11/1-30/44, 4; Morison, *Leyte*, 345–346.
113. UBWD, 11/1-30/44, 5.
114. FD.
115. Boise-AA Leyte, 10/21/44-11/3/44, 10–12.
116. UBWD, 11/1-30/44, 6–10.
117. FD.
118. UBWD, 11/1-30/44, 14.
119. This may have been the last flight of the *Boise*'s SOC Seagulls, as sometime in September they swapped for the new OS2U Kingfisher scout planes, although logs continued to reference their aircraft simply as "SOC." Larkins, *Battleship and Cruiser Aircraft*, 160; UBWD, 11/1-30/44, 15–16.
120. UBWD, 11/1-30/44, 18.
121. "Roberts, John S. 10/30/1892-04/09/1953" Tombstone, Arlington National Cemetery.
122. UBWD, 11/1-30/44, 19–20.
123. UBWD, 12/1-31/44, https://catalog.archives.gov/id/139792551?objectPage=2, 1–4.
124. UBWD, 12/1-31/44, 4.
125. UBWD, 12/1-31/44, 5.
126. Morison, *Leyte*, 374.
127. UBWD, 12/1-31/44, 6; USS BOISE-For Reps of AA Acts in Leyte Gulf Philippines, 12/5-6/44 (Boise-AA Leyte), https://catalog.archives.gov/id/139766011?objectPage=3, 1–3.
128. UBWD, 12/1-31/44, 6; Boise-AA Leyte, 12/5-6/44, 4–6.
129. UBWD, 12/1-31/44, 6.
130. UBWD, 12/1-31/44, 6.
131. FD.
132. There is no biography of Downes career, but several sources indicate previous submarine service, including the submarine on his tombstone. "Willard Merrill Downes," *Find a Grave*, https://www.findagrave.com/memorial/100374091/-willard_merrill-downes; Morison, *Bismarcks Barrier*, 146; "Willard Merrill Downes," *The United States Navy Memorial*, https://navylog.navymemorial.org/downes-willard.
133. UBWD, 12/1-31/44, 7; Boise-AA Leyte, 12/5-6/44, 7–9.
134. RP, Fitch, FFPC, 10; Mark Fitch Interview; Letter Envelope, Warren D. Freeman to Don Fitch. March 3, 1975. FFPC.
135. UBWD, 12/1-31/44, 9.
136. UBWD, 12/1-31/44, 9; Morison, *Leyte*, 375–388.
137. UBWD, 12/1-31/44, 10.
138. Morison, *The Liberation of the Philippines*, 17–21.
139. Smith, *Triumph in the Philippines*, 43–45.
140. UBWD, 12/1-31/44, 11.
141. USS Nashville–War Diary, 12/1-31/44, https://catalog.archives.gov/id/139809259?objectPage=10, 9; James, *The Years of MacArthur*, Vol. 2, 608
142. UBWD, 12/1-31/44, 12; USS BOISE–Form Reps of AA Acts in Philippine Area 12/10, 13, 15, & 20/44 (Boise-AA Philippine), https://catalog.archives.gov/id/139793890?objectPage=4, 4–12.
143. FD.
144. Morison, *The Liberation of the Philippines*, 25; USS BOISE–Rep of Ops in support of Amphibious Landings on Mindoro Is, Philippines 12/13-15/44 (Boise–Mindoro), https://catalog.archives.gov/id/139804780?objectPage=2, 2.
145. Boise-Mindoro, 12; Smith, *Triumph in the Philippines*, 48.
146. Boise-Mindoro, 13; Boise-AA Philippine, 13–15; Morison, *The Liberation of the Philippines*, 29–30.
147. BOISE-Mindoro, 13.
148. FD.
149. UBWD, 12/1-31/44, 15–16.
150. UBWD, 12/1-31/44, 17.
151. Morison, *The Liberation of the Philippines*, 37–42.
152. UBWD, 12/1-31/44, 19.
153. RP, Fitch, Fitch Family Private Collection, 10.

Chapter 8

1. Generals Marshall, Eisenhower, and Arnold were all promoted to General of the Army along with MacArthur, while Admirals Leahy, King, and Nimitz were promoted to Fleet Admiral. Admiral Halsey was promoted to 5 stars the following December, and General Bradley achieved the rank in 1950. "Marshall and the Five-Star Rank," The George C. Marshall Foundation, December 15, 2017, https://www.marshallfoundation.org/articles-and-features/marshall-five-star-rank/.
2. *Gamble at Los Negros: The Admiralty Islands Campaign: 29 February 1944*, NHHC, https://www.history.navy.mil/browse-by-topic/wars-conflicts-and-operations/world-war-ii/1944/-admiralty-islands.html.

3. James, *The Years of MacArthur*, Vol. 2, 383.

4. S-Day landed four American divisions in the first wave, while D-Day (officially Operation Overlord) landed three American divisions and three Allied divisions in the first wave along with three airborne divisions that dropped the preceding night.

5. Smith, *Triumph in the Philippines*, 19.

6. John C. McManus, *To the End of the Earth: The U.S. Army and the Downfall of Japan, 1945* (Caliber, 2023), 16.

7. Smith, *Triumph in the Philippines*, 29–30.

8. Operations Plan. CANF SWPA No. 17–44. Commander Allied Naval Forces, Southwest Pacific Area and Commander Seventh Fleet, Luzon Attack Force, Task Force Seventy-seven Forces Headquarters, Hollandia, Dutch New Guinea, 20 November 1944, 1200, in *Luzon Campaign*, Vol. 1, United States Air Force Academy collections.

9. Samuel Eliot Morison, *The Liberation of the Philippines: Luzon, Mindanao, the Visayas 1944–1945*, vol 13: *History of United States Naval Operations in World War II*, 1948, Reprint (Little, Brown, 1989), 98

10. Morison, "The Liberation of the Philippines," 101–103, 110, 113.

11. USS Boise–Report of Operations in Support of the Occupation of Luzon Island, Philippines, 1/4–31/45 (Boise-Luzon), https://catalog.archives.gov/id/139908377?objectPage=6, 6.

12. FD.

13. *Boise Muster Roll*, https://catalog.archives.gov/id/125563586?objectPage=1458, 1458.

14. McManus, *To the End of the Earth*, 3.

15. MacArthur, *Reminiscences*, 239.

16. Boise-Luzon, 7; Morison, "The Liberation of the Philippines," 115.

17. Boise-Luzon, 8.

18. Boise-Luzon, 8.

19. James, *The Years of MacArthur*, Vol. 2, 619–620.

20. Roger Egeberg, *The General: MacArthur and the Man He Called "Doc"* (Oak Mountain Press, 1993), 100.

21. USS TAYLOR—Rep of ops in Support of the Seizure & Occupation of Luzon Is, Philippines, 1/4–31/45, including AA acts on 1/7, 8, & 10/45, & sinking of Jap midget submarine on 1/5/45 (Taylor-Luzon), https://catalog.archives.gov/id/139864326?objectPage=31, 31.

22. Taylor-Luzon, 32.

23. MacArthur, *Reminiscences*, 239; Morison, "The Liberation of the Philippines," 115; USS Phoenix–War Diary, 1/1–31/45, https://catalog.archives.gov/id/139860937?objectPage=4, 4.

24. Boise-Luzon, 9; FD.

25. Boise-Luzon, 9.

26. The Phoenix log suggested that the Nick may have been the same aircraft previously chased away by anti-aircraft fire. Phoenix–War Diary, 1/1–31/45, 4–5; Boise-Luzon, 9–10; USS BOISE–Form reps Of AA acts While en route to & at Lingayen Gulf, Luzon Is, Philippines 1/7–12/45 (Boise–AA Lingayen) , https://catalog.archives.gov/id/139889921?objectPage=3, 1, 3.

27. While *Boise* reported the aircraft as an "Irving," *Phoenix* identified it as a "Val." Boise-Luzon, 10; Phoenix–War Diary, 1/1–31/45, 5.

28. Phoenix–War Diary, 1/1–31/45, 5.

29. Boise-Luzon, 11.

30. Morison, "The Liberation of the Philippines," 116.

31. James, *The Years of MacArthur*, Vol. 2, 620.

32. Morison, "The Liberation of the Philippines," 116.

33. Boise-Luzon, 11.

34. Boise-Luzon, 11.

35. Boise–AA Lingayen, 7.

36. Egeberg, *The General*, 100–103.

37. Egeberg, *The General*, 104.

38. Dyar interview; Fenton interview.

39. Morison, "The Liberation of the Philippines," 116.

40. USS CALLAWAY–War History, https://catalog.archives.gov/id/77631012?objectPage=7, 7.

41. Phoenix–War Diary, 1/1–31/45, 6.

42. USS Kadashan Bay–War History, https://catalog.archives.gov/id/77690409?objectPage=20, 19–20.

43. Boise-Luzon, 12.

44. Boise-Luzon, 12; Morison, "The Liberation of the Philippines," 303–310.

45. USS KITKUN BAY–Rep of air ops Covering amphibious assault force en route Lingayen Gulf, Luzon Is, Philippines, 12/31/44–1/8/45, including enemy suicide crash dive off West coast of Luzon Is, Philippines on 1/8/45 (Kitkun Bay–Luzon), https://catalog.archives.gov/id/139828311?objectPage=3, 3.

46. Boise–AA Lingayen, 9–10; Boise-Luzon, 13; Kitkun Bay–Luzon, 3–4; Morison, "The Liberation of the Philippines," 326.

47. Boise–AA Lingayen, 11–12.

48. Boise-Luzon, 13.

49. FD.

50. Egeberg, *The General*, 99–100.

51. Chief of Naval Operations, "Amphibious Landings in Lingayen Gulf," *Aerology and Amphibious Warfare: NAVAER 50-30T-9*, July 1945, https://www.history.navy.mil/research/library/online-reading-room/title-list-alphabetically/a/amphibious-landings-lingayen-gulf.html.

52. Smith, *Triumph in the Philippines*, 69.

53. Morison, "The Liberation of the Philippines," 128, 131.

54. Boise-Luzon, 14.

55. Boise-Luzon, 37.

56. USS Hodges–War Diary, 1/1–31/45, https://catalog.archives.gov/id/139895290?objectPage=6, 6.

57. *Columbia VI (CL-56): 1942–1959*, NHHC, https://www.history.navy.mil/research/histories/ship-histories/danfs/c/columbia-vi.html.

58. Boise–AA Lingayen, 13–14.

59. FD.

60. DB likely misidentified two battleships. While *West Virginia* and *Colorado* were present, both the *Tennessee* and the *Maryland* were

operating elsewhere. As for the cruisers, the *Astoria* was operating elsewhere while the *Australia* and *Minneapolis* were present. Morison, "The Liberation of the Philippines," 303–304.

61. Morison, "The Liberation of the Philippines," 127.

62. Milo Sandoval, "The History of Pangasinan: A Storied Provincial Capitol," *Our Pangasinan*, February 9, 2023, https://www.ourpangasinan.com/history/the-history-of-pangasinan-a-storied-provincial-capitol/.

63. Information on Filipino reactions to the landing and collateral damage gathered from official memorials in Lingayen, Philippines. The story of the guerrilla trying to signal American forces is commemorated in the painting James Turnbull, *Spirit of 1945*, 1945, oil on canvas, 26 × 20 in., https://www.history.navy.mil/content/history/nhhc/our-collections/art/exhibits/conflicts-and-operations/wwii/art-of-naval-amphibious-operations-from-wwii/spirit-of-1945.html.

64. Boise–Luzon, 14.

65. Photos and plaques from Veterans Memorial Park, Lingayen Beach, Pangasinan, Philippines.

66. *Reports of General MacArthur: Japanese Operations in the Southwest Pacific Area*, Vol II, Part II, Center for Military History Publication 13-2, Facsimile Reprint 1994, 467.

67. Morison, "The Liberation of the Philippines,"131–132, 138.

68. Boise–Luzon, 14–15.

69. Boise–Luzon, 15.

70. Photo, Pangasinan Memorial; James, *The Years of MacArthur*, Vol. 2, 621.

71. The "MacArthur Landing Park" in Dagupan has a memorial and large picture of the general. A half mile west near an inlet is a prominent statue of the General atop a pedestal known as the "Old Site of MacArthur Park." A few hundred yards further west is yet another memorial, now on private property, that claims "Luzon Landing. On this shore. Known as Blue Beach. Bonuan. Dagupan City.

72. Author observations of Corregidor; McManus, *To the End of the Earth*, 17, 19.

73. Military History Section Headquarters, Army Forces Far East. *Philippine Area Naval Operations: Part IV, January 1945–August 1945*. Japanese Monograph Series. No. 114. 1–4.

74. The *Boise* log concluded that while the smoke screens were largely effective, the nature of *Boise*'s mission to host General MacArthur and move between formations meant that they often found themselves without cover and assumed they were the only heavy warship visible to enemy planes. They recommended in the future that they carry their own smoke pellets and thus create their own smoke screen. Boise–Luzon, 39; Samuel J. Cox, *The Invasion of Luzon–Battle of Lingayen Gulf, January 1945*, NHHC, H-040-3, January 2020, https://www.history.navy.mil/about-us/leadership/director/directors-corner/h-grams/h-gram-040/h-040-3.html.

75. Morison, "The Liberation of the Philippines," 138.

76. *Reports of General MacArthur: Japanese Operations in the Southwest Pacific Area*, Vol II, Part II, Center for Military History Publication 13-2, Facsimile Reprint 1994, 571–572 & notes, https://history.army.mil/books/wwii/MacArthur%20Reports/MacArthur%20V2%20P2/ch17.htm.

77. Boise–Luzon, 16.

78. Morison, "The Liberation of the Philippines," 139–140; Boise–Luzon, 16.

79. Boise–Luzon, 16, 41; Boise–AA Lingayen, 17.

80. Morison, "The Liberation of the Philippines,"142–143.

81. Boise–Luzon https://catalog.archives.gov/id/139908377?objectPage=176, 17.

82. FD.

83. *USS Boise Muster Rolls*, https://catalog.archives.gov/id/125563586?objectPage=146, 146, 1465; Boise–Luzon, 19; Dyar Interview.

84. Boise–AA Lingayen, 21–22.

85. Boise–Luzon, 19; Kit C. Carter and Robert Mueller, *The Army Air Forces in World War II: Combat Chronology 1941–1945*, Albert F. Simpson Historical Research Center Maxwell (AFB: Air University, 1973), 536–545.

86. McManus, *To the End of the Earth*, 19; Boise–Luzon, 20.

87. USS Richard W Suesens–War Diary, 1/1–31/45, https://catalog.archives.gov/id/139861126?objectPage=3, 2–3.

88. Boise–Luzon, 21.

89. *RP*, Fitch, FFPC.

90. *RP*, Fitch, FFPC, 10–11.

91. FD, Boise–Luzon, 22–32, 36.

92. Boise–Luzon, 33–34; Morison, "The Liberation of the Philippines," 187–188.

93. Boise–Luzon, 35–36; Morison, "The Liberation of the Philippines," 189.

94. UBWD, 2/1–28/45, https://catalog.archives.gov/id/139915938?objectPage=2, 1.

95. FD.

96. UBWD, 2/1–28/45, 3; USS Boise–Report of Operations in Support of the Assault Landings on Southern Bataan & Corregidor Island, Luzon Island, Philippines, 2/13–17/45 (Boise–Corregidor), https://catalog.archives.gov/id/139906347?objectPage=2, 2.

97. Carter and Mueller, *The Army Air Forces in World War II: Combat Chronology 1941–1945*, 570–571.

98. Author observations of Corregidor.

99. Author observations of Corregidor.

100. Smith, *Triumph in the Philippines*, 335–339.

101. Boise–Corregidor, 4.

102. Morison, "The Liberation of the Philippines," 199.

103. UBWD, 2/1–28/45, 3; Boise–Corregidor, 6, 28.

104. Boise–Corregidor, 7.

105. Boise–Corregidor, 8; UBWD, 2/1–28/45, 4.

106. Boise–Corregidor, 9.

107. Boise–Corregidor, 10–12.

108. Boise–Corregidor, 12.
109. Boise–Corregidor, 12.
110. Boise–Corregidor 3, 13–14.
111. UBWD, 2/1–28/45, 5; FD.
112. Boise–Corregidor, 15.
113. Boise–Corregidor, 15, 16.
114. Boise–Corregidor, 16; Smith, *Triumph in the Philippines*, 333.
115. Boise–Corregidor, 17.
116. The leaflet wording quoted comes from a surviving leaflet dated 17 February 1945. It is highly probable that leaflets dropped on preceding dates relayed the same message, if not used the exact same wording. "'Bataan Appeal' Leaflet," 17 February, 1945, Psychological Warfare Branch, GHQ, in *WWII Anti-Japan Propaganda*, Collection, Pacific University Oregon, https://washingtoncountyheritage.org/s/world-war-ii-propaganda/item/126054#:~:text=A%20propaganda%20leaflet%20issued%20by%20the%20Allied%20Forces,soon%20after%20General%20MacArthur%20landed%20in%20October%2C%201944; Boise–Corregidor, 17.
117. Boise–Corregidor, 17.
118. Morison, "The Liberation of the Philippines," 202.
119. The official U.S. Army report from the war suggested 20 percent planned casualties, and Rock Force commander Colonel Jones estimated 50 percent. Keven Maurer, *Rock Force: The American Paratroopers Who Took Back Corregidor and Exacted MacArthur's Revenge on Japan* (Caliber, 2020), 74.
120. Boise–Corregidor, 19.
121. The official Army report recorded the first paratrooper touching down at 0833. Smith, *Triumph in the Philippines*, 341; Boise–Corregidor, 20; FD.
122. Smith, *Triumph in the Philippines*, 338; Boise–Corregidor, 20.
123. Boise–Corregidor, 20.
124. Smith, *Triumph in the Philippines*, 341–342.
125. Smith, *Triumph in the Philippines*, 341.
126. Morison, "The Liberation of the Philippines," 203; Smith, *Triumph in the Philippines*, 345.
127. Smith, *Triumph in the Philippines*, 344.
128. Boise–Corregidor, 20.
129. Morison, "The Liberation of the Philippines," 204.
130. Boise–Corregidor, 21.
131. Boise–Corregidor, 22.
132. Smith, *Triumph in the Philippines*, 345.
133. Boise–Corregidor, 23–24.
134. Boise–Corregidor, 24.
135. Smith, *Triumph in the Philippines*, 346.
136. Nathan N. Prefer, *The Luzon Campaign, 1945: MacArthur Returns* (Casemate, 2024), 117.
137. Smith, *Triumph in the Philippines*, 347–348.
138. "Rock Force Memorial," Corregidor, Philippines.
139. Boise–Corregidor, 24–25.
140. UBWD, 2/1–28/45, 9–11.
141. Ian W. Toll, *Twilight of the Gods: War in the Western Pacific, 1944–1945* (W.W. Norton, 2020), 486.
142. Williamson Murray and Allan R. Millett, *A War to Be Won: Fighting the Second World War*, paperback ed. (Belknap, 2001), 476–478.
143. Prefer, *The Luzon Campaign, 1945*, 258.
144. FD.
145. *RP*, Fitch, FFPC, 11.
146. Morison, "The Liberation of the Philippines," 222.
147. USS Boise–Rep of Ops in Support of the Invasion of Zamboanga Peninsula, Mindanao Is, Philippines 3/8–12/24 (Boise–Zamboanga), https://catalog.archives.gov/id/139956576?objectPage=10, 10–11, 61.
148. Morison, "The Liberation of the Philippines," 222; Boise–Zamboanga, 14–15, 20–21, 26.
149. Boise–Zamboanga, 23–24.
150. Smith, *Triumph in the Philippines*, 596–597.
151. FD.
152. Morison, "The Liberation of the Philippines," 233–236.
153. COMCRUDIV 15–War Diary, 3/1–31/45, https://catalog.archives.gov/id/139974192?objectPage=8, 7.
154. Scott, *Rampage*, 316, 395–402.
155. Nearly all accounts of the battle speak of the smell. Scott, *Rampage*, 422; James, *The Years of MacArthur*, Vol. 2, 653.
156. James, *The Years of MacArthur*, Vol. 2, 655; Dyar Interview.
157. FD.

Chapter 9

1. FD.
2. ABSD-4-War History, https://catalog.archives.gov/id/77580951?objectPage=7, 1, 4, 7.
3. DB's handwriting is difficult to read in this case, so the sailor's name in the text may not be correct. FD.
4. ABSD-4-War History, https://catalog.archives.gov/id/77580951?objectPage=4, 4.
5. USS BOISE–Rep of ops in support of the invasions of Sadau & Tarakan Is, Borneo, 4/26/1945–5/3/1945 (Boise–Tarakan), https://catalog.archives.gov/id/140010696, 1.
6. Morison, *The Liberation of the Philippines*, 255–258; Harry A. Gailey, *The War in the Pacific: From Pearl Harbor to Tokyo Bay* (Presidio Press, 1995), 469–470.
7. Boise–Tarakan, 2–3.
8. Boise–Tarakan, 3.
9. Boise–Tarakan, 9–10.
10. Murray and Millett, *A War to Be Won*, 482.
11. Boise–Tarakan, 12; UBWD, 5/1–31/45, https://catalog.archives.gov/id/140069584?objectPage=3, 3.
12. Gavin Long, ed., *The Final Campaign, series 1, vol. VII: Australia in the War of 1939–1945* (Adelaide: Griffin Press, 1963), 412.

13. Long, *The Final Campaign*, 414, 416–417.
14. Boise-Tarakan, 13–14; Morison, *The Liberation of the Philippines*, 262.
15. Boise-Tarakan, 14.
16. Rottman, *FUBAR*, 30.
17. UBWD, 5/1–31/45, 6.
18. UBWD, 5/1–31/45, 8.
19. MacArthur, *Reminiscences*, 260.
20. USS BOISE–Rep of Opers in Support of the Assault Landings in the Brunei Bay Area, Borneo, 6/10–11/45 (Boise-Brunei), https://catalog.archives.gov/id/101711121?objectPage=17, 17; UBWD, 6/1–30/45, https://catalog.archives.gov/id/77464667?objectPage=4, 2.
21. FD.
22. UBWD, 6/1–30/45, 3–4.
23. MacArthur, *Reminiscences*, 255.
24. Morison, *The Liberation of the Philippines*, 264.
25. Boise-Brunei, 5.
26. UBWD, 6/1–30/45, 6.
27. Fenton Interview.
28. UBWD, 6/1–30/45, 7; Boise-Brunei, 9.
29. Long, *The Final Campaign*, 467.
30. UBWD, 6/1–30/45, 7.
31. *USS Boise (CL 47)*, Navsource Online: Cruiser Photo Archive, Photo 0404720, original with MacArthur Library and Museum, https://navsource.org/archives/04/047/04047.htm; UBWD, 6/1–30/45, 8.
32. UBWD, 6/1–30/45, 10–11.
33. UBWD, 6/1–30/45, 13–14.
34. FD.
35. UBWD, 6/1–30/45, 14–15.
36. FD, UBWD, 6/1–30/45, 16.
37. UBWD, 7/1–31/45, https://catalog.archives.gov/id/77484453?objectPage=3, 2–3.
38. FD.
39. Prefer, *The Luzon Campaign*, 256; Toll, *Twilight of the Gods*, 640, 675.
40. Other sources suggest different numbers of troops. This staff study includes the number in the text and another 356,902 troops in the "follow--up echelons." General Headquarters Southwest Pacific Area, *Basic Plan for Olympic Operation*, 28 May 1945, in the Ike Skelton Combined Arms Research Library Digital Library, https://cgsc.contentdm.oclc.org/digital/collection/p4013coll8/id/6061/, 10.
41. McManus, *To the End of the Earth*, 294.
42. Toll, *Twilight of the Gods*, 697.
43. Murray and Millett, *A War to Be Won*, 523.
44. Toll, *Twilight of the Gods*, 706–708.
45. Toll, *Twilight of the Gods*, 715–718; National Archives, "The Atomic Bombing of Hiroshima and Nagasaki," https://visit.archives.gov/whats-on/-explore-exhibits/atomic-bombing-hiroshima-and-nagasaki.
46. Murray and Millett, *A War to Be Won*, 524.
47. V-J Day, 1945 photo collection, TESSA, Digital Collections of the Los Angeles Public Library, https://tessa2.lapl.org/digital/collection/photos/search/searchterm/V-J%20Day%2C%201945./field/subjec/mode/exact/conn/and.
48. UBWD, 8/1–31/45, https://catalog.archives.gov/id/77500438?objectPage=2, 2.
49. Toll, *Twilight of the Gods*, 751–752.
50. Starnes interview.
51. Toll, *Twilight of the Gods*, 750, 756–762.
52. UBWD, 9/1–30/45, https://catalog.archives.gov/id/77540567?objectPage=1, 1–5; FD.
53. UBWD, 10/1–31/45, https://catalog.archives.gov/id/77565378?objectPage=2, 1.
54. UBWD, 10/1–31/45, 3–4.
55. UBWD, 10/1–31/45, 4; *RP*, Fitch, FFPC, 11.
56. "'Home Alive By '45': Operation Magic Carpet," National World War 2 Museum, October 2, 2020, https://www.nationalww2museum.org/war/articles/operation-magic-carpet-1945.
57. UBWD, 10/1–31/45, 5–6.
58. Bonnie Docherty, "USS Boise Crew Members Gather in Natick: Navy Veterans Drop Anchor to Reminisce about World War II." Unknown newspaper clipping, 1997, FFPC.
59. UBWD, 10/1–31/45, 6.
60. Speech, President Harry S. Truman address on foreign policy at the Navy Day Celebration in New York City, October 27, 1945, Recording, Harry S. Truman Library and Museum, online, https://www.trumanlibrary.gov/soundrecording-records/-sr64-18-president-trumans-address-foreign-policy-navy-day-celebration-new.
61. "Navy Day 1945, New York City," Painting, 80-G-K-6547, NHHC, https://www.history.navy.mil/content/history/nhhc/our-collections/photography/numerical-list-of-images/nara-series/80-g-k/80-G-K-06000/80-g-k-6547-navy-day-1945--new-york-city.html.
62. Elliot Rosenberg, "Navy Day in New York, 1945: The Biggest Display of Military Might the Nation had Ever Seen," *Wall Street Journal*, October 26, 2015, https://www.wsj.com/articles/navy-day-in-new-york-1945-1445899687.
63. *RP*, Fitch, FFPC, 12.
64. UBWD, 10/1–31/45, 7.
65. "Navy Training Course Certificate" 11 November 1945, FFPC.
66. FD.
67. COMNAVEU–War Diary, 11/1–30/45, https://catalog.archives.gov/id/77576597?objectPage=5, 2–3.
68. "'Home Alive By '45': Operation Magic Carpet," National World War 2 Museum, October 2, 2020, https://www.nationalww2museum.org/war/articles/operation-magic-carpet-1945.
69. "Passenger Regulations: U.S.S. Boise, 8 November 1945," Fitch Papers, IMHM, 2008.60.1/17.
70. "'Home Alive By '45': Operation Magic Carpet," National World War 2 Museum, October 2, 2020, https://www.nationalww2museum.org/war/articles/operation-magic-carpet-1945.
71. FD; Mark Fitch interview; Donald Fitch, "Agreement to Extend Enlistment," 20 June 1944, FFPC; Boise (CL-47), 1/28/39–7/1/46, 107.
72. FD.

Epilogue

1. Mason C. Doan, *American Housing Production, 1880–2000: A Concise History* (University Press of America, 1996) 53–54.
2. "Passenger Regulations: U.S.S. *Boise*, 8 November 1945," Fitch Papers, IMHM, 2008.60.1/17.
3. *U.S.S.* Boise *Memorial Service* program, September 26, 1987, FFPC, 12.
4. Lieutenant Carlos E. Zartmann, AN, "The Argentine Navy (Pictorial)" *Proceedings*, July 1960, Vol. 86/7/689, U.S. Naval Institute, https://www.usni.org/magazines/proceedings/1960/july/argentine-navy-pictorial.
5. Antonio Luis Sapienza, *Revolucion Libertadora: Volume 2: The 1955 Coup that Overthrew President Peron*, Latin America War Series (Helion & Company, 2023), 91–93, 100–102.
6. Robert Farley, "Meet the General Belgrano: The Only Ship Ever Sunk by a Nuclear Submarine," *The National Interest*, June 25, 2021, https://nationalinterest.org/blog/reboot/meet-general-belgrano-only-ship-ever-sunk-nuclear-submarine-188481.
7. "The 'Armada' Trial, According to Prosecutors, Shows the Operation of Illegal Repression in the Region," *Telam, Agencia Nacional de Noticias*, 12 August 2015, https://web.archive.org/web/20180308041816/http://memoria.telam.com.ar/noticia/-armada---2a—ronda-de-alegatos—con-descripcion-de-ccd_n5482.
8. *U.S.S.* Boise *Memorial Service* program, September 26, 1987, FFPC, 12.
9. "USS Boise, 11 Battle Stars And All, At End," *The Courier*, Saturday August 15, 1981, FFPC.
10. U.S.S. *Boise* display, IMHM, Boise, Idaho.
11. Letter from D. B. "Scoop" Fitch to The Executive Committee: U.S.S. Boise, February 7, 1989. FFPC.
12. "Christening of USS BOISE SSN764," Pamphlet, Newport News Shipbuilding, October 20, 1990, in FFPC, 14.
13. "Attack Submarines–SSN," U.S. Navy, 15 Mar 2024, https://www.navy.mil/Resources/Fact-Files/Display-FactFiles/Article/2169558/attack-submarines-ssn/.
14. "Bash from Bottle of Bubbly Christens N-Sub Boise," *The Salt Lake Tribune*, Monday, October 22, 1990, copy found in FFPC.
15. "Armada I (Fracassi)," Sentences, Sentences in Trials Against Humanity, *Lesa Humanidad*, Ministerio de Justicia y Derechos Humanos, Gobierno de la Provincia de Buenos Aires, https://derechoshumanos.mjus.gba.gob.ar/sentencia/129-armada-i-fracassi/.
16. "Rear Admiral Edward J. ("Mike") Moran, USN (Retired) (1893–1957)," *Department of the Navy–Naval Historical Center*, https://ibiblio.org/hyperwar/OnlineLibrary/photos/persus/uspers-m/ej-moran.htm; "Edward Moran, Ex-Admiral, Dies," *New York Times*, Apr 25, 1957; "Adm Edward Joseph 'Mike' Moran," *Find a Grave*, https://www.findagrave.com/memorial/87714007/edward_joseph-moran.
17. "Vice Adm. Leo Thebaud, 90; Led a Cruiser Division," *The New York Times*, Apr 20, 1980; "Admiral Thebaud Dies," *The Montreal Gazette*, April 21, 1980, https://news.google.com/newspapers?nid=1946&dat=19800421&id=ihQyAAAAIBAJ&sjid=aaQFAAAAIBAJ&pg=3189,72558.
18. "Stephan B. Robinson: Navy Captain," *New York Times*, Nov 10, 1990; "Capt Stephan Boutwell Robinson," *Find a Grave*, https://www.findagrave.com/memorial/43724181/stephan_boutwell-robinson.
19. Don B. Fitch, *USS Boise*, Reunion Newsletter, November 12, 1987, FFPC.
20. "Death: Donald B. Fitch," *Deseret News*, July 10, 1998.
21. A search through the first and last names of the crew who died in the battle did not clearly reveal who Mark was named after, and DB never shared who it was.
22. Mark Fitch interview.
23. "Yesterday's Heroes: At Peace Today … No Regrets," *The Salt Lake Tribune*, Sunday, November 11, 1962, https://newspapers.lib.utah.edu/details?id=26486489.
24. Mark Fitch interview.
25. "Maj. Gen. Maurice L. Watts–Utah TAG–1964–1980," Portrait, Utah National Guard., https://www.flickr.com/photos/utahnationalguard/8700381264/in/album-72157633382094571.
26. Personal Letter, Major General Maurice L. Watts to Donald Fitch, 16 April 1980, FFPC.
27. Personal Letter, Justice F. Henri Henriod to Donald Fitch, postmarked 31 Dec. 1978, FFPC.
28. Mark Fitch interview.
29. Personal Letter, Captain Stephan B. Robinson (USN Ret.) to Donald Fitch, 24 February 1971, FFPC.
30. Mark Fitch interview.
31. "Barbary Queen Entertains," *The Idaho Statesman*, Tuesday, October 12, 1971.
32. D.B. Fitch, *U.S.S. Boise: Second Reunion*, Newsletter, November 1971, FFPC.
33. Larry McMullen, "The Time Machine," *Philadelphia Daily News*, October 5, 1973, FFPC.
34. Postcard, Donald Fitch to Mrs. D. B. Fitch, Apr 3, 1975.
35. H.T. Jenkins, Jr., letter to Don B. Fitch, 10 May 1975, FFPC.
36. Letter to Pat Markuson, USS *Denver*, from Donald Fitch, April 19, 1975, FFPC.
37. Letter. James D. Johnston to Don [Fitch] and the USS *Boise*, May 25, 1987, FFPC.
38. "Death: Donald B. Fitch," *Deseret News*, July 10, 1998.
39. "USS Boise: Navy Crew, Historians Puzzle Over Artifacts," *The Idaho Statesman*, Saturday, September 26, 1987; *U.S.S. Boise Memorial Service* program, September 26, 1987, FFPC; *Tenth Reunion: U.S.S. Boise Cl-47*, pamphlet, Sept 23–26, 1987, FFPC.

40. Dirk Kempthorne, Mayor of Boise, "Proclamation: U.S.S. Boise Crew Member Day," 26 Sept 1987, in FFPC.
41. "*USS Boise: 10th Reunion*," Photo Album, FFPC.
42. Photo, Delta High School Class of 1941: 1991 Reunion, FFPC.
43. Donald B. Fitch Funeral Registry, FFPC.
44. Mark Fitch interview.

Bibliography

Official Documents

Bates, Richard W. *The Battle for Leyte Gulf, October 1944: Strategical and Tactical Analysis.* Vol. 1, *Preliminary Operations Until 0719 October 17th, 1944, Including Battle off Formosa.* Bureau of Naval Personnel, 1953.

Chief of Naval Operations. "Amphibious Landings in Lingayen Gulf." *Aerology and Amphibious Warfare* NAVAER 50-30T-9 (1945). https://www.history.navy.mil/research/library/online-reading-room/title-list-alphabetically/a/-amphibious-landings-lingayen-gulf.html.

Command Summary of Fleet Admiral Chester W. Nimitz, USN: Nimitz "Graybook." 8 vols. U.S. Naval War College, 2013. Internet Archive.

The Java Sea Campaign: Combat Narratives. Office of Naval Intelligence, 1943. U.S. National Archives.

Military History Section Headquarters, Army Forces Far East. *Philippine Area Naval Operations: Part IV, January 1945–August 1945.* Japanese Monograph Series. No. 114.

Reports of General MacArthur: Japanese Operations in the Southwest Pacific Area, Vol. 2, Part 2, Center for Military History Publication 13-2, Facsimile Reprint 1994.

USS *Boise*. Various Reports. U.S. National Archives.

USS *Phoenix* War Diary. U.S. National Archives.

USS *Salt Lake City* War Diary. U.S. National Archives.

Interviews

Blinn, Welford C. (Commander, USS *Pope*). Interview by U.S. Navy. October 22, 1945. https://catalog.archives.gov/id/278475679.

Butler, W.C. (Gunnery Officer, USS *Boise*, CL-47). Interview by U.S. Navy. October 18, 1943. https://catalog.archives.gov/id/278477619.

Campbell, Roy Allen, *Roy Allen Campbell Collection.* Interview by Carl Cox. July 14, 2010. Library of Congress, Veterans History Project. https://www.loc.gov/item/afc2001001.75599/.

Dyar, Joseph Eugene (Turret Officer, Ensign, USS *Boise*), *Joseph Eugene Dyar Collection.* Interview by Daniel Lacasse. January 15, 2003. Library of Congress, Veterans History Project. https://www.loc.gov/item/afc2001001.07912/.

Fenton, Joseph Franklin (Engineer, USS *Boise*), *Joseph Franklin Fenton Collection.* Interview by Constance Jones. December 2007. https://www.loc.gov/item/afc2001001.82111/.

Fitch, Mark O. (Son of Donald "DB" Fitch). Interview by the author. January 26–29, 2021.

Hirsch, Raymond (Boatswain's Mate, USS *Boise*), *Raymond Hirsch Collection.* Interview by Joanna Roussis. May 28, 2004. Library of Congress, Veterans History Project. https://www.loc.gov/item/afc2001001.13485/.

Kikunori Kijima. Interrogated by Captain C. Shands, USN. November 27, 1945. Interrogation Nav No. 106, USSBS No. 464, in "Interrogations of Japanese Officials: Volume 2," *United States Strategic Bombing Survey (Pacific), OPNAV-P-03-100.* Government Printing Office. 1946.

Klemm, Frederick Robert (Machinist Mate, USS *Boise*), *Frederick Robert Klemm Collection.* Interview by Leslie Harrold. January 27, 2004. Library of Congress, Veterans History Project. https://www.loc.gov/item/afc2001001.10835/.

Lowry, Raymond Orton (Gunner's Mate 1st Class, USS *Boise*), *Raymond Orton Lowry Collection.* Interview by Joshua Horner. November 10, 2009. Library of Congress, Veterans History Project. https://www.loc.gov/item/afc2001001.69948/.

Moran, Captain Edward J. (Commander, USS *Boise*). Interview by U.S. Navy. February 15, 1943. https://catalog.archives.gov/id/278490145.

Morris, Brian (Chief Quartermaster, USS *Stockdale* (DDG-106)). Interview by author. February 17, 2025.

Mulvey, William (Sailor, USS *Boise*). Interview by James Smither. September 15, 2009. Grand Valley State University. https://digitalcollections.library.gvsu.edu/document/29314.

Olivar, Julian (AO3/(AW/IW), USS *Wasp*). Interview by the author. March 13, 2022.

Oshier, Edward Roth (Commander, USS *Boise*). *Edward Roth Oshier Collection.* Interview by Jolene Pierson. August 8, 2007. Library of Congress, Veterans History Project. https://www.loc.gov/item/afc2001001.54941/.

Piano, Michael (Commander, USS *Gabrielle Giffords*, LCS-10). Interview by the author. August 22, 2020.

Starnes, James (Ensign, USS *Boise*). Interview. June 10, 2010. Digital Collections of the National WWII Museum, Oral Histories. https://www.ww2online.org/view/james-starnes#segment-1.

Unpublished and Privately Published Eyewitness Accounts

The personal papers of Donald "DB" B. Fitch contained written accounts from several men that are not attributable to any specific person. However, the booklet printed for multiple *Boise* reunions includes references, including the statement "Personal notes from former crewmembers: Darrell Allen, Donald R. Elbert, Donald B. Fitch, George Flores, Arthur E. Griggs, Melvin Howard, John Macomber and Wallace Nicely."

D'Angelo, Anthony S., Papers. D'Angelo Family Private Collection.

Eubank, Eugene, Major General, Oral History. United States Air Force Academy Oral History Collection. File no. 313.

Fitch, Donald B., Papers. Fitch Family Private Collection.

Fitch, Donald B., Papers. Idaho Military History Museum.

Grant, Harold W., Lieutenant General, Oral History. United States Air Force Academy Oral History Collection. File no. 408.

Hotchkiss, Gilbert. Letters and correspondence. National Museum of the American Sailor.

Moneymaker, Garnett Bailey, and Henry Shapiro. *Garnett Bailey Moneymaker Collection*. 1937. Personal Narrative. https://www.loc.gov/item/afc2001001.83353/.

Tripp, Robert, Papers. Tripp Family Private Collection.

Books and Articles

Atkinson, Rick. *An Army at Dawn: The War in North Africa, 1942-1943*, Henry Holt, 2002.

Atkinson, Rick. *The Day of Battle: The War in Sicily and Italy, 1943-1944*, Henry Holt, 2008.

Blumenson, Martin. *Salerno to Cassino*. United States Army in World War II: The Mediterranean Theater of Operations. Center of Military History, 1969.

Cannon, M. Hamlin. *Leyte: The Return to the Philippines*. United States Army in World War II: The War in the Pacific. Office of the Chief of Military History, 1954.

Carter, Kit C., and Robert Mueller. *US Army Air Forces in World War II: Combat Chronology, 1941-1945*. Albert F. Simpson Historical Research Center. Air University, 1973.

Carter, Worrall Reed. *Beans, Bullets, and Black Oil: The Story of Fleet Logistics Afloat in the Pacific During World War II*. Department of the Navy, 1953.

Conn, Stetson, Rose C. Engelman, and Byron Fairchild. *Guarding the United States and Its Outposts*. Government Printing Office, 1964.

Cox, Samuel J. "The Invasion of Luzon–Battle of Lingayen Gulf, January 1945." Naval History and Heritage Command, H-040-3 (2020). https://www.history.navy.mil/about-us/leadership/director/directors-corner/h-grams/h-gram-040/h-040-3.html.

Dear, I.C.B., and M.R.D. Foot, eds. *The Oxford Companion to World War II*. Paperback edition. Oxford University Press, 2002.

Dull, Paul S. *A History of the Imperial Japanese Navy, 1941-1945*. Naval Institute Press, 1978.

Dyer, Vice Admiral George Carroll, USN (ret). *Amphibians Came to Conquer: The Story of Admiral Richmond Kelly Turner*. Vols. 1 and 2. Government Printing Office, 1972.

Egeberg, Roger. *The General: MacArthur and the Man He Called "Doc."* Oak Mountain Press, 1993.

Frank, Richard B. *Guadalcanal: The Definitive Account of the Landmark Battle*. Penguin, 1990.

Frank, Richard B. *Tower of Skulls: A History of the Asia-Pacific War, July 1937–May 1942*. Norton, 2020.

Friedman, Norman. *US Cruisers: An Illustrated Design History*. Naval Institute Press, 1984.

Gailey, Harry A. *MacArthur's Victory: The War in New Guinea, 1943-1944*. Presidio Press, 2004.

Gailey, Harry A. *The War in the Pacific: From Pearl Harbor to Tokyo Bay*. Presidio Press, 1995.

Garey, Jennifer A. *San Diego's Naval Training Center*. Images of America series. Arcadia Publishing, 2008.

Garland, Albert N., Howard McGaw Smyth, and Martin Blumenson. *Sicily and the Surrender of Italy*. United States Army in World War II: The Mediterranean Theater of Operations. Office of the Chief of Military History, 1965.

Ginter, Steve. *Curtiss SOC Seagull*. Naval Fighters Number 89. Ginter Publishing, 2011.

Glines, Carroll V. *The Doolittle Raid: America's Daring First Strike Against Japan*. Schiffer, 1991.

Hamilton, Nigel. *War and Peace: FDR's Final Odyssey; D-Day to Yalta, 1943-1945*. Mariner Books, 2020.

Hara, Tameichi, Fred Saito, and Roger Pineau. *Japanese Destroyer Captain: Pearl Harbor, Guadalcanal, Midway; The Great Naval Battles as Seen Through Japanese Eyes*. Naval Institute Press, 1967.

Holland, James. *Sicily '45: The First Assault on Fortress Europe*. Griffon Merlin, 2020.

Hornfischer, James D. *Neptune's Inferno: The US Navy at Guadalcanal*. Bantam, 2012.

Hornfischer, James D. *Ship of Ghosts: The Story of the USS Houston, FDR's Legendary Lost Cruiser, and the Epic Saga of Her Survivors*. Bantam, 2006.

James, D. Clayton. *The Years of MacArthur: Vol. 1, 1880-1941*. Houghton Mifflin, 1970.

James, D. Clayton. *The Years of MacArthur: Vol. 2, 1941-1945*. Houghton Mifflin, 1975.

Kaplan, Philip. *World War Two at Sea: The Last Battleships*. Pen and Sword, 2014.
Langelo, Vincent A. *With All Our Might*. Eakin Press, 2000.
Larkins, William T. *Battleship and Cruiser Aircraft of the United States Navy, 1910–1949*. Schiffer Publishing, 1996.
Lawson, Robert L. *The History of US Naval Air Power*. Temple, 1985.
Long, Gavin, ed. *The Final Campaign*. Series 1, vol. 7 of *Australia in the War of 1939–1945*. Griffin Press, 1963.
MacArthur, Douglas A. *Reminiscences*. Bluejacket Edition. Naval Institute Press, 2001.
McManus, John C. *Fire and Fortitude: The US Army in the Pacific War, 1941–1943*. Caliber, 2019.
McManus, John C. *Island Infernos: The US Army's Pacific War Odyssey, 1944*. Caliber, 2021.
McManus, John C. *To the End of the Earth: The US Army and the Downfall of Japan, 1945*. Caliber, 2023.
Miller, John, Jr. *Cartwheel: The Reduction of Rabaul*. United States Army in World War II: The War in the Pacific. Office of the Chief of Military History, 1959.
Mitcham, Samuel W., and Friedrich von Stauffenberg. *The Battle of Sicily: How the Allies Lost Their Chance for Total Victory*. Orion Books, 1991.
Morison, Samuel Eliot. *Breaking the Bismarcks Barrier, 22 July 1942–1 May 1944*. Vol. 6 of the *History of United States Naval Operations in World War II*, Reprint, Little, Brown, 1988.
Morison, Samuel Eliot. *The Liberation of the Philippines: Luzon, Mindanao, the Visayas, 1944–1945*, Vol. 13 of the *History of United States Naval Operations in World War II*. 1959. Reprint. Little, Brown, 1990.
Morison, Samuel Eliot. *New Guinea and the Marianas, March 1944–August 1944*. Vol. 8 of the *History of United States Naval Operations in World War II*. 1953. Reprint, Little, Brown, 1990.
Morison, Samuel Eliot. *The Rising Sun in the Pacific, 1931–April 1942*. Vol. 3 of the *History of United States Naval Operations in World War II*. 1948. Reprint, Little, Brown, 1988.
Morison, Samuel Eliot. *Sicily, Salerno, Anzio, June 1943–June 1944*. Vol. 9 of the *History of United States Naval Operations in World War II*. 1954. Reprint, Little, Brown, 1990.
Morison, Samuel Eliot. *The Struggle for Guadalcanal, August 1942–February 1943*. Vol. 5 of the *History of United States Naval Operations in World War II*. 1948. Reprint, Little, Brown, 1989.
Morris, C. G., and H. Cave. *The Fightin'est Ship: The Story of the Cruiser* Helena *in World War II*. Reprint. Zenger, 1979.
Morris, Frank D. *"Pick Out the Biggest": Mike Moran and the Men of the* Boise. Houghton Mifflin, 1943.
Murray, Williamson, and Allan R. Millett. *A War to Be Won: Fighting the Second World War*. Paperback edition. Belknap, 2001.
Naval History and Heritage Command. *The Battles of Cape Esperance, 11 October 1942, and Santa Cruz Islands, 26 October 1942: Combat Narratives*. WWII 75th Anniversary Series. Naval History and Heritage Command, 2017.
O'Hara, Vincent P., and Trent Hone, eds. *Fighting in the Dark: Naval Combat at Night, 1904–1944*. Naval Institute Press, 2023.
Prange, Gordon W., Donald M. Goldstein, and Katherine V. Dillon. *At Dawn We Slept: The Untold Story of Pearl Harbor*. 60th Anniversary Edition. Penguin, 1991.
Prefer, Nathan N. *The Luzon Campaign, 1945: MacArthur Returns*. Casemate, 2024.
Pyle, Ernie. *Brave Men*. Henry Holt, 1944.
Scott, James M. *Rampage: MacArthur, Yamashita, and the Battle of Manila*. Norton, 2018.
Smith, Robert Ross. *The Approach to the Philippines*. United States Army in World War II: The War in the Pacific. Office of the Chief of Military History, 1953.
Smith, Robert Ross. *Triumph in the Philippines*. United States Army in World War II: The War in the Pacific. Office of the Chief of Military History, 1963.
Stankovich, Mike. "The Hardest Choice." *Naval History*. U.S. Naval Institute. Winter 1988. 2/1/2: 30–33.
Stille, Mark. *US Navy Light Cruisers, 1941–45*. Osprey, 2016.
Taaffe, Stephen R. *MacArthur's Jungle War: The 1944 New Guinea Campaign*. University Press of Kansas, 1998.
Toll, Ian W. *The Conquering Tide: War in the Pacific Islands, 1942–1944*. Norton, 2015.
Toll, Ian W. *Pacific Crucible: War at Sea in the Pacific, 1941–1942*. Norton, 2012.
Toll, Ian W. *Twilight of the Gods: War in the Western Pacific, 1944–1945*. Norton, 2020.
Ugaki, Matome. *Fading Victory: The Diary of Admiral Matome Ugaki, 1941–1945*. University of Pittsburgh Press, 1991.

Newsreel

World War II Public Domain. *November 1942 Newsreel: Guadalcanal; USS Boise (CL-47); Patton in North Africa, etc. (full)*. YouTube. https://www.youtube.com/watch?v=5EFtXH_QVfk&t=220s.

Other Sources

Naval History & Heritage Command, www.history.navy.mil/index.html.
The Naval Technical Board, www.navweaps.com/index_tech/index_tech.htm.

Index

Numbers in ***bold italics*** indicate pages with illustrations

ABDA Command 20–21, 27–28
aircraft: German (Do-217 103; Focke-Wulf (generic) 103; Ju-87 *Stuka* 92; Ju-88 95; Me-109 91; Me-210 95; Messerschmitt (generic) 90; Japanese (A6M *Zero/Zeke/Hamp* 37, 123, 158, 163; D3A *Val* 134, 143, 145, 147, 153, 214*n*27; G4M *Betty* 124; H6K *Mavis* 52; Ki-21 *Sally* 147; Ki-45 *Nick* 147, 153–154, 214*n*26; Ki-49 *Helen* 142; Ki-57 *Topsy* 121; Ki-61 *Tony* 155; U.S. (A-20 *Havoc* 165–166, 168–170; B-24 *Liberator* 121, 127, 165–166, 168–169, 173; B-25 *Mitchell* 24, 35–36, 124; B-26 *Marauder* 119, 144; B-29 *Superfortress* 115, 127, 182–183; C-47 *Skytrain* 169–171; F-4 *Corsair* 147; P-38 *Lightning* 103, 124, 147, 168; P-47 *Thunderbolt* 153, 165, 168, 169; PBY *Catalina* 27, 42, 51, 54–55, 160; SOC-3 *Seagull* 7, 25, ***26***, 27, 29, 33, 38, 42–46, 54–56, 65, 80, 82, 88, 89, 91–93, 98, 100, 108, 114–119, 121, 127, 132–137, 144, 165–172, 177–180, 202*n*4, 213*n*119; SON *see* SOC; TBM *Avenger* 152
Aitape, New Guinea 116
Aleutian Islands 38, 113
Alexishafen, New Guinea 112
Algiers, Algeria 85, 97–100, 104–105, 107
Allen, Terry 93–95, 97
American Samoa *see* Samoa
Amphibious Vehicle, Tracked (LVT) 117, 159
Andrus, Clift 97
Arnold, Henry "Hap" 34, 213*n*1
Ashby, Minnesota 1, 70, 206*n*162
Asiatic Fleet 16–18, 20, 33, 196

Auckland, New Zealand 38, 40–41
Australian Army 111–112, 177
Australian Army units: 9th Infantry Division 177, 179; 26th Brigade Group 177

Badong, Estaneslas 162
Balboa, Panama 72, 108, 183
Balolong, Pedro 160
Balikpapan, Dutch East Indies 18–19, 21–23
Barbey, Daniel 132
Bartlett, R.C. 56, 65, 67
Bataan 16, 20, 33–34, 154, 163–165, 167–168, 202*n*29
Beardslee, George 135, 193
Beau, Stan 176
Berkey, Russell S. 113–115, 118–119, 132, 135, 137–138, 140, 143, 145–146, 151–153, 155, 166–168, ***167***, 176, 178, 180
Biak 119–120, ***120***, 122–126, 128–129
Binder, Arthur D. 69
Bizerte, Tunisia 100, 102, 104
Black Cat squadron 112, 124–125
Blinn, Welford 23
Boal, J.K. 43–46
Boise crewmembers (Badong, Estaneslas 162; Bartlett, R.C. 56, 65, 67; Boal, J.K. 43–46; Boone, Clayton 141; Butler, W.C., Jr. 42, 65, 87, 192, 206*n*157; Campbell, Roy 18, 202*n*54; Cassidy, William 135; Donahue, Philip A. 69, 206*n*156; Downes, Willard M. 145–146, 152–153, 156, 163, 168, 180, 183, 213*n*132; Drake, Estill 107; Duncan, Theron 69, 206*n*156; Dyar, Joseph 155; Evarts, Milo 69, 206*n*157; Fenton, Joseph 18, 62, 110, 155, 179; Fletcher, A.A. "Red" 43, 46; Griffin, R.A. 76; Harding, William T. 91; Hartman, C.C. 183, 185, 188; Hiner, Harold 194; Hunnicutt, Al 194; Kasell ***181***; Kelley, Woodrow 69; Klemm, Frederick 8, 62; Laffan, John 37, 39, 206*n*156; Langelo, Vincent A. 41, 128, 203*n*57; Ledford, James Clarence 109; Lewis, Cyril 88–89, 91; Macomber, John 42; Martin, W. R. ***66***; McCandlish, B.V. 9; Moneymaker, Garnett 18, 58, 61, 64, 71, 82, 128, 200*n*16; Moran, Edward J. "Mike" 24–26, ***25***, 29–32, 37, 39, 41–43, 45, 53, 55–61, 64–66, 69–71, ***74***, 74–75, 80, 189, 191, 203*n*59, 206*n*157; Mulvey, William 62; Oldham, Charles 27, 81; Olinger, Charles ***78***; Perry, Berry 64; Petreycik, J. S. 43, 46; Poole, Mino 69, 206*n*157; Ralston, Carl T. 69 ; Roberts, John S. 104–105, 107–108, 115–116, 121, 127, 135, 138, 144; Robinson, Stephen B. 4, 9, 14, 22, 24, 191, 193; Schofield, Howard 162; Starnes, James 18, 42, 183; Thebaud, Leo Hewlett 80–81, 85, 90, 95, 97–100, 102, 104–105, ***105***, 191; Thomas, William "Beaverhead" 60, 63, 69, 206*n*157; Tripp, Robert 70, 206*n*162; Tyndal, Bill 63; Tyndal, Ed 63; Watson, John F. 194; Wollenberg, F. R. "Punchy" 43–46; Wolverton, Tom 39, 58, 61, 64, 69, 118, 135, 141, 144–145
Bombay, India 26–27, 29–32, ***31***, 38
Boone, Clayton 141
boot camp 10–11
Bora Bora, French Polynesia 72, 108

Index

Borneo, Dutch East Indies 16, 18, 176–177, 179
British Army 13, 20–21, 46, 75, 86, 90, 98, 100–102, 105, 151, 172; Commandos 100–101, 105; 1st Airborne Division 100, **101**, 102
British Navy 30, 83, 100–102, 105, 176
Brooklyn-class cruisers 5–7, 35–37, 41, 46, 81, 85, 100, 103, 150, 185, 189
Brooklyn Navy Yard 107, 185
Brunei 18, 179, 194
Buddington, A.F. 155
Buna, New Guinea 41, 111–112, 115
Bureau of Ships (BuShips) 78–79
Butler, W.C., Jr. 42, 65, 87, 192, 206*n*157

Cactus *see* Henderson Airfield
Campbell, Roy 18, 202*n*54
Cape Esperance 55, **66**, 66–68, **68**, 70–71, **77**, **79**, 81, 110, 114, 149, **186**, 188, 189, **190**, 192, 205*n*127, 206*n*156-157
Cape Gloucester 112
Captain's Mast 39, 203*n*57
Casablanca 107
Cassidy, William 135
Castelluccio di Gela 87, 91, 96
Cebu, Philippines 18, 173, 178–179
Ceylon (Sri Lanka) 24, 26–27, 29, 32–33
Child's Guide to Triphibious Operations 90
China 10, 17, 21, 35, 75, 182
Churchill, Winston 86
Clark Air Base 150, 164
Colombo, Ceylon 24, 26–27, 32–33
combat air patrol (CAP) 136, 145, 147–148, 163, 166, 168, 177
Conrath, Paul 85, 89, 92–93, 97
Coral Sea 48
Corregidor, Philippines 2, 16, 33, 154, 165–173, **167**, 202*n*29
Crutchley, Victor 123–125
Cunningham, Andrew 100–101

Darby, William O. 86–88, 94
Darwin, Australia 19, 21
Davidson, L.A. 81, 100, 104, 191
Dieppe, France 86
Diggers *see* Australian Army
Dirty War 188–189
Donahue, Philip A. 69, 206*n*156
Doolittle, James H. "Jimmy" 34–36, 41, 47
Doorman, Karel 27, 48
Downes, Willard M. 145–146, 152–153, 156, 163, 168, 180, 183, 213*n*132
Drake, Estill 107
Duncan, Theron 69, 206*n*156
Dutch East Indies 3, 20, 22, 28, 115, 131
Dyar, Joseph 155

Egeberg, Roger 152, 154
Eichelberger, Robert 150, 178, 182–183
Eisenhower, Dwight D. 34, 92, 96–97, 100, 127, 150, 213*n*1
Espiritu Santo, New Hebrides 51, 54–55, 71
Evarts, Milo 69, 206*n*157

Fenton, Joseph 18, 62, 110, 155, 179
Fiji 20, 51, 108
Fletcher, A.A. "Red" 43, 46
Formosa, China 115, 131
Fremantle, Australia 32–33

Galela Bay, New Guinea 129, **130**
Gavin, James 89–90, 96
Gela, Sicily 2, 83, 86–96, 98, 102, 110, 193
German Air Force 29, 91–92, 95–96, 100, 102–103
German Army: Hermann Goering (HG) Division 85, 89–92, 94, 95
Germany 10, 13, 82, 98, 182
Glassford, William 18, 21–22
Gorman, Arthur "Hard Nose" 89
Goto, Aritomo 56–57, 59, 67, 69
Grant, Harrold 90
Great Marianas Turkey Shoot *see* Philippine Sea
Griffin, R.A. 76
Guadalcanal 2, 40–41, 46, 48–56, **49**, 67–71, 75–76, 81–83, 118, 138, 163, 188, 192, 194, 209*n*33
Guam 3, 14, 18
guerrilla 159, 164, 173, 215*n*63

Hall, John 85, 97
Halmahera, Dutch East Indies 129, **130**
Halsey, William "Bull" 34–35, 131, 136, 141–142, 147, 183, 213*n*1
Hansa Bay, New Guinea 115–116
Harding, William T. 91
Hart, Thomas C. 17–18, 20–22
Hartman, C.C. 183, 185, 188
Henderson Airfield **49**, 51–54, 69
Hewitt, Henry 19, 86, 104

Hiner, Harold 194
Hirohito, Michinomiya 48, 182
Hiroshima, Japan 182
Hitler, Adolf 13, 148, 177, 208*n*96
Hold That Ghost 72
Hollandia, New Guinea 115–119, 122
Hotchkiss, Gilbert 11
Humboldt Bay, New Guinea 116, **117**, 118–120, 122–123, 125, 127, 129, 131
Hunnicutt, Al 194

Identify Friend or Foe (IFF) 38, 118
Imperial Japanese Navy *see* Japanese Navy
Imperial Japanese Navy ships *see* Japanese ships
Indochina 14, 20, 154
Intramuros, Manila 14, 174
Ironbottom Sound 50, 69, 205*n*127
Itagaki, Akira 170
Italian Army: Livorno Division 85, 90–92, 94
Italian Navy 100, 102
Iwo Jima, Japan 46, 104, 172

Japanese Army 3, 21, 51, 161
Japanese Army units: 18th Army 115
Japanese Navy 3, 17, 48, 114–115, 122, 124–125, 131, 136–138, 141, 144, 151, 188, 212*n*59
Japanese Navy units: Carrier Division 2 46–47; Combined Fleet 46–47; Cruiser Division 6 69; 1st Submarine Squadron 47; 2nd Fleet 47
Java, Dutch East Indies 16, 20–22, 24, 33
Java Sea, Battle 27–28
Johnston, James D. 194
Jones, George 171–172, 216*n*119

kamikaze 134, 142–147, **148**, 151, 153–156, 158, **159**, 160, 162, 164, 168, 176, 178, 182
Kasell **181**
Kelley, Woodrow 69
Kenney, George 178
Kijima, Kikunori 69
Kilkis see *Mississippi (BB-23)*
Kimmel, Husband E. 8, 9
Kimura, Masanori 149
King, Edward 33
King, Ernest 20, 34, 51, **74**, 74–75, 135, 213*n*1
Kinkaid, Thomas 128, 136, 163
Kiska, Alaska 41, 46
Klemm, Frederick 8, 62

Index

Knox, Frank 9, 17, 200n27
Krueger, Walter 132, 163, 182–183
Kurita, Takeo 136–137, 141–142
Kyushu, Japan 177, 182

Laffan, John 37, 39, 206n156
Landing Craft, Infantry (LCI) 117, 119–120, 136, 159, 161–162, 168
Landing Craft, Support (LCS) 177
Landing Ship, Tank (LST) 90, 92, 118, 120, 122, 133, 147–148, **148**, 161
Lange, Otto 102
Langelo, Vincent A. 41, 128, 203n57
Larsen, Dale 192
Ledford, James Clarence 109
Leonardi, Dante Ugo 93
Lewis, Cyril 88–89, 91
Leyte, Philippines 131–137, **139**, 140–146, 149, 160, 176, 180, 193, 212n68, 212n72
Licata, Sicily 86, 88, 96
Lingayen Gulf, Philippines 2, 20, 150–152, 155–156, **157, 158, 159**, 158–160, 162–164, 169, 172, 178–179
London Naval Conference 5
Long Lance torpedo, Type 93 49, 59
Lucas, John 90
Luftwaffe *see* German Air Force
Luzon, Philippines 20, 131–132, 147, 150–152, 154, 156–164, **157**, 169, 173, 182, 193

MacArthur, Gen. Douglas A. 16–20, 33–34, 107, 111–113, 115–120, 122, 126–127, 129, 131–133, 136, 144, 147, 150–157, **152**, 160–166, 172, 174, 176, 178–183, **181**, 202n29, 213n1, 215n71, 215n74
Macomber, John 42
Madang, New Guinea 112
Makassar, New Guinea 19, 22–23
Makin Island, Gilbert Islands 41, 46
Malinta Hill 165, 170–171
Malta 93, 100, 104
Manila, Philippines 3, 14, 16–18, 20, 33, 150–151, 154, 161–162, 164–166, 172–176, 178–180
Manila Bay *see* Manila
Manus Island, Admiralty Islands 116, 118, 144
Mare Island, California 32, 37–38

Marianas Islands 115, 125–127, 136
Mariveles, Philippines 165, 167–169
Marshall, George C. 96, 213n1
Martin, W. R. **66**
McCandlish, B.V. 9
Melbourne, Australia 33, 36
Mers-el-Kebir, Algeria 85, 107
Messina, Italy 86, 98, 104
Midway 38, 41–42, 48, 74
Mikawa, Gunichi 49–50, 55
Milne Bay, New Guinea 108, 111–112, 114, 128
Mindanao, Philippines 3, 132, 137, 147, 151, 173, 178, 179
Mindoro, Philippines 147–149, **148**, 153, 165, 169–170, 173, 178
Moneymaker, Garnett 18, 58, 61, 64, 71, 82, 128, 200n16
Montgomery, Bernard 86, 98
Moran, Edward J. "Mike" 24–26, **25**, 29–32, 37, 39, 41–43, 45, 53, 55–61, 64–66, 69–71, **74**, 74–75, 80, 189, 191, 203n59, 206n157
Morgan, O.W. 56
Morotai, Dutch East Indies 129, **130**, 132
Mulvey, William 62

Nagasaki, Japan 182
Nagumo, Chuichi 32
New Caledonia 71
New York City 72, 76, 107–108, 183–185, **184**, 187
Nimitz, Chester 20, 41, 46, 66, 112, 115–116, 125, 129, 131, 136, 142, 182–183, 213n1
Niscemi, Sicily 89–95
Nishimura, Shoji 23, 136–138, 140
Noemfoor Island, New Guinea 125–126

Objective Y, DIME Sector 89, 91, 94
Okinawa 104, 131, 176, 182
Oldendorf, Jesse 136–138, 140–141, 151
Oldham, Charles 27, 81
Olinger, Charles **78**
Operation Avalanche 100, 102
Operation Bagration 127
Operation Brewer 150
Operation Cartwheel 112
Operation Downfall 178, 182
Operation Husky 83, 85–86, 91, 97–98, 208n96 (CENT Sector 86, 89; DIME Sector 86–89, **87**, 91–92, 95–97; JOSS Sector 86)
Operation KON 122, 124–125

Operation Magic Carpet 183, 185, **186**, 187–188
Operation Mike I 150, **152, 157**
Operation Mike VII 164
Operation Oboe I 177
Operation Olympic 178, 217n40
Operation Reckless 116–118, **117**
Operation SHO-1 136, 212n59
Operation Slapstick 100, 102, 104
Operation Torch 73
Operation Victor IV 173
Operation Watchtower 40–41, 46, 48
Owsley (Fitch), Betty Lou Eileen 192–194, **195**
Ozawa, Jisaburo 32, 136, 141–142

Pago Pago, American Samoa 37, 72
Palermo, Sicily 98–99, 102, 104–105, **105**
Panama Canal 34, 72, 108, 183–184
paravanes 99, 132, 177
Patrol Torpedo boats 82, 125, 137–138, 140, 146, 149–150, 161–162, 170–171, 179
Patton, George S. 86, 90, 92, 94, 96–98
Pearl Harbor 3, 9, 11, 13, 14, 18, 20, 21, 34, 37, 41, 46, 51, 73, 108, 137, 142, 180, 194, 200n27, 203n76
Perry, Berry 64
Petreycik, J.S. 43, 46
Philadelphia 71–76, **74**, 81, 107, 187, 193
Philippine Sea 126, 136, 142
Pick Out the Biggest 39, 203n59
Ponto Olivo Airfield 86, 96
Poole, Mino 69, 206n157
prisoner of war (POW) 28, 46, 89, 96, 177, 182–183
propaganda 21, 69, 160, 203n59
PT boats *see* patrol torpedo boats
Pyle, Ernie 88

Rabaul, New Britain 41, 49, 69, 112, 150
radar systems: FH *see* Mk-8; Mk-3 Fire Control Radar (FCR) 7, 80, 189; Mk-8 (FH) 140, 173, 179; Mk-35 FCR 7, 57, 135; Mk-57 80, 99; Mk-63 80, 99; SC 7, 56; SG 7, 38, 49, 56, 80, 138, 205n67; SK 124, 156
Ralston, Carl T. 69
reunions **181**, 193–194, **195, 196**, 196
Roberts, John S. 104–105,

228 Index

107–108, 115–116, 121, 127, 135, 138, 144
Robinson, Stephen B. 4, 9, 14, 22, 24, 191, 193
Roosevelt, Franklin D. 3, 10, 13, 19, 33, 36, 72, 131, 176
Roosevelt, Theodore, Jr. 93

Sakonju, Naomasa 123–124
Salerno, Italy 100, 102, 104–105
Salt Lake City 4, 9, 10, 14, 75, 131, 181, 187, 192, 194
Samar Island, Philippines 136, 141–142
Samoa (American) 20, 37, 72
San Diego 9–11, 193
San Fabian, Philippines 156, *157*, 160
Savo Island, Guadalcanal 49–50, 55–56, 65, 69, 78
Sawar, New Guinea 119
Schofield, Howard 162
Scoglitti, Italy 86, 89
Scott, Norman 54–59, 64–65, 67–69, 71, 74, 205n67, 206n156
Seeadler Harbor, Admiralty Islands 118–119, 125, 127–130, 144, 176
Shand, William Henry 131, 143, 163, 165
Shellback Ceremony 19, 108
Shima, Kiyohide 137, 140–141, 212n68
ships: Argentinian (*General Belgrano* 188; *Nueve de Julio* 188); Australian (*Australia* 114, 116, 119–120, 123–123, 126, 128–130, 132–134, 151, 160, 215n60; *Canberra (D33)* 49, 130; *Perth* 27–28; *Shropshire* 114, 116, 119–120, 129–130, 132, 136–137, 140, 143, 158); British (*Abdiel* 101–102; *Abercrombie* 102; *Ajax* 40; *Cornwall* 26, 33; *Dorsetshire* 26, 33; *Electra* 27; *Enterprise* 25; *Exeter* 27, 40; *Glasgow* 26; *Hermes* 26, 33; *Howe* 102; *Jupiter* 27; *King George V* 98, 102; *Prince of Wales* 20; *Repulse* 20; *Truant* 25; *Vampire* 33); Dutch (*De Ruyter* 27; *Java* 27; *Klipfontein* 38, 108; *Kortenaer* 27; *Torrens* 38; *Van Ghent* 22); German (*Bismarck* 98; *Graf Spee* 40); Japanese (*Abukuma* 137, 140; *Aoba* 50, **66**, 66–67, 122; *Ashigara* 137, 141; *Chokai* 49–50, 69; *Fubuki* **66**; *Furutaka* **66**, 66–67; *Fuso* 122, 137; *Haruna* 69; *Hatsuyuki* 67; *Hatuharu* 65; *Hinoki* 154; *I-15* 52; *I-19* 52; *I-26* 51, 56; *Itukusima* 65; *Kinugasa* 50, 67, 69; *Kiso* 42; *Kiyoshimo* 149; *Kongo* 69; *Kuretake Maru* 23; *Mogami* 62, 66, **137**; *Musashi* 136; *Nachi* 66, 137; *Nitta Maru* 35; *PC-37* 23; *Shigure* **139**; *Shiratsuyu* 125; *Sumanoura Maru* 23; *Tama* 42; *Tatsukami Maru* 23; *Yamashiro* 137–138, **139**; *Yubari* 65; New Zealand (*Achilles* 40, 52; *Leander* 52–53); U.S. (*Abbot* 171; *Abner Read* 143; *Advance Base Sectional Dock-4* 176; *Ammen* 143; *Argonne* 72; *Arizona* 41, 51, 203n76; *Astoria* 50, 78, 158, 215n60; *Atlanta* 71; *Barker* 41; *Barnett* 38, 92; *Benson* 99; *Birmingham* 85; *Biscayne* 88; *Boise (SSN-764)* 189; *Boston* 130; *Bristol* 99; *Brooklyn* 97–98; *Brownson* 112; *Buchanan* 55; *California* 41, 51, 130, 140, 158, 203n76; *Calloway* 155; *Cape Flattery* 38; *Cavalier* 165; *Champlin* 73; *Chester* 71; *Chicago* 50; *Claxton* 169; *Cleveland* 73, 130; *Cofer* 177; *Coghlan* 156; *Columbia* 73, 158; *Colorado* 51, 214n60; *Dashiell* 147; *Denver (CL-58)* 130, 151, 162, 165; *Denver (LPD-09)* 193–194; *Drayton* 145; *Duncan* 55, 57, 66–67; *Durham Victory* 142; *Edwards* 156, 162; *Ericcson* 38; *Enterprise* 35–36, 51, 185; *Farenholt* 55, 57; *Farragut* 54; *Fletcher* 155; *Fuller* 22; *George F. Elliot* 38, 48; *Gleaves* 104; *Guardfish* 42; *Helena* 51, 55–57, 67, 71, 109, 111, 204n51; *Heywood* 38; *Honolulu* 6, 37, 46, 134; *Hope* 145; *Hornet (CV-8)* 34–36, 51–52, 54; *Hornet (CV-12)* 130; *Houston* 16, 18, 27–28 *Hughes* 146; *Hutchins* 120–121; *Idaho* 51, 130; *Indiana* 73, 130; *Indianapolis* 19, 46; *Jarvis* 48, 203n1; *Jeffers* 86–87; *Jenkins* 177; *John D. Ford* 22–23; *Jupiter* 38; *Kadashan Bay* 155; *Kitkun Bay* 155–156; *Laffey* 55; *Langley* 107–108; *La Salle* 209n33; *Lavallette* 168; *LCI-974* 161–162; *LCT-1075* 146; *Leutze* 161; *Lewis Hancock* 107; *Long Island* 51; *Louisville* 46, 136, 148–149, 158; *LSM-20* 145; *LSM-23* 145; *LST-215* 96; *LST-313* 92, 94; *LST-472* 147; *LST-738* 147; *LST-912* 154; *LST-925* 161; *Ludlow* 99; *Maddox* 92; *Manila Bay* 151; *Marblehead* 16, 22, 24, 28; *Marcus Island* 147; *Maryland* 51, 130, 158, 203n76, 214n60; *Matsonia* 38; *McCalla* 55, 67; *McCawley* 52; *Minneapolis* 51, 53, 130, 149, 215n60; *Mississippi (BB-23)* 29; *Mississippi (BB-41)* 51, 130, 144, 158, 160; *Missouri* 183, 185; *Monrovia* 86, 162; *Montpelier* 151, 162, 165, 167–168; *Mount Olympus* 158; *Mugford* 145; *Mullany* 123–124; *Nashville* 34–36, 42–43, 46, 111, 114, 116, 118, 123–124, 129–130, 132–133, 136, 143–144, 147, 150; *Nevada* 51, 203n76; *New Jersey* 128; *New Mexico* 51, 158; *New Orleans* 7; *Nicholas* 151–152, 166, 168, 177; *Nicholson* 107; *North Carolina* 52, 54; *O'Bannon* 170; *O'Brien* 52; *Oklahoma* 41, 51, 203n76; *Ommaney Bay* 151; *Parrott* 22–23; *Patterson* 50; *Paul Jones (DD-230)* 22–23; *Paul Jones (DD-10)* 80; *PC-1600* 155; *Pelias* 38; *Pennsylvania* 51, 130, 158, 203n76; *Philadelphia* 81–82, 85, 99–100, 102–105, 185; *Phoenix* 33, 37, 111–112, 114, 116, 123–126, 128–130, 132, 136–138, 140, 143–146, 148–153, 155, 162, 165, 167–168, 173, 177, 188, 214n26; *Pope* 22–23; *Portland* 145, 148, 158; *President Polk* 29, 202n4; *Princeton* 136; *PT-109* 82; *PT-127* 138; *PT-323* 147; *Quincy* 50, 78; *Radford* 168; *Remey* 107; *Renshaw* 185; *Rhind* 107; *Robert Rowen* 95; *Robinson* 161; *Rowan* 99, 103; *S-36* 22; *St. Lo* 142; *St. Louis* 37, 46; *Salt Lake City* 55–57, 62, 71–72; *Salute* 180, 194; *Sampson* 122; *San Francisco* 54–56, 67, 71; *San Juan* 49; *Santa Fe* 113; *Saratoga* 51; *Savanah* 6, 8, 82, 85, 93, 96–98, 100, 102–104, 185; *Shaw* 112; *Shubrick* 91; *Stanton* 86; *Suesens* 131, 143, 163, 165; *Taylor* 152–153, 166, 168, 170–171, 177–178; *Tennessee* 51, 130, 140, 158, 203n, 214n60; *Trathen* 126; *Utah* 41, 203n76; *Vincennes* 50; *War Hawk* 161; *Warrington* 72; *Washington* 71, 209n33; *Wasp (CV-7)* 52–54; *Wasp (CV-18)* 130; *West Virginia* 41, 51, 133, 140,

203n76, 214n60; *Wharton* 11; *Wichita* 130; *William S. Ladd* 146; *Winooski* 180; *Young* 22
Shore Patrol 14, 38, 76
Sicily 83–89, *84*, 95–100, 115, 178, 188, 208n96
Singapore 20–21, 25–26
Soeffker (Fitch), Jenna Vee Lundahl 194–195, **195**
Solomon Islands 40–41, 46, 51, 81, 189
Soviet Union 14, 86, 97, 127, 182
Sprague, Clifton 141
Sri Lanka *see* Ceylon
Stalin, Joseph 14, 97, 172
Stalingrad, Soviet Union 75
Starnes, James 18, 42, 183
Subic Bay, Philippines 164–166, 168, 172–173, 176–178
suicide boats 161–162, 169
Surigao Strait, Philippines 136–138, **139**, 141, 143–144, 146–147, 178, 212n68
Sutherland, Richard 160
Sydney, Australia 113–114, 127

Tacloban, Philippines 132, **139**, 191
Talbot, Paul 22–23
Tanahmerah Bay, New Guinea 116, 119
tanks: M-4 Sherman 94; Mark III 85, 89; Mark IV 85, 89; Renault 35 91; Tiger (German) 83, 85, 89
Tarakan Island, Dutch East Indies 177
Taranto, Italy 100–102, **101**, 105, 191
Tate, W.J. 56
Thebaud, Leo Hewlett 80–81, 85, 90, 95, 97–100, 102, 104–105, **105**, 191
Thomas, William "Beaverhead" 60, 63, 69, 206n157
Tjilatjap, Dutch East Indies 22, 24
Tokyo Express 51, 55, 69, 164
Tripp, Robert 70, 206n162
Truman, Harry S. 185, 191, 202n29
Tulagi, Guadalcanal 48, 56
Turner, Richmond Kelly "Terrible" 41, 52–53
Tyndal, Bill 63
Tyndal, Ed 63

Ugaki, Matome 46
Ulithi, Caroline Islands 143, 180
U.S. Army units: 1st Army 182; 1st Cavalry Division 132; 1st Infantry Division 86–88, 93, 96; 3rd Infantry Division 98; 6th Army 132–133, 182; 6th Infantry Division 127, 157; 7th Infantry Division 132; 8th Army 150, 164; 24th Infantry Division 116, 132, 147; 31st Infantry Division 129; 32nd Field Artillery Battalion 94; 32nd Infantry Division 132; 34th Infantry Regiment 170; 36th Infantry Division 102; 41st Infantry Division 116–117, 119–120, 173; 42nd "Rainbow" Division 17; 77th Infantry Division 132; 82nd Airborne Division 86, 89–90, 92–93, 96; 96th Infantry Division 132; 151st Regimental Combat Team (RCT) 168; 163rd Regimental Combat Team (RCT) 119; 503rd Parachute Infantry Regiment (PIR) 147, 169–172, 216n119; 504rd Parachute Infantry Regiment (PIR) 96; Alamo Force 112, 132; Americal Division 173; Cyclone Task Force 126; Rangers 86–88, 91, 94, 132; Rock Force *see* 503rd Parachute Infantry Regiment; X Corps 132–133; XI Corps 164; XXIV Corps 132
U.S. Army Air Force units: 5th Air Force 116, 178; Far East Air Force *see* 5th Air Force
U.S. Marine Corps units: 1st Marine Division 40, 48; 7th Marine Regiment 52–54
U.S. Navy units: 3rd Fleet 130–132, 136; 7th Fleet 107, 111, 114, 116, 122, 128, 131, 135–136; 8th Fleet 85; 16th Reserve Fleet 188; Close Covering Group (Berkey) 132, 134, 137, 147, 151 (Cruiser Division 8 81) Cruiser Division 9 9; (Cruiser Division 10 104; Cruiser Division 15 111–115)
Pacific Fleet 3, 9, 16, 18, 36, 41, 51, 81 (Pacific Fleet Battle Force 8, 9; Task Force 5 [Striking Force] 18–19, 24
Task Force 34 142
Task Force 58 116, 180
Task Force 61 52, 54
Task Force 64 54–57, 59, 64–65, 67, 71, 74
Task Force 65 52–54
Task Force 74 114, 119, 122–125, 128
Task Force 75 114, 119, 122–123, 128
Task Force 77 116, 119
Task Force 78 132
Task Force 79 155 (Task Force 8 41, 46; Task Force 81 85)

Vogelkop Peninsula, New Guinea 126–127
von Senger, Fridolin 98

Wainright, Jonathan 34, 164–165, 183, 202n29
Wakde, New Guinea 119–120, 122–123
Wake Island 3, 18, 41
Watson, John F. 194

Watts, Maurice L. 193
Wellington, New Zealand 40
Wilkinson, Theodore 163
Wollenberg, F. R. "Punchy" 43–46
Wolverton, Tom 39, 58, 61, 64, 69, 118, 135, 141, 144–145
Woolloomooloo, Australia 113, 128

Yamamoto, Isoroku 14
Yamashita, Tomoyuki 161, 174

Zamboanga, Philippines 173, 179

www.ingramcontent.com/pod-product-compliance
Lightning Source LLC
Chambersburg PA
CBHW060341010526
44117CB00017B/2922